THE INTERNATIONAL MONETARY SYSTEM,

1945–1976

THE

INTERNATIONAL

MONETARY

SYSTEM,

1945-1976

An Insider's View

Robert Solomon

HARPER & ROW, PUBLISHERS

New York / Hagerstown / San Francisco / London

1817

Grateful acknowledgment is made for permission to reprint the following:

Excerpt from "The Payments Adjustment Process and the Exchange Rate Regime: What Have We Learned?" by Marina V. N. Whitman, *AER, Papers and Proceedings,* May 1975, by permission of the American Economic Association.

Excerpt on page 85 from *The Economist,* London.

Excerpt from "Reflections on the International Monetary Reform," by J. Marcus Fleming, Essays in International Finance No. 107, December 1974, International Finance Section, Princeton University.

FIRST EDITION

Designed by Sidney Feinberg

Library of Congress Cataloging in Publication Data

Solomon, Robert.
  The international monetary system, 1945–1976.
  Bibliography: p.
  Includes index.
  1. International finance. I. Title.
HG3881.S5574   332.4'5   76–10094
ISBN 0–06–013898–X
77 78 79 80 10 9 8 7 6 5 4 3 2 1

Contents

Preface

This book offers an analytical interpretation of evolving international monetary relations since the end of World War II; its purpose is to improve the future by illuminating the past. Although the quest for an improved international monetary system is hardly a rallying cry for the ordinary citizen, the fact is that the structure and functioning of that system have an impact on all our lives. A better understanding of the history of that system is essential to the shaping of its future.

The international monetary arrangements agreed to in 1944 at Bretton Woods reflected U.S. dominance—political, industrial, and financial. As the economies of Europe and Japan recovered and went on to thrive, and as the developing countries threw off colonialism and began to act as independent economic entities, the deficiencies of the Bretton Woods system were gradually revealed in a series of monetary crises beginning in the mid-1960's. The efforts made to cope with these deficiencies were too little and too late.

Economic policies and practices that had been adopted both in the United States and abroad in the early postwar years to foster economic recovery and balance-of-payments strength in Europe and Japan persisted into the 1960's when they were no longer needed. Meanwhile, the United States took on a costly military burden in Vietnam but failed to adopt adequate domestic measures to prevent the inflationary consequences. For these reasons the Bretton Woods system broke down in 1971. A two-year exercise in reform was conducted by the Committee of Twenty in 1972–74. Although the Committee produced a broad vision of a reformed system, the sharp acceleration of inflation and the outbreak of the oil crisis in 1973–74 led to a decision to make reform an evolutionary process. In January 1976, agreement was reached on evolutionary steps regarding the role of gold; more important, a long-standing doctrinal dispute on the nature of the exchange rate regime was resolved.

This, then, in barest outline, is the history that is recounted in the pages that follow.* Although the viewpoint is international—I try to present the sometimes conflicting and often changing perceptions and objectives of policy-making officials concerned with international monetary questions in the United States and abroad—more emphasis is given to developments in the United States than in other countries. The largest entity and the central country in the system necessarily deserves the most detailed attention.

It is one of the themes of this book that there are no deep-seated national interests standing in the way of an improved international monetary system. The issues are technically complex, the forums for consultation and negotiation are unwieldy, and effective communication is exceedingly difficult. But these problems are surmountable, especially when the participants have a healthy dose of empathy.

A word is in order on the limits of this book. Although the Eurodollar market is mentioned often, the reader will find here no systematic analysis of the functioning of that market or other Euro-currency markets; that would require a separate book. Similarly, the problems of European integration are not dealt with in detail. Canada is mentioned from time to time, but its problems and various aspects of the U.S.-Canadian relationship are ignored. And little is said about the developing countries; their major problems lie outside the international monetary realm.

I should like to express my gratitude to the Board of Governors of the Federal Reserve System for encouraging me to write this book and for having given me, over the years, the responsibilities that made possible my participation in international monetary affairs. It was my friend Robert Holland, until recently a Governor of the Board, who first suggested that I write the book. The Board has not attempted to influence in any way what I have wished to say. By the same token, none of the analyses or judgments in this book should be attributed to the Board or its staff.

I wish to thank Roy Blough, Arthur Burns, Richard Cooper, Dewey Daane, Henry Fowler, Robert Roosa, James Tobin, Paul Volcker, and George Willis for providing me with recollections of events or developments of which

*An International Monetary Chronology will be found at the end of the book, beginning on page 339.

I had no direct knowledge. Needless to say, they bear no responsibility for what I have written.

For having read and provided helpful suggestions on all or most of an earlier draft, my sincere thanks to Ralph Bryant, Dewey Daane, Lewis Dembitz, Fern Solomon, Robert Triffin, and Edwin Truman. My former colleagues in the "Bureau" of the Committee of Twenty, Sir Jeremy Morse, Alexandre Kafka, and Edward George, provided helpful reactions to a first draft of Chapter XIV.

For her cheerful diligence and good nature, my secretary, Jan Anderson, has my lasting gratitude.

Finally, with love, I dedicate this book to my mother, Betty Solomon, who maintains a lively interest in world events though she has attained a certain maturity of years.

THE INTERNATIONAL MONETARY SYSTEM,

1945–1976

I

The International Monetary System:
What It Is and Why It Matters

Like the traffic lights in a city, the international monetary system is taken for granted until it begins to malfunction and to disrupt people's daily lives. During the first ten or fifteen years following World War II, while serious problems of postwar economic recovery were confronted and overcome, especially in Europe and Japan, the monetary aspects of international economic relations attracted little public attention. When monetary difficulties did arise, they were dealt with by specialized international institutions and by technicians in individual countries.

Not until the 1960's did acute problems emerge and come to the attention of the public at large. A series of events—annual crises culminating in a devaluation of the British pound in 1967, a crisis of weakness for the French franc and of strength for the German mark in 1968–69, the Nixon import surcharge and suspension of gold convertibility in August 1971, two formal devaluations of the dollar, the adoption of floating exchange rates in March 1973, and, finally, the quadrupling of the price of oil in late 1973—brought international monetary questions to newspaper headlines and into the conscious concern of the man and woman in the street. In recent years international monetary matters have even begun to show up as subjects of *New Yorker* cartoons—an infallible measure of public interest. Further evidence of such interest may be found in the Archbishop of Canterbury's plea to his flock to "pray earnestly" for the pound sterling as well as for the country.[1]

Because monetary developments affect the citizenry, the attention of high government officials became engaged. As Valéry Giscard d'Estaing, then Min-

ister of Finance and now President of France,* said in 1973, "the problem of
money had been treated as a matter for the experts and formed the subject of
plans that were a delectable blend of sophistication and obscurity. Now it has
become a problem for governments and is even being debated by statesmen.
At stake is the expansion of international trade, that is to say, the growth of
the world economy."[2] In France in November 1975, government leaders of the
five largest industrial nations met at Rambouillet to discuss economic and
financial matters, and the end result of the meeting was an agreement on the
future exchange rate system—not the kind of issue that would have arrested
the attention of such men a few years before.

The Impact of Monetary Events

International monetary developments affect individuals as workers, consumers, travelers, businessmen producing goods for domestic or foreign markets, and investors at home or abroad. The channels which transmit the impact
of monetary events to people in their various roles in society are numerous.

Employment opportunities for some workers are improved when exports
thrive and are weakened for other workers when foreign products compete
effectively in price or quality with domestic output; exports and imports are
influenced by what is happening to gross national product at home and abroad
as well as by exchange rates, prices, and controls over international transactions.

A particular monetary change—for example, a movement in the exchange
rate—may benefit an individual in one of his roles but leave him worse off in
another. The individual as consumer may have a different view of, and a
different interest in, what happens in the international monetary sphere from
that of the individual as worker. One sees many foreign cars in the employee
parking lots of automobile plants in Michigan and, no doubt, there are foreign-
made television sets and numerous other imported products in the homes of
American workers. Similarly, the son or daughter of a French worker wears
American-made blue jeans and the Swiss worker may, these days, have an
American-made digital watch. A higher exchange rate for the dollar improves
the welfare of the American consumer by making foreign products less expensive; at the same time it may weaken employment opportunities in some

---

*It is no accident that finance ministers in recent years have succeeded to the post of head of
government; in addition to Giscard d'Estaing in France, there are Helmut Schmidt in Germany,
James Callaghan in Great Britain, and José Lopez Portillo in Mexico.

industries as other consumers choose foreign over domestic products. And the same is true in other countries.

The prices that the consumer pays for both home-produced and foreign goods are affected by monetary developments, including changes in exchange rates. As these words are being written the Italian Government is struggling to prevent its currency (the lira) from depreciating further in order to avoid additional upward pressures on prices in that country.

If the worker or his foreman or one of the executives of his company travels abroad, he becomes conscious of exchange rates. How far his dollar (or franc or mark or yen) will stretch in paying for his expenses as a tourist depends upon the rate of exchange. If the traveler happened to be abroad during one of the many monetary crises between 1965 and 1973, he might have found it difficult or even impossible to encash his traveler's checks or to change one currency for another. If he went to France in 1968 he was asked to declare, on arrival and departure, the amount of foreign currency he was carrying.

Business activity is heavily influenced by international monetary conditions. Decisions to develop a new product for sale at home or abroad or to establish a factory in a foreign country depend in part on expectations about prices, exchange rates, interest rates, and the possible imposition of controls on exports or imports or on capital movements. Interdependence among nations has intensified; exports and imports have increased faster than total production. Consequently, there is greater interest in the functioning of the international monetary system.

Although the subject matter may seem to be and often is technical, there is much human drama in the relationships among those whose business it is to try to manage or at least cope with international monetary problems. The past decade has witnessed a series of negotiations and high level meetings— some routine, some called on an emergency basis—at which finance ministers and central bank governors have sat down together and worked out solutions to problems that affected all their countries. While political and economic interests often diverged, a vital centripetal force was the realization that all must sink or swim together—that economic interdependence exists and brings shared benefits.

Fear of the unknown was another important unifying influence in the various crises that arose. When faced with crises—as happened all too often —high officials pulled together, sometimes to try to preserve the status quo even when that was unrealistic, sometimes to adopt innovations. What all were motivated to avoid was a free-for-all—a reversion to the climate of the 1930's when countries often acted without taking account of the repercussions of their policies on their neighbors and the ultimate feedback on themselves.

The jet airplane makes it possible to decide today that finance ministers or central bank governors, or their deputies, should meet tomorrow. Despite jet lag and the fatigue it brings, senior monetary officials are able to get together, frequently and at short notice, to deal with problems of mutual concern. I myself, as the Federal Reserve Board's senior staff economist in the international field, logged 90 round trips across the Atlantic Ocean in the years 1963–1975, in addition to making several voyages to Japan and South America.

Domestic Monetary Systems

In characterizing the international monetary system, it helps to look first at its domestic counterparts. The development over time of the international system tends to repeat or parallel the historical development of monetary systems within individual countries, much as the evolutionary development of the human species from its early pre-human origins is similar to the development of the individual human being from conception to birth. (In biology, ontogeny is said to recapitulate phylogeny.) The analogy is turned around in the monetary field, where the development of the broader concept, the system, seems to "recapitulate" an evolution that occurred earlier within individual units of the system. Two illustrations of such recapitulation are the decline in the role of gold, first in domestic monetary systems and then internationally, and the assumption of growing responsibility for management of the economic system by central governments and, in the international sphere, by the International Monetary Fund (IMF).

Textbooks dealing with domestic monetary systems tell us that money has three functions: it serves as a medium of exchange, a unit of account (or measure of value), and a store of value (one of many media in which wealth may be held). Within individual countries and among countries, money is a lubricant that eases and facilitates transactions in goods and services. It also makes possible the transfer of purchasing power from lenders to borrowers and back again. Without money we would have to resort to barter, an extremely cumbersome means that would not permit the high degree of specialization that has developed within modern economies and in trade between them.

Domestic monetary systems now involve a single currency: the dollar in the United States, the franc in France, the yen in Japan, the cruzeiro in Brazil. Within each domestic system, a central bank exercises management to a degree that varies both quantitatively and qualitatively among countries. Managing the domestic monetary system normally entails regulating the amount and cost of money and credit available from the banking system to finance the myriad transactions that occur every day in a modern economy. The domestic management of money is important because it affects the willingness and ability of businesses and consumers to borrow and lend—and therefore to spend. Too much money and credit can lead to too much spending and inflation. Too little money and credit can lead to too little spending and recession.

The role of central banks in domestic economies has evolved over time. Initially they did no more than provide the economy with money in which the public could place confidence. Only later did they deliberately manage the volume of money and credit to influence spending, their aim being to help domestic economies achieve stable growth with a minimum of inflation or recession.

The International Monetary System

The Holy Roman Empire has been said to have been neither "holy" nor "Roman" nor an "empire"; the international monetary system is not fully "international" (since Russia and China, among other countries, barely participate), is broader than "monetary," and is less formal than a fully coherent "system." We may define the international monetary system as the set of arrangements, rules, practices, and institutions under which payments are made and received for transactions carried out across national boundaries. The international "system" is concerned not only with the supply of international money but with the relationships among the hundred or so currencies of individual countries and with the pattern of balance-of-payments relationships and the manner in which they are adjusted and settled. Thus the "system" is broader than "monetary" in that it is concerned with trade relationships and fiscal and other national policies as well. But to call it a "system" is to impute more formality to it than it deserves, even though it embodies a set of rules enunciated in the Articles of Agreement of the International Monetary Fund.* International monetary relations are governed not only by these Fund rules but also by agreements and consultations among nations through other international institutions: The General Agreement on Tariffs and Trade (GATT), Organization for Economic Cooperation and Development (OECD), Bank for

---

*The term "international monetary order" has been suggested by Robert Mundell. Richard Cooper, pointing out that the entity we are discussing can be both disorderly and unsystematic, prefers "international monetary regime."

International Settlements (BIS) and other regional organizations, and the United Nations Conference on Trade and Development (UNCTAD).

A major reason why the international monetary system is afflicted with problems is that the nations that participate in it are politically independent but economically and financially interdependent. This discrepancy defines the functions of the international monetary system; at its best, the system acts to reconcile the conflicting economic policies of its politically independent members.

In order to perform this reconciling function, the system is concerned, first, with those economic policies of its members that affect other nations—with how nations act, deliberately or otherwise, to influence their balance-of-payments positions (each country's balance of payments being the mirror image of the balance of payments of the rest of the world with it). Of particular importance here is exchange rate policy, since each country's exchange rate with another country is also the exchange rate of the other country with it. The system is concerned, second, with how nations settle their accounts with one another—how they pay or receive money in some form to finance deficits and surpluses. Third, the system is concerned with the amount and form of international money; in this respect it is closest to the characterization we have given to domestic monetary systems, though by "international money" we mean not just cash but all the various financial instruments nations hold as reserves. In practice, the U.S. dollar has tended to fulfill for the international monetary system all three of the functions of money identified above.

In broad terms, then, the international monetary system involves the management, in one way or another, of three processes: (1) the adjustment of balance-of-payments positions, including the establishment and alteration of exchange rates; (2) the financing of payments imbalances among countries by the use of credit or reserves; and (3) the provision of international money (reserves).

Any monetary system—even one involving a minimum of deliberate management—requires a set of rules of behavior. The gold-standard system, whether or not it ever existed in the idealized form described in textbooks, involved little management at the international level but depended on a set of rules governing the policies of individual countries. A system of freely floating exchange rates, which would not need explicit provision for settling imbalances or providing reserves, would also require a rule proscribing official intervention in the foreign exchange markets. In the present system, and probably in the future system, there is a role not only for general rules or guidelines but also for more active day-to-day management at the international level.

Why Does the International Monetary System Matter?

The key to the answer to this question lies in the concept of international interdependence. "No man is an island," and even nations that are islands are affected by economic events and policies in other countries. It was often said, twenty years ago and more, that when the United States sneezes, Europe catches pneumonia. Interdependence is no longer as asymmetrical as it was in the early postwar years, but the economic and financial linkages among nations are closer now.

Exports and imports have grown at a faster rate than domestic output in almost all countries. International travel has increased enormously. Money moves from one currency to another, by a variety of channels, in amounts unimaginable twenty years ago. Living standards and employment have come to depend on the ability to export and to import and to provide the capital flows that help finance such trade and the stock of capital on which it is based.

In these circumstances, a strike, a bank failure, an increase in interest rates, a recession, inflation, the discovery of a new resource, or the development of a new or improved product in any one nation can have a significant impact on other nations. When the government of one country adopts a policy to deal with a problem, other countries will have an interest in the impact of that policy on them. Will it influence their imports, their exports, or the flows of funds across national boundaries? What effect will these changes have in turn on domestic output, employment, prices, and living standards?

The international monetary system provides the framework within which these various economic relationships among nations operate. A well-functioning monetary system will facilitate international trade and investment and smooth adaptation to change. A monetary system that functions poorly may not only discourage the development of trade and investment among nations but subject their economies to disruptive shocks when necessary adjustments to change are prevented or delayed—much as an earthquake is said to represent a sudden release of subsurface tensions that build up as edges of geological plates first lock and then slip as they shift in relation to each other. So the international monetary system matters because it affects the ways in which nations impinge on each other and in which they manage their economic interdependence.[3]

In the course of this book we shall have numerous opportunities to observe the struggle of nations, individually or collectively, to cope with their economic and monetary interdependence. While interdependence creates problems, the

belief is widespread that it brings reciprocal advantages, economic and political, to the nations that participate. One outstanding example of a political
benefit was the reconciliation of France and Germany in the period following
World War II. Starting with the efforts of Jean Monnet to create the European
Coal and Steel Community in 1950, France and Germany have since become
major trading partners. It now seems unthinkable that—one hesitates to use
the word—war could break out again between those two countries.

In this connection it is useful, and perhaps refreshing, to note that the
problems of the international monetary system have relatively little bearing on
national security in the military aspect. Virtually all of the monetary debate
and controversy of the past decade has been among nations that are national
security allies or neutrals. The potential military adversaries of the United
States and its allies have played no significant role in the development and
discussions involving the international monetary system in recent years.

This is not surprising, since Russia and China are more self-sufficient and
less interdependent with other economies than are the United States and,
especially, Europe, Japan, and most developing countries. In time, Russia and
China may join the system. Their entry is unlikely to change drastically its
basic character. These facts lend support to the point, noted in the preface, that
improvement or reform of the international monetary system, difficult though
it may be to agree upon, is not likely to be thwarted by deep-rooted differences
in national interest.

II

Recovery and Renewal: The System
from Bretton Woods to the End of the 1950's

When peace was restored in 1945, the outlines of the postwar international monetary system had already been agreed upon. This was largely the result of intensive work during the war by Lord Keynes and his colleagues in the United Kingdom and by Harry Dexter White and his colleagues in the United States.

John Maynard Keynes was the foremost economist of his generation. He first achieved world fame upon publication of *The Economic Consequences of the Peace* (1919), a condemnation of the Treaty of Versailles. His subsequent major works on economics, *Monetary Reform* (1924), *A Treatise on Money* (1930), and *The General Theory of Employment, Interest, and Money* (1936), established his eminence in economics. *The General Theory* created a revolution in the thinking of economists and, in turn, had a profound impact on economic policies of governments throughout the world. In addition to producing these seminal books, Keynes found time to write numerous essays and biographical sketches, to contribute to the daily and weekly press, to manage the finances of Kings College of Cambridge University, to serve as editor of a distinguished professional journal, to promote the arts, and to be associated with both the British Treasury and the Bank of England. After the publication of *How to Pay for the War* (1940)—a book that applied his theories, aimed initially at economies in recession, to coping with excess demand—Keynes joined the Treasury and soon was involved in postwar monetary planning.[1]

Harry Dexter White earned a Ph.D. in economics at Harvard, where his dissertation won the prestigious Wells Prize. (It was published in 1933 as *The French International Accounts, 1880–1913*.) After teaching at Harvard and Lawrence College in Appleton, Wisconsin, White joined the U.S. Treasury in

1934. During the next thirteen years he rose in the Treasury ranks, receiving a presidential appointment as Assistant Secretary in 1945. A forceful man, he saw to it that the Treasury dominated U.S. policy in international financial matters. Like Keynes, White turned his attention to postwar monetary plans early in the war.[2]

Late in 1942 Keynes and White began to exchange drafts, and from the ensuing negotiations there ultimately emerged a compromise proposal which was agreed to at the International Monetary and Financial Conference of the United and Associated Nations, held at Bretton Woods, New Hampshire, in July 1944. This agreement, signed by 44 nations, is the constitution, the Articles of Agreement, of the International Monetary Fund. (The Articles of Agreement of the World Bank were established at the same time.)

The postwar monetary planners underestimated the difficulties that Europe would face in restoring economic viability; at least, the plan they were able to agree upon was not designed to cope with the immediate post-war problems of relief and reconstruction.[3] Nor did they foresee the political friction that would develop between the Soviet Union and its wartime allies. The U.S.S.R. had been represented at the Bretton Woods Conference and signed, but never ratified, the Agreement. The combination of these two factors—more intractable economic recovery problems than had been expected and the splitting of the world into hostile ideological camps—was mainly responsible for a series of special measures under which the United States (and also Canada) extended direct financial assistance to Western Europe. The first of these efforts was the Anglo-American Loan Agreement of 1945. It was followed by a Greek-Turkish Aid program, "interim aid" to Europe, and finally by the Marshall Plan.

In his speech initiating the Marshall Plan, Secretary of State George C. Marshall said, "the rehabilitation of the economic structure of Europe quite evidently will require a much longer time and greater effort than had been foreseen."[4] Until Europe and Japan achieved recovery from the devastation of war, the design of the international monetary system envisaged at Bretton Woods could not be fully implemented.

The failure to foresee fully the severity of postwar transitional problems was epitomized in the inability of the United Kingdom to carry out the provisions of the Anglo-American Loan Agreement, under which the United States loaned Britain $3.75 billion to assist it "to meet transitional postwar deficits in its current balance of payments," while Britain agreed, among other provisions, to make sterling convertible for current transactions within one year after the effective date of the agreement—that is, by July 15, 1947.

(Convertibility would foster multilateral trade by permitting countries that exported to or otherwise earned funds from the United Kingdom to use the proceeds to make purchases elsewhere.) As it turned out, Britain had to suspend convertibility within one month because of the rapid drain on its dollar resources.[5] It was not until December 1958 that the United Kingdom and a number of other European countries reestablished the convertibility of their currencies.

This chapter has two purposes: (1) to describe the design of the postwar monetary system agreed to at Bretton Woods and to identify its deficiencies and (2) to trace the major economic and monetary developments from the end of World War II to the end of the 1950's—the period of the "dollar shortage." This background is essential to an understanding of subsequent international monetary problems. "What Is Past Is Prologue" is engraved on the National Archives Building on Constitution Avenue in Washington. A taxi driver, asked by a passenger to explain the meaning of this motto, is reported to have replied "You ain't seen nothing yet."

The Fund Agreement

Those responsible for designing the International Monetary Fund had aimed at establishing a system of multilateral trade and payments compatible with the maintenance of high levels of income and employment. Consistent with this purpose, they wanted to prevent a repetition of the so-called beggar-thy-neighbor policies of the 1930's, when countries used trade restrictions, subsidies, and competitive depreciation of exchange rates in attempts to solve domestic unemployment problems by increasing their trade surpluses—thereby shifting their domestic problems to other countries. Keynes and White had other motivations and other fears, too, and they didn't always agree. A reading of the Keynes plan[6] shows that he was attempting to establish a thoroughly reformed system, while the U.S. representatives, fearing that the United States, undamaged by the war, would find itself providing unlimited finance to the rest of the world (the "milch cow of the world in general," as Keynes characterized the U.S. concern[7]), were cautious and conservative in viewing the proposed innovations that issued from Keynes' office in the British Treasury. (As we shall see later, American proposals for monetary reform put forward in 1972 bear a striking similarity to Keynes' ideas formulated 30 years earlier.)

As it emerged from the negotiations of 1943–44 the Fund Agreement, while providing transitional arrangements in recognition of the disruption of the economies and the financial systems of many countries as a result of the war, contained the following essential features:

1. A new permanent institution, the International Monetary Fund, was to be established to promote consultation and collaboration on international monetary problems, to administer the Articles, and to lend to member countries in balance-of-payments deficit.

2. Each Fund member would establish, with Fund approval, a par value for its currency and would undertake to maintain market exchange rates for its currency within one percent of the declared par value. A related provision was that countries that freely buy and sell gold in settlement of international transactions were "deemed" to be adhering to the requirement that they maintain exchange rates within the one percent margins. Thus the United States, the only country that met this condition, was not expected to intervene in the foreign exchange markets; rather, other countries would intervene, mainly by buying or selling dollars against their own currencies, to keep their rates within one percent of their parities with the dollar.

3. Except for a transitional arrangement permitting a one-time adjustment of up to ten percent in initial par values, members would change their par values only after having secured Fund approval. And such approval would be given only if the country's balance of payments was in "fundamental disequilibrium"—a term that was not defined in the Articles and has never been officially defined. While it would be inaccurate to describe this as a system of "fixed" exchange rates, it is clear that exchange rate adjustment was not to be undertaken lightly. Temporary and cyclical imbalances were to be financed by the use of reserves or through borrowing from the Fund and were to be corrected by policies other than exchange rate adjustment.

4. After a transitional period, currencies would be convertible in the sense that countries would undertake to redeem balances of their currencies acquired by other members; such convertibility would be into either gold or the currency of the member requesting conversion. Restrictions on payments for current transactions and all discriminatory currency practices were to be discouraged, if not eliminated.

5. The Fund would be in a position to lend to countries in deficit, out of its holdings of gold and currencies arising from subscriptions by its members in relation to their "quotas" (to be determined according to each member's size in the world economy). But the Fund was not to lend to finance outflows of capital (this provision was insisted upon by

the Americans), and countries were permitted, if not encouraged, to use controls to suppress undesired capital flows (a reaction to the "hot money" movements of the 1920's and 1930's).

6. If a country's currency became "scarce" in the Fund, the latter could authorize other countries to adopt exchange controls on imports and other current account purchases from the surplus country. This sanction against countries in large surplus was offered by the Americans at a late stage of the negotiations in response to a charge by Keynes and his colleagues that the proposed system was asymmetrically severe toward countries in deficit.[8] In practice, as Keynes predicted,[9] the scarce currency clause of the Fund Articles has never been invoked. Its use might have been justified immediately after the war, when Europe (and Japan, which did not become a member of the Fund until 1952) was experiencing a "dollar shortage." But many countries were then already applying discriminatory restrictions against imports from the United States, and the United States acted quickly, through the Marshall Plan, to alleviate the scarcity of its currency.

It is easy, 30 years later, to criticize the Fund Agreement (its deficiencies will be discussed at the end of this chapter), but the historical significance of the Bretton Woods agreement should be recognized. As Louis Rasminsky, Governor of the Bank of Canada, said in 1969, "Something very important happened at Bretton Woods in 1944, and that was that the world consciously took control of the international monetary system."[10] In the words of Austin Robinson, "What was Bretton Woods about if it was not the creation of a world in which countries did not close their eyes to the repercussions of their actions on others?"[11] For the first time a potentially worldwide central monetary institution had been established and a universal set of rules of monetary behavior had been formulated. What had been created was the embryo of a world central bank.[12]

Bretton Woods established both the IMF and the International Bank for Reconstruction and Development but, as Keynes believed, the Fund was really a bank, and the Bank a fund.

Early Postwar Economic and Monetary Developments

The cessation of World War II left Europe and Japan in a state of industrial and financial destitution. While the degree of war damage to factories, railroads, roads, harbors, and homes varied from country to country, it was universally severe. Imports were vitally needed not only to feed and clothe the populations but also to begin the process of renewing and replacing capital equipment and infrastructure so that domestic economic activity could be restored. But export capacity was dependent on industrial recovery and foreign exchange reserves were low.

The United States, whose industrial and agricultural capacity had expanded during the war, was the place to which war-torn countries looked for imports of food and manufactures. U.S. exports rose rapidly, and in 1947 this country had an export surplus of almost $10 billion, which was more than 4 percent of its GNP (an equivalent export surplus in 1975 would have been $60 billion). But Lend-lease had been terminated in 1945, and despite the activities of the United Nations Relief and Rehabilitation Administration (UNRRA), to which North America was the major contributor, and despite other U.S. aid programs, the foreign exchange reserves of Europe and Japan were being rapidly depleted. In the two years 1946–1947, the rest of the world used about $6 billion of its gold and dollar holdings to finance its deficit with the United States. The gold and dollar reserves of Europe fell by one-fourth in this period.

Meanwhile, political weakness in a number of continental European countries engendered fears of increased Communist influence. And the winter of 1946–47 was one of the most severe in Europe's history. In Henry Fairlie's words, revisionist historians

> forget the condition of the continent whose future was in the balance. They forget it all: the cold and the hunger and the disease; the factories which were in ruins, the others which had been dismantled, the rest which were idle because there was no fuel; the unemployed and the refugees—they forget even these, the displaced persons, as we learned to call them, for whom there was no room, indeed no inn; they forget the scavenging that had become a way of life. They even forget the weather, the terrible winter of 1947, which seemed to have no end; when I could walk, if a personal memory will be allowed, over the hills of Northumberland in what ought to have been the warmth of a new spring, but which was instead still a freezing cold, kicking the carcasses of the sheep which had frozen to death, and that I could as easily have walked through the cellars of Europe, kicking the unburied corpses of human beings.[13]

In these circumstances, the United States offered the Marshall Plan—formally the European Recovery Program*—which was announced in rather

---

*It was soon dubbed the ERP. The proclivity of Americans to use initials had an amusing sidelight. The original legislation provided for a "United States Special Representative" in Europe to help administer the ERP. When it was discovered that the initials of his title might turn out to be awkward for their bearer, Averell Harriman, the name was changed to Office of the Special Representative (OSR).

low-key terms by Secretary of State Marshall at the Harvard commencement exercises in June 1947. This was to be a systematic four-year arrangement under which the United States would make available grants and loans that would finance the recovery and assure the viability of the European economies. The European countries in turn were expected to organize and commit themselves to a self-help program of cooperative action that would make U.S. assistance effective and successful. "The objectives which the framers of the Marshall Plan set themselves were the rehabilitation of the ruined countries and the reconstruction of the European economies with a view of containing Communism and reducing the dangers of domestic subversion."[14]

Ernest Bevin, British Foreign Secretary, characterized the Marshall speech as "an announcement of the greatest historic significance. It rightly placed responsibility on Europe to make the next move and formulate a plan of reconstruction. The three immediate problems to be considered in any plan were food, coal, and transport." Bevin went on to observe that the United States was in the same position in 1947 as Britain at the end of the Napoleonic Wars. At that time Britain held, according to Bevin, about 30 percent of the world's wealth; the United States in 1947 held even more. Britain for 18 years after Waterloo "practically gave away her exports," but this resulted, he said, in stability and a hundred years of peace.[15]

The European countries set to work on their side of the bargain and established an Organization for European Economic Cooperation (OEEC). Between mid-1948 and mid-1952, the United States provided $11.6 billion in the form of grants and $1.8 billion in the form of loans to the countries of Europe. In the case of Japan, grants amounted to $950 million and loans to $275 million.[16]

Several characteristics of the Marshall Plan had particular significance for the subsequent evolution of the international monetary system.

1. As part of the recovery effort, European countries were encouraged by the United States to liberalize trade among themselves while maintaining restrictions on imports from the so-called dollar area. The intra-European liberalization effort was supplemented by a European Payments Union (EPU), again with American sponsorship, designed to facilitate the liberalization and expansion of multilateral intra-European trade and payments while enabling European countries to conserve their scarce dollar reserves.
2. Aid recipients were urged by the United States to expand their exports to the dollar area, and the devaluations of 1949 were a part of this effort.

In September 1949 the United Kingdom and most European countries devalued their currencies against the dollar by about 30 percent. While these actions were urged and applauded by U.S. officials, it may now be questioned whether, at least in the case of some countries, the devaluation was not excessive.

3. Countries receiving Marshall Plan assistance were encouraged not to spend it all for imports but to hold a portion of the dollars so as to rebuild their depleted reserves. In other words, pursuit of balance-of-payments surpluses was established as a laudable objective.

4. Administration of the Marshall Plan led to the close involvement of American officials in the economic policies of recipient countries. In each country a U.S. mission was established, headed by a director with ambassadorial rank and staffed with experts on industry, trade, finance, etc. In these conditions it was perhaps unavoidable that youthful and exuberant Americans often found themselves negotiating with and even instructing European ministers and senior officials not only on the use of Marshall funds but on the general economic policies of the recipient countries. The donor-recipient relationship is a prickly one in any circumstances, and no doubt it produced in some cases arrogance on the one side and resentment on the other. The arrogance took the form of implying that if Europe would only remake itself in the American image, its problems would be solved much more easily; the resentment followed naturally from this attitude as well as from the need to accept charity. Yet the relationship was fruitful. Said an astute European commentator, Raymond Aron:

To this voluntary contribution I would add the way in which the Americans continuously and almost as a matter of course supplied examples of know-how, in respect to productivity, for instance. The American propensity to consider their own system exemplary, though it may lead to the direct havoc in politics or morals, proved most fortunate for the European and Japanese economies; the productivity missions which toured the United States, and the closely knit relationships which sprang up on both sides of the Atlantic, had beneficial repercussions on the Old Continent. After 1945 the Europeans had more to learn than to teach. The Americans, by very virtue of their philosophy, considered it a matter of course to teach others the secret of their own success. As the predominant economy, the United States had the advantage, from its partners' point of view, of believing in freedom and communication rather than secrecy and bureaucracy.[17]

These and other features of U.S.-European economic and financial relations in the early postwar period can be understood only in the light of then-existing attitudes concerning the economic prospects of Europe and Japan relative to those of North America. Apart from the need to repair and replace war damage, which imposed an economic handicap on Europe and Japan, it was widely assumed that the United States would, for many years, outpace the rest of the world in the development of new technology and in the rate of growth of productivity.

Charles Kindleberger saw it this way: "Different rates of technological progress in the United States and abroad, and in particular faster technological progress in the United States than abroad, call for a continuous dynamic adjustment which other forces in the world economy resist."[18] Kindleberger went on to say:

> Only a few economists, on the other hand, believe that the structural disequilibrium produced by World War II is a permanent condition requiring assistance from the dollar area in perpetuity, or continuous interference with the price mechanism and discrimination in trade with the dollar area. This is not to suggest that the secular dollar shortage is not a problem which may require its own remedies. Given a structural disequilibrium, however, most observers are in agreement that it must be possible to adjust production and consumption over time with the help of the law of comparative advantage so that a new equilibrium position can be reached.[19]

The widely held view that a dollar shortage was likely to last for a long time was bolstered by the apparent condition of some of the major European countries. England, burdened financially with heavy external liabilities created during the war, had been thought to have been going downhill industrially since World War I.[20] Germany, formerly a formidable industrial power, was now divided geographically and in ruins; in addition, the heavy immigration of "displaced persons" from Eastern Europe was then viewed as a burden. France, although less damaged physically, was regarded as a nation whose industrialists were not interested in improving productivity, preferring instead to be protected by high tariffs against external competition which might disrupt existing business relationships and practices; meanwhile France's resources were being drained off in a war in Indochina. (To many of those whose job it was to follow developments in the French economy, including the present writer, it seemed inconceivable that France would ever be able to free itself from dependence on financial assistance from the United States.) Italy, with a high unemployment rate and an impoverished southern region, was not taken seriously as an industrial power and soon came under American criticism for utilizing too little of the Marshall Plan funds allocated to it. While Belgium recovered early and threw off discriminatory import restrictions against North America, it is a small country that could neither influence nor characterize Europe. In Asia, Japan's cities lay in ruins and, in any event, it had the prewar reputation of producing cheap and shoddy products.

These views led in turn to the expectation that the world would for many years experience a "dollar shortage." It was believed that American products would remain especially attractive, in terms of price, quality, and availability, and would easily outcompete the products of Europe and Japan in their own markets, in other countries, and in the United States. Thus the United States would continually tend to have an export surplus greater than the rest of the world could find the dollars to finance. Hence the dollar shortage. This in turn justified under the Marshall Plan those policies identified above: discriminatory import restrictions against the "dollar area," special incentives for Europe and Japan to promote exports to the United States and other "dollar" countries, and major devaluations.

The expectation of a continuing dollar shortage led the American government to establish incentives for U.S. corporations to invest abroad, where dollars and U.S. technology were badly needed; similarly, American banks and capital markets were invited to find ways to lend abroad. At the same time, other countries were encouraged to build up their dollar holdings in order to have adequate reserves in case of need—to protect, for example, against a U.S. recession that might reduce U.S. imports and the dollar earnings of the rest of the world. And while it did not justify, it perhaps explained the high-handed attitude of some Americans in their dealings with Marshall aid recipients.

Economic and Balance-of-Payments Results Under the Marshall Plan, 1948–1952

The record of the European economic recovery is well known. For the countries participating in the ERP, industrial production rose 39 percent from 1948 to 1952. At the same time, the physical volume of exports more than doubled while the volume of imports increased by about one-third. When all current account transactions, including U.S. military expenditures, are considered, the net balance on goods, services, and private remittances of the OEEC countries showed a small surplus ($600 million) in 1952.[21] A number of the ERP countries had begun to add to their gold and foreign exchange reserves. And the level of living improved markedly in Europe; by 1952–53 prices had stabilized in most countries, helped along by a revival in the use of monetary policy.

These developments in Europe—as well as the improvements in Japan's external position, aided by expenditures related to the Korean War—had their reflection in the balance of payments of the United States. The U.S. trade surplus declined from $10.1 billion in 1947 to $2.6 billion in 1952. U.S. Government grants plus capital outflows, official and private, exceeded the surplus on goods and services. Beginning in 1950, the overall U.S. balance of payments was in deficit.

Although the U.S. balance of payments had been nudged into deficit, no one knew and no one cared. In fact, the U.S. balance of payments was not characterized as being in "deficit." Rather, official statistics and commentary *(Annual Reports* of the IMF and articles in the *Federal Reserve Bulletin)* used the term "net transfers of gold and dollars to the rest of the world." Attention was focused on the improving position of Europe and Japan, and there was rejoicing in the fact that some countries were succeeding in acquiring and holding on to dollars, thereby restoring their depleted reserves. When some countries began to use their dollar accruals to purchase gold from the United States, this too was welcomed, since the distribution of world gold reserves was thought to be highly skewed: at the end of World War II the United States held 60 percent of world gold reserves.

The marked improvement in the position of Europe and Japan was recognized as reflecting in part the large increase in U.S. overseas military expenditures that began after the outbreak of the Korean War. The IMF pointed out, in its *Annual Report* covering the year 1952, that these expenditures could not be counted on to continue over "the somewhat longer run." Furthermore, it noted, many countries still maintained restrictions on imports from the dollar area.[22] It was estimated that while two-thirds of intra-European trade was free of restrictions by mid-1952, only 11 percent of imports of OEEC countries from the dollar area had been so liberalized as of the beginning of 1953.[23]

Europe's recovery and external improvement in the years 1948–1952 made it suitable to terminate U.S. economic grants to the OEEC countries, but it was generally believed that a serious disequilibrium in world payments—"the dollar problem"—remained to be corrected. The Commission on Foreign Economic Policy (Randall Commission), established by Act of Congress in 1953, reported:

During the period 1946 through 1953, the United States transferred to the rest of the world through gifts and loans $33 billion of goods and services, exclusive of

military items. This total was equal to more than one fourth of all American
exports. The fact that after so large a program of assistance, carried out over so
long a period, the rest of the world still finds it necessary to maintain drastic
restrictions on trade and payment, directed particularly against this country, indicates strikingly the gravity of the world's dollar problem.[24]

After reviewing the progress made in Europe, the Commission continued:

Surveying the postwar experience as a whole, the Commission believes, as already
stated, that much remains to be done to achieve a dependable international balance.
It believes that the problem must be attacked on many fronts and that too much
dependence should not be placed on any one line of attack. There is no single or
simple solution. The final solution will probably depend even more on the efforts
of other countries than on our own. It will involve their continuing internal efforts
to achieve sound and strong economies and their external efforts to correct their
international imbalance.[25]

The Commission recommended a series of measures that included guarantees and tax relief to American corporations and individuals, designed to
encourage them to invest abroad. To promote the attainment of convertibility,
the Commission also recommended measures to increase the reserves of other
countries, especially the United Kingdom. Such measures might include more
active utilization of the International Monetary Fund and the exploration of
the possibility of standby credits between the Federal Reserve System and
foreign central banks.

In these circumstances, the earning of overall balance-of-payments surpluses by other countries was regarded as normal and as a sign of successful
policies, domestic and international. The United States, on the other hand, was
considered able to ignore its balance of payments. It was the strongest industrial country, its current account surplus was large, and if other countries had
not been maintaining discriminatory import controls against U.S. products,
the surplus would have been even larger. Virtually every country wanted to
hold dollars, and those central banks that bought gold, a non-earning asset,
were welcome to it. It was taken for granted that the dollar price of gold would
remain at $35 per ounce, where it had been since 1934. While other countries
devalued their currencies in 1949, it was assumed that the U.S. exchange rate
in terms of gold was immutable, given the passive stance of the United States
in balance-of-payments policy and given the central role of the dollar as the
reserve currency in the international monetary system.

Economic and Monetary Developments in the Later 1950's

With the termination of the Marshall Plan, U.S. economic assistance to Western Europe fell off sharply. This was partly offset by an increase in U.S. military expenditures in Europe, which in 1954–1959 amounted to about $1.5 billion per year. At the same time, loans and grants to less developed countries, including security support assistance, increased. Thus U.S. government grants and loans to the world as a whole, which in 1950–1952 had averaged $3.1 billion per year, were maintained at an average rate of $2.25 billion per year for the rest of the decade.[26]

Economic progress in continental Europe was impressive. Angus Maddison characterized it in this way: "In continental Europe the decade of the 1950's was brilliant, with growth of output and consumption, productivity, investment and employment surpassing any recorded historical experience, and the rhythm of development virtually uninterrupted by recession."[27]

Output (gross domestic product in constant prices) per man hour, which rose at an average rate of 2.4 percent per year in the United States in the 1950's, increased 3.9 percent in France, 6 percent in Germany, 4.1 percent in Italy, 3.7 percent in the Netherlands, and 4.2 percent in Switzerland. In the United Kingdom the rate was 2 percent, a much smaller acceleration than occurred on the Continent.[28]

Two additional features of Europe's thriving expansion were significant. Defense spending was of much smaller importance in Europe (and Japan) than in the United States. Of the increase in GNP from 1950 to 1960, almost 15 percent went to defense spending in the United States, whereas comparable figures in the larger European countries ranged from 2.8 percent in Germany to 6.4 percent in the United Kingdom.[29] This may help to explain the second feature, that Europe (and again Japan) devoted a much higher proportion of annual output to capital investment than did the United States.

As a result, industrial production in the OEEC countries increased by more than 60 percent between 1952 and 1960.[30] The U.S. recessions of 1953–54 and 1957–58 had relatively little impact on overall economic activity in Europe. "Since 1950," Maddison wrote in 1964, "the United States has had three business recessions, none of which has had a serious impact on European payments or more than a minor impact on European demand and output. The most severe was in 1958 and coincided with an extremely mild recession in Europe, but the U.S. recession contributed to it rather than caused it."[31] In fact, during the recession of 1958, U.S. exports to Europe were more seriously affected than were European exports to the United States.[32] Thus the adage, "when the United States sneezes, Europe catches pneumonia," turned out to be greatly exaggerated. This realization must have contributed to the self-confidence and spirit of independence that became evident in Europe in the late 1950's and, as we shall see, had an important influence on U.S.-European monetary relations in the 1960's.

Meanwhile, after a period of price stability in 1952–53, most European countries experienced some degree of inflation for the rest of the decade. For OEEC member countries combined, the GNP price deflator rose 20 percent from 1953 to 1959.[33] Among the larger countries, the advance varied from 10 percent in Italy to 15 percent in Germany, 21 percent in the United Kingdom, and 34 percent in France. In the United States the rise in the deflator over the same period was 14 percent. An experts group appointed by the OEEC[34] attributed the European inflation to two causes: a period of excess demand lasting one to two years (1955–56 in Germany, 1956–58 in France) and in some countries—the United Kingdom, the Netherlands, and Scandinavia—wage increases in excess of productivity advance.

Balance of Payments Trends

While GNP in real terms rose 30 percent from 1953 to 1959 in the OEEC countries combined, the volume of exports increased 59 percent (and a further 13 percent from 1959 to 1960). For the original members of the European Economic Community (Belgium-Luxembourg, France, Italy, Germany, and the Netherlands) the increase in the volume of exports was 89 percent in the period 1953–1959. The liberalization of trade among OEEC countries in general and among EEC countries in particular provided a stimulus to demand and to efficiency. In a sense, European countries, at least those on the Continent, pulled themselves up by their bootstraps when they opened their markets to each other. This action made possible not only increased exports but a spur to increased productivity resulting from economies of scale in a larger market and exposure to the competition of imports from more efficient producers.[35] In the process the countries of Europe increased their interdependence.

Britain seems to have been an exception to this generalization. We have already noted its slow advance of productivity compared with major nations on the Continent. An analysis by Lamfalussy indicates that Britain's share in the exports of all industrial countries declined between 1953 and 1959, while the share of the EEC countries increased markedly. He attributes this outcome to a deterioration in the competitive position of the United Kingdom, accounted for in turn by the slower growth of productivity, since wages rose at about the same rate in Britain as in the EEC countries on the average. Lamfalussy summarizes his argument in terms of a "virtuous" circle of growth in the EEC: "competitive advantage in world markets, leading to faster growth of exports; export-oriented growth, raising the share of investment in the national product; higher investment ratio, calling forth a faster growth in the productivity of labor and leading, therefore, to renewed competitive advantage in world markets."[36] In Britain he finds a "vicious" circle, in which developments were the obverse of those on the Continent.

The trade deficit of the OEEC countries with the rest of the world, which had been reduced during the Marshall Plan period, showed little further net change during the rest of the 1950's. The deficit averaged $4.8 billion during the years 1953–1959, compared with $5.1 billion in 1952. But receipts from U.S. military transactions plus invisible receipts, which had already provided the OEEC countries with a small ($600 million) current account surplus in 1952, increased during the remainder of the decade. By 1959, the surplus on current transactions had risen to over $3.5 billion. Most of this increase was accounted for by non-trade transactions. Net receipts on account of invisible transactions rose from $2.1 billion in 1952 to $4.1 billion in 1959. Tourist receipts were of special importance for France and Italy, while the United Kingdom experienced an increase in investment income. Italy also benefitted from heavy remittances from emigrants. Germany was the only major country whose invisible accounts showed a deterioration between 1952 and 1959, despite a substantial increase in receipts from the provision of services to foreign military personnel on German soil. At the same time, Germany's trade position improved dramatically in the 1950's and by 1959 it had a current surplus of about $1.6 billion.[37]

During most of the 1950's, private capital flows were of small magnitude in the balance of payments of the European countries. There was a small inflow of U.S. private capital but this may have been more than offset by unrecorded capital outflows from Europe. On the other hand, U.S. capital flows to other areas—notably Latin America—probably found their way in part to Europe in the form of purchases of European exports or financial instruments. Most OEEC countries maintained strict controls against capital outflows. In 1957, Germany took the lead toward a freer regime of capital movements by allowing German residents to export capital in any form anywhere in the world.[38]

A substantial improvement in Europe's balance of payments in 1958 led to a sizable increase in reserves. In these circumstances, most European countries found it possible, at the end of 1958, to declare their currencies convertible. That is, they permitted nonresidents who earned their currencies, as a result of current transactions, to convert them into any other currency at exchange rates within the official margins. Only Germany permitted convertibility as well for the proceeds of capital transactions.[39]

With European currencies convertible (Japan took the step only in 1964), capital flows to Europe became both feasible and attractive to American businesses and financial institutions. Interest rates came to influence the flow of capital to and from Europe. By 1960, U.S. private capital flows to Western Europe reached $1.5 billion, compared with an average of just over $400 million in the three previous years.[40] Europe, now in surplus on current transactions, was also attracting capital inflows from the United States.

The French Crisis of 1956–1958

France, whose output increased rather little in the early 1950's, experienced a surge of domestic investment in 1955, followed by a step-up in defense spending in 1956. As a result excess demand developed, output accelerated, and prices rose. The GNP deflator, which had advanced little more than one percent per year from 1952 to 1955, rose by more than 5.5 percent from 1956 to 1957 and by a further 12.1 percent the following year.[41] Under the pressure of excess demand, imports increased rapidly and a moderate trade surplus in 1955 gave way to substantial deficits in 1956 and 1957 despite the imposition of import restrictions. Foreign exchange reserves declined sharply and France found it necessary to draw on the International Monetary Fund, to borrow from the EPU, and to defer debt repayments to the United States.

A series of stabilization measures in 1957–58, along with two devaluations of the franc, finally restored stability, led to a replenishment of foreign exchange reserves, and set the stage for a renewed period of rapid economic expansion.

Two features of this experience deserve attention. France drew from the Fund in 1957 and again in 1958 under standby arrangements carrying conditions regarding French policies. French officials believed that the conditions imposed upon them by the Fund were more stringent than what had been asked of the United Kingdom in late 1956, when speculative capital flows, under the impact of the Suez crisis, contributed to a severe drain on Britain's reserves. Having come to the Fund hat in hand and then undergoing what they regarded as a humiliating experience, French financial officials were psychologically receptive to President de Gaulle's expressed determination to make France economically strong and to combat what he regarded as Anglo-Saxon domination of international monetary affairs.

The second feature of consequence is that the French franc was devalued by a total of 29 percent against the dollar and most other currencies during this crisis. This substantial devaluation may well have been excessive. In any event, it provided France for several years with ample leeway to pursue expansionary policies without having to be overly concerned with domestic price developments. At the same time, it permitted France to participate with other EEC countries in the "virtuous" circle of growth.

Developments in Japan

The relative neglect of Japan in the preceding pages corresponds somewhat to the prevailing attitude toward that country in the 1950's. Japan was not at the center of things, it did not create disturbances that attracted attention to itself, and its leaders adopted a "low profile" in world affairs. Europeans tended to regard Japan as a ward of the United States.

Although Japan had gone about rebuilding its burned-out cities and restoring industrial and agricultural output, the American attitude in 1950 toward further progress in Japan's per-capita income was characterized in a report to the President in this way:

> The chief obstacles are the disadvantageous competitive position of certain segments of Japanese export industry (arising out of obsolete plant and equipment and aggravated by inefficient and wasteful use of manpower), the reduction in the size of Japan's merchant fleet, the international political problems associated with the re-entry into foreign countries of Japanese merchant vessels and foreign traders, and over the longer run, the rapid rate of population growth.

However, the report continued, "Japan can supply the underdeveloped areas, where its chief markets must be found, with an important part of the capital and consumer goods needed for development purposes."[42]

As it turned out, national income per capita, in real terms, rose at a compound annual rate of almost 9 percent from 1951 to 1959. Several factors combined to render Japan's economic development much more favorable than the above quotation suggests. For one thing, the Korean War created a heavy demand for Japanese goods and, at the same time, relieved balance-of-payments strains. Industrial production rose by an amazing 33 percent from 1950 to 1951 and a further 9 percent in 1952. By 1959, industrial production was 144 percent above the 1952 level, a compound average annual increase of more than 13 percent.[43]

The rapid increase in output and income—encouraged by growing exports and by U.S. military procurement in Japan of goods and services—provided both the incentive and the financing for enlarged business investment expenditures. Gross fixed capital formation rose rapidly after 1951 both in absolute terms and as a proportion of total output; it increased from about 17.5 percent of GNP in 1950 to 27 percent in 1959.[44] Even more so than Europe, Japan was free from the burden of defense spending. And history and geography combined to hold down the proportion of national output devoted to housing.

Meanwhile, Japan's birth rate fell off with remarkable steepness. Encouraged by official policies, including the availability of abortion facilities, the birth rate declined from 28.1 per 1000 in 1950—about what it had been in 1940 —to about 17 per 1000 in the early 1960's. The rate of increase of population declined from 1.6 per cent in 1950 to 1 percent or less in the late 1950's and early 1960's.[45] At the same time there occurred a large shift of the labor force from agriculture to industry. And Japanese industry, by investing heavily and adopting advanced technology available abroad, achieved an explosive rate of growth of productivity. Lamfalussy's "virtuous circle" of growth was exhibited dramatically in Japan.

In these circumstances, Japan's exports increased rapidly. Its share of world exports and imports doubled in the 1950's. The United States became Japan's largest single market, taking more than one-fourth of its exports by 1959. Continental Europe, on the other hand, maintained restrictions on some imports from Japan and accounted for only about 6.5 percent of Japan's exports in 1959.[46]

Rapid growth of exports and output also made Japan a large importer, but exports grew more rapidly, and by the end of the 1950's Japan had a trade surplus of a few hundred million dollars. The other items in Japan's balance of payments were of relatively small magnitude, on balance; Japan's reserves increased slowly, though with fluctuations, during the 1950's. In that period, Japan accounted for only a small part of the overall surpluses that were the counterpart of the deficits in the U.S. balance of payments.

The International Monetary System at the End of the 1950's

The 1950's, then, were a decade of dramatic change in Europe and Japan. The near-hopeless status of their economies at the inauguration of the Marshall Plan had given way to economic recovery and expansion and to significant improvement in the balance of payments. The gold and foreign exchange reserves of Western Europe and Japan virtually doubled between 1952 and 1959, when they reached more than $22 billion (of a world total of $57 billion).[47]

Yet, habits and practices adopted in the early postwar years persisted, even though Europe and Japan were now in a far different economic position. As late as 1958 and early 1959, when France removed quotas on 90 percent of its imports from the countries of Europe, it removed them on only 50 percent of its imports from North America.[48] Discrimination against U.S. exports still appeared appropriate and justified. Only in 1961 did the countries of Western Europe abandon hesitantly the postwar transitional provision of the Fund Articles that authorized member countries to maintain restrictions on payments and transfers for current international transactions (Article XIV).

Toward the end of the decade, in 1958 and 1959, the U.S. deficit increased as a result of a (temporary) reduction in the surplus on goods and services. The overall deficit was $2.9 billion in 1958 and $2.2 billion in 1959.* Of these amounts, about three-fifths was financed by U.S. gold sales to foreign monetary authorities. The International Monetary Fund began to characterize the U.S. balance-of-payments position as a "problem."[49] Similarly, the *Economic Report of the President* published in January 1960 discussed the U.S. balance-of-payments problem and reported on American efforts to persuade other countries to reduce their restrictions on imports from the United States as well as on a first U.S. step toward tying foreign aid to American exports. The same report contained an analysis suggesting somewhat defensively that, except for automobiles, iron and steel, and aircraft, U.S. exports had maintained their competitive position in foreign markets between 1954–56 and 1958.

Concern about the balance of payments also played a role in the restrictive fiscal and monetary policies adopted in the United States in 1959.[50]

The *Federal Reserve Bulletin* for October 1960 spoke of the need for further increases in the export surplus to establish "reasonable equilibrium in U.S. transactions with the rest of the world." It went on to say:

> The gold stock of the United States is big enough to absorb the impact of large swings in current and capital transactions, so long as underlying forces continue to work in the direction of adjustment. These forces include rising international liquidity [an increase in IMF quotas had recently been agreed], continuing reductions of foreign barriers to U.S. goods, continuing efforts of U.S. businessmen to improve the competitive position of their products in domestic and foreign markets, and continuing avoidance of inflation in the United States.[51]

---

*Unless otherwise indicated, the overall balance-of-payments position is measured on the "official settlements" basis—that is, by the change in U.S. reserve assets plus the change in U.S. liabilities to foreign monetary authorities.

If some of this advice sounds familiar, it may be recalled that similar counsel had been offered by Americans to Europeans a decade earlier.

The OEEC, in its report for 1959, observed that the gold and foreign exchange holdings of member countries had increased $3.7 billion in 1958 and $1.4 billion in 1959, and said:

> The growth of the gold and dollar holdings of European countries over most of the last decade has represented a beneficial and necessary redistribution of world reserves. But the continuation of large overall European surpluses on the scale experienced during the past two years would pose considerable problems for the rest of the world. . . . The United States could not for very long provide an outflow of reserves on the present scale, although its reserves are still large in regard to any probable fluctuations in its balance of payments and to claims on the dollar as a reserve currency.[52]

The decade thus ended with the first stirrings of concern and adoption of measures to deal with the deficit in the U.S. balance of payments. The dollar shortage was over.

What replaced the dollar shortage was sometimes referred to as a "dollar glut." But it is useful to examine whether the new situation—a concern with U.S. balance-of-payments deficits—was simply the mirror image of the earlier dollar shortage. Was it the dollar shortage with a minus sign? U.S. deficits had been incurred since 1950, but the dollar shortage continued until the late 1950's. And although the overall U.S. deficit became larger in 1958–60, it declined again in the early 1960's. While some Europeans spoke of imported inflation in the early 1960's, U.S. deficits can hardly be said to have provided the world with excessive reserves in the 1960's. What then had changed?

What had changed was that European countries no longer had an excess —and repressed—demand for U.S. goods. Furthermore, the *level* of their reserves had been restored. Although none of them appeared to want to see their reserves reduced, they felt a greater security about being able to finance temporary deficits in their payments balances. The dollar shortage had been a reserve shortage and had reflected a lack of competitiveness of European products with those produced in America. Both of these adverse conditions had disappeared. At the same time, some Europeans began to worry about the *quality* of their dollar reserves; that is, they feared that, in time, U.S. liabilities would increase too much in relation to U.S. gold reserves, thereby leading to a devaluation of the dollar or, perhaps, inability to convert dollars into gold.

Finally, there must have been a political element in the changed attitude toward the dollar. With strength and self-respect restored, it was only natural that continental Europeans would react to their earlier position of weakness and subservience to an all-dominant America by finding fault with America's currency. Renewed strength brought with it a desire for greater symmetry in international monetary arrangements. One way to express this desire was to complain about excess accumulations of dollars. Thus the dollar glut was not simply the opposite of the dollar shortage. It was qualitative rather than quantitative, and it had political overtones.

A favorite pastime of a number of international economists in the 1960's was to poke fun at those of their colleagues who had written about the dollar shortage in the previous decade. Albert Hirschman commented on this attitude: "To consider the dollar shortage theories entirely refuted simply because the dollar shortage is no more, reminds one of the patient who after submitting to a variety of fairly radical treatments finally recovers his health and then exclaims: 'I told you that there was nothing wrong with me.' "[53]

Before turning to the 1960's, it will be useful to summarize the main features of the international monetary system as it appeared at the end of the 1950's in comparison with what had been incorporated in the Fund Articles of Agreement.

1. The par value system was in operation. Except for the special case of the Canadian dollar, which floated from 1950 to 1962, most countries were observing par values and prescribed margins. By 1960, virtually all of the industrial countries were implementing their obligation to maintain exchange rates within their territories at one percent above or below par—in practice, most European countries maintained margins of about three-fourths of one percent—by standing ready to intervene in the foreign exchange market to buy or sell dollars. The dollar had become the most widely used intervention currency. Another consequence of the use of the dollar as the main intervention currency was that when any country was in surplus, that surplus showed up as an increase in the country's dollar holdings. There was a tendency to assume that the corresponding deficit was in the United States. In fact the corresponding deficit could have been incurred by any country that used the dollar as intervention currency.

2. The dollar had also become the principal reserve currency. Between the end of 1949 and the end of 1959, U.S. liabilities to foreign monetary authorities increased $7 billion, bringing them to $10.1 billion. British liabilities (sterling balances) hardly changed during the decade, remaining at about $10 billion.

3. Par value changes had not been frequent. The general devaluation of 1949, initiated by Britain and followed in varying degrees by other countries, was looked upon as exceptional, representing a one-shot adjustment to postwar conditions and, in fact, was strongly encouraged by the United States. After that, Canada decided in 1950 to let its currency float, and France devalued in two steps in 1957–58. No other industrial country changed its par value. Par value changes and multiple currency practices occurred much more often among developing countries, in cases where inflation was rapid or where the terms of trade moved adversely.

4. The currencies of the industrial countries were convertible, though it took longer for this to be achieved than had been expected when the Fund Articles were written. The transitional arrangements (Article XIV), which permit "restrictions on payments and transfers for current international transactions," were abandoned by the major industrial countries in 1961 but were and are still being used in most developing countries. Going beyond what was envisaged at Bretton Woods, after 1958 "the scope for international movements of commercial bank funds and other private capital in response to financial incentives was widened, and a closer degree of interdependence was thus established between the capital and money markets of the industrial countries. These conditions made the conduct of monetary management more complex, and, in the consideration of national policies, called for closer attention to what was being done in other countries."[54]

5. The Fund, after the Marshall Plan period, began to exercise its lending functions as envisaged in the Articles. Borrowings from the Fund, notably by the United Kingdom and France, had been large in 1948, before Marshall Plan disbursements got going. Only about $100 million was drawn in 1949; nothing was drawn in 1950. In the years 1951–1955, borrowings averaged less than $100 million per year and, except for a Japanese drawing in 1953, were entirely by developing countries. The United Kingdom and France borrowed heavily in 1957 and 1958. In 1957, total drawings from the Fund came to almost $1 billion. They fell off again in 1958 and 1959. Of the $3.4 billion of gross Fund drawings from its inception to the end of 1959, about $3 billion was in U.S. dollars.[55] This provided the United States with a claim on the Fund that was used in the 1960's in financing U.S. deficits.

In general, apart from the continued recourse to transitional arrangements by some countries (Article XIV), by 1960 the Fund was operating more or less as envisaged at Bretton Woods. Yet weaknesses were beginning to show up in the international monetary system—weaknesses that reflected, in part, deficiencies in the system established at Bretton Woods.

A major weakness in the Bretton Woods arrangements was that they failed to provide explicitly for a systematic means by which world reserves could grow with world trade and the world economy. Throughout the 1950's, world reserves *did* grow, as the result of new gold production in excess of nonmonetary uses and, more important, as the result of deficits in the U.S. balance of payments. These deficits averaged $1.1 billion per year from 1949 through 1959. By definition, the reserves of the rest of the world increased by the same amount. And, to the extent that other countries held dollars rather than purchase gold from the United States, total gross world reserves increased as a result of the U.S. deficits (other countries' reserves went up while U.S. reserves did not go down). In fact, U.S. gold sales to foreign countries, on a net basis, came to $5.7 billion during the years 1949–1959, an annual average of $515 million. Increases in official dollar liabilities averaged $635 million per year. These movements were not steady over time; in several years—for example, 1952, 1956, and 1957—other countries sold gold to the United States in order to replenish their dollar holdings. But, during the years 1949–1959, the United States added just over $600 million per year, on average, to world reserves through its balance-of-payments deficits.

Thus the United States took on one major role of a world central bank, fulfilling a function left unspecified in the Bretton Woods agreement: the United States created international money by expanding its liquid liabilities to the rest of the world. Of the $8.5 billion increase in world reserves in the years 1949–1959, the United States provided $7 billion through the increase in its liabilities to foreign monetary authorities.

There has been considerable discussion in the literature and in official debates of whether the U.S. deficit was demand-induced or supply-induced;[56] that is, whether it was the desire of the rest of the world to increase its reserves that led to U.S. deficits or whether U.S. policies—or the absence of them—forced dollars on the rest of the world, which other countries felt required to hold for fear that converting those dollars into gold would create a crisis. We shall return to these questions after we have reviewed developments in the 1960's and early 1970's, but for the moment it is worth noting that the rate of increase of world reserves in the decade of the fifties hardly seems excessive. From the end of 1948 to the end of 1959, world reserves grew at a compound annual rate of 1.5 percent. For all countries except the United States, combined reserves increased at a rate of 5.3 percent per year. Considering the rates at which incomes, output, and trade were expanding, it is fair to say that the United States was not flooding the world with reserves.

Nevertheless, a degree of uneasiness had begun to develop and to be expressed. Robert Triffin stated elegantly the dilemma of the existing monetary system: the world was dependent on U.S. deficits for growth of reserves; if this process continued, U.S. reserve liabilities would increase relative to U.S. reserve assets (net reserves would decline steadily) and this, in time, would lead to instability as official holders of dollars began to fear that the value of their reserves might change in relation to gold; on the other hand, if U.S. deficits were eliminated, the world would be deprived of its major source of reserve growth, with depressing effects on world trade and economic activity. The answer, according to Triffin, was to "internationalize" foreign exchange reserves under the aegis of the IMF and to empower the Fund to meet "the legitimate liquidity requirements of an expanding world economy." Triffin acknowledged that his proposals were broadly similar to those of Keynes in 1943.[57]

A second weakness of the Bretton Woods system—though some would ascribe this to the way in which the system was managed rather than to its structure as defined in the Fund Articles—concerned the balance-of-payments adjustment process. As individual countries encountered balance-of-payments problems—this invariably meant deficits—the problems were dealt with on an individual basis, the international community providing both credits and advice, usually through the Fund. Exchange rate adjustment was a rare event among the industrial countries; when it did occur, the amount was large. Virtually no one was looking at the adjustment process from a systemic viewpoint, asking whether the balance-of-payments policies and the aims of individual countries were compatible with each other and with a stable international monetary system.

A third weakness, which was to become much more dramatically evident in the late 1960's and early 1970's, was the failure of the system to cope with large disequilibrating capital flows. Both France and Britain had experienced major speculative outflows in the 1950's; furthermore, it was becoming evident that interest rate differentials could induce sizable movements of capital. The Fund's Articles had assumed that controls would suppress such flows. As it turned out, it was neither possible nor, as most countries viewed it, desirable to control capital flows without controlling all international transactions. Leads and lags in commercial payments had already shown up as a potent disequilibrating force.[58]

Thus, although world trade had expanded markedly and the monetary system was operating smoothly on the whole, the major international monetary problems of the 1960's and early 1970's had begun to make their appearance.

At the end of the 1950's, Europe and Japan were thriving economically and Europe in particular had regained self-confidence. The Treaty of Rome establishing the European Economic Community had been signed in 1957. There prevailed in Europe both a euphoria over successful economic performance and a hesitancy to accept it as lasting.

Perhaps the most vivid symbol of the change in monetary relationships that had occurred over the decade was the contrast between the purposes of two trips to Europe by American Treasury Secretaries. In November 1960 Secretary of the Treasury Robert B. Anderson and Under Secretary of State C. Douglas Dillon flew to Europe to discuss with European officials, especially in Germany, ways to reduce strains on the American balance of payments. Among the subjects covered were relief of U.S. troop costs in Germany, relaxation of European restrictions on imports of American farm products, and a possible increase in German procurement of military items in the United States.[59] Eleven years earlier, Secretary of the Treasury John W. Snyder had triumphantly stepped off a ship in England where, as chief financial officer of the most powerful nation in the world, he planned to engineer a devaluation of sterling and other European currencies.

III

The First Half of the 1960's:

The United States on the Defensive

The period from 1960 to 1965 was marked by recession and recovery in the United States, by several institutional innovations designed to protect the dollar and to bolster international cooperation, by concern over inflation in Europe, and by lively and confused debates, sometimes acrimonious, between European and American officials on international monetary matters. These developments are the subject of this chapter; the first steps toward international monetary reform, taken in the same period, will be examined in Chapter IV.

The Transition Year 1960

In the United States, 1960 was an election year and a year in which the economy moved into a recession following what came to be called an abortive recovery in 1958–59.

U.S. imports levelled off and then declined after mid-1960 with the fall-off of economic activity and with the introduction of "compact" cars by Detroit to compete with imported automobiles. Exports surged ahead as economic expansion continued vigorously in Europe and Japan and import restrictions against the dollar area were liberalized further. As a result the U.S. balance on current transactions (goods, services, and private transfers) strengthened again, moving from a small deficit in 1959 to a surplus of $3.5 billion in 1960. But net capital outflows increased even more. In particular, short-term capital outflows grew substantially as U.S. interest rates fell relative to those abroad. Foreign short-term private dollar holdings in the United States, which had built up fairly steadily in the 1950's—from $3.1 billion at the end of 1949 to $7.1 billion at the end of 1959—declined about $0.5 billion in the second half of 1960.[1] Thus, despite the improved current balance, the overall deficit increased from $2.2 billion in 1959 to $3.4 billion in 1960. Foreign monetary authorities purchased almost $2 billion of gold from the United States in 1960, mainly in the latter part of the year.

The counterpart of the U.S. deficit appeared principally in Western Europe. Germany alone experienced an increase in reserves of $2.2 billion in 1960. Its large surplus on goods and services increased slightly and, more important, Germany was the recipient of an inflow of short-term capital in response to the pull of higher interest rates as well as in anticipation of a possible appreciation of its currency, the Deutsche mark (hereafter simply the mark). Other European countries—Belgium, France, Italy, the Netherlands and Switzerland—also experienced sizable reserve increases, as did Japan.

At the annual meetings of the Fund and World Bank in September 1960, there was much talk of the weakness of the dollar and of the need for continental European countries, Germany especially, to increase their capital outflows. Reporting on the meetings, *The Economist* discussed the pros and cons of a dollar devaluation and found the cons to be overwhelming.[2] But the question was being discussed, along with the possibility of an appreciation of the mark.

This uneasiness was reflected in the London gold market, where the price, which had been close to the U.S. Treasury's selling price of $35.0875, suddenly shot up in October and briefly reached the $38–$40 range. Among the explanations offered for the run-up in the gold price was uncertainty about the outcome of the American election and the economic policies that would follow. Central banks, which had been regular buyers in the London gold market, stopped buying when the market price rose above $35.35, since the Fund's Articles of Agreement ruled out central bank purchases above the official price (plus a small margin) and sales below the official price (minus a margin). But private speculators from continental Europe and the United States were reported to be purchasing heavily.[3] The rise in the gold price tended to weaken the exchange rate of the dollar, and foreign central banks found themselves buying dollars in order to maintain their exchange rates within official margins.

By early November—before the U.S. election—the London gold price fell to about $36, in part the result of substantial sales by the Bank of England but perhaps also in reaction to a statement by Senator John F. Kennedy on October 31: "If elected President, I shall not devalue the dollar from the present rate. Rather, I shall defend its present value and its soundness." Other parts of the Kennedy statement stressed the persistence of the American deficit and of gold losses during the Eisenhower Administrations.[4] The statement was designed, it would appear, to refute the notion that the rise in the London gold price and the uncertainties in exchange markets were reactions to the possibility of Kennedy's election.

In November the United States and seven other countries started to sell gold in London on an ad hoc basis to help stabilize the market price.[5] This arrangement was later formalized in the gold pool (described below).

Also in the latter part of 1960 the Federal Reserve System began to alter its approach to open market operations—which had been confined to purchases and sales of Treasury bills and had been characterized as a "bills only" policy—so as to supply reserves to the banking system "without exerting undue downward pressure on short-term Treasury bill rates that might stimulate further outflow of funds."[6]

The rise in the London gold price plus heavy purchases of gold from the United States by foreign monetary authorities in 1960, despite the fact that the underlying balance of payments was showing a dramatic improvement, appeared to have a sobering effect (to put it mildly) on Secretary of the Treasury Anderson and other high officials of the outgoing administration. This led in November to a presidential directive setting forth a series of measures aimed at strengthening the balance of payments. The measures included reducing the number of dependents abroad of military personnel, cutting back Defense Department procurement abroad, and further tying of U.S. development assistance to American exports. At the same time, the International Monetary Fund was urged to use "other strong currencies" in its lending operations and European countries were asked to open up their capital markets to foreign borrowers.[7] Soon afterward came the Anderson-Dillon European mission, on which President-elect Kennedy declined to send a representative.[8] That mission was publicly characterized as less than fully successful—and in fact seems to have been somewhat humiliating. Gilbert Burck wrote in *Fortune:* "When a banker is forced to advertise the fact that he's in a bad way, he does not inspire confidence in the people who have money on deposit."[9]

The incoming administration also appeared to be worried about the balance of payments. According to both Theodore Sorensen and Arthur Schlesinger, President-elect Kennedy became far more concerned about the problem during the transition period between the election and his inauguration. He used to tell his advisers, according to Schlesinger, that the two things that scared him most were nuclear war and the payments deficit! The danger of a run on the dollar was a decisive influence in Kennedy's choice of C. Douglas

Dillon, a Republican and Under Secretary of State in the Eisenhower Administration, as Secretary of the Treasury.[10]

These developments of 1960 raised a question that would be germane to succeeding years: Did American officials overreact to the balance-of-payments deficit, with its accompanying gold outflow, thereby aggravating the problem they were trying to cope with?

The reasons for concern were clear. The surplus on current transactions had disappeared in 1959. There could well have been a lag in recognizing the dramatic improvement in 1960 and doubts about its durability. And while the U.S. gold stock had declined $1.7 billion in the years 1950–1957, it fell $5.1 billion in the three years 1958–1960. A "run on the bank" was not an impossible eventuality.

Nevertheless, there are reasons for thinking that the reaction was excessive. The world had no adequate alternative to U.S. deficits as a source of reserve growth, and "the worsening of the payments position in 1958–59 compared with 1956–57 was basically a cyclical phenomenon accentuated by the reopening of the Suez Canal."[11] By 1960 the underlying balance of payments was strengthening markedly and the overall deficit was mainly the result of short-term, and therefore potentially reversible, capital flows. A substantial part of the U.S. deficit was reflected in Germany's surplus plus the surplus of other Continental countries. In my judgment, the measures of retrenchment in U.S. payments abroad, including uneconomic policies such as aid-tying, plus public handwringing, probably aggravated outflows of speculative capital from the United States and at the same time relieved the burden on countries in surplus to take more vigorous measures to reduce the imbalance on their side.

The Approach of the Kennedy Administration

Elected with a very thin majority, President Kennedy faced, in the economic field, both a domestic recession and an external deficit. The combination of a weak electoral base and a fundamental policy dilemma between domestic and external objectives was not conducive to bold policy initiatives. Perhaps this is why the new President's inaugural address, lofty though it was, referred not at all to domestic affairs and, in its discussion of the U.S. role in the world, ignored the balance of payments.

In dealing with the domestic recession, the President was constrained by his own rhetoric. Having called in his inaugural address for sacrifices, and having suggested that his fellow Americans "ask not what your country can do for you—ask what you can do for your country," he would have found it awkward to launch a bold stimulative program involving, say, a cut in taxes.

Timidity and uncertainty also characterized the approach to the country's external problem. For example, in a meeting of the President's economic team, including Treasury Secretary Dillon, shortly after the inauguration, there was general agreement that the President should request legislation to repeal the "gold cover requirement" of the Federal Reserve Act, under which the Federal Reserve System had to hold gold certificates in an amount equal to at least 25 percent of its deposit and note liabilities. Such a repeal would have freed the entire gold reserve for potential international use, thereby reassuring official dollar holders abroad of the determination of the United States to maintain the $35 price of gold. It is reported that Kenneth Galbraith and Theodore Sorensen persuaded President Kennedy to reject this recommendation on the ground that it would frighten conservative Americans, who would say that the Democrats always tinker with monetary arrangements as soon as they come into office.[12]

The President-elect had had the benefit of a task force report on the balance of payments with which he was "impressed but not satisfied."[13] The report, prepared under the chairmanship of George Ball and dated December 27, 1960, was not published. This is probably explained by a reluctance in the new administration to reveal some of the specific recommendations or observations of the Ball report, which might have been regarded as too bold or likely to aggravate the balance-of-payments problem. The report, for example, recommended that the Secretary of State arrange for informal consultations with American companies before they made substantial overseas investments—a hint of capital controls which might have stimulated anticipatory capital outflows. It recommended legislation embodying proposals for systematic machinery to restrain cost-price spirals. It recommended a change in the U.S. agricultural program from price support to income support, to enhance the competitiveness of U.S. farm products in world markets. It proposed that countries accumulating foreign exchange as a direct result of expenditures by other countries in furtherance of the common defense or of development assistance should take a series of measures to increase imports and other payments abroad. But, surprisingly and without explanation, the report rejected the idea that the United States should urge Germany to revalue its currency.

The Ball report also suggested study of the desirability and feasibility of giving a gold-value guaranty to foreign official holders of dollars, but it explicitly refrained from recommending such a step. Finally, in a section entitled "International Monetary Reform," it suggested study within the government of alternative ways of meeting the world's growing reserve needs, and it summarized a series of possible reforms, ranging all the way to a world central bank, along the lines of the proposals of Robert Triffin, who was a member of the Task Force.[14] There is reason to think that the details on international monetary reform were not to the liking of Secretary of the Treasury Dillon; he was quoted in *Fortune* as saying, in reaction to reform proposals such as those of Triffin or E. M. Bernstein, "The United States should continue as banker for the world."[15]

Douglas Dillon, whose father was a wealthy investment banker, entered public life in 1953 as Ambassador to France and in 1959 was Under Secretary of State. He showed an ability to grasp difficult problems, was briskly efficient, and was given to dogged hard work. He also had the distinction of owning Château Haut-Brion, one of the five greatest vineyards of Bordeaux. In the Kennedy years, Dillon and Robert Roosa at the Treasury served as counterweight to the more daring proclivities in economic policy of Walter Heller and his colleagues at the Council of Economic Advisers.

Dissatisfaction with the Ball report quickly led President Kennedy to commission a new bipartisan study of ways to reconcile steps to turn around the economy with those that could be taken to correct the balance-of-payments deficit. The new report, dated January 18, 1961, was prepared by Allan Sproul, Paul McCracken, and Roy Blough (and is reprinted as an Appendix to Robert Roosa's *The Dollar and World Liquidity*). It had the "salutary effect," according to Roosa, of ending "any lingering expectations that the President would embrace one or another kind of panacea at the outset—such as a change in the gold price, or an immediate call for an international monetary conference, or massive 'funding' of short-term dollar liabilities, or direct controls over capital flows."[16]

The new President's position on the balance of payments was set forth in a special message to the Congress on February 6, 1961, just four days after a message on the domestic economy which proposed a number of relatively mild measures to encourage economic recovery.

The President's balance-of-payments message characterized the United States as "the principal banker of the free world" and drew the conclusion that "The United States must in the decades ahead, much more than at any time in the past, take its balance of payments into account when formulating its economic policies and conducting its economic affairs." After describing the enlargement of the deficit in 1958–1960 and the recent improvement in the underlying balance, the message took stock of the ample international financial resources of the United States, including the entire gold reserve, though it did not recommend repeal of the gold cover requirement. (The Ball report had proposed that this measure be taken only when confidence in the dollar was increasing and in conjunction with measures to improve the balance of payments and reserve position of the United States.) The message pledged that the $35 price of gold would be maintained, "exchange controls over trade and investment" would not be invoked, and that U.S. security and assistance programs would be carried forward.

The President noted that in the future "it may not always be desirable or appropriate to rely entirely" on gold, dollars, and sterling as sources of needed growth of world reserves. He directed the Secretary of the Treasury to initiate studies promptly, in cooperation with other leading countries, to "consider ways in which international monetary institutions—especially the International Monetary Fund—can be strengthened and more effectively utilized, both in furnishing needed increases in reserves, and in providing the flexibility required to support a healthy and growing world economy." Here was a first public hint of international monetary reform, a subject on which, according to Sorensen, the President had more enthusiasm than his Secretary of the Treasury.[17]

The message went on to say that the United States was prepared to borrow from the IMF if necessary, that the President would request Congressional action to exempt dollar deposits of foreign monetary authorities from the Federal Reserve's interest rate ceilings, and, as recommended by the Ball task force, that he had authorized the Secretary of the Treasury to issue dollar-denominated securities, at special rates of interest, to foreign monetary authorities (these came to be called "Roosa bonds," having been negotiated by Robert V. Roosa, the Under Secretary of the Treasury for Monetary Affairs, who had been a member of the Ball task force). Other measures included export promotion, cost and price stability, export guarantees and financing through the Export-Import Bank, encouragement of foreign travel and foreign investment in the United States, a reduction of duty-free imports by American tourists from $500 to $100 (a measure opposed by the Ball task force), and a close review of expenditures abroad by U.S. Government agencies (which came to be known, oddly enough, as the "gold budget"). Finally, the President rescinded the action of the previous administration limiting the number of military dependents abroad.[18]

In general, the specific measures proposed in the Kennedy balance-of-payments program did not represent a substantial departure from the approach of the previous administration. The February 6 message did, however, recognize that U.S. deficits were a needed source of growth of world reserves;

it said that "any sustained future outflow of dollars into the monetary reserves of other countries should come about only as the result of considered judgments as to the appropriate needs for dollar reserves." And the message suggested that it might not always be desirable or appropriate to rely on this source for increases in reserves.

The Economist characterized the message as "heavy on words and light on action" and a holding operation for a period in which positive measures would be taken at home to get the U.S. economy out of recession. But *The Economist* picked up and emphasized the paragraph dealing with alternative ways of providing for growth of world reserves, reporting that the British Treasury and the Bank of England were prepared to send their "best brains" to Washington to consult on this matter.[19]

Meanwhile the U.S. Treasury and the Federal Reserve proceeded with a series of steps of a more or less defensive character. Debt management and monetary policies were to be conducted in a manner that would sustain short-term interest rates while permitting downward influences to be exerted on longer-term rates. This came to be called "Operation Twist." Whether it had a significant influence in altering the relationship between short-term and long-term interest rates, and therefore in discouraging capital outflows while encouraging domestic investment and housing outlays, has been questioned;[20] but its purposes were clear enough.

Another measure was the negotiation of advance repayments of Marshall Plan and other debts owed to the U.S. government by European countries that were in balance-of-payments surplus.

A network of "swap" arrangements (reciprocal credit facilities) with foreign central banks was initiated by the Treasury in 1961 and taken over by the Federal Reserve in 1962. This network, with the Federal Reserve Bank of New York at its hub, acting under directives from the Federal Open Market Committee in close consultation with the Treasury, was designed to finance or accommodate short-term capital flows that would otherwise create instability in the monetary relations among the major countries. In 1962, swap arrangements were established with nine foreign central banks and the Bank for International Settlements.

The swap network amounted to $900 million at the end of 1962 and over the years it expanded to reach a total of more than $20 billion by 1976. A drawing on the Federal Reserve by a foreign central bank was equivalent to a short-term borrowing of dollars, adding to the borrowing country's reserves available for use in the foreign exchange market to finance a balance-of-payments deficit. When the Federal Reserve drew on another central bank, it

normally used the proceeds to redeem dollars already held by that central bank
—dollars that might otherwise have been presented to the U.S. Treasury to
purchase gold. Thus the foreign central bank substituted a claim on the Federal Reserve, denominated in its own currency, for "uncovered" dollar holdings. In effect the United States provided a guaranty to the foreign central bank
against a depreciation of the dollar to the extent of its swap drawings. The
existence of the swap network was one reason for regular attendance by
Federal Reserve officials at the monthly meetings of central bank governors
at the Bank for International Settlements (BIS) in Basle, Switzerland.

In a further step, the ad hoc gold selling arrangements referred to earlier
were formalized in a gold pool established by the United States and seven other
countries for the purpose of stabilizing the free market price of gold in London.[21]

Meanwhile, the OEEC was being transformed into the Organization for
Economic Cooperation and Development (OECD); in his balance-of-payments message, President Kennedy had proposed U.S. membership. This led
to regular consultations with officials of other industrial countries in the various organs of the OECD, notably the Economic Policy Committee (EPC) and
Working Party 3.

The Chairman of the Council of Economic Advisers headed the U.S.
delegation at the EPC, which usually met three times a year. The Under
Secretary of the Treasury for Monetary Affairs, accompanied by a senior
Federal Reserve official (initially Ralph A. Young, Director of the Board's
Division of International Finance), headed the delegation to Working Party
3, which met with greater frequency. The latter group was chaired first by
Emile Van Lennep, Treasurer-General of the Netherlands, and then by Otmar
Emminger, Vice President of Germany's central bank. The membership of
Working Party 3 was confined to the ten largest countries of the OECD; it was
to be the forum in which, over the years and to the present, monetary and
balance-of-payments problems and policies of the larger countries were examined, compared, and debated by finance ministry and central bank officials.
The many monetary crises of the 1960's and 1970's were aired in this group
(we shall have more than one occasion to return to its activities in later
chapters); in the early 1960's the Working Party was the forum in which
European criticisms of the U.S. balance-of-payments deficit and its alleged
causes were brought out and in which American officials countered with
critiques of European policies, especially the failure to develop adequate capital markets which would reduce Europe's dependence on capital from abroad.

The final element in what Roosa has called the "outer perimeter defenses" created in 1961 was the enlargement, through a borrowing arrangement, of the potential resources of the IMF. The idea originated with the IMF staff and was proposed by the Managing Director, Per Jacobsson.[22] Should it have become necessary for the United States to borrow heavily from the Fund in the event of a substantial speculative flight from the dollar, the Fund's resources of other usable currencies would not have matched the U.S. drawing rights in the Fund. In November 1961, for example, the United States had a potential right to borrow $5.8 billion from the IMF, but the Fund's holdings of the currencies of the major industrial countries other than the United Kingdom (which had itself just borrowed from the Fund) amounted only to about $1.6 billion.[23]

A series of involved negotiations—which took place mainly in Paris—between American and European officials, with Jacobsson in the wings trying to preserve the role and authority of the Fund, led to an agreement called the General Arrangements to Borrow (GAB). Under the GAB, ten countries would stand ready, in specified conditions, to lend a total of $6 billion to the Fund. (Switzerland, not a Fund member, later associated itself with the arrangement.) Of the $6 billion, the U.S. share was $2 billion and Britain's share $1 billion, leaving $3 billion divided among Germany, France, Italy, Japan, Canada, the Netherlands, Belgium, and Sweden.

Full details of these negotiations have never been disclosed, to the author's knowledge, but enough is known to justify the observation that the European negotiators, led by French Finance Minister Wilfrid Baumgartner, took the opportunity to express their new-found power relative to the United States. They were not prepared to lend passively to the Fund, which they regarded as dominated by the United States. Instead they insisted on procedures under which they, as lenders, would have the chance to consult and make decisions among themselves upon receiving a proposal from the Managing Director of the IMF. The voting procedures provided that the prospective borrower—assumed to be the United States—would not vote.

The procedures specified that the deputies of the finance ministers of the ten countries would meet and use "the facilities of the international organizations to which they belong in keeping each other informed of developments in their balance of payments that could give rise to the use of the Supplementary Resources." In other words, Working Party 3 and the deputies of the Group of Ten would play an important role in the decisions whether or not to lend to the Fund and how to apportion any loan among participants.[24] In deciding whether or not to lend to the Fund they would, in most cases, also be determining whether the Fund would be in a position to lend to the country in need of financing.

Some other members of the Fund found this arrangement less than pleasing. The Australian Executive Director spoke of a "very exclusive club" and the Indian Director feared that the Fund Board might find itself obliged to concur in decisions taken elsewhere.[25] But the Dutch Director described the agreement as a compromise between the ideology of the Fund as a global monetary institution and a newer ideology which sought solutions through closer cooperation between the main industrial countries.[26]

While the Treasury was busily improvising defenses, other members of the administration—Walter Heller and James Tobin at the Council of Economic Advisers, George Ball at the State Department, and Carl Kaysen at the White House—were advocating, in internal discussions, more fundamental initiatives in which the United States would work with other countries in reforming the international monetary system. One purpose they had in mind was to liberate U.S. domestic policy instruments that could be used more actively to combat the recession.[27]

U.S. Policies in the Face of Domestic Recession and External Deficit

By what the new administration must have regarded as a stroke of good fortune, the recession reached its low point in the first quarter of the Kennedy Presidency. (According to GNP data as recently revised, the trough of the recession came in the fourth quarter of 1960.) Real output began to increase in the spring of 1961 and the unemployment rate fell off from its peak of 7 percent in May to 6 percent at the end of the year. The expansion of business activity in 1961 was more rapid than the increase in the economy's potential; the so-called GNP gap, as computed by the Council of Economic Advisers, thus contracted in the course of 1961. But the rate of expansion slackened in 1962, and in 1963 the growth of the economy was no faster than the expansion of capacity. Thus a considerable degree of slack remained, mirrored in the unemployment rate, which fluctuated between 5.5 and 6 percent until late 1964.[28]

At the same time prices were remarkably stable. Wholesale prices of industrial goods edged down slightly and consumer prices crept up about one percent a year, mainly reflecting increases in the cost of services. The Economic Reports of the President pointed out, again and again, that the United States was showing the best price record of any industrial country (with the occasional exception of Canada).

The overall balance-of-payments deficit declined from almost $3.5 billion in 1960 to $1.3 billion in 1961 and $2.7 billion in 1962.* Most of the improvement from 1960 to 1961 was in the surplus on goods and services, which increased as the recession further reduced the demand for imports. Although imports began to rise again after mid-1961 with the recovery of the economy, exports and other receipts from abroad also increased. Private capital outflows continued in 1961 at about the same rate as in 1960 but short-term capital outflows declined in 1962, reflecting in part a fall-off in borrowings by Japan from American banks.

The relatively slow growth of the economy in 1962–63 kept imports from rising rapidly, and the surplus on current transactions remained strong—between $4 and $5 billion. But beginning in the autumn of 1962 there was a distinct increase in the volume of foreign security issues in the United States, largely by borrowers in Canada, Japan, and Europe. This helped to swell the overall deficit and led to considerable concern in the Treasury and Federal Reserve as dollars accumulated heavily in the hands of foreign monetary authorities. A part of these holdings was refunded into Roosa bonds, and a part was covered by Federal Reserve swap drawings. Net foreign gold purchases were relatively small in 1963—less than $400 million, which was more than accounted for by France—compared with about $800 million in 1961 and 1962 and with almost $2 billion in 1960. In part this was the result of the fact that the gold pool, originally established as a coordinated mechanism to sell gold in order to keep the market price from rising, was able to make net purchases in the market in 1962 and 1963 and to distribute the gold to members of the pool, including the United States.

Against this background of economic and balance-of-payments developments, several policy actions were taken. In a message to Congress on taxation in April 1961, the President proposed an innovation, the investment tax credit, which was designed to encourage business investment outlays. The proposal was greeted with initial suspicion in the business community and the measure was not enacted until October 1962. Apart from its intrinsic merits, the invest-

---

*A Review Committee for Balance of Payments Statistics, chaired by Edward M. Bernstein, was appointed by the Budget Bureau in April 1963. Among its many recommendations was the adoption of the "balance settled by official transactions" as an overall measure of the balance-of-payments position; *The Balance of Payments Statistics of the United States,* Report of the Review Committee for Balance of Payments Statistics to the Bureau of the Budget, April 1965. The concept has also been called "balance on official settlements" and "balance on official reserve transactions." It measures the balance of payments as settled by transactions of monetary authorities. Thus a U.S. deficit on official settlements measures the decrease in gold and other official reserve assets of the United States plus the increase (or minus the decrease) in U.S. liabilities to foreign monetary authorities.

ment tax credit, which was in essence a 7 percent subsidy from the Federal Government on business expenditures for new equipment, served as one means of reconciling the divergent objectives of encouraging more rapid economic growth while protecting the balance of payments. For with this incentive to business capital formation in place, there was less need to lower long-term interest rates further (with consequences for capital outflows from the United States).

In his State of the Union message in January 1962, the President requested "standby authority, subject to Congressional veto, to adjust personal income tax rates downward within a specified range and time, to slow down an economic decline before it has dragged us all down," as well as standby authority to accelerate Federal capital outlays upon a given rise in the rate of unemployment. This attempt to make fiscal policy more flexible was no doubt motivated in part by balance-of-payments considerations, since it would have reduced reliance on monetary policy for domestic anti-recession purposes. In the event, Congress did not grant these powers.

Under pressure from the Treasury Department, with its concern over the balance of payments and its desire to demonstrate to the world that the United States was pursuing fiscal discipline, the President in January 1962 proposed a balanced budget for fiscal year 1963. The tax receipts in this proposed budget were estimated on the assumption of a "brisk recovery" in the economy. In fact the assumption was for a 10 percent increase in nominal GNP from 1961 to 1962. As it turned out, the increase was somewhat less than 7 percent and the shortfall in tax receipts produced a budget deficit in fiscal year 1963 little different from that in the previous year. But this is not to criticize the administration's approach to fiscal policy; on the contrary, the approach, while bowing to conservative legislators, the business community, and foreign observers, took account of the inevitable effect of the rate of economic activity on the budget outcome. Walter Lippmann characterized the President's budget as a landmark because "for the first time in our history it states that the balancing of the budget—whether with a surplus, a deficit, or with neither—is a question of economic policy and of deliberate decision. It is not, as so many regard it, a question of right or wrong."[29]

There is a tendency nowadays to look back longingly and enviously on the first half of the 1960's, when the economy was expanding and prices were stable. It is well to remind ourselves that unemployment was then thought excessive and that a considerable gap persisted between the actual and potential performance of the economy.

Yet the administration was not prepared to act boldly. A slowdown in the rate of economic expansion in the summer of 1962 motivated the Council of Economic Advisers to recommend a tax cut to the President. The debate in the administration, with the Treasury opposed, led the President to reject an immediate call for a tax cut but to announce on August 13, 1962—in a radio and television report to the American people on the state of the national economy—that, while tax rates were too high and "a drag on economic recovery and economic growth," the right time for a bill to reduce taxes and reform the tax structure was not then but January 1963. And, in January, a phased tax reduction was proposed.

Meanwhile, the Federal Reserve pursued a relatively easy monetary policy, with the result that money and credit expanded steadily. Short-term interest rates crept up very slightly from their low point in early 1961 (the bottom of the recession), while long-term rates edged down slowly but steadily. On July 16, 1963, Federal Reserve discount rates were raised from 3 to 3.5 percent, and the reasons for this were entirely international: "to minimize short-term capital outflows prompted by higher interest rates prevalent in other countries."[30]

Two days later, the President announced a new balance-of-payments program that included a proposal for a "temporary" tax on purchases of foreign securities by Americans (the interest equalization tax), designed to stem the large volume of foreign capital issues in the United States that occurred after mid-1962 and were expected to continue in the latter part of 1963. This was the first element in a network of capital controls that the United States was to call into use as the 1960's unfolded. Other features of the July 1963 balance-of-payments program included a further tying of foreign aid to U.S. exports, a reduction in overseas military expenditures, and a decision to request a standby credit of $500 million from the IMF.

The economy's expansion after 1961 was not sufficient to reduce unemployment to acceptable levels (an "interim" goal was set at 4 percent). The tax reduction and reform recommended by President Kennedy in January 1963 was not enacted until February 1964, when President Johnson succeeded in pushing it through Congress. Although the rate of economic expansion apparently began to accelerate somewhat around the middle of 1963, the tax reduction of early 1964 provided a strong stimulus to total demand in the economy. From the first quarter of 1964 to the first quarter of 1965, GNP in constant prices increased 5.4 percent. Over the same period the rate of unemployment fell from 5.5 percent to 4.8 percent. By the end of 1965, the unemployment rate was down to 4.1 percent.

But by then influences of a more ominous nature had begun to make themselves felt. President Johnson's decision to increase American involvement in Vietnam brought with it a very large increase in military orders and expenditures in the United States. From the first quarter of 1965 to the first quarter of 1966, defense expenditures rose $6.4 billion, about 10 percent. New orders placed by the Defense Department increased 30 percent over the same period.[31] These orders began to affect the economy before they showed up in the national accounts as defense expenditures. By the fourth quarter of 1965, GNP in real terms was growing at an annual rate of almost 8.5 percent and the unemployment rate was dropping rapidly. In these circumstances prices began to rise. There had been a moderate up-creep of prices in the second half of 1964, but the price advance became larger and more generalized in 1965–66.

The U.S. balance of payments was showing little change. The announcement of the interest equalization tax had a striking impact in discouraging American purchases of foreign securities. Furthermore, the surplus on goods, services, and private transfers increased from $4.4 billion in 1962 to $7.7 billion in 1964, before declining to $6.1 billion in 1965 as imports accelerated with the pickup in economic activity. Other forms of capital outflow increased, notably loans to foreign borrowers by U.S. banks and direct investment abroad by U.S. corporations. The rapid growth of bank loans to foreigners in 1964, particularly medium-term loans, was the result both of growing interest by U.S. banks in international activity and of policies of credit restraint applied in a number of foreign countries.[32] While these outflows were increasing in 1964, there was an inflow to the United States of private liquid funds— reflecting at least in part movements out of sterling—but these were registered as increased liabilities that added to the U.S. deficit as it was most commonly measured at that time. On the official settlements basis, however, the deficit fell from $2.7 billion in 1962 to $1.5 billion in 1964 as a whole. In the last quarter of 1964 and the first quarter of 1965 the deficit increased again to more than $2 billion at an annual rate.

In these circumstances, the U.S. Government on February 10, 1965, announced a new balance-of-payments program involving voluntary restrictions on foreign loans by banks and other financial institutions, application of the interest equalization tax to bank loans of over one-year maturity, and voluntary restraint on the financing of overseas direct investment by U.S. corporations. This program had an immediate impact of some magnitude, producing an official settlements surplus in the second quarter of 1965 and reducing the deficit for the year to $1.3 billion.

The U.S. deficit on the official settlements basis over the years 1960–1965 averaged $2 billion per year. Of this amount, half was reflected in increases in foreign official holdings of dollars. U.S. gold sales averaged just under $1 billion per year, declining during 1960–1964 and increasing sharply again in 1965 as a result of a change in French policy on holding dollars.

The expansion of U.S. liabilities was increasing world reserves, on average, by about $1 billion, or less than 2 percent, per year. (See Table 1.) The reserves of the rest of the world increased at an average rate of just under 5 percent per year as the result of U.S. deficits during 1960–1965. Taking into account all sources of reserve growth, the reserves of the rest of the world increased 7.5 percent per year in the period 1960–1965. Over the same period, the GNP of the European members of OECD was increasing at a rate of 9.5 percent in current prices and just over 5 percent in constant prices. By 1964 the preoccupation of European officials with the dollar problem had lessened. Meanwhile, a distinct change had taken place in the reserve positions of developing countries: After remaining virtually unchanged on balance in the 1950's, the reserves of developing countries began to increase in the 1960's.

Developments in Europe and Japan

While the U.S. economy went into recession followed by slow recovery in the early 1960's, economic activity surged ahead in most European countries. Total exports expanded despite the reduction in Europe's exports to North

TABLE 1.   **Major Sources of World Reserve Growth, 1960–1965***
             (Billions of Dollars)

	1960	1961	1962	1963	1964	1965	Average Annual Change
Increase in U.S. liabilities to foreign monetary authorities	1.0	0.7	1.1	1.5	1.4	—	.95
Increase in official gold reserves of countries	0.1	0.9	0.3	0.9	0.7	1.0	.65
Reserve positions in the Fund	0.3	0.6	−0.4	0.1	0.3	1.2	.35
Change in official liabilities of U.K.	0.1	—	−0.6	0.3	−0.1	−.01	−.07
Other	1.4	−0.1	0.3	1.1	0.1	−0.1	.45
Total	2.9	2.1	0.7	3.9	2.4	2.0	2.33

SOURCE: International Monetary Fund.
*Covers member countries of IMF plus Switzerland.

America, and intra-European trade increased rapidly as the Common Market countries lowered their tariffs against one another. While Britain, Italy, and Japan experienced temporary setbacks in economic expansion, continental Europe continued on its virtuous circle of growth in the early 1960's. The Common Market countries increased their industrial production about one-third from 1959 to 1963, a rate twice as fast as that of the United States.

The United Kingdom recovered smartly from the recession of 1958 and by 1960 its output was approaching capacity limits. Restrictive monetary and fiscal policies were applied in early 1960 and industrial output remained on a plateau for the next three years. While imports also levelled off, British exports failed to increase very much despite booming markets on the Continent. Hence domestic policies were tightened further; a wage pause was introduced in mid-1961 in the hope of strengthening the balance of payments. The pay pause (which gave way to an incomes policy in 1962) had some success in dampening wage advances, but they continued to exceed gains in productivity. Nevertheless, Britain's balance of payments improved enough to permit an expansionary policy to be introduced in late 1962 and 1963 and, as a result, output began to rise again. Thus Britain experienced another of its several "stop-go" episodes.

Japan developed a sizable balance-of-payments deficit in 1961 as its exports were weakened by the U.S. recession and its imports were stimulated by a domestic boom. Restrictive policies slowed the growth of the economy in 1961–62 while Japan borrowed heavily abroad to finance its deficit. The balance of payments improved and industrial expansion resumed rapidly in 1963. At that time, Japan's strong balance of payments had not yet emerged and its reserves were relatively low.

The fairly steady economic expansion of the continental European countries began to be accompanied by an accelerated rise in food and industrial prices in 1961. Except in Italy and Belgium, the main explanation for the upward price pressures was wage increases in excess of the advance of productivity.[33] By 1963–64 inflation had come to be regarded as a key problem in Europe. From the fourth quarter of 1962 to the fourth quarter of 1963 wholesale prices rose 3.5 percent in Belgium, 4.5 percent in France, and more than 6 percent in the Netherlands; in Germany the increase was less than one percent, but it accelerated somewhat in 1964. (In the United States wholesale prices were stable over this period.)

Beginning in mid-1963 monetary policies and, in some countries, fiscal policies shifted toward restraint in the face of increasing prices. The result was a tendency toward rising short-term interest rates in continental Europe in

1963–64,[34] which helps to explain the growing volume of capital outflows from the United States in that period.

Europe's Balance of Payments

The current surplus of the OEEC countries had risen to more than $3.5 billion by 1959, when the U.S. current balance was at its lowest level since the end of World War II. By 1965, the current surplus of the European countries had declined to $1.3 billion. Thus the increase in the American balance on goods, services, and private remittances from about zero in 1959 to about $6 billion in 1965 had as its counterpart a reduction in the current balance of the European OECD countries by about $2.25 billion. Meanwhile, Japan's current surplus increased irregularly from $400 million in 1959 to more than $1 billion in 1965. About half of the counterpart of the stronger current balance of the United States must have shown up as increased deficits in the developing countries.

It will be recalled that at the end of the 1950's Germany accounted for a large share—about one-half—of the aggregate current surplus of the OEEC countries and that speculative funds had begun to move into marks. Germany faced an internal-external dilemma that was the mirror image of that in the United States. The German economy was booming—GNP in real terms rose more than 8.5 percent in 1960—and the overall balance of payments was in large surplus. Fiscal policy was not used actively to curb the boom and, as a consequence, restrictive monetary policy measures were brought into play. The result was an inflow of capital from abroad as German banks and businesses reacted to the Bundesbank's restrictive policies and investors abroad took advantage of higher interest rates in Germany. Although the monetary authorities attempted to discourage capital inflows by forbidding the payment of interest on foreign deposits, and by similar measures, it was estimated that the total amount of credit received from abroad by the German economy in 1960 was $1.3 billion.[35] As a result of this inflow on top of the substantial current surplus, Germany's reserves increased more than $2 billion in 1960 and a further $400 million in the first quarter of 1961, even though the German authorities began to ease their tight money policies in late 1960.

The German Government finally attempted to resolve the dilemma by revaluing the mark by 5 percent on March 6, 1961. The Netherlands guilder followed the next day. In both cases, official statements emphasized the once-for-all nature of the exchange rate actions.

But the revaluations were minimal—the BIS characterized them as of "modest size"[36]—and exchange markets reacted accordingly. Both Germany and Switzerland experienced heavy speculative inflows, mainly at the expense of sterling, in the weeks following the German and Dutch revaluations. At that time central banks took steps to lend to each other, offsetting the movement of private funds; this led to the formation of the swap network described earlier in this chapter.

The German surplus, on both current and capital account, declined sharply in the second half of 1961 and in 1962, as imports rose rapidly and capital flowed out. Over the three years 1962–1964, the current surplus averaged about $800 million per year, half of what it had been in 1959–1961. But private capital continued to flow into Germany and was only partially offset by governmental flows to developing countries and advance debt repayments to the United States. Thus Germany's reserves rose again, beginning in early 1962, though much more slowly than before.

Italy, which had been enjoying rapid expansion with relatively stable prices, experienced a sudden wage explosion in late 1962 as labor shortages began to be felt in the industrialized northern part of the country. The wage explosion had two effects: it raised unit labor costs and, as a result, prices; and it redistributed income to Italian workers, permitting an extraordinary burst of buying—a ratcheting up of workers' living standards to include higher meat consumption and purchases of cars.[37] Automobile sales increased by two-thirds in one year.[38] In the circumstances, imports of both industrial and agricultural products soared, and Italy's current account surplus, which had averaged about $400 million per year in 1960–1962, gave way to a deficit of almost $700 million in 1963. Restrictive fiscal and monetary policies were imposed and industrial output began to fall in late 1963, continuing until the autumn of 1964. This led to an improvement in the current account and to a deceleration in wage and price advances.

But before Italy's difficulty was overcome, the financing of its balance of payments, which was affected by capital outflows as well as the surge of imports, created a serious problem. At first the overall deficit was financed by borrowings by Italian banks in the Eurodollar market, and then by the use of foreign exchange reserves. Reserves fell heavily in the fourth quarter of 1963 and early 1964 as speculation developed on a depreciation of the Italian lira.

In mid-March Guido Carli, Governor of the Bank of Italy, went to Washington, where a credit package of $1 billion to Italy was announced. The lenders were the United States, Britain, and Germany. The bailing out of Italy at the initiative of the United States created chagrin among some of Italy's Common Market partners; the need for Italian officials to go to Washington in an emergency did nothing to enhance the image of a unified Common Market. Furthermore, some of Italy's European neighbors probably believed that the lira should be devalued, while U.S. officials were anxious to preserve the existing pattern of exchange rates. In the event, speculation against the lira subsided and the balance of payments returned to surplus in the latter part of 1964. In the spring of 1965 industrial output resumed its upward trend. Thus Italy overcame its international crisis, which reflected in part a structural adjustment to a higher level of living for the Italian people, without devaluing its currency. In retrospect the decision to avoid devaluation appears justified; Italy's current account once again moved into large surplus in the second half of the 1960's and the economy grew rapidly.

The U.S.-European Dialogue

With occasional exceptions (such as Italy in 1963–64), most continental European countries were net recipients of private capital on top of current account surpluses. This tendency was reinforced by the upward movement in interest rates in Europe in 1963–64 as central banks took steps to restrain rising prices.

Two issues came to be debated, mainly in Working Party 3, between European and American officials: (1) To what extent was the United States, through its continuing overall balance-of-payments deficit, and specifically its relatively expansionary monetary policy, "exporting inflation" to other countries? (2) To what extent was the inflow of capital to Europe, which accounted in part for its balance-of-payments surplus, the result of inadequately developed European capital markets?

To American officials, the charge by Europeans that inflation was "imported" from the United States seemed like a convenient *post hoc ergo propter hoc* argument. The United States had a deficit and Europe was experiencing inflation; how easy it was to blame the one on the other and thereby avoid looking for domestic reasons for the inflation!

We countered the European view by pointing to the stable price level, the moderate rate of monetary expansion, and the *surplus* on current transactions of the United States. By what process was the United States exporting inflation? What it came down to was the inflow of capital to Europe and the outflow from the United States. This then involved the second issue, Europe's undeveloped capital markets. (In any event, the rate of growth of world reserves as a result of the U.S. deficits was hardly excessive.)

The debate on specific policies and institutional structures in the United

States and Europe took place against the background of general European dissatisfaction with the persistent U.S. balance-of-payments deficit and particular French dissatisfaction with large-scale investment in Europe by American corporations.

French policy on incoming investment by foreign corporations was schizophrenic in the 1960's.[39] Until 1962, such investment was welcomed so long as it was financed by funds from abroad; then the Gaullist concern over American domination began to be asserted. But France faced the dilemma that if a proposed American investment were disapproved by the Finance Ministry, the investment could be made instead in a neighboring EEC country and the products exported to France in any event. Efforts by the French Government to persuade the Common Market to adopt a general Community policy on American investment came to nothing in the face of opposition by other EEC countries. Moreover, the attitude of the French Government was not shared by specific French communities where new American firms might be established. The failure of this Gaullist objective was dramatized when Jacques Chaban-Delmas, Prime Minister under President Georges Pompidou, hailed the decision of the Ford Motor Company to establish a plant in Bordeaux, where he was mayor.[40]

Ironically, every time President de Gaulle and his aides talked about measures to keep American investment out of Europe, President Kennedy secretly wished they would.[41] The result would have been an improved U.S. balance of payments without the political onus of restraining business plans falling on the Kennedy Administration.

European criticisms in Working Party 3 focused on U.S. monetary policy, which was alleged to provide excess liquidity to the American economy and to keep interest rates too low, with the result that U.S. investors had an incentive to place funds abroad. This in turn swelled both the overall U.S. deficit and European surpluses. American officials, in turn, argued that European countries were relying too heavily on monetary policy and not enough on fiscal policy to restrain aggregate demand. Thus each side charged the other with letting its monetary policy be excessively influenced by and devoted to its domestic economy, to the detriment of the balance of payments. In addition, American officials repeatedly charged that Europeans tended to regard the U.S. deficit, rather than the European surplus, as the aberration that needed correction.

In general, American officials were on the defensive in these discussions. They laid stress on the special burdens the United States was carrying in the fields of defense and aid to developing countries and on the inability to raise

U.S. interest rates sharply without impeding recovery from the recession. Once the plans for a tax cut were announced, it was possible to look forward to a shift in the mix of fiscal and monetary policy that would reduce the incentive for capital to move out of the United States. In the meantime, the announcement of the proposed interest equalization tax in the summer of 1963 calmed European concerns. In 1964 the attention of European monetary officials shifted first to the Italian problem and then to the emerging balance-of-payments difficulties of the United Kingdom.

French Views on Gold

In early 1965, the French Government decided to convert into gold some $300 million of its dollar holdings and thereafter to step up its monthly purchases of gold from the United States. These actions prompted a question at one of President de Gaulle's magisterial press conferences, on February 4, 1965. He was asked whether he favored a reform of the international monetary system and, if so, how.

The lengthy reply brought out the by then well-known French criticisms of the existing system—notably the privileged position of the United States, which permitted among other things "a kind of expropriation" of enterprises in other countries. In this period of relative calm, de Gaulle pointed out, it was opportune to change the system and establish international trade

> on an unquestionable monetary basis that does not bear the stamp of any one country in particular. On what basis? Truly it is hard to imagine that it could be any standard other than gold, yes, gold, whose nature does not alter, which may be formed equally well into ingots, bars, or coins, which has no nationality, and which has, eternally and universally, been regarded as the unalterable currency par excellence. . . . Certainly the terminating of the gold exchange standard without causing a hard jolt and the restoration of the gold standard as well as the supplementary and transitional measures which will be essential, particularly the organizing of international credit on this new basis—all that must be examined calmly.

Perhaps to the consternation of some of his own officials, President de Gaulle identified the IMF as "a very suitable framework for such negotiations." But he also paid tribute to the Group of Ten and, finally, to the Six, upon whom it would devolve "to work out among themselves, and to win outside acceptance for, the sound system which would be in conformity with common sense and respond to the reviving economic and financial power of our very old continent."

This pronouncement was something of a bombshell in financial circles. In substance it did not diverge from the position French officials had been promoting, but it was generally interpreted as a call for a further step toward a full gold standard. Given the authority from which these words came, the reactions were to be expected. The U.S. Treasury issued a statement on the same day rejecting a return to the gold standard and reaffirming the U.S. intention to maintain the official price of gold. In London, *The Economist* saw in President de Gaulle's remarks evidence that Jacques Rueff's influence had gained the upper hand over that of officials in the Ministry of Finance and the Bank of France.[42]

De Gaulle's pronouncement must be viewed against his foreign policy stance. One observer has written:

> the two most important concerns of French foreign policy under former President de Gaulle were the insurance of French independence of action and the cultivation of France's role as a leading world power. He apparently deemed attainment of either role as being inconsistent with French cooperation in a U.S.-dominated military alliance or in a dollar-dominated monetary system. The country's pursuit of its national interests inexorably brought it into conflict with the policies and interests of the United States, particularly because a primordial fact of Gaullist foreign policy was its insistence that the United States was far too powerful, and, regardless of its intentions, could not keep from trying to dominate the affairs of other nations. De Gaulle's abhorrence of U.S. hegemony and power meant that the achievement of the independence and world-leadership role for France, which he so craved, presupposed restoration of some semblance of a balance of power in the Atlantic community in particular and in the world in general. His anti-U.S. thrusts were therefore not vicious ends in themselves but unemotional means to attain French values in an all too Americanized world.[43]

De Gaulle's press conference statement was echoed a week later by Finance Minister Valéry Giscard d'Estaing. But that was not the final word. On June 15, 1965, Giscard d'Estaing gave a lecture at the Institut d'Etudes Bancaires et Financières in Paris which, in its tone and nuance, was less "hard-nosed" (to use an American expression that the French Minister would probably have found distasteful) than the declarations he and the President of the Republic had made in February. While gold was still given pride of place at the center of the system, the Minister acknowledged that there existed a number of theses on the subject of how the role of gold should be preserved. Then, in a clear rejection of the approach of Jacques Rueff, he said, "I in fact believe that gold by itself is not enough." He went on to present the disadvantages of a substantial increase in the official gold price—one of them being that the reserve currency countries would experience an increase in their assets relative to their liabilities and might relax their efforts to balance their external accounts. He also recognized the uneven impact among countries of a gold price increase. If this alternative is rejected, then "we must undertake to establish a new international payments system."

Finally, in his discussion of the balance-of-payments adjustment process, Giscard d'Estaing put forward the possibility of "widening the present margins for fluctuation of exchange rates around parity"—a surprising and unexplained departure from orthodoxy.

Apparently a debate was occurring within the French Government; that would account for the subtle seesaws we observed. The outcome was that by early 1966 Giscard d'Estaing was replaced as Finance Minister by Michel Debré, a former Prime Minister and an orthodox Gaullist.

Valéry Giscard d'Estaing, who will reenter our narrative, was head of the small but influential Independent Republican Party when he was appointed Finance Minister in January 1962 at the age of 36. Patrician in appearance and manner, trained in France's finest schools, Giscard's comprehension and mastery of technical issues usually gave him a distinct advantage in debates with finance ministers of other countries. But as leader of a minority party in the Gaullist coalition, and later during the Pompidou Presidency, his ability to influence policy in his own country was limited. In international monetary matters, he was more inclined to pragmatism than his Gaullist colleagues Michel Debré and Maurice Couve de Murville, who—for political or doctrinal reasons—embraced the views of Jacques Rueff.

The Brookings Report

American officials became less defensive as the decade of the 1960's moved toward mid-point. One reason for this was their growing optimism about the prospects for the U.S. balance of payments. This optimism was based in part on a thorough study of those prospects, undertaken for the U.S. Government by the Brookings Institution in 1962 and published in 1963.[44] A distinguished group of economists, under the leadership of Walter Salant, provided an assessment of the outlook for the balance of payments in 1968.

The report projected that the U.S. basic balance (the balance on goods and services and long-term capital, official and private) would improve from a deficit of $850 million in 1961 to a surplus of $2.7 billion in 1968. The major factors underlying the projected improvement were (1) the assumption that wages and prices would rise faster in Europe than in the United States as the result of a labor shortage in Europe and (2) the expectation that the net flow of private capital from the United States would decline, largely because the rate of profit would rise in the United States as compared with Europe.

The Brookings report went on to consider the implications of its projection. If the United States was to be in basic surplus, the world would need an alternative means by which to increase official reserves. In effect, Triffin's proposition (see page 32) was accepted by the Brookings scholars. The report also blessed fixed exchange rates but cautioned that correction of imbalances, under fixed rates, would take time, and adequate reserves and credit facilities would be needed. If agreement on a satisfactory "liquidity mechanism" could not be obtained, the report recommended—as an "inferior" alternative to fixed exchange rates—"a modified system of flexible exchange rates consisting of a dollar-sterling bloc and an EEC bloc," with relatively fixed rates among the members of each bloc and the discontinuance of the tie between gold and the dollar.[45] (It can be presumed, with some confidence, that this alternative policy recommendation was not greeted with enthusiasm at the Treasury Department.)

The present relevance of the Brookings report is that it provided a rationale to those U.S. policy makers who believed that prospects for the U.S. balance of payments were favorable; this in turn justified defense of the status quo with respect to exchange rates. Indeed, as we have seen, the current account position of the United States did improve markedly in the first half of the 1960's. What the authors of the Brookings report could not have foreseen was the impact of Vietnam on the U.S. economy beginning in 1965.

Attitudes Toward Exchange Rates

While interest and concern were constantly expressed in the first half of the 1960's regarding the need for avoiding and correcting persistent payments imbalances, remarkably little attention was given to exchange rates. A report in 1964 by the Deputies of the Group of Ten (to be reviewed in Chapter IV) identified various instruments of policy that might be used to correct "sustained" deficits or surpluses: budgetary and fiscal policies; incomes policies; monetary policies; other measures relating to international capital transactions (e.g., measures designed to affect capital movements, advance repayments of inter-governmental debts); commercial policies (e.g., temporary unilateral tariff reductions); and policies directed to particular sectors of the economy (e.g., housing or hire purchase, governmental transactions affecting the balance of payments). This listing was followed by the statement: "Such instruments must be employed with regard for obligations in the field of international trade and for the IMF obligation to maintain stable exchange parities which are subject to change only in cases of fundamental disequilibrium."

The IMF itself, discussing the relationship between international liquidity and the process of adjustment in its *Annual Report* for 1964, suggested a number of ways in which payments imbalances "of more than transitory character" may be corrected. Countries tending toward persistent deficits "should be willing to pursue less expansionary policies than they would otherwise prefer," and countries in similar surplus "should be willing to pursue, within limits, a more expansionary policy than they would have been inclined to adopt for purely domestic reasons." Use of a wide variety of policy instruments was advocated, including greater flexibility of fiscal policy so that monetary policy could be directed more to its effects on the international movement of capital. There followed a listing of other policies similar to that in the deputies' report; then: "Adjustments in exchange rates are of course not precluded by the par value system, and are indeed foreseen by the Articles in the event that a country has fallen into fundamental disequilibrium; *but such situations should arise less frequently to the extent that the policies described above are followed.*" (Emphasis added.)[46]

The Fund's *Annual Report* for 1965 included an interesting chapter on "The International Monetary System and International Liquidity." In the discussion of balance-of-payments adjustment, exchange rates were mentioned as one of the policy instruments usable by countries either in deficit or in surplus, but in each case *it was the last policy instrument on the list.* The report noted: "With the exception of one large-scale and widespread devaluation in 1949, which was part of the postwar readjustment process, there have been relatively few changes in agreed par values."[47]

Even the U.S. Council of Economic Advisers, which has normally been somewhat more adventurous than other government agencies in international matters, said in its 1964 report:

> While the Articles of Agreement of the IMF permit exchange-rate adjustment in case of a "fundamental disequilibrium"—an imbalance that is chronic and intractable at the existing exchange rate—most countries are reluctant to take this step. For a reserve currency country, this alternative is not available. For other major industrial countries, even occasional recourse to such adjustments would induce serious speculative capital movements, thereby accentuating imbalances.[48]

Robert Roosa, in a series of lectures at the Council on Foreign Relations just after leaving office in 1965, argued strongly for fixed rates of exchange but proposed that central banks should permit wider fluctuations in *forward* exchange rates. If this were done, he believed, it would not be necessary to widen the one percent margin above and below parity for spot exchange provided for in the IMF Articles. Roosa continued:

> The advantage of the present arrangements, as their widened use in recent years has begun to make clear, is that the necessary disciplines of fixed rates can be maintained for the individual countries concerned, while the force of transitional speculation can, at least in significant part, be absorbed through wider swings in the forward markets for the same currency.[49]

We have also noted that the Brookings report of 1963 had expressed a preference for fixed rates of exchange, provided the system was supplied with adequate liquidity to permit a gradual adjustment of imbalances. On the other hand, a report of Working Party 3 on adjustment—commissioned by the Group of Ten in 1964 and published in August 1966—included changes in exchange rates as one of the instruments of policy for countries in imbalance either on the surplus or deficit side.[50] This report, and the debates carried on in the course of its preparation, helped to instill in officials' minds a more symmetrical view of payments imbalances. The responsibilities of countries in surplus were brought to attention.

A number of private economists differed with the official view. Milton Friedman had been arguing for flexible exchange rates for years. In a commentary on the Brookings report presented to the Joint Economic Committee of the U.S. Congress, Randall Hinshaw of Claremont Graduate School concluded:

> Partly because I am less optimistic than the authors are about the American balance of payments, I am less impressed than they appear to be with the virtues of fixed exchange rates—particularly since our competitors, when confronted with serious payments difficulties, are far more likely to alter these rates than we are. The result, for us, may well be the worst of both worlds.[51]

Few of the other contributors to the Joint Economic Committee's compilation of reactions to the Brookings report advocated exchange rate adjustment, though many of them expressed doubts about the more optimistic of the two Brookings projections.

How are we to explain what appears to have been in the early and mid-1960's a widespread acceptance of the proposition that for industrial countries exchange rate changes should be either ruled out altogether or regarded as a step to be taken only *in extremis?*

First, there was an almost universal belief that the fixed price of gold at $35 per ounce was a basic underpinning of the system. To almost everyone, this ruled out a unilateral devaluation by the United States. According to Theodore Sorensen, some of President Kennedy's advisers privately told him that even devaluation was not unthinkable, that it would be a drastic change in the system but preferable to wrecking it altogether. The President responded that he did not want that weapon of last resort even mentioned outside his office; by disrupting the international monetary system, devaluation would call into doubt the good faith and stability of the nation and the competence of its President.[52]

Aside from questions of "good faith" and prestige, there was an overriding *economic* reason to oppose a devaluation of the dollar involving a rise in the price of gold. It was that so much of the world's foreign exchange holdings consisted of dollars retained by monetary authorities on the assumption that the dollar would maintain its value in relation to gold. If the dollar price of gold were changed, the entire monetary system would have to be altered, for it could not be expected that foreign monetary authorities would go on holding dollars in the belief that the dollar's gold value would not be changed again. This does not mean that the continued convertibility of the dollar into gold at the fixed price was an end in itself; rather, as Richard Cooper pointed out in his statement on the Brookings report, "it was an efficient means to serve our real ends," which were to promote the movements of goods, services, and productive capital among nations.[53] Nevertheless, suspension of the gold convertibility of the dollar could not be undertaken without bringing with it other drastic changes in the system.

In addition to this constraint on U.S. action, there were reasons why exchange rate adjustment by other countries did not appear feasible in the first half of the 1960's. As the current account surplus of the United States increased after 1960, the U.S.-European imbalance came to be looked upon mainly as a capital flow problem. There was a tendency—for a number of reasons, cyclical and structural—to regard the outflow of private capital from the United States as excessive. Although an overvalued dollar might help to explain some of the capital outflow,[54] it was also likely, given the strong U.S. surplus on goods and services, that European countries would not be prepared to see their currencies revalued upward against the dollar, no matter how that change might be brought about. Although this view imputed to European officials might not be justified on economic grounds, it was a reasonable description of their beliefs, particularly since Europe's surplus on goods and services had decreased markedly by 1964.

As we shall see, it was only when the U.S. current account surplus began to dwindle in the second half of the 1960's that the subject of greater exchange rate flexibility came to be discussed seriously in official circles.

IV

Stirrings of International Monetary Reform

We have noted that President Kennedy, in his first balance-of-payments message, encouraged multilateral consideration of ways in which the international monetary system might be strengthened and that the response in London was enthusiastic. While authorities in the United States were preoccupied in 1961 and 1962 with creating the defense perimeter described earlier, officials in London were considering far-reaching reforms. This led to an initiative by Reginald Maudling, new British Chancellor of the Exchequer, at the annual meeting of the IMF in Washington in September 1962. After reviewing monetary developments—and graciously describing the U.S. deficit problem as "less one of a balance of payments than of a balance of generosity," in view of large U.S. outlays abroad for defense, aid, and investment—and paying tribute to recent innovations, Maudling stressed the need of a growing world economy for a growing volume of international liquidity. Rather tentatively, he proposed that the Fund establish a "mutual currency account" into which countries in surplus—and therefore accumulating dollars or sterling—could deposit these currencies in exchange for another asset. That asset would carry the usual guaranty that attaches to countries' claims on the Fund and would be usable as a reserve. More important, according to Maudling, it would "enable world liquidity to be expanded without additional strains on the reserve currencies."[1]

Although the Americans had not been briefed officially on this proposal until just before the meeting, they had heard "rumblings" about it and some of them at least were disturbed—for two reasons. First, Roosa was in the process of strengthening the multilateral buttresses of the dollar through a

proposal to add to U.S. holdings of foreign currencies and by introducing a
new type of "Roosa bond" denominated in the currency of the foreign monetary authority that purchased it (thereby giving the holder a guaranty against
a devaluation of the dollar). Second, and more important, Roosa viewed the
Maudling proposal as a way to "permit holders of sterling or dollars to 'run'
from them into a special deposit account in the International Monetary Fund
on their own initiative."[2]

Failing to persuade the British to have "second thoughts" on the nature
and timing of their proposal, Roosa, on the instruction of President Kennedy,
wrote an article that was published in the monthly *Business Review* of the
Federal Reserve Bank of Philadelphia just before the Fund meeting. In rather
strong language, the article criticized both the substance and timing of "revolutionary approaches." It examined and rejected three such approaches: (1) a
doubling or tripling of the dollar price of gold, as advocated by Jacques Rueff;
(2) a system of guarantees, in terms of gold value, of foreign dollar holdings;
and (3) "immediate launching of plans" to pool international reserves in a
"new supranational bank." Instead, he advocated continuation of the step-by-
step approach to strengthen the system and "avoid the hazards of despair and
economic disruption so likely to result from the displacement of the dollar as
the universally recognized supplement and alternative to gold in meeting the
international liquidity reserve needs of the world."[3]

Pointing to the General Arrangements to Borrow (GAB) and other defenses against a "run" on the dollar (Roosa identified the system as a "convertible gold dollar system," while Maudling spoke of *two* reserve currencies),
Roosa went on to say:

> Once the United States has its balance of payments fully under control, the rate
> of increase in the supply of dollars available to serve the international liquidity
> requirements in the world can also be managed. Whether or not there is a corre-
> sponding proportionate increase in the underlying supply of gold in the world's
> monetary reserves, additional increases in the supply of dollars can rest upon an
> accumulation by the United States of incremental amounts of the currencies of
> other leading countries.

Thus Roosa saw no need for fundamental institutional reform. The dollar
was to continue as the world's reserve currency, and growing reserve needs
could be met even in the absence of U.S. balance-of-payments deficits. When
in balance or surplus, the United States would acquire other currencies, and
this in turn would permit the rest of the world to go on accumulating dollars
as reserves. This was Roosa's way of cutting through the Triffin dilemma,

under one horn of which elimination of the U.S. deficit would leave the world starved for reserves.

Although his rejection of the Maudling proposal in 1962 was rather brusque, Roosa, writing in 1967, recognized that "in the end the Maudling initiative proved a most valuable catalyst."[4] For it led the United States in 1963 to propose a study in the Group of Ten of additional steps to assure the adequacy of international liquidity over the long run. Officials in various capitals were sounded out in the first half of 1963.

The Managing Director of the IMF, Per Jacobsson, was not especially pleased to have an examination of the monetary system take place outside the Fund. But Jacobsson died in May 1963, and under his successor, Pierre-Paul Schweitzer, the Fund undertook to intensify its own studies of international liquidity and related questions.

President Kennedy's balance-of-payments message of July 18, 1963, which announced the proposed interest equalization tax, endorsed a study of "possible improvements" in the monetary system and, in fact, adverted to the Triffin dilemma by stating that "one of the reasons that new sources of liquidity may well be needed is that, as we close our payments gap, we will cut down our provision of dollars to the rest of the world."[5]

As a result, the Ministers and Governors of the Group of Ten agreed, at the annual meeting of the IMF in early October 1963, that their deputies should "undertake a thorough examination of the outlook for the functioning of the international monetary system and of its probable future needs for liquidity." They agreed "that the underlying structure of the present monetary system—based on fixed exchange rates and the established price of gold—has proven its value for present and future arrangements" and this proposition was taken as given in the study conducted by the deputies over the next ten months.[6] Robert Roosa was chosen chairman of the deputies. The group met monthly from October 1963 to June 1964, when it completed a report to the Ministers and Governors.

The Study of the Group of Ten Deputies

The monthly meetings of the deputies took place mostly at the French Finance Ministry, which occupies one wing of the palace of the Louvre in Paris. Thus the Americans supplied the chairman and the French supplied the site of the meetings. The Americans and British also provided the language; it was agreed that all discussion would be in English, thereby avoiding simultaneous translation and encouraging informality and untrammeled dialogue.

(Only in later years were French officials under strict instruction to use no language but their own in formal international meetings.*)

The logistics of the meetings were such that there were 20 deputies around the table—a senior treasury and a central bank official from each of the members of the Group of Ten—plus observers from the Swiss National Bank, the IMF, the OECD, and the BIS. Behind the deputies of each country sat two or three advisers, and there were also five "secretaries," officials from countries that were members of the group.

The deputies' meetings provided an opportunity for a frank and confidential exchange of views on the working of the international monetary system —the first systematic examination of the system by governments since Bretton Woods. The dissatisfaction of some European members of the Group of Ten —notably the French—with the existing reserve currency system was aired frankly. Some of these objections had already been expressed by Finance Minister Giscard d'Estaing, at the IMF annual meeting in October 1963. In particular he criticized the existing system (1) for its lack of "automatic machinery" to bring about a prompt return to balance-of-payments equilibrium, and for the inflationary consequences of this failing; (2) for its lack of "reciprocity" between reserve centers and other countries; and (3) for the inequity involved in the differing composition of countries' reserves as between gold and currencies. But, at least in retrospect, his tone was conciliatory, and he paid tribute to the economic progress that had been achieved under the existing system, saying, "I do not want us to give in to this kind of intellectual nomadism by virtue of which one tries to escape from an existing system as soon as weaknesses become apparent in it, while forgetting the substantial benefits that it has brought, and the perils which it has helped avoid."[7]

In the course of the deputies' meetings from October 1963 to June 1964, the French objections to the existing system were clarified and a specific proposal for a new reserve asset, the "collective reserve unit" (CRU), was put forward.[8] This asset was to be linked to gold and created and used outside the IMF by the members of the Group of Ten.

In the deputies' debates, the French representatives stressed the disorderly way in which reserves were created by deficits of reserve centers, the potential

---

*Just as he objected to the use of the dollar as world currency, President de Gaulle disliked the use of English as world language. There is a story, probably apocryphal, that when a Japanese Cabinet Minister called on him, de Gaulle asked what was the second language of Japan. When told it was English, he asked whether the Japanese Government would consider adopting French as the second language. The Japanese visitor replied that he thought consideration could be given to this suggestion, provided that France would consider making Japanese its second language.

instability of the system, the lack of "discipline" on reserve centers, and the inflationary effects of all this. This led them to distinguish between "glad" and "not so glad" holders of reserve currencies, the latter being countries that refrained from converting "unwanted" dollars into gold in a spirit of cooperation with the United States and in fear of creating an international crisis. Finally, until reserve currencies could be phased out and replaced by a collective reserve unit, it was desirable to introduce a form of "collective discipline" under which the other members of the Group of Ten would agree on the extent to which they would be willing to finance additional American deficits.

The U.S. deputies, Robert Roosa and J. Dewey Daane of the Federal Reserve Board, took the position that reserve currency status had been thrust upon the U.S. dollar, not deliberately sought; that the balance of payments was improving; that the United States was an important source of capital for the rest of the world; that, though a country may derive advantages from being a reserve center, it is also subject to constraints on its policies, given that its currency is convertible into gold for foreign monetary authorities (that, in particular, it cannot devalue). Finally, in reaction to the French proposal for a new international currency unit, they stressed the important role of credit facilities among the various forms of international liquidity.

The views of other countries' representatives ranged between those of France and the United States. Deputies of other Common Market countries shared some of the French views but not their political stance on the U.S. role in the world.

The published report of the deputies to their Ministers and Governors glossed over the basic differences that had been expressed during the months of intensive discussion. Treasury Secretary Dillon was anxious to avoid a public confrontation with the French; thus the report presented to the Ministers for their meeting of June 15–16 was edited and toned down by the "secretaries" of the deputies group before publication on August 10 as an annex to a ministerial statement.[9]

The published deputies' report first addressed itself to the process of correcting payments imbalances, proposing that Working Party 3 of the OECD undertake a study of how balance-of-payments equilibrium could be better preserved and imbalances more quickly corrected. The terms of reference for this study did not mention exchange rates.

The report went on to describe existing forms of international reserves and credit facilities. The deputies agreed that "gold will continue to be the ultimate international reserve asset" but also stated that "we cannot prudently expect new gold production to meet all liquidity needs in the future." As for the dollar, it was stated that the "deficit in the U.S. balance of payments now appears to be shrinking and the contribution of dollar holdings to the growth in international liquidity seems unlikely to continue as in the past." But there was "no immediate prospect of any other currency assuming the function of an international reserve currency." Thus "the need may in time be felt for some additional kind of international reserve asset." The deputies therefore established a Study Group on the Creation of Reserve Assets under the chairmanship of Rinaldo Ossola of the Bank of Italy, one of the two Italian deputies.

In addition to commissioning two studies, the other major recommendation of the deputies was to establish a system of "multilateral surveillance" over "the various elements in international liquidity—whether of a private or official character—available or created for the financing of surpluses and deficits." All members of the Group of Ten would provide the BIS with statistical data on the means used to finance surpluses and deficits. These data would be combined and circulated confidentially to individual members of the Group of Ten and to Working Party 3, where they would be subject to "a full exchange of views." The purpose of this was "to provide a basis for multilateral surveillance of the various elements of liquidity creation, with a view to avoiding excesses or shortages in the means of financing existing or anticipated surpluses and deficits in the balance of payments, and to discussing measures appropriate for each country in accordance with the general economic outlook." This procedure was what had survived of the French proposal for "collective discipline."

Only one paragraph out of 55 in the deputies' published report referred to differences in views among the countries:

> Given the complexity of the problem referred to us, it is not surprising that a number of views were expressed as to the areas which most deserve further study or action for the longer run improvement and strengthening of the international monetary system. Some Deputies considered that it was mainly in the field of the provision of owned reserves under the gold exchange standard that changes and improvements were desirable. They noted that the present system might imply a reliance on a continuing accumulation of reserve currency holdings, and they stressed the disadvantage of depending for the creation of reserves on the balance of payments deficits of a reserve currency country rather than on the needs of the international monetary system as a whole. Other Deputies stressed the primary desirability of building upon the accomplishments and flexibility of the present system. They noted that reserve currencies were unlikely to make the same contribution as in the past to the growth of international liquidity and believed that principal reliance should be placed on strengthening the international credit com-

ponent of the present system, and on the increase in reserve assets created when
official credits are extended either through the Fund or in some other form.[10]

Readers of the report had little difficulty in identifying the principal proponents of these viewpoints.

How the deputies' study would have evolved if Robert Roosa had not been
chairman is an intriguing, though unanswerable, question. Roosa's principal
antagonist, persistent but gentlemanly, was André de Lattre, at that time
Directeur du Trésor in the French Ministry of Finance. De Lattre pushed hard
at times but was often either isolated or in a small minority, while Roosa had
the capacity to absorb the thrusts of his adversary and convert them, usually
through lengthy discourse, into a proposition that the United States could live
with. The subsequent removal of de Lattre from office has been attributed to
dissatisfaction at higher levels of the French Government—perhaps the highest level—with the outcome of this exercise.

But the ministerial statement of August 1, 1964—released on August 10
to coincide with publication of the IMF *Annual Report*—revealed none of the
basic disagreements that had engaged the deputies during their months of
debate. It simply ratified the deputies' proposals (summarized above) and
expressed agreement on a "moderate" increase in IMF quotas when that
subject should come up for scheduled consideration in the Fund in 1965. The
agreement on the enlargement of quotas was a compromise between the initial
American position, widely shared by others, for a 50 percent increase, and the
initial French view that no increase was necessary. Dillon and Giscard d'Estaing apparently split the difference in a last-minute conversation before a
Group of Ten meeting.

IMF Study of Liquidity

The results of the Fund's study of international liquidity in 1963–64 were
summarized in two chapters in its 1964 *Annual Report*. These chapters included an analysis of the relationship between international liquidity and the
balance-of-payments adjustment process and an appraisal of the adequacy of
international liquidity in terms of both demand and supply. This analysis
treated the role of the dollar in rather favorable terms and reportedly aroused
the displeasure of some of the representatives of Common Market countries,[11]
even though it included a sentence that paraphrased the remarks of Minister
Giscard d'Estaing about the benefits the system had brought and the perils it
had helped to avoid. In considering further changes in the system, the Fund

report, not unexpectedly, stressed the advantages of "the multilateral institutional approach to the creation and administration of international liquidity." Finally, after describing the various ways in which the Fund, as then constituted, provided international liquidity, the report went on to sketch possible new approaches to the creation of reserves through the Fund.

Report by 32 Economists

Sparked by a statement by Secretary Dillon (at a press conference during the 1963 annual meeting of the IMF) to the effect that individual economists outside government would not play a role in the projected study by the Group of Ten, three academic economists organized a group of 32 nongovernmental economists from eleven countries to undertake a study "designed to interpret their disagreements in a form potentially useful to decision-makers." Under the leadership of Professor Fritz Machlup of Princeton, the group held four conferences, two at Princeton and two at the Villa Serbelloni in Bellagio, Italy (hence it was sometimes referred to as the Bellagio Group), and by June 30, 1964, it completed a report.[12]

The report was not an agreed-upon statement but an analysis of problems, a presentation "in idealized form" of four different approaches toward improving the international monetary system, and a statement of a broad consensus on policy formulated by fourteen of the economists at the final meeting of the group in June 1964.

The analysis of the system was carried out under three main headings: adjustment (of imbalances), liquidity, and confidence (or the problem of instability arising from possible conversions from one reserve asset to another). The four alternative approaches to dealing with the problems revealed in the analysis were: (1) a semi-automatic gold standard; (2) centralization of international reserves in the IMF (or another institution); (3) multiple currency reserves, which would involve diversifying the reserve currency function among a number of countries and agreeing to rules on the ratios in which various reserves would be held; and (4) flexible exchange rates, with some degree of management by monetary authorities.

The four propositions on policy on which there was said to be extensive but not unanimous agreement were:

1. That balance of payments disturbances differ substantially in source and duration and that the differences among them call for differentiated responses. If public policy could be perfectly designed, it would seek to finance—without

triggering the adjustment mechanism—such payments imbalances as will, in time, be reversed without adjustments by the economy; it would, conversely, seek to initiate adjustment when international payments are affected by disturbances of an enduring kind.

2. That adjustments of payments imbalances of an enduring kind should be initiated promptly. They should be executed with the smallest possible loss of income and employment, and to this end, adequate interim financing should be available. Exchange rates should be allowed to change more frequently than currently contemplated by major governments.

3. That the financing of reversible disturbances requires the use of official reserves (save under a system of freely flexible exchange rates) and that the mechanism of reserve creation should be overhauled to adjust the expansion of reserves to needs. The process by which nations acquire reserves should not disrupt international trade and payments or interfere with the pursuit of domestic economic objectives; the rate of reserve creation should be sufficient to sustain the growth of world production without inducing price inflation.

4. That the protection of the large outstanding foreign-exchange component of the world reserve pool against sudden or massive conversions into gold should receive a high order of priority.

One can discern here two areas of divergence from the content of the reports of the Group of Ten and the IMF. More stress was placed on the desirability of changing exchange rates as a means of balance-of-payments adjustment. And more concern was expressed about the instability that could arise from conversion of the "overhang" of foreign exchange reserves. (In general the report of the Bellagio Group holds up well in the light of subsequent developments.)

Reform Catches On

At the Fund's 1964 annual meeting in Tokyo, some major shifts in intellectual attitudes became apparent. Suddenly ministers and central bank governors were talking about reform of the system and, in the process, revealing the basic differences of position that the Ministers and Governors of the Group of Ten chose to ignore in their August statement releasing the deputies' report. A number of the ministers from Group of Ten countries presented their interpretation of "multilateral surveillance."

Secretary Dillon, after stressing both the progress achieved in the domestic U.S. economy and the reduction in the external deficit, emphasized the importance of credit facilities, including bilateral credit arrangements, as an element in international liquidity. We must, he said, "constantly guard against the over-simplified conclusion that a simple addition to the international money supply—or an agreed limitation upon it—or a contraction of it—will provide an adequate solution." He did, however, acknowledge both the Group of Ten and IMF studies of reserves and observed that the "results of these studies should put us in a position to meet any need for enlarged supplies of unconditional liquidity that may develop over the coming years."[13]

In a subsequent press conference in Tokyo on September 11, Secretary Dillon aligned the United States solidly behind Schweitzer on the desirability of decisions in the IMF, rather than in the Group of Ten, on international liquidity. He also joined Schweitzer in rejecting the notion that inflation in Europe was the result of the payments deficits of reserve centers. Finally, he expressed clearly what was probably his basic position on new reserve assets: the IMF quota increase agreed to in Tokyo should take care of the international liquidity problem for the next few years. It was possible, maybe likely, that as the U.S. deficit disappeared, there would be a need to create new reserve assets. "We would like to look ahead and come to some conclusions which would strengthen the monetary system of the world in the long run."

Minister Giscard d'Estaing set out more clearly than he had a year earlier his objections to the "present gold exchange standard." The system was "an empirical creation" which permitted reserve currency countries to finance lasting balance-of-payments deficits without adequate corrective mechanisms. As a result, he said, it may lead to the spread of international inflation and to pressure on creditor countries to "create a deficit" in their own balance of payments to compensate for the outflow of reserve currencies, "a phenomenon for which they have no responsibility whatever."

A reformed system should, he continued, be set in concentric circles. The inner circle is gold; its importance "does not arise from any charm in the metal itself" but from the fact that it is "the only monetary element outside the scope of government action." But gold alone cannot meet the needs of the world. If and when "fiduciary means must be added to gold," they should be of an objective nature governed by strict rules concerning their creation and volume, and "the group of those with whom would rest the responsibility and burden" for creating and controlling such assets "should act in close cooperation with the Fund and with due regard to the interest of the world community as a whole." The substitution of this system for the gold exchange standard should be brought about gradually. And, finally, Giscard d'Estaing recognized that "it is normal that various central banks will go on keeping, in their reserves, dollars, pounds sterling, or French francs, owing to the particular financial relationship they maintain with the countries issuing such currencies."[14] In this last point, what the French Minister presumably had in mind was that, even if the Group of Ten countries eliminated the use of currencies as reserves, other countries, particularly those less developed, might continue to belong to a currency area to which they had historical ties.

Reginald Maudling, British Chancellor of the Exchequer, undertook to rebut some of the propositions of the French Minister. In particular he defined multilateral surveillance as a step forward in international consultation but without establishing a veto on the setting up of new credit facilities or on the use of existing facilities. He also defended the "empirical character" of the existing system and expressed doubts about the benefits of strengthening the role of gold. As did Secretary Dillon, he thought there was a danger in "too much emphasis on owned reserves as opposed to credit facilities." In view of the British balance-of-payments position in the summer of 1964 (described in the next chapter), it is not surprising that international credits were on Maudling's mind.

In his closing remarks, Pierre-Paul Schweitzer placed himself on the other side of the table from his fellow countryman, Minister Giscard d'Estaing. Schweitzer welcomed the broad support that had been expressed for the "multilateral institutional approach" as opposed to the limited group approach to reserve creation espoused by the French. He also doubted that the inflationary pressures experienced by a number of industrial countries could properly be attributed "to the payments deficits of other countries, or even to those features of the international monetary system which have made such payments deficits somewhat easier to finance."[15]

Thus by the autumn of 1964 the official controversy on the international monetary system was out in the open and some of the major issues were clear.

The French position favored reemphasizing the role of gold and replacing reserve currencies with a new asset linked to gold. The interest of France in a new asset arose not so much from a concern that world reserves might be inadequate but from a desire to provide a substitute for the dollar. Although the French position followed Jacques Rueff this far, it did not go all the way with him and advocate an increase in the official price of gold.

The British and the Americans defended the existing system while agreeing that their deficits should be reduced or eliminated. Secretary Dillon was lukewarm about a new reserve asset, preferring to stress international credit as a means of financing balance-of-payments deficits and surpluses.

Other members of the Group of Ten favored an end to the growth of reserve currency balances but did not follow the French in advocating the extinction of existing balances; some of them favored a new reserve asset to provide for growth of world reserves when U.S. deficits no longer performed that function.

The representatives of developing countries, in addition to supporting an increase in Fund quotas and other matters in the Fund of special interest to them, called for consideration of international liquidity questions within the Fund itself. "It is precisely because of its multilateral and open character that the Fund provides the most appropriate forum for this purpose."[16]

Against this background of official positions, the members of the Group of Ten's Study Group on the Creation of Reserve Assets were already at work.

The Ossola Group, 1964–1965

The Study Group's mandate from the deputies asked that it examine various proposals for the creation of reserve assets, taking full account of "their implications for the functioning of the present international monetary system" and of the broad considerations set forth in Paragraph 40 of the deputies' report:

> compatibility with the evolution of the system, their contribution to greater stability, their ability to direct liquidity to the point of greatest legitimate need at any given time, their ability to adapt the volume of reserves to global needs as opposed to individual shortages, the acceptability and soundness of the claims they offer as a reserve asset, their effect on relations of the Group with the rest of the world, the machinery required for controlling the volume and distribution of reserves created, and the desirability of a group approach as opposed to a worldwide approach.

The Study Group was not expected to make recommendations but to "assemble the elements necessary for an evaluation of the respective proposals."

Chaired by Rinaldo Ossola, the Group consisted (except for Ossola) not of deputies but of officials one or two levels lower, from ministries of finance and central banks. The United States was represented by George Willis, longtime senior official in the Treasury Department, and me, with the assistance of Donald McGrew, U.S. Treasury representative in Paris. Because of illness in his family, Willis was unable to attend the last few meetings of the Group. Assembling at regular intervals, either at the Finance Ministry in Paris or amidst the ornate decor of the Bank of Italy in Rome, the Group completed its report at the end of May 1965.

Meeting our deadline in the spring of 1965 often required that we work on into the late evening. I have vivid recollections of wearily seeking out restaurants in Paris or Rome that would serve dinner at 11 P.M.—or later—and then trying to get a decent night's sleep in order to be fresh for the debates of the next day.

In the period of almost a year during which the Group met, the various proposals that had been dimly adumbrated during the previous year were sharpened and elaborated. We found that, while various specific proposals for creating reserves had been published,[17] thorough analysis of the mechanics and the effects of different techniques had not been carried out. Thus the Group's efforts involved some intellectual breakthroughs in respect to the entire process of "deliberate reserve creation." And the report clarified and analyzed the means by which ordinary Fund drawings usually increase world reserves (in the form of gold tranches or super gold tranches).

The cleavage between France and the United States, which had surfaced publicly during the previous year, was of course reflected in the deliberations of the Ossola Group. But the good nature of the chairman and the personal qualities of the members created a remarkable spirit of empathy and warmth, which made the experience pleasurable and facilitated a reasonably clear and dispassionate presentation of the issues. A decade later, those who participated in the Ossola Group retain a bond of friendship, strengthened by a sense of having been "present at the creation" of the Special Drawing Right (SDR).

In the early stages of the Group's work, the U.S. representatives were on the defensive, stressing the dangers of a radical departure from the existing system. As time went on, we developed and presented specific plans for creating reserve assets by adapting the existing procedures of the International Monetary Fund. Meanwhile, Claude Pierre-Brossolette, the able representative of the French Finance Ministry, was handicapped by the fact that both President de Gaulle and Minister Giscard d'Estaing had made public statements in early 1965 that had de-emphasized the CRU.

Basing itself on the agreed propositions (a) that future flows of gold into reserves cannot be fully relied upon to meet future needs for an expansion of reserves associated with a growing volume of world trade and payments and (b) that the contribution of dollar holdings to reserve growth "seems unlikely to continue as in the past," the Group described, analyzed, and compared various techniques for the deliberate creation of reserve assets under three broad headings: (1) creation of new reserve assets by a group of countries— the CRU outside the Fund or a similar limited-group scheme associated with the Fund, (2) creation of new assets or drawing rights in the IMF—under which four possible techniques were included, and (3) creation of reserve assets in the Fund in exchange for countries' holdings of currency—under which two schemes were set forth, one of which was Maudling's mutual currency account. All the reserve assets considered had the characteristic that they would be held and used only by monetary authorities (in contrast with both gold and reserve currencies).

The French proposal for collective reserve units (CRU), first presented to the deputies in 1963–64, was described in detail. The CRU would be an asset created outside the IMF by and for the use of a limited group of industrial countries—presumably the Group of Ten, but possibly open to participation by a few other countries. CRU would be held and used in a uniform ratio with gold; they would be created on the basis of *unanimous* decision by the participants. They would be distributed to participants in proportion to their gold reserves, though it was recognized that other bases of distribution were possible, including either total reserves of participating countries or IMF quotas. If either of these alternative methods were used, it would be necessary for the participants to redistribute gold and CRU among themselves so as to maintain a uniform ratio of CRU to gold among the participating countries. As used to finance deficits and surpluses, CRU would move in a fixed ratio with gold. If, for example, one country sold gold to another during a given period, then on a subsequent settlement date there would be a "reshuffling" of CRU and gold to reestablish the uniform ratio; the outcome would be that the country in deficit would have transferred gold and CRU in the established uniform proportion to the country in surplus.[18]

Even those who opposed this scheme had to admire its elegance. It was a product of French "cartesian" logic, and it reflected and embodied French objections to the existing system and French objectives for a reformed system. One can imagine its authors asking themselves, How can we create a new asset the effect of which will be identical with the effect of an increase in the price of gold? That, in fact, is what the scheme achieved. Reserves of participating countries would be increased in proportion to their gold reserves, and the new asset would move among countries in a ratio to gold equivalent to the "camouflaged" increase in the gold price. Further, the scheme was to be outside the IMF, a reflection of the French view that the Fund was dominated by Anglo-Saxons and of the practical consideration that in a worldwide organization it would be awkward to create reserves exclusively for the Group of Ten. Finally, the rule of unanimity was another reaction to what the French regarded as the overwhelming power of the United States, even in the Group of Ten.

The French proponents of the CRU argued that the adoption of this scheme would make it clear that an increase in the price of gold was excluded, thereby ending uncertainty and speculation on this question. Others answered that the close link to gold in the distribution and use of CRU would enhance the role of gold. Since the distribution of CRU would be in proportion to gold holdings, countries would have an incentive to maximize their gold reserves by converting existing currency balances into gold. This would have a particularly heavy impact on the United States, the issuer of the principal reserve currency and the only country that stood ready to convert its currency into gold. Even if the distribution were on another basis—for example, IMF quotas —the requirement that CRU be used only in a fixed proportion to gold would lead to substantial gold movements in balance-of-payments financing; among other effects, this was likely to induce countries outside the limited group to convert their currency balances into gold in order to have enough gold to use with CRU.[19] As it turned out, the French proposal garnered no support in the Group, even from other members of the Common Market.

A limited group scheme associated with the Fund, put forward by one of the Dutch representatives on a personal basis, contained a great number of variants. In one variant it would be virtually indistinguishable from the CRU; at the other extreme, it merged with the schemes to be outlined below, with the exception that participation would be limited "to a small group of industrial countries, which might or might not be larger than the Group of Ten."[20]

The other major proposals involved a direct adaptation of the IMF and were intended to create reserves in the form of drawing rights automatically usable by Fund members. The United States took the lead in putting forward proposals in this category. One of them was designed to be put into effect without amendment of the Fund's Articles of Agreement. Under that scheme, the Fund would simply extend beyond the usual limits the automatic drawing rights of members; each country receiving such additional drawing rights— which would be treated as reserves—would provide an equal line of credit to the Fund. While this loan procedure appeared cumbersome, it was no different in essence from the way in which other reserves are used: any country receiving reserves from another (whether gold or reserve currencies) provides its own currency in exchange.

A second proposal provided for IMF quota increases without the usual 25 percent payment in gold; instead, members of the Fund would pay over a gold certificate that would lie dormant in the Fund. As a result each quota increase would expand countries' automatic drawing rights (gold tranches) without requiring them to give up gold to the Fund.

In both of these schemes, countries that had borrowed from the Fund beyond the point to which automatic drawing rights were extended would receive a potential rather than an actual increase in reserves; it would become actual only when they had repaid their borrowings. This provision was dubbed a "self-qualifying" principle; it had the appeal of excluding from the benefits of deliberate reserve creation countries that were in persistent deficit. The idea was that reserves were to be created to finance *temporary* swings in payments balances, not chronic imbalances.

These two proposals envisaged the deliberate creation of reserves analogous to the existing gold tranche and super gold tranche positions. Countries would use these reserves by drawing currency from the Fund, thereby transferring reserves to the country whose currency was drawn.[21] It turned out to be a small step from this type of proposal to that of a reserve in the form of a claim on the Fund that was directly transferable among countries (a Fund unit). This is what the SDR is. As the Ossola report pointed out in its comparison of units and drawing rights, "Technically, the one form of asset can be made to do all that the other can do, and, for some members, the difference of form itself, as opposed to other characteristics of the scheme, is not a substantial issue."[22] At that time, however, many American officials had an aversion to new reserves in the form of "units." This aversion sprang from their adverse reaction to the French proposal, which called for a unit, and from a feeling that a unit transferable directly among countries, rather than by drawing currencies from the Fund, would be too obvious a substitute for dollars.

The arguments countering these proposals included: giving the Fund power to create and distribute reserve assets at its initiative might impair its major role as a lending institution concerned with the policies of the countries that came to it to borrow; reserves would be created for too wide a range of countries, some of which "might not be able to assume the obligations and responsibilities required for the functioning of the system"; use of the claims on the Fund would involve cumbersome procedures; weighted voting (rather than unanimity) would give a decisive influence to a very few countries; and use of claims on the Fund as reserves lacks the disciplinary effects provided by a link to gold.[23]

Two other proposals for creating reserves involved "special operations" by the Fund, either Fund investment in member countries or deposits or loans placed with the Fund by member countries for use by the Fund for special loans or credits. In both cases member countries would acquire a claim on the IMF usable as reserves.[24]

Finally, the Group considered two proposals designed not to increase reserves but to provide holders of currency with an alternative asset. One would involve Fund drawings by reserve centers; in essence, reserve centers would use their gold tranche drawing rights or credit tranches to redeem other countries' holdings of their currencies. The other proposal (the mutual currency account first proposed in 1962) would provide a depository facility into which countries could place reserve currencies and receive an asset "expressed as the equivalent of a given weight of gold."[25]

The report of the Study Group concluded by identifying four fundamental issues on which "a range of views" existed:

(i) the question of a link between gold and a new reserve asset, the closeness of that link, and its effects on the existing system;
(ii) the width of membership for purposes of management and distribution of the asset;
(iii) the role of the IMF as regards deliberate reserve creation;
(iv) the rules for decision-making concerning the creation of reserve assets.

The pros and cons of each of these issues were presented in the body of the report. The arguments against reserve creation in the Fund were supplied "mainly by one of our members," whose nationality the reader of the report had little difficulty in identifying. The French had greater support, among other European members, for a limited group approach. There were two reasons for this predilection among European officials (it was not entirely absent among Americans) toward confining reserve creation and especially decision-making to the Group of Ten countries. One was a concern among Europeans that, in a worldwide system, the United States and the developing countries might team up and vote for excessive creation of new reserves. (We shall have occasion to take note of this issue again.) The second reason reflected a muddled notion that only countries with "usable currencies" should be involved in deliberate reserve creation. When one stopped to analyze the meaning of "usable currency," one was driven either to confine reserve creation to the United States and Britain or to extend it well beyond the Group of Ten. Among Europeans, there was a tendency to believe that virtually all developing countries would spend fully any reserve assets created in their favor. Yet, as it happened, many developing countries, though they were borrowers of long-term funds to finance their development, were accumulating reserves in the early 1960's even in the absence of deliberate reserve creation.

The report was completed in late May and circulated to the deputies in June. Thus it had its impact on governments well before it was published on August 10, 1965.

An American Initiative

The discussion and debate in 1965 concerning the international monetary system took place against the background of a distinct improvement in the U.S. balance of payments and of a change in the team at the top level of the U.S. Treasury.

Robert Roosa had resigned at the end of 1964 as Under Secretary for Monetary Affairs, though he stayed on unofficially for a few weeks to help in the formulation of the new balance-of-payments program. Roosa was succeeded on February 1 by Frederick Deming, a career Federal Reserve official (as was Roosa) and at the time President of the Federal Reserve Bank of Minneapolis. Secretary Dillon resigned as of April 1 and was succeeded by Henry H. Fowler, Dillon's second-in-command at the Treasury Department from 1961 until early 1964.

"Joe" Fowler, who has a law degree from Yale, had divided his career between private law practice and governmental service. A courtly gentleman whose deliberate but lucid way of speaking bears traces of his origins in Roanoke, Virginia, Fowler approaches problems with the thoroughness of a trial lawyer preparing himself for any contingency that might arise as he presents or defends a case in the courtroom. As Secretary of the Treasury, he sought expert advice and was remarkably patient in listening to different points of view before making up his mind. He was deeply involved in domestic economic policy and worked incalculably hard to persuade Congress to enact the tax increase of 1968. A major feature of his tenure as Secretary of the Treasury was a shift in the U.S. position on a new international reserve asset.

Part of the background for this shift was provided by Robert Roosa, who had joined Brown Brothers, Harriman & Co., a prestigious private bank many of whose partners had over the years done service in Washington. In May 1965, Roosa gave three lectures at the Council on Foreign Relations that were then published as a book in the summer.[26] A key passage was this: "For it should be clear by this time that I do agree with those who wish urgently to pursue the search for new methods of broadening and adding to the facilities now available." He continued: "The promising scope for additional reform lies in the development of new arrangements for creating some additional type of acceptable reserve asset."[27] It was as though Bob Roosa felt unleashed now that he was no longer in the Treasury. Perhaps Secretary Dillon had held the other end of the leash; though, after leaving office, Dillon too spoke of the need for increasing world reserves through a strengthened international monetary system (in a speech at Middlebury College, June 14, 1965). Roosa's book outlined a specific plan for a new reserve asset, a unit in the International Monetary Fund—which he jestingly dubbed the "crusa" at a press conference.

In March 1965 the annual report of the Joint Economic Committee of the U.S. Congress called for speedy elimination of the U.S. balance-of-payments deficit and improvements in the international monetary system. These improvements might include both "broadening the limits of permissible exchange rate variation" and new methods of providing international liquidity. In the latter connection, the Committee urged "serious consideration of the possibility of creating a new reserve unit."[28]

William McChesney Martin, Chairman of the Board of Governors of the Federal Reserve System, had, from the beginning of my participation in the Ossola Group, encouraged me to pursue an open-minded exploration of the question of reserve creation. On June 25, 1965, in a commencement speech at the Stonier Graduate School of Banking at Rutgers, he spoke of the "broad principles that ought to guide us as we give consideration to proposed changes in international monetary arrangements." His approach was characterized in this way: "Change, development, progress are the law of life. There is no reason for any of us to insist on maintenance of the status quo. Although the present international monetary system has served the world well, it, like all institutions, must evolve and adapt to changing circumstances." After characterizing and commenting on European views of the U.S. balance-of-payments position—and noting, incidentally, that those who complain about investment by U.S. corporations would probably complain just as loudly if the U.S. payments deficit did not exist—he went on to recognize that the amount of dollars that flow abroad as a result of our balance-of-payments position does not necessarily or automatically correspond to the needs of the rest of the world for currency reserves. Thus "we at the Federal Reserve can well understand those who say in effect that international money will not manage itself." Finally, he stressed the importance of a flexible approach rather than a restrictive one that would "turn back the clock of monetary history" to an excessive reliance on gold, of a recognition of the diversity among nations in size, structure, policies, and values, and of a reliance on adaptation of the IMF "if and when the need is felt for additional reserve assets." This does not sound like the hard-bitten conservative whom Herblock—political cartoonist of *The Washington Post*—always depicted as wearing a Herbert Hoover collar.

Against this background—the improving U.S. balance of payments, the Ossola report, and the growing tide of interest in reform of the international liquidity mechanism—the new Secretary of the Treasury electrified the world in early July by announcing that the President had authorized him to say that "the United States now stands prepared to attend and participate in an international monetary conference that would consider what steps we might jointly take to secure substantial improvements in international monetary arrangements." To this end, Secretary Fowler announced, the President had appointed an Advisory Committee on International Monetary Arrangements, which included Douglas Dillon as Chairman, Roosa, Kermit Gordon, Edward Bernstein, André Meyer of Lazard Frères, David Rockefeller of Chase Manhattan Bank (who was accompanied or represented by Paul Volcker), and Charles Kindleberger of M.I.T. Secretary Fowler also noted that he had conferred with the British Chancellor of the Exchequer, James Callaghan, was expecting to meet soon with the Japanese Finance Minister, and before the autumn meetings of the Fund and Bank would visit officials of other Group of Ten countries.[29]

Meanwhile, President Johnson had authorized the establishment within the government of a study group consisting of senior officials from the Treasury, State Department, Council of Economic Advisers, the Federal Reserve Board, and the White House, to be chaired by the Under Secretary of the Treasury for Monetary Affairs. The Study Group, which came to be known as the Deming Group, was, according to the President's memorandum, to work in strictest secrecy in developing and recommending a comprehensive U.S. position and negotiating strategy "designed to achieve substantial improvement in international monetary arrangements." It was also asked to give urgent and thorough consideration to the special situation of the United Kingdom,

> which is of major foreign policy concern. Specifically, it should consider what steps the United States could take to arrange for a relief of pressure on sterling, so as to give the United Kingdom the four- or five-year breathing space it needs to get its economy into shape, and thereby sharply reduce the danger of sterling devaluation or exchange controls or British military disengagement East of Suez or on the Rhine.[30]

Thus the U.S. Government made a quantum jump, as it were, in its attitude and objectives with respect to reform of the international monetary system; it abandoned its defensive posture and took the initiative in its dealings with other countries.

Secretary Fowler's trip through Europe in the late summer of 1965 permitted an exchange of views with finance ministers and central bank governors. There was apparently no enthusiasm in Europe for an international monetary conference at an early date. European officials felt that it was necessary, first, to reconcile differences of view among members of the Group of Ten.[31] During these consultations, the notion of "contingency planning" for a possible future shortage of international liquidity was developed as a way of reconciling Secretary Fowler's call for a conference and the general feeling in Europe that there was no imminent shortage of world reserves. During this trip Secretary Fowler also had to deal with the brewing sterling crisis (described in the next chapter).

At the annual meeting of the IMF in September 1965, a diversity of views was expressed. The European finance ministers and central bank governors generally asserted, in the words of Italian Minister Columbo, that "there is no case at present for any further increase in the volume of unconditional or conditional liquidity."[32] Minister Columbo did, however, suggest that the Maudling plan be considered as a way of converting sterling balances into claims on the IMF. (A sterling crisis had been overcome just weeks before the convening of the Fund annual meeting.) French Minister Giscard d'Estaing expressed interest but the Chancellor of the Exchequer and other British officials failed to respond to these overtures. According to *The Economist,* "The kind explanation is that they are interested but dare not appear so"[33] (presumably out of fear of precipitating another run on sterling). Another issue on which the continental European officials appeared united pertained to the "width of membership" in a reserve-creating scheme; they favored a limited group.

Giscard d'Estaing warmly welcomed Secretary Fowler's move to join the French initiative for reforming the international monetary system but warned against ambiguity as to the "desired orientation" of the reform. "Otherwise the will to reform would suggest the picture of a family, so far united, announcing enthusiastically an intention to take a trip, while half its members are firmly determined to go North, toward the snow, and the other half to the South, where the sun shines." His orientation was toward correcting the "inequalities" in the system and reinforcing its "rules of operation," which involved, among other things, sufficient corrective action by countries in balance-of-payments deficit. He repeated the arguments in favor of the CRU but added a further criterion for its distribution: the proportion of national income allotted to aid to developing countries.[34] *The Economist* said Giscard d'Estaing reached "new heights in the development of elegance, precision and the loftiest idealism in the pecuniary interest of France," since France leads the world in the proportion of its national income devoted to development assistance, as such computations are made. This minor amendment of the CRU, along with a proposal to "organize" certain raw material markets, was designed to make the limited-group approach more acceptable to those countries that had been left out.

Secretary Fowler avoided specifics in his address to the Fund meeting but stressed the agreement in the Group of Ten to proceed, in consultations on reform, to a second phase that would involve the combined efforts of the Executive Board of the Fund and the deputies of the Group of Ten. This phase would be designed to ensure that "the basic interests of all members of the Fund in the new arrangements for the future of the world monetary system will be adequately and appropriately considered and represented before significant intergovernmental agreements" are concluded.[35] These carefully chosen words did not commit the United States to a worldwide scheme for reserve creation, but they differed in tone from the presentations by the continental European Ministers.

The Australian Finance Minister was probably representing the views of the great majority of Fund members outside the Group of Ten when he diplomatically but forcefully attacked the Group of Ten for its lack of representativeness. It could "claim no mandate to legislate for the rest of the world." Yet, he continued,

> a common feature of many of the proposals is that countries inside the Group could receive an immediate and direct increase in reserves. The benefit of this increased liquidity to countries outside the Group would be delayed and indirect. Some of those outside the Group are ready and able to assume the obligations involved. They would feel discriminated against if they were denied the opportunity to join in the arrangements made and share in the mutual extension of credits. Even where countries outside the Group were not in a position to accept the obligations involved in participation, they would wish to be assured that their legitimate interests were being taken into account.

He went on to support Schweitzer's statements that "international liquidity is the business of the Fund" and that "new facilities should be available to all countries which can meet reasonable and agreed tests."[36]

Amidst this welter of views, the Ministers and Governors of the Group of Ten were able to agree on a communiqué. They noted and welcomed the fact that the U.S. balance-of-payments deficit "is being corrected" and concluded that "it is important to undertake, as soon as possible, contingency planning so as to ensure that the future reserve needs of the world are adequately met." They instructed their deputies to resume their discussions on an intensified basis now that the report of the study group on reserve assets had been completed. The deputies were requested to determine "what basis of agreement can be reached on improvements needed in the international monetary system, including arrangements for the future creation of reserve assets, as and when needed, so as to permit adequate provision for the reserve needs of the world economy." The deputies were asked to report by the spring of 1966. The communiqué continued:

> The Ministers and Governors recognize that, as soon as a basis for agreement on essential points has been reached, it will be necessary to proceed from this first phase to a broader consideration of the questions that affect the world economy as a whole. They have agreed that it would be very useful to seek ways by which the efforts of the Executive Board of the Fund and those of the Deputies of the Group of Ten can be directed toward a consensus as to desirable lines of action, and they have instructed their Deputies to work out during the coming year, in close consultation with the Managing Director of the Fund, procedures to achieve this aim, with a view to preparing for the final enactment of any new arrangements at an appropriate forum for international discussions.[37]

Perhaps as reasonable an interpretation as any of this outcome was that of *The Economist:*

> The emerging agreement that some form of new international reserve asset is required represents, truly, a distinct advance—and in the perspective of history this recognition may be seen as a decisive step towards a more rational international monetary order. But the present leisurely moves look anything but in perspective for the more relevant present.
>
> The possible creation of a small amount of new international money for a small group of countries some time in the late 1960's has little immediate significance for the two most serious financial problems before the world. The first is the position of the pound sterling, safe for the short-term, delicate beyond that. The second— and much more harrowing—is the increasingly critical position of the world's poor. The conference was warned diplomatically by the Italians about the first, urgently by the President of the World Bank about the second. The people who counted took equally little notice of either.[38]

We shall now suspend our account of the gradual move toward agreement on a new reserve asset in order to take note of other developments in the world economy, notably the problems of the pound sterling.

$$V$$

The Travail of Sterling, 1964–1968

Britain's struggle to maintain the foreign exchange parity of the pound in the mid-1960's reflected a serious deficiency of the monetary system—the assumed inability of a major economic power to alter its exchange rate. The resolution of the crisis of sterling contributed to a change of thinking in official circles on the virtues of fixed exchange rates.

The Economic and Political Background

The British economy entered a phase of rapid economic expansion in 1963. Industrial production increased more than 14 percent from the end of 1962 to the end of 1964 and GNP in real terms rose 11 percent under the impact of a surge in fixed investment outlays and an accompanying increase in inventory accumulation. Wages and prices rose only moderately, but imports increased almost one-fourth while exports rose half that much.[1] As a result, the current account balance shifted from a surplus of more than $600 million in 1962 to a deficit of almost $650 million in 1964,[2] and long-term capital outflows increased considerably. Nevertheless, Britain's gold and foreign exchange reserves hardly changed in the first half of 1964, largely because other countries, particularly those in the sterling area, increased their sterling holdings, and other forms of short-term capital flowed to London.

Beginning in the summer of 1964, however, sterling weakened in the foreign exchange markets and British reserves began to be used. A standby credit of $1 billion from the IMF was renewed in August. In September, British authorities arranged a series of swap credits—sometimes referred to as

Basle credits, since they were worked out among central banks whose officials met regularly at the Bank of International Settlements in Basle—with several European central banks and the Bank of Canada. These came to $500 million, an amount equal to the outstanding swap with the Federal Reserve. By the end of September, the Bank of England had drawn $200 million of the $1 billion of swap credits available.[3]

An election was due in Britain in 1964, and this inhibited the incumbent Conservative government from acting to stem the deteriorating balance-of-payments position. Apart from an increase from 4 to 5 percent in the bank rate of the Bank of England in February and a 10 percent increase in taxes on tobacco and alcohol in the April budget, government policy was immobilized until after the election of October 15—which brought the Labour government to power.

While Britain's political constraints were recognized, European and American officials privately expressed their concern to their British counterparts throughout 1964. Robert Roosa visited London in early May to confer with then Chancellor of the Exchequer Reginald Maudling. During this visit, Maudling arranged for Roosa to lunch with the "shadow" Chancellor, James Callaghan, who assured Roosa that a Labour government would not devalue sterling.[4] Working Party 3 was also preoccupied with the British problem in the spring and summer, and the British representatives manfully explained the situation. Everyone understood that little could be expected in the way of policy actions before the election; thus British officials arranged in August and September for financing the balance of payments.

The Labour Party's Stance

Harold Wilson took office on October 16, with Callaghan as Chancellor of the Exchequer and George Brown as Minister of a new Department of Economic Affairs. They were confronted immediately with staff estimates of a larger balance-of-payments deficit than they had expected—a deficit on current and long-term capital account of $2.25 billion for 1964—and with an exchange market under pressure: the Bank of England had to draw an additional $215 million on swap credits in October.

The fateful decision for the new government was whether or not to devalue sterling. Some of the economists close to Wilson were strongly in favor of devaluation[5] on the ground that this was the only way to improve Britain's competitive position in export markets and at home (where imports were flooding in).[6]

The case against devaluation had both economic and political aspects. On the economic side, it was argued that an economy operating at full capacity was in no position to release resources for an improvement in the trade balance. Anyway, some claimed, Britain's trade problem stemmed not so much from a price disparity as from excess demand and poor salesmanship by exporters. Furthermore, there was a question whether other countries would not follow the pound if it were devalued. On the political side, the Americans were known to be strongly opposed to British devaluation—and Prime Minister Wilson was anxious to strengthen his relationship with the United States. Finally, Wilson did not want his party to be identified as the "devaluation party." On Saturday evening, October 17, the decision was firmly taken to defend the existing sterling parity. From then on the subject became known as "The Unmentionable."[7]

Sterling Crisis of 1964

On October 26, 1964, the government issued a White Paper which revealed the magnitude of the balance-of-payments deficit it had inherited and announced imposition of a 15 percent surcharge on imports of manufactured goods together with a small rebate of taxes on exports. On November 11 an interim budget was presented to Parliament, proposing an immediate rise in gasoline taxes and stating an intention to increase personal and corporate taxes later and to introduce a capital gains tax. What was missing was an immediate and comprehensive fiscal policy program to dampen the boom (and thereby improve the balance of payments).

These announcements produced adverse reactions both among officials abroad and in private markets. While the U.S. Treasury pronounced a favorable verdict on the import surcharge, Europeans complained strongly not only about the substance of the surcharge but about the lack of advance consultation. Financial markets showed their distrust of sterling by selling it short one way or another, which required the Bank of England to sell foreign exchange heavily, drawing on central bank swaps. It was in this period of turbulent speculation that George Brown, picturing an international conspiracy of financiers against the Labour government, coined the expression "the gnomes of Zurich."[8]

When the bank rate was not raised on the traditional Thursday in the week of November 16, sterling came under heavy pressure; on Monday, November 23, after coordination with U.S. monetary authorities, the Bank of England raised the bank rate two points to 7 percent—the first time since 1931 that the rate had been changed on a Monday. Exchange markets were calmed only momentarily; by Monday afternoon the Bank of England was again required to sell dollars to support sterling. By Tuesday, the Bank of England had fully used up its $1 billion in swap credits from other central banks.

With the active participation of Robert Roosa in the U.S. Treasury and the Federal Reserve Bank of New York, and with the approval of an emergency telephone meeting of the Federal Open Market Committee on November 24, an international credit package of $3 billion was announced on November 25. It consisted of $500 million from the United States—a $250 million increase in the Federal Reserve swap line and a standby credit in equal amount from the Export-Import Bank—and $2.5 billion from ten central banks in Europe, Canada, and Japan, plus the BIS. European participation was generally enthusiastic, except in the case of France, which agreed reluctantly and, President de Gaulle said, for the last time.[9] This credit package was in addition to the $1 billion drawing from the IMF announced on November 20, which involved the first use of GAB. (This Fund drawing was used by Britain to repay the earlier central bank credits that had been utilized before November 26.)

The $3 billion credit package did the trick in persuading foreign exchange markets that the sterling exchange rate would be held. Sterling recovered sharply, despite occasional setbacks, in late 1964 and early 1965.

Sterling Crisis of 1965

But the respite was short-lived. Although the balance of payments improved in 1965 as the surcharge discouraged imports, the economy continued to experience excess demand and wages rose rapidly despite the inauguration of a voluntary wage-price policy in February 1965. Sterling weakened in March, partly as a reflection of the restrictive balance-of-payments measures adopted by the United States in February, and the Bank of England once again had to draw on its swap credits with the Federal Reserve and other central banks. A somewhat restrictive budget was announced in early April and later that month the Bank of England tightened monetary policy and introduced a ceiling on expansion of credit by banks and other financial institutions. This took the pressure off sterling temporarily. In May, the United Kingdom drew $1.4 billion—the remainder of its quota—from the IMF, which again invoked the GAB. The proceeds were used once again to repay debts under swap arrangements with central banks. In June 1965, the bank rate was reduced from the crisis level of 7 percent to 6 percent, presumably as a sign of confidence on the part of the authorities. It apparently had little effect.

As the summer approached and somewhat unfavorable trade figures were announced, a crisis atmosphere began to develop again in the foreign exchange markets for sterling. In the circumstances, the Federal Open Market Committee in June authorized its Special Manager, Charles Coombs, to undertake quiet and informal consultations with other central banks regarding assistance to the United Kingdom if the need should arise.[10]

After heavy reserve losses resulting from speculative activity against sterling, the British Government in late July 1965 announced additional measures to restrain demand: a tightening of consumer credit controls, restrictions on some forms of private construction, and some slowdown in government outlays. Again the favorable reaction in exchange markets was short-lived. By early August, sterling was hit hard: in the first week of that month the Bank of England had to use $225 million to support the exchange rate.[11]

Meanwhile, behind the scenes, an active discussion was taking place within the British Government and between British and American officials on the need for a more stringent incomes or wage-price policy. Wage rates in manufacturing industries had risen 7 percent from the summer of 1964 to the summer of 1965.[12] The Chancellor of the Exchequer had visited Washington in late June, and throughout July and August there was considerable communication between London and Washington at various levels, including intensive talks between the heads of the two central banks, Lord Cromer and William McChesney Martin, on the possibilities of a stringent incomes policy.[13]

Gradually a program was formulated involving an incomes policy with "teeth" on the British side and, on the American, leadership in assembling an additional rescue package for sterling by the United States and other countries.

George Brown took on the task of selling the new wage-price policy to labor and industry, using as leverage the necessity to assure Washington that both sides would support a stronger incomes policy.[14] Finally, on September 2, a new statutory policy was proposed that involved pre-notification of increases in prices and wages (or other terms of labor contracts) and governmental power to defer such increases.

On September 10, 1965, the Federal Reserve, a number of European central banks, and the Bank of Japan—but not the Bank of France—began to purchase sterling in the market, on the basis of agreements with the Bank of England regarding guarantees of the sterling they acquired. No specific limits were announced for such purchases, though the agreement involved about $1 billion.[15] This "squeeze on the bears"—a rise in the price of sterling at a time when many market participants had sold sterling in the expectation of a fall in its price—worked like magic; the central banks had to purchase only minimal amounts of sterling.[16] The market reacted favorably to the combination of the new incomes policy and the concerted central bank action. "A sigh of relief went up in London and Washington: the fears of devaluation had finally been blown away."[17]

By February 1966, the reversal of speculative capital flows, plus an improved balance of payments, enabled the Bank of England to repay much of the debt it had incurred in 1965, including the full $750 million of its swap drawings on the Federal Reserve.[18]

Although some influential officials in Britain remained opposed to these spectacular moves in defense of the sterling parity (they would have preferred to let the currency float) senior officials in Washington and New York were still virtually unanimous in supporting the policy. The foundation for this view was the fear that if sterling were devalued or floated down, probably followed by other currencies, enormous pressures would fall on the dollar as market participants came to expect a devaluation of the dollar or a suspension of its convertibility into gold. The ultimate consequences were highly unpredictable, but among the concerns of American officials was the possibility that a breakdown of the monetary system, based as it was on the dollar as the major reserve currency, would lead to a reversion to restrictions on trade and payments as countries tried to protect themselves against a series of currency devaluations. As we shall see in later chapters, this fear of the unknown was to have its effect on American policy until August 1971.

As might be expected, some who favored a complete revamping of the system were opposed to the sterling rescue operation. It is reported that Jacques Rueff urged this view on President de Gaulle,[19] which may explain the absence of the Bank of France from the consortium of central banks that came to the rescue of sterling in September 1965.

Crisis Again in 1966–1967

The United Kingdom did not fail to come up with a sterling crisis, once again, in 1966. Although there was less scope for economic expansion in Britain in 1965–66 than in other countries, the unemployment rate declined to a relatively low level and wage rates rose rapidly despite the wage-price policy that had so laboriously been put together in the autumn of 1965. Moreover, high interest rates in the United States and Germany in 1966 tended to attract funds out of sterling. Despite the introduction of a restrictive budget in May, sterling came under pressure in the exchange markets. A seamen's strike added to the uncertainty by disrupting trade, and the situation reached crisis proportions in July, when the British authorities had to draw heavily on the Federal Reserve swap line as well as on credit lines with other central banks.

This time sentiment in the British Government was more widespread for letting the pound float or for devaluation. Not only professors working temporarily in Whitehall but a number of ministers, including George Brown, now held this view. Floating was not, however, regarded as an alternative to restrictive domestic policies; it was recognized that these were needed in any event. As Crossman put it, "it had become clearer and clearer that the scale of the package [of expenditure cuts] required to float the pound was not very different from that required to save it."[20] That is, domestic resources had to be released to provide for an increase in exports relative to imports.

As it turned out, Wilson and Callaghan prevailed once again and the decision was made to hold the exchange rate.

On July 20, 1966, the Wilson government, reelected in March, introduced a severe program of restraint aimed at putting sterling back on its feet once and for all. It involved restrictions on consumer credit, an increase in sales and income taxes, limitations on new building activity, reduced government expenditures both at home and abroad, and a limit on tourist allowances. Described as "perhaps the most drastic stabilization program ever to be put forward by a democratic government in peace time,"[21] the new measures were designed to reduce total demands on domestic resources by £500 million ($1.2 billion or about 1.5 percent of GNP) in 1967. In addition, there was to be a six-month standstill on all prices and incomes, to be followed by a further six-month program of severe restraint on prices and wages.

Although the new measures had no immediate impact on sterling in the exchange markets, they did affect the economy and the balance of payments. Industrial production stabilized and the trade deficit fell sharply in the fourth quarter of 1966. Sterling gradually strengthened, helped by reductions in interest rates in the United States and Germany in late 1966 and early 1967. But first it had been necessary, in September, to announce an enlargement of the Federal Reserve reciprocal swap facility with the Bank of England (from $750 to $1350 million) and unspecified increases in credit lines to the Bank of England from other countries. At the same time the Federal Reserve increased its credit facilities with all of its other swap partners except the Bank of France.

By March 1967, the Bank of England had fully repaid its swap drawings and other borrowings from the Federal Reserve and the U.S. Treasury, as well as credits from other central banks. In May it repaid to the IMF $400 million of indebtedness stemming from its borrowings in 1964.

Once again the respite was short-lived. The "six-day" Arab-Israeli war in June created expectations of a switching of Arab funds out of sterling, which other holders of sterling acted to anticipate. The closing of the Suez Canal was seen as a setback for sterling, since it increased shipping costs. President de Gaulle's rejection in May of the proposed entry of Britain into the Common Market may also have had an effect on long-term confidence in sterling. Recession and falling imports in the United States and Germany affected world trade in general and British exports in particular. In addition, the import surcharge that the British Government had imposed in 1964 was lifted in November 1966, leading to a surge of buying from abroad in the first part of 1967. In the summer and fall of 1967, American banks began to borrow once again in the Eurodollar market, thereby driving up interest rates in that market and attracting funds out of sterling.[22]

Meanwhile, the British stabilization program of July 1966 led to rising unemployment, which exceeded 2 percent of the labor force in the summer of 1967. While not necessarily excessive from the viewpoint of improving economic efficiency in Britain, this level of unemployment must have been politically onerous to the Wilson government.

All this was reflected in the exchange markets. The Bank of England, while letting the exchange rate creep down, had to use reserves to support it. In the first 19 days of July, the Bank used about $400 million for this purpose.[23] For the three months May–July, the Bank used $800 million, covering $660 million of this amount by drawing on credits from other central banks and publishing a reserve decline of $140 million.[24]

The reserve drain abated in August following the announcement of relatively favorable trade statistics for July. As a result, the 1967 annual meeting of the IMF, at Rio de Janeiro in September, concentrated mainly on an Outline of a Facility Based on Special Drawing Rights in the Fund; "there did not appear to be any fears of an immediate crisis."[25] One straw in the wind might have been an indication the British Chancellor of the Exchequer would carry back to London after a meeting of the Ministers and Governors of the Group of Ten at Rio: The prospects were that interest rates in other major countries were more likely to rise than decline.[26] With unemployment increasing, the British Government faced the unpalatable prospect of either raising interest rates or putting up with an outflow of short-term funds.

A dock strike that began in mid-September added to Britain's woes. The Bank of England had to use $345 million to support sterling in September, most of which was concealed from the public by official borrowing from central banks and by a one-day loan (at the end of the month) from the U.S.

Treasury. Between May and September, the Bank of England had borrowed $1.7 billion in addition to entering into commitments with the foreign exchange market to purchase sterling forward (that is, to pay dollars for sterling at specified prices at specified future dates).[27]

The rate of reserve drain accelerated in October. With reluctance, the bank rate was raised one-half of one percent on October 19 and another one-half of one percent on November 9, but the government was hesitant to apply additional deflationary pressure to the economy. On November 14 it was announced that in October Britain had incurred the largest trade deficit in its history. But by that time, Wilson and Callaghan had apparently decided to devalue.[28] The combination of a stagnant domestic economy and a bleak outlook for the balance of payments explains the decision.

On Saturday, November 11, two senior British officials, Sir Denis Rickett of the Treasury and Jeremy Morse of the Bank of England, were in Washington to communicate to their American counterparts that the alternatives were substantial *long-term* credits or devaluation.[29] Whether the British Government was actually prepared to take on long-term credits at that point is unclear; it is possible that the visit was intended to sound out and prepare the Americans for devaluation under the cover of presenting alternatives. In any event, various credit packages were discussed.

Over the same weekend the Governor of the Bank of England, Sir Leslie O'Brien, attended the usual monthly BIS meeting in Basle, where credits to the United Kingdom were examined, as well as the magnitude of a possible devaluation—between 10 and 15 percent.[30]

In both Washington and Basle (between which the telephone was in active use) there was discussion of an IMF credit of $1.4 billion plus central bank credits of unspecified maturity of another $1 billion. European central bankers were unwilling to agree to the latter and at least one of them suggested a $3 billion credit from the IMF. A credit of this size would have required the IMF to waive its normal rules concerning maximum use of Fund credit in relation to a country's quota, and it was turned down by the Managing Director of the Fund, Pierre-Paul Schweitzer.[31]

Throughout the following week, most senior Treasury and central bank officials of the Group of Ten countries were in Paris for regularly scheduled meetings of OECD's Working Party 3 and Economic Policy Committee and of the Deputies of the Group of Ten. In and around these meetings Fred Deming, U.S. Under Secretary of the Treasury, tried very hard to put together a credit package, using as nucleus an authorization from Washington to participate to the extent of $500 million in a multilateral loan to Britain.

But the die had been cast; a number of British officials had already left London for various capitals to inform other governments of the decision to devalue. If it had not been so, the events of Friday, November 17, would have been decisive. On Thursday afternoon, Callaghan was asked in the House of Commons whether negotiations were proceeding on an international loan. He gave an evasive answer and this was interpreted correctly by market participants. Consequently, Friday saw an avalanche of sterling sales. It is estimated that the Bank of England, on that one day, paid out more than $1 billion of reserves in supporting sterling at a rate that was to be abandoned the next day.[32]

Ironically, while this market turmoil was in process, the deputies of the Finance Ministers and of the central bank governors of the ten richest nations were sitting in the OECD's Château de la Muette in Paris discussing a number of points regarding the SDR—points on which the Fund's Executive Directors were finding it difficult to agree. Large numbers of reporters milled outside, assuming no doubt that we were wrestling with the fate of the pound.

The decision to devalue was, until Callaghan's statement in the House, very well concealed. Though uncertainty prevailed, I am aware of no non-British official who knew before Friday, November 17, that a definitive decision had been made. That day, when the Group of Ten Deputies meeting broke for lunch, I decided on the basis of an inexplicable hunch to try to get the late afternoon plane to New York and then to proceed to Washington. With Fred Deming and Dewey Daane remaining in Paris (Deming decided to go to London later that day), I felt the need to get home just in case something happened, even though Deming seemed supremely confident that nothing would.

I had a pleasant and restful flight across the ocean. When I finally got to National Airport in Washington, at about 9:30 P.M., I was surprised to be met by my colleague Ralph Bryant. He told me that Chairman Martin had been informed early that afternoon that sterling would be devalued the next day, Saturday, by 14.3 percent (from $2.80 to $2.40). I was expected to attend a meeting on Saturday morning in the office of Winthrop Knowlton, Assistant Secretary of the Treasury. I phoned Chairman Martin's house to let him know I was back and was told that he had already gone to sleep. Wise man!

My initial reaction to the news I received at the airport was one of relief. We and our hard-pressed British colleagues had lived for three years with this trauma, and now it was finally over—or so I thought.

Aftermath of Sterling Devaluation

Contingency planning for a possible devaluation of sterling had gone on intermittently in the U.S. Government for two years. Thick black notebooks in the hands of senior officials provided procedural and substantive guidance. The first objective of the United States was to limit the number of currencies that followed sterling and, for those that did, to minimize the magnitude of their devaluations. This purpose was of course shared by the British authorities, and they had already taken some steps to assure it.

We conjectured that the inevitable speculation against the dollar that would follow would probably focus more on gold than on European currencies. The rational speculator would probably reason that, if the dollar were to be devalued against gold, most European currencies would follow, and therefore little was to be gained by moving out of dollars into European currencies other than sterling. But we could not be sure of this; we had to be prepared for the possibility of large accumulations of dollars by European central banks.

We were more certain that there would be heavy movements of private funds into gold. In fact, the gold pool had been under considerable pressure in the months preceding the devaluation of sterling. The immediate concern over the devaluation weekend was to communicate to financial officials around the world the firm intention of the United States to hold to the $35 price of gold.

President Johnson issued a statement on Saturday, November 18, "unequivocally" reaffirming the commitment of the United States to buy and sell gold at the existing price. That afternoon, the Federal Reserve Board met to approve an increase in the discount rate. Meanwhile, the administration was using the crisis, as we shall observe later, as an additional bit of leverage on the Congress to take action on the President's recommended tax increase.[33]

A week after the devaluation, governors of the central banks of countries that were active members of the gold pool—Belgium, Germany, Italy, the Netherlands, Switzerland, the United Kingdom, and the United States (but not France)—met in Frankfurt. Fred Deming was present and pushed for adoption of the gold certificate proposal (described in Chapter VII). The Group issued a statement that, taking note of President Johnson's reaffirmation of the U.S. commitment on the price of gold, announced decisions to coordinate their actions to ensure orderly conditions in exchange markets and to support the existing pattern of exchange rates.[34] They also agreed, apparently with some hesitation, to continue their support of the gold pool.[35] Meanwhile, a "command post" of central bank foreign exchange operators was established at Frankfurt to coordinate official operations in forward exchange markets. Forward sales of their own currencies against dollars were one way in which European central banks could demonstrate to the market their intention to hold their existing exchange rates. In addition, such offerings of foreign currencies against dollars would tend to mitigate upward pressure on interest rates in the Eurodollar market, thereby easing the strain on the reserves of some countries that might have been tempted to devalue in the wake of the British devaluation.[36]

To cope with potential pressures against the dollar, the central banks agreed to substantial increases in their reciprocal swap credits with the Federal Reserve, to the extent of $1.75 billion. In the case of some countries, notably Japan and Sweden, the increase was designed to help them maintain their exchange rates against downward market pressures. For others, the purpose was the usual one of providing an exchange value guaranty for acquisitions of dollars. The swap line of the Bank of France remained unchanged at $100 million.

In the week following the devaluation, a return flow of funds into sterling enabled the Bank of England to acquire about $750 million, but this was only three-fourths of what had been lost on the Friday before devaluation. Clearly not all those who had reduced their sterling holdings (or sold short) in the months before the devaluation were rushing to cover their positions. Even though the British authorities had accompanied the devaluation with a package of restrictive domestic measures—tighter credit and an increase in the bank rate from 6.5 to 8 percent, continuation of the price-wage policy, more stringent terms on consumer instalment purchases, and a projected tax increase and curtailment of government expenditures in the spring budget—no one in the market seemed to expect that sterling would rise above its new maximum level of $2.42. With the market rate at the ceiling immediately after the devaluation, there was no incentive to rush back into sterling. By December, the Bank of England was selling dollars to keep the rate from falling too rapidly away from the ceiling of $2.42. British reserve availability had been supplemented by a new standby credit from the IMF in the amount of $1.4 billion—the remaining amount of its IMF quota—plus substantial central bank credits, for a total of about $3 billion.

Chancellor Callaghan, conforming to tradition, resigned shortly after the devaluation.

In January 1968 a reduction in government spending was announced that included an ultimate phaseout of military installations east of Suez and a

cutback in welfare outlays. In March the budget of the new Chancellor, Roy
Jenkins, included increases in indirect taxes designed to reduce the growth of
consumer spending—a tax increase amounting to more than £900 million on
a full-year basis. A ceiling on increases in wages and other forms of income
was also announced. Harold Wilson has called this "the most punishing Budget in Britain's peacetime history."[37]

Despite the devaluation and the stringent monetary and fiscal measures
designed to shift resources to improve the balance of payments, sterling remained weak in exchange markets during much of 1968 and again the Bank
of England had to draw heavily on credit facilities. The weakness of sterling
was a reflection not only of the usual initial perverse effects of devaluation on
trade, but also of the turmoil in the gold market in the early part of 1968, of
losses by the Bank of England in paying off on forward contracts it had entered
into before November 18, 1967, and of a running down of sterling balances by
members of the sterling area. This latter problem was dealt with by a guaranty
arrangement, backed by the central banks of European countries, Japan, Canada, and the United States, that was negotiated in mid-1968 and announced
in September; essentially, the arrangement committed the United Kingdom to
maintain the dollar value of the sterling held in official reserves at the time of
the negotiations.[38]

In this atmosphere, particularly in the first half of 1968, doubts arose about
the viability of Britain's new exchange rate. The Federal Reserve's chief foreign exchange operator, Charles Coombs, after battling for three years to "save
the pound,"[39] had in the spring of 1968 "increasingly come to share the view
of the market" that the new parity of $2.40 was untenable and that the British
Government was "in a hopelessly bankrupt position." He recommended to the
Federal Open Market Committee that it limit further credits to the Bank of
England and urge Britain to draw on the Fund so as to pay off its debts to the
Federal Reserve. Coombs was afraid that the Federal Reserve would be stuck
with a frozen asset.

On the basis of staff analyses done at the Board, I presented a different view
to the Open Market Committee. The Board's staff believed that the combination of the devaluation and the domestic measures adopted by the British
Government established the preconditions for a sizable improvement in Britain's trade position. I stated this to the Committee as strongly as I could and
urged it to continue to support the United Kingdom. The Open Market
Committee accepted this analysis and directed Coombs to keep the Bank of
England's credit line open.[40]

As it turned out, the Board's staff analysis was correct. By early 1969,

Britain moved out of deficit and into growing surplus. The current surplus exceeded $1 billion in 1969. The Bank of England was soon in a position to begin to pay off the heavy debts that had been incurred in 1967–68. From a peak of $8 billion at the end of 1968, Britain's official indebtedness was reduced to $1.6 billion over the next 27 months.[41] But throughout 1969, sterling remained vulnerable to speculative pressures associated with market expectations concerning the German mark and the French franc and with high interest rates in the Eurodollar market. Further measures of fiscal and monetary restriction were required.

Nevertheless the British devaluation demonstrated, if such demonstration were needed, that exchange rate adjustment combined with domestic measures to facilitate a shift of resources could indeed be effective in altering a country's balance-of-payments position.[42]

But the travail of sterling also illustrated and embodied in a number of ways the deficiencies of the existing international monetary system: It exhibited the potential for, and the impact of, speculative capital flows in the accounts of a major trading country. It showed the vulnerability of a reserve currency country; Britain's economic position had weakened dramatically but it retained enough of the vestiges of a reserve center to be subject not only to normal capital flows but to movements out of its currency by monetary authorities. It pointed up the weaknesses of an exchange rate system in which a change of parity of a major currency became a policy issue of the highest order that engaged heads of state; in such a system a change in the exchange rate could be excessively delayed, permitting the build-up of a large imbalance which, when action was finally taken to correct it, required massive shifts of resources. In Britain in 1966–67, the magnitude of the imbalance was masked by the sluggish state of the domestic economy.

We conclude our review of the sterling devaluation by noting two favorable features of the experience: international monetary cooperation was shown to be operative and effective in the various crises that arose and—a related point —the devaluation of sterling was followed by only fourteen other countries, most of them having close economic and financial ties with Britain. No major country followed sterling down, whereas in 1949 the 30 percent sterling devaluation was considerably diluted when most European countries followed in whole or in part.

A further consequence of the sterling devaluation of 1967 was that the complacent view that the exchange rates of the larger countries could be regarded as fixed—a view that prevailed in official circles in the early 1960's —was undermined. It would be completely shattered in the next two years.

VI

The Build-up of Monetary Crisis:
The United States, Germany, and Japan

The period 1965–1971 was one of turmoil which revealed the need for, and to a degree hastened the process of, international monetary reform. In this chapter, moving back and forth in time, we will trace the course of the American, German, and Japanese economies and the accompanying balance-of-payments developments, taking note in passing of such major events as the devaluation of sterling and the gold crisis of late 1967 and early 1968. In subsequent chapters we will examine further important developments of the period, including the ongoing SDR and other reform negotiations.

The Economic Impact of Vietnam

The U.S. economy was expanding very rapidly at the end of 1965, under the impact of the 1964 tax reduction and the rapid build-up of military outlays related to Vietnam. In early 1966 the unemployment rate fell below 4 percent and the rate of capacity utilization in manufacturing reached 91 percent, higher than at any time since 1955. Wholesale prices of industrial products rose at an annual rate of 1.4 percent in the second half of 1965 and 3.4 percent in the first half of 1966. Food prices were also advancing.

Although the sudden acceleration of the economy in the second half of 1965 took economic analysts by surprise, in August William McChesney Martin, Chairman of the Federal Reserve Board, had a premonition. In his judgment, "it was necessary for the [Federal Open Market] Committee to bear in mind that, while there had been no declaration of war, a war-time psychology might be developing more rapidly than was generally realized."[1] Interest rates began to rise in the late summer without any overt tightening of Federal Reserve policy. By early October, Chairman Martin was conferring with the President, Treasury officials, and Gardner Ackley, Chairman of the Council of Economic Advisers (CEA), about an increase in the discount rate and in "Regulation Q" ceilings on interest rates payable by banks on time deposits. All expressed opposition to a change in monetary policy at that time.[2] But Martin's hunch was right: "How much stimulus Vietnam would give the economy was still conjectural, but he was inclined to think it was likely to be larger, rather than smaller, than the current guesses."[3]

By late November, Chairman Martin believed that "the time for decision had arrived." He told the Federal Open Market Committee on November 23 that he, as one member of the Board of Governors, was prepared to approve an increase in the discount rate if such a proposal were made by any of the Federal Reserve Banks.[4] On December 6, Federal Reserve discount rates were increased from 4 to 4.5 percent and Regulation Q ceilings were raised.

President Johnson expressed his indignation publicly, Martin flew to Texas to confer at the LBJ ranch, and an amicable press conference was held at which all was sweetness and light: The Federal Reserve's action prevailed and in February there was a series of further moves toward a tighter monetary policy.

Arthur Okun observed in 1969 that "Economists cannot feel proud of their diagnostic or predictive performance during the second half of 1965." On the timing of the Federal Reserve's discount rate action, the President had said that his view (and that of the Secretary of the Treasury and the Chairman of the CEA) was that the decision on interest rates should be a coordinated one in January, when the nature and impact of the administration's budgetary and Vietnam decisions would be known. Although the Federal Reserve's verdict that the time to apply restraint had come was regarded by administration economists as debatable at the time the Fed was deciding, "once the plant and equipment survey was in front of them" (in early December)—showing a surge of planned investment outlays—"they recognized that the Fed was right on that score."[5]

The President was told by his economic advisers at the end of 1965 that a general increase in income taxes was desirable to avoid excess demand, even on the basis of the estimates of defense spending available to them, which "underestimated the magnitude of the escalation by a wide margin."[6] President Johnson, in 1968, said he could not have persuaded Congress to enact a tax increase in early 1966. Others claimed that the President was reluctant to have his Vietnam policy brought under Congressional scrutiny, which probably would have happened in the course of a debate on a tax increase. He may also have been concerned that, as a partial substitute for a tax increase, Congress might cut back his "Great Society" programs.

"The economists in the administration watched with pain and frustration as fiscal policy veered off course. . . . The January 1966 budget marked the first defeat of the new economics by the old politics since Kennedy's decision in August 1962 to delay a tax cut recommendation."[7] The late Kermit Gordon, in a speech in 1974, called the failure to enact a tax increase in early 1966 the worst blunder in U.S. economic stabilization policy since World War II.[8] It set the stage for the economic disorder of the next few years, with concomitant effects on the external position of the United States.

But the immediate impact on the balance of payments was superficially favorable. Although the surplus on current transactions fell from $6.1 billion in 1965 to $3.9 billion in 1966 as imports accelerated with the rapid growth of domestic demand, high interest rates and the pressure on banks to meet the loan requirements of their customers led to heavy inflows of funds from abroad. In particular, American banks adopted the new practice of borrowing heavily from the Eurodollar market through their overseas branches. Such borrowings rose from about $1.5 billion at the beginning of 1966 to about $4 billion at the end of the year.[9] The result was an intensified demand for funds and a rise in interest rates in the Eurodollar market, which in turn attracted funds from European and other countries. Consequently the United States in 1966 had its first overall balance-of-payments surplus since 1957. Despite this surplus, the United States sold about $600 million of gold in 1966—almost entirely accounted for by sales to France—but this amount was more than matched by a fall in U.S. liabilities to foreign monetary authorities, including the repayment by the Treasury of a substantial volume of Roosa bonds and repayment by the Federal Reserve of swap debts to other central banks.[10]

With excess demand clearly evident and actions in the fiscal policy area weak, the Federal Reserve progressively tightened monetary policy during the first nine months of 1966. Interest rates, both short- and long-term, rose to the highest levels since the 1920's. The major impact was on housing construction as thrift institutions—savings and loan associations, mutual savings banks, and life insurance companies—experienced a diversion of funds to securities markets. New housing starts fell from a seasonally adjusted annual rate of 1.6 million in the fourth quarter of 1965 to less than 1 million a year later. By the fourth quarter of 1966, industrial production levelled off and then declined as businesses sharply reduced the rate at which they were accumulating inventories.

The inventory adjustment temporarily reduced demand in the economy in the first half of 1967. But defense expenditures, after increasing by $13 billion, or 25 percent, in the course of 1966, rose by a further $9 billion over the next year to the fourth quarter of 1967. After monetary policy eased in the latter part of 1966, homebuilding recovered somewhat. By the autumn of 1967 industrial output began to rise again. Unemployment remained below 4 percent for most of 1967 and declined further in 1968, reaching a low point of 3.3 percent in late 1968 and early 1969. The demand for labor was thus intense. In the circumstances, wage rates accelerated. Average hourly earnings, which rose about 4 percent from 1965 to 1966, increased by more than 6 percent in 1968 and again in 1969. The index of wholesale prices of industrial products, which had been stable from 1959 to 1964, rose almost 11.5 percent over the next five years, more than in most European countries and Japan. Consumer prices rose 18 percent over the same period, 1964–1969, as increases in the prices of foods and services outpaced those of industrial goods.[11]

The President's budget presented in January 1967 finally called for a surcharge of 6 percent on individual and corporate income taxes, to take effect later in the year. In part the purpose of the proposal was to shift the mix of fiscal and monetary policies so as to relieve some of the pressure on housing. In August 1967, with the economy rebounding and defense expenditure estimates rising, the President asked that the Congress enact a 10 percent surcharge. According to Okun, "At this point, the nation had an excellent second chance to get on the path of non-inflationary prosperity. That chance depended upon prompt congressional enactment of the tax increase, and the entire strategy failed when legislative action did not take place."[12]

The proposed tax increase did not become law until June 1968, with the 10 percent surcharge retroactive to April 1 for individuals and to January 1 for corporations. It was combined with a ceiling on Federal expenditures, for the first time in U.S. history. "The threat of international financial crisis may well have been the single most decisive factor in getting Congress to move on fiscal restraint."[13] Sterling had been devalued and the dollar was under strong pressure in the early months of 1968.

Monetary policy had continued to ease in the first half of 1967 and interest rates had declined from the peak levels reached in the autumn of 1966. Consequently, the exceptionally small net capital outflows of 1966 gave way to larger outflows in 1967, and the net borrowings from abroad by American banks declined. The surplus on current transactions, though it improved slightly in the first half of 1967 as inventory accumulation fell off sharply, decreased further for the year as a whole. Military expenditures abroad, insofar as they had a direct balance-of-payments effect, increased $800 million in 1966 and an additional $600 million in 1967, accounting for half of the reduction in the surplus on goods, services, and private transfers between 1965 and 1967. The result was that the United States had an overall deficit of $3.4 billion in 1967, after a surplus of $200 million in 1966. The 1967 deficit was swelled, to the extent of $500 million, by the sale of U.S. private securities held by the British Treasury.

U.S. gold sales in 1967 took place mainly to support gold pool operations designed to hold down the market price of gold before and especially after the devaluation of sterling in November 1967. Meanwhile the Treasury adopted the questionable policy of persuading some foreign monetary authorities to place a portion of their dollar holdings in U.S. assets with a maturity of more than twelve months. Such assets were not recorded as "liquid," and the policy served to reduce the so-called liquidity deficit of the United States. In less polite terms, the policy could be described as "window dressing" the balance-of-payments statistics. For the two years 1967–68, foreign monetary authorities increased their "non liquid" dollar holdings by about $2.25 billion. The balance on the official settlements basis was not affected by this practice.

The U.S. Economy and the Balance of Payments, 1967–1971

The economy rebounded after mid-1967. Real GNP increased more than 5 percent from the second quarter of 1967 to the second quarter of 1968, and prices, as measured by the GNP deflator, rose more than 4 percent. Imports, surging ahead at the most rapid rate since the Korean War, increased 23 percent from 1967 to 1968. In 1968 imports of finished manufactures—including automobiles, other consumer goods, and capital equipment—moved up to constitute more than half of total imports.

In spite of a sizable increase in exports to expanding markets abroad, the surplus on current transactions dropped sharply to only $750 million in 1968, less than one-fourth of what it had been in 1967 and only one-tenth of its total in 1964—a deterioration that was mainly a reflection of the surge of imports.

The sharp fall-off in the U.S. trade surplus in 1968 was masked by an enormous improvement in the capital accounts which threw the overall balance of payments into a surplus of $1.6 billion. Several influences were at work on capital flows. As a result of the pressure on the dollar and heavy gold sales in late 1967 following the devaluation of sterling, President Johnson on January 1, 1968, announced a stringent set of controls on outflows of capital by American businesses, banks, and other financial institutions.[14] The announced aim was to reduce the balance-of-payments deficit by $3 billion in 1968. The most spectacular feature of the program was a mandatory requirement that there be no outflow of dollars from the United States to finance corporate direct investment in continental Western Europe and other developed nations. The result was that the financing of corporate direct investment abroad involved an outflow of funds from the United States of about $2.5 billion less in 1968 than in 1967.

This program, together with the predicted effects of the sterling devaluation on Britain's balance of payments, was expected to strengthen the payments balance of the two countries combined by as much as $4 billion. This would mean a movement in the opposite direction, by $4 billion, in the balance of payments of the rest of the world. It was inevitable that the primary impact would be on continental Western Europe.

As I reported to the Federal Open Market Committee on February 6, 1968, the reaction of European officials to the program was constructive and heartening. They accepted the discriminatory capital controls in good grace and recognized that their own policies would have to be adjusted to accommodate both the income effects of the U.S.-British actions and the heavier borrowing by American firms together with the reduction in U.S. bank credits to Europe. If these adjustments also led to a loss of foreign exchange reserves, the Europeans seemed prepared to accept this result too.[15] The lesson that surplus as well as deficit countries needed to act if an imbalance in external payments was to be corrected—"it takes two to tango"—seemed to have been learned. This was a considerable change in attitude from that of the early 1960's, for which the Working Party 3 study should be given some of the credit.

A second major influence on capital flows in 1968 was a substantial increase, already emerging in 1967, of foreign purchases of U.S. stocks. Among the reasons adduced for the greater attractiveness of Wall Street to foreign investors in 1968 were the political unrest in France and the movement of Soviet troops into Czechoslovakia. Foreign investors increased their net purchases of American stocks from $800 million in 1967 to $2 billion in 1968.[16]

Finally, capital flows reacted to U.S. monetary policy, which was tight during most of 1968 except for a short period in the summer after the tax increase became effective. American banks stepped up their borrowings from abroad, notably from their own branches in the Eurodollar market in London. This accounted for an inflow of almost $2 billion in 1968.

These tendencies persisted in 1969 and produced another overall payments surplus, to the extent of $2.7 billion, despite a further reduction in the trade balance. In the two years 1968–1969, U.S. liabilities to foreign monetary authorities fell by $2.3 billion and U.S. gold holdings were reduced by only

$200 million, as U.S. gold sales in 1967 and early 1968 were offset later in 1968 and in 1969 by purchases of gold from Germany and France. Meanwhile, the U.S. reserve position in the IMF improved by $1.9 billion.

At the end of 1969, dollar holdings of foreign monetary authorities were less than $300 million higher than they had been five years earlier. Despite domestic inflation and the erosion of its trade surplus, *the United States had stopped adding to world reserves through its balance of payments.*

As funds were attracted to the United States, a number of European countries experienced contractions in their reserves in 1969, and several European central banks drew a total of $2.4 billion on their swap lines with the Federal Reserve.[17]

American officials found themselves in the unaccustomed position of listening to complaints from some European officials about the impact of tight U.S. monetary policy on their economies and about the losses of reserves they were experiencing. Thus the rhetoric that welcomed the U.S. balance-of-payments program in 1968 was not fully matched, in 1969, by European reactions to a U.S. payments surplus.

In the United States the inflow of funds through U.S. bank borrowing abroad did not significantly blunt the restrictive effects of stringent Federal Reserve policies. This was a difficult point to get across, since inflows of this type in other countries would have the effect of undermining monetary policy. But the fact that the dollar was the main reserve currency meant that, as U.S. banks borrowed from abroad, the reserves of foreign central banks were reduced. This in turn involved the sale in the United States of U.S. Treasury bills and other assets in which foreign central banks held their reserves. These sales tended to offset and mop up the greater availability of funds that the U.S. banks came into possession of as a result of their borrowings abroad.

The Federal Reserve authorities were concerned about the heavy Eurodollar borrowings by U.S. banks. They were sensitive to complaints from abroad. They realized that larger U.S. banks might be benefitting at the expense of smaller banks. And they feared what might happen to the balance of payments when monetary policy was later relaxed and the borrowed dollars flowed back to Europe.

Therefore, in late June 1969, the Federal Reserve announced its intention to establish a reserve requirement on increases in bank borrowings from foreign branches as well as a reserve requirement on borrowings from foreign banks. The 10 percent marginal reserve requirement, which went into effect in September, served to discourage further inflows. The marginal nature of the requirement, under which banks had a reserve-free base, was designed to discourage too rapid a repayment of such borrowings in the future.

The economy continued to expand, though at a decelerating pace, until the autumn of 1969. For the year as a whole, unemployment averaged 3.5 percent of the labor force. Despite the tax increases signed into law in June 1968, said Arthur Okun, "the boom proved remarkably stubborn, and the experience was a sobering one for many economic diagnosticians, forecasters, and policy planners. If I seem defensive in reviewing the results, it is only because I am."[18]

Ultimately, fiscal and monetary policies began to have a significant effect on aggregate demand. Federal government expenditures virtually stopped rising at the end of 1968 and fell in real terms by 7 percent from the last quarter of 1968 to the last quarter of 1969. This, combined with the increase in tax rates, resulted in a substantial shift in the "high employment budget" from a deficit of $10.5 billion in 1967 to a surplus of $11.7 billion in 1969.[19] Homebuilding declined in 1969 and the advance of consumer spending slowed as individuals felt the effects of the tax increase. Total output in the economy reached a peak in the third quarter of 1969 and then turned down in a mild recession.

Unemployment rose from 3.5 percent at the end of 1969 to 5 percent in the summer of 1970. Throughout 1971, unemployment hovered between 6.3 and 6.6 percent as real output climbed slowly under the policy of "gradualism" pursued by the Nixon Administration. But the upward thrust of prices and wages continued despite the relatively slack economy and the high rate of unemployment. Consumer prices rose about 6 percent in 1970 and more than 4 percent in 1971. Average hourly wages advanced 4.6 percent in 1970 and 7.2 percent in 1971.

It was during this period that Arthur Burns, who had become Chairman of the Federal Reserve Board in January 1970, began to call publicly for a price-wage policy, to the displeasure of officials of the Nixon Administration.* His argument was that high unemployment by itself would not bring down the rate of wage and price advances, and he cited the experience of other countries to bolster his case.

The restrictive fiscal policy that had finally been put in place in 1968 was eased as the 10 percent tax surcharge expired in the first half of 1970. Monetary

---

*Anonymous officials in the White House began to threaten the Federal Reserve's independence and even to spread the false story that Burns had been trying to get his own salary raised. (*Wall Street Journal,* July 29, 1971, p. 26.) Upon investigation, it was learned that the "aide" who had called in a reporter to spread these stories was named Colson. This was the first time I came across this name.

policy began to shift away from restraint in February 1970. Short-term interest rates declined gradually in the first half of 1970 and more rapidly in the second half, when they were joined by long-term rates. Short-term rates changed little in 1971 but, on average for the year, the three-month Treasury bill rate, for example, was about 2.33 percentage points lower in 1971 than in 1969. The pressure on bank reserves eased off markedly, putting banks in a position to repay debt.

At the same time, economic activity was surging ahead in Europe and Japan and interest rates were rising. In Germany particularly, interest rates advanced rapidly in early 1970 and German companies turned to the Euro-currency markets for financing that was either not available or too expensive at home.

In these circumstances, American banks began to repay their borrowings from their foreign branches despite the disincentive that had been built into the marginal reserve requirement. Over the year 1970, U.S. banks repaid more than $5 billion to their branches, and this reflow continued in 1971. The Federal Reserve staff produced various proposals designed to discourage the outflow by, in effect, compensating the banks for holding on to their liabilities to their overseas branches. But such measures smacked of a subsidy and would necessarily have benefitted banks with branches abroad—which tend to be the larger banks. In lieu of action by the Federal Reserve, the Treasury and the Export-Import Bank offered special securities to banks in an effort to soak up some of their Eurodollar funds.

While the surplus on current transactions increased somewhat in 1970 (to $1.4 billion from near zero in 1969) this was a temporary phenomenon associated with the recession. Toward the end of 1970, the current surplus was falling again.

All in all, the balance of payments was in deficit to the extent of $9.8 billion in 1970; the largest element in the reversal from 1969 was the switch from borrowing by U.S. banks to repayment. Thus the veil which had kept attention from the deteriorating export surplus in 1968 and 1969 was lifted to reveal the brutal truth.[21] The year 1971 saw a continuation of these trends. The trade surplus disappeared in the winter of 1970–71 and the surplus on current transactions in the spring. By then strong speculative pressures against the dollar had developed.

As a counterpart to these developments, Germany's reserves increased rapidly in 1970–71 despite various measures, including reductions in the discount rate, to discourage capital inflows. In May 1971 the German authorities decided to abandon the par value and let the mark float. The Netherlands guilder followed. But most other European countries and Japan sat tight, and the outflow of dollars became a hemorrhage.

Finally, on August 13, President Nixon and his chief economic officials assembled at Camp David. On Sunday night, August 15, the President announced the suspension of the convertibility of the dollar into gold for foreign monetary authorities, a temporary 10 percent surcharge on dutiable imports, and a price-wage freeze. (We shall examine later the events that led to these momentous decisions.)

Economic Trends in Europe and Japan, 1965–1971

Developments in the economies and balance-of-payments positions of other industrial countries both reflected and influenced what was happening to the position of the United States. But the evolution in other countries had its own significance for each of them—and was far from uniform.

In late 1965 and early 1966 almost all of the industrialized countries were experiencing vigorous expansion. Where this was leading to pressures on capacity and intensified inflation (in the United States, Canada, Germany, and Britain), restrictive monetary policies were adopted. In general, world interest rates rose to record levels for the postwar period.

Germany

The expansion came to a halt first in Germany, where output fell after March 1966. Over the next twelve months industrial production declined more than 8 percent and unemployment rose to the highest levels since 1959, despite the fact that Germany by 1966 was employing a large number of foreign workers who could be permitted or induced to return to their home countries when employment opportunities worsened in Germany. Thus Germany went into a recession in 1966 that started earlier, lasted longer, and fell deeper than the mild decline in the United States in early 1967. The German recession had both political and balance-of-payments consequences. A controversy over budget policy led to the replacement of a Christian Democratic government by a "grand coalition" of Christian and Social Democrats, in which the Economics Minister (Karl Schiller) was a Social Democrat and the Finance Minister (Franz Joseph Strauss) was a Christian Democrat—a combination that did not generate harmony, poetic, musical, or economic.

The recession led to the reappearance of a large surplus in Germany's trade with the rest of the world. In part this surplus reflected a normal cyclical drop in imports; but the recession brought on a distinct slowdown in wage increases, which in turn permitted prices to stabilize and Germany's competitive position to improve in 1966–67. Exports to the United States, France, Italy, and other countries rose rapidly. The trade surplus, which had declined after the 1961 revaluation, and amounted only to about $400 million in 1965, rose to $4.4 billion in 1967.[22]

German policy changed slowly in reaction to the recession. In 1967, Germany shared with the United States and the United Kingdom the onus of searching examination in Working Party 3. From the time the Working Party was established in 1961, Germany was the only country in surplus to be put on the defensive and subjected to persistent probing by officials of other countries.

It was not until January 1967 that the Bundesbank began to act aggressively to counteract the recession. Thereafter it adopted a series of stimulative measures, including four reductions in the discount rate and several cuts in reserve requirements. Fiscal policy in Germany had been hobbled for years by a combination of factors: Public opinion, still influenced by the disastrous price explosion of the 1920's, associated deficits with inflation. The Federal structure of the government made it difficult to adjust budgets for the purposes of economic stabilization. And to some extent existing law imposed inhibitions on the ability of the central government to budget for a deficit. A new Economic Growth and Stabilization Law, enacted in June 1967, provided more scope for the use of counter-cyclical budget policy.[23] At the same time Economics Minister Schiller, by means of persuasive public statements reminiscent of and perhaps inspired by Walter Heller's performance in the United States in the early 1960's, helped to make German public opinion more receptive to the active use of fiscal policy for economic stabilization purposes.

Two special budgetary actions designed to encourage economic recovery were taken in February and September 1967. These measures, combined with the ease of monetary policy, helped to produce a recovery in output beginning in the autumn of 1967.

While industrial production increased more than 11 percent from 1967 to 1968, the trade surplus did not shrink. The volume of imports increased with the recovery of domestic spending, but exports also rose rapidly as France, Italy, and the United States sharply increased their imports.

Thus in 1968, as in 1961, Germany was confronted with a fundamental dilemma: how to reconcile a buoyant domestic economy with a strong balance of payments. Output was advancing rapidly, unemployment was falling, and foreign workers were returning. Although prices were stable, the possibility of excess demand loomed ahead; any action to brake the boom would enlarge the already enormous surplus on goods and services. And a tightening of monetary policy would slow down or reverse the outflow of capital that was financing the export surplus. In these circumstances, expectations of a revaluation of the mark began to develop in 1968.

It was against this background that, in the course of the periodic negotiations between German and American officials regarding ways to "offset" the balance-of-payments costs to the United States of troops stationed in Germany, the German Government pledged in 1967 not to purchase gold from the U.S. Treasury. A letter to this effect was sent from President Karl Blessing of the Bundesbank to Chairman Martin, backed up by a further letter from the Chancellor of the German Republic to Blessing. This exchange of correspondence took place in March 1967 and was released to the public on May 2 by the U.S. Treasury and the Federal Reserve. The "Blessing letter" was to take on considerable significance in later years when Germany's dollar holdings increased.

The Emergence of Japan's Surplus

The explosive rate of growth of the Japanese economy, which began in the 1950's, continued in the next decade with minor interruptions. (A standard joke defined a Japanese recession as a slowdown in growth to a rate normal for most other countries.)

The factors that accounted for Japan's remarkable economic performance (see Chapter II) continued in the 1960's. But now Japan was not only absorbing advances in technology from abroad; it was beginning to produce "made in Japan" technological and design innovations that were showing up in exports of electronic equipment, cameras, watches, ships, and automobiles. By the end of the 1960's, the name Toyota no longer brought forth the derisive smiles of ten years earlier.

With a rate of economic growth at least twice that of most other industrialized countries, Japan was narrowing the gap between the living standards of its citizens and those of Europe and North America. Japan joined the OECD in 1964. In 1970, it replaced India as one of the five largest members of the IMF (each of which is entitled to appoint an Executive Director to represent it exclusively), along with the United States, the United Kingdom, Germany, and France.

While Japan's growth was phenomenal, it managed to hold down its rate of inflation. Export prices were no higher on balance in 1969 than in 1959, having dipped and risen again during the period. Wholesale prices of manufactured capital goods were similarly stable, while prices of manufactured consumer goods rose at an average annual rate of just over 2 percent. On the other hand, consumer prices of goods and services rose by more than 5 percent per year.[24] (The disparity in the movement of consumer and wholesale prices is explained in large part by the fact that productivity growth was less rapid in the service industries and agriculture than in manufacturing, yet the former industries had to compete for labor whose wage advances were keyed to the productivity growth in manufacturing.)

Japan's relatively favorable price experience, plus the striking advances in quality and design, provided the basis for its now renowned export performance. And this performance was encouraged by government policies and attitudes, including tax incentives and export financing.

In volume, Japan's exports more than quadrupled between 1959 and 1969 and then increased by a further one-third in the next two years. Germany, which was hardly backward in export performance, experienced an increase in export volume of 250 percent from 1959 to 1969, compared with almost 460 percent for Japan.[25]

While Japan's imports increased rapidly, they began to be outpaced by exports in the second half of the 1960's. In 1968 in particular, Japan seems to have benefitted from a marked improvement in its competitive position. Its exports increased by 25 percent whereas the markets to which it exported grew by only 15 percent. Japan's disproportionately large export growth was matched by a loss of market share on the part of the United States, France, and the United Kingdom.[26] Japan's trade surplus, which was quite small until 1964, was $1.9 billion in 1965 (a "recession" year), fell back to $1.2 billion in 1967, then increased to $2.5 billion in 1968, $3.7 billion in 1969, and $4 billion in 1970.

The remarkable export performance led to a doubling of Japan's share in the imports of the rest of the world between 1960 and 1970. By 1970, Japan accounted for 15.5 percent of U.S. imports. Penetration of European markets had increased even more rapidly, though Japan's share of Western European imports was still only 2.6 percent in 1970.[27] A number of factors, including distance, smaller individual markets, and trade restrictions, accounted for the relatively low volume of Europe's imports from Japan. The United States was Japan's "natural market" after Australia and the nearby countries of Asia. By 1970, U.S. trade with Japan, which showed a small surplus in the early 1960's, was in deficit by $1.2 billion. This gave rise to considerable acrimony between the two countries. Japan continued to maintain numerous import restrictions but, on the other hand, had agreed to limit its exports of textiles and steel to the United States.

(While the United States complained about the size of Japan's overall surplus in the late 1960's, and U.S. controls on capital outflows were applicable to Japan as to other developed countries, some elements in the U.S. Government, paradoxically, criticized Japan's restrictions on inward direct investment. The schizophrenic American approach—explained by the desire of American companies to establish themselves in Japan as they had in Europe —may have left Japanese officials a little puzzled.)

By 1968 Japan's situation, with a booming economy and a growing export surplus, was beginning to resemble Germany's. Japan's gold and foreign exchange reserves, which had remained remarkably steady at around $1.6 billion through 1967—Japan had shifted from a net borrower to a net lender of private capital in 1965—more than doubled in the next three years. Although total reserves of $3.7 billion were relatively small for a country of Japan's economic size, the magnitude of its current surplus and the *rate of increase* of its reserves were clearly unsustainable, in the sense that they were incompatible with the balance-of-payments objectives of other countries.

Restrictive domestic policies brought on a distinct slowdown in the expansion of the Japanese economy beginning in late 1970. Imports also slackened and the trade surplus jumped from $4 billion in 1970 to almost $8 billion in 1971. Meanwhile Japan experienced a capital inflow, much of it speculative, given the spreading discussion of the need for a revaluation of the yen. Total reserves rose $3 billion in the first half of 1971. In June 1971, Japan announced an "eight point program" designed to reduce its overall surplus and forestall an upward revaluation of the yen. As I could not resist saying to my colleagues at the time, Japan did not have a yen to revalue. But it was too late; August 1971 was close at hand.

Thus, as the weakness of the underlying U.S. payments position was unmasked in 1970–71, Japan, along with Germany, emerged as a country with an excessively large surplus. The deterioration of the U.S. trade position from the early 1960's to 1971 could be more than accounted for by the increased trade surpluses of Japan and Germany. But it did not follow from this that, to restore the U.S. trade position, all that was necessary was that Germany and Japan take action—presumably exchange rate action—to reduce their trade surpluses. If the effects of German and Japanese revaluations were to be reflected in an improved U.S. position, it was necessary that other countries move their exchange rates up with the yen and the mark; otherwise those countries would be devaluing along with the dollar and much of the reduction in the surpluses of Germany and Japan would accrue to them.

VII

The Great Gold Rush of 1967–1968

The devaluation of sterling in November 1967 had the expected effect on private gold markets. Since the United States had openly supported and, in some views, abetted Britain's efforts to hold the $2.80 parity of sterling, it was only natural that there would be questions about the other reserve currency, the dollar. Those who wished to protect themselves against, or to speculate on, a change in the value of the dollar could easily do so by buying gold in private markets, where the gold pool was keeping the price from rising significantly above the official price of $35 per ounce. (In the United States, such buying of gold was illegal.)

Rationale and Operations of the Gold Pool

Even before the devaluation of sterling in November 1967, the gold pool had had to sell gold intermittently to keep the free market price at or below $35.20. The gold pool (as described earlier) was an arrangement among eight countries, including the United States, to sell or buy gold in the free market in order to keep the price close to the official price of $35 per ounce. In the first ten months of 1967, pool sales, concentrated mainly in October, came to more than $400 million.[1] The participants agreed periodically to additional contributions in amounts of $50 million each. Of the original members, France discontinued active participation in the summer of 1967, but this became public knowledge only after the sterling devaluation. Figures of gold pool losses—erroneous figures—then began to turn up in French newspapers, along with rumors that other European central banks would soon leave the pool.

Then Algeria purchased $150 million of gold from the United States, presumably at French instigation. France itself purchased no gold in 1967 or 1968.

What was the rationale for the U.S. policy, supported with varying and waning enthusiasm by the other members of the gold pool, of selling gold in London to prevent the market price from rising significantly above the official price?

American officials believed that if the free market price were to rise sharply, expectations of an early increase in the official price would be engendered. This would lead central banks holding dollars to come to the U.S. Treasury to ask for conversion into gold. Even if this did not happen in great volume, a central bank that needed to sell gold would sell in the market while those that wished to buy gold would come to the United States. It could even be imagined that some central banks would engage in arbitrage—buying from the United States at $35 and selling in the market at a higher price. Each of these consequences would reduce U.S. gold reserves and would sooner or later lead the United States to suspend the convertibility of the dollar into gold, with unpredictable results. It is hard today to put ourselves in the shoes of officials who feared —deeply feared—that suspension of dollar convertibility would lead to chaos in international financial relations and the danger of spreading restrictions on trade and payments. In 1967 and 1968, maintenance of the status quo regarding gold seemed imperative if an open, secure, and prosperous world economy was to be preserved.

Based on this rationale, American officials developed a number of proposals for coping with the gold rush. One set of proposals involved an attempt to limit—through licensing—access of private purchasers to the London gold market. The main objection to this approach was that the free market would then be likely to migrate to another center where the authorities were unwilling or unable to control access to the market.

Two plans were developed by the Federal Reserve Board's staff. In early 1967 I conceived and circulated a proposal to link continuation of the gold pool with the creation of a new reserve asset (similar to what was to become the SDR). By autumn this approach, identified in Washington as the Solomon Plan* or the "gold certificate plan," was adopted by the U.S. Government as an official proposal. The essential objective of the plan was to convince the gold-buying public that the members of the gold pool were prepared to continue to sell gold in the market and therefore that further speculative buying

---

*Not to be confused with another Solomon Plan for reserve creation in the Fund, to be discussed later. (Neither plan was adopted in the form in which I put it forward.)

was fruitless. To make this credible, the members of the gold pool would create among themselves a new reserve asset, a "gold certificate," to replace the gold they were selling in the market. Thus the extinction of reserves that accompanied gold pool sales would be brought to an end, for the certificates would be usable as reserves in place of gold.

I had discussed the proposal with a number of European central bank colleagues in the autumn of 1967 and found considerable interest. But one of them pointedly told me that "not everyone is as rational as you and I."

After the devaluation of sterling, the plan was forcefully proposed by American officials at the Frankfurt meeting of November 26 and was discussed again at the Basle meeting of central bank governors on December 9–10, where it received mixed reactions. As Alfred Hayes, President of the Federal Reserve Board of New York, reported to the FOMC, "perhaps the most fundamental objection, however, was that while the plan was intended to make participation in the gold pool more palatable by offering central banks something better than dollars for their gold, most of the banks were reluctant to give up gold on any basis."[2] In fact, most of the gold was being given up by the United States.

On the Monday following the BIS meeting, Fred Deming went to Basle to support Dewey Daane's efforts to persuade the European central bankers to accept the gold certificate plan. The intrusion of a Treasury official into what had always been an unadulterated central bankers' forum, plus distorted newspaper stories on the nature of the discussions, resulted in a sharp though brief flurry of speculative buying in the gold market. It also resulted in a determination by some of the central bankers not to allow another such break in the tradition that Basle was where central bankers met on their own.

Meanwhile, both the Board staff and Governor Carli of the Bank of Italy had developed an alternative plan, which we at the Board called "the green stripe plan." The idea was to abandon the gold pool and to segregate monetary gold—that held by central banks and treasuries—from privately held gold. Figuratively, a green stripe would be painted on each bar of monetary gold; monetary authorities would then buy and sell—at the official price of $35 per ounce—only gold with a green stripe on it. Thus they would use the existing stock of monetary gold as a reserve asset but would stay out of the free market as either buyers or sellers. This insulation of official transactions from the free market would, it was hoped, prevent the ill effects of any rise in the free market price. This proposal was adopted as the two-tier system in March 1968. But before that happened, a considerable amount of turmoil was to occur.

Although speculative pressures concentrated on the free gold market after the sterling devaluation, the market calmed following the Frankfurt meeting.

There, in addition to the declaration described earlier, agreement was reached to impose restrictions, notably in Switzerland, on forward buying of gold and on credit-financed buying. Nevertheless, the pool had to sell more than $800 million of gold in November. In order to supply its share on time, the United States found it necessary to use the Air Force to airlift gold to London.[3]

Heavy sales by the gold pool countries fed on themselves as gold buyers began to expect an abandonment of the gold pool arrangements. What had started out as a bet on a devaluation of the dollar had become a bet that the countries participating in the pool were unwilling to go on supplying gold to the market without limit. And it was virtually a one-way bet; speculators had little to lose compared with their potential gains.

These expectations were strengthened by the fact that the United States still had a "gold cover" requirement against Federal Reserve notes. Legislation to eliminate this requirement had been requested, but as long as it was on the books, there was a tendency to look at the amount of "free gold" (in excess of the cover) that the United States had available. This amount was shrinking rapidly. The fact that the Federal Reserve had the legal right to suspend the requirement did little to calm speculation based on the belief that the gold pool would be abandoned.

Gold pool sales subsided temporarily in January 1968 after the announcement of the new U.S. balance-of-payments program. William McChesney Martin made a strong speech in mid-February rejecting an increase in the official price of gold as a solution either to international payments imbalances or to the problem of providing for the growth of world reserves.[4] But South African sales in the market were falling off and some pool members bought gold from the United States to replace what they had supplied to the pool.[5] The feeling was growing that the pool would not continue in operation.

Speculation was abetted by a statement by Senator Jacob Javits, issued on February 28, proposing that the United States suspend convertibility of the dollar into gold and abandon the gold pool.

Whatever the reasons, after gold pool sales of less than $250 million in January and February, speculative purchases picked up in early March and became a torrent. Newspapers were studded with reports, editorials, and columnists' views on the gold problem. Radio news carried reports on the "gold rush." Bankers from Albany to Zurich were quoted. On Friday, March 8, pool sales amounted to $180 million.[6] Chairman Martin had decided in the middle of the week to attend the weekend BIS meeting and to take me with him.

It was a hectic time. I had been up half the night of March 6–7, substituting for Chairman Martin at a meeting at Treasury with high officials from Canada who felt that either their country would have to be exempt from the January 1 balance-of-payments program or the Canadian dollar would have to float. Secretary Fowler finally agreed to the Canadian exemption, with some safeguards to protect the U.S. balance of payments. After a few hours' sleep, I packed a suitcase and went to the office to attend to business before leaving for the airport for the overnight flight to Basle. After a few more hours of fitful sleep in our hotel rooms on Friday, March 8, Martin and I strolled around Basle, discussing the position he would take in the weekend meetings and observing the prosperous Swiss burghers, who showed no outward awareness of the international crisis that had brought us to Basle. But my powers of observation may have been less than acute; I was tired, and I was thankful that I had no obligations until the next morning. After dining with Martin, who managed to consume a banana split while I finished the wine, I wearily fell into bed at 10:00 P.M.

During the weekend, Chairman Martin, by raising the specter of a collapse of the international monetary system, persuaded his fellow central bank governors to continue pool operations; but he was unable to win them over to the gold certificate plan. A "reaffirming" statement was issued to the press. The market quieted down somewhat for one day.* Then pool losses quickly built up again, climaxing at almost $400 million on Thursday, March 14. That did it. After much transatlantic telephoning, the Bank of England decided to close the London gold market on Friday, and Chairman Martin invited the pool members to come to Washington for a meeting on the weekend.

That same Thursday, the FOMC had held a telephone conference to consider a proposal by Charles Coombs to enlarge the Federal Reserve swap lines by $2 billion in order to cover expected speculative capital flows out of dollars and into some European currencies that would result from the decision to close the gold market. The Board staff expressed opposition to this proposal on the ground that, in the prevailing international crisis, all the major central banks should be willing to act cooperatively and hold the dollars they were receiving on an uncovered basis. The United States should not, we argued, go heavily into debt as a result of speculative capital flows related to the gold crisis. To repay those debts might require heavy use of U.S. reserves or a large

---

*Chairman Martin and I, waiting for a plane at the London airport on Monday, were curious about the market reactions to the weekend meeting. I phoned the Bank of England but had to go to considerable lengths to identify myself before I was able to get the desired information for the Chairman of the Federal Reserve Board. Such was the sensitivity of the Bank to market leaks and to the ingenuity of journalists.

U.S. drawing from the IMF. In the back of our minds was the belief that a change in exchange rate relationships might be necessary, and it did not make sense for the United States to provide heavy guarantees in preservation of the existing relationships. The FOMC, with three members dissenting, agreed to the Coombs proposals.[7]

In that same week Congress finally passed the bill eliminating the gold cover requirement on Federal Reserve notes.

From the time sterling was devalued in November 1967 until the gold market was closed on March 15, 1968, the gold pool had sold $3 billion of gold, of which sales the United States' share was $2.2 billion.[8] If we look at gold holdings of the "active" gold pool countries from the end of September 1967 to the end of March 1968, we find a reduction of $3.5 billion, or about one-eighth of their combined gold reserves. U.S. gold holdings fell $2.4 billion and those of the United Kingdom by about $340 million (of which $250 million reflected a sale to the United States in November 1967[9]). Germany's gold reserves went down $312 million and Switzerland's $238 million. For both the United States and Britain, the reduction came to 18 percent of their gold holdings as of September 30, 1967. For Germany the drop was 7 percent and for Italy 1 percent. But, it should be stressed, it was only the United States that experienced a reduction in its *total* reserves as a result of the operations of the gold pool. The other members received dollars in exchange for their contributions to the pool and thus experienced a change in the composition rather than the amount of their reserves. They may not have been happy with this change in composition, but their position was different from that of the United States. Only to the extent that their own residents bought gold were the reserves of other gold pool countries affected, but this would have happened even in the absence of the gold pool.

Establishment of the Two-Tier System

The central bank governors, some of them accompanied by Treasury officials, assembled in the Federal Reserve's Board Room at 10:00 A.M., Saturday, March 16, 1968. Pierre-Paul Schweitzer, Managing Director of the IMF, and Gabriel Ferras, General Manager of the BIS, were also present. While central bankers are almost always described as being "somber,"* "somber and tense" was particularly apt for this occasion. All were aware that a turning point had

---

*Sir Leslie O'Brien once characterized an optimistic central banker as someone who saw the situation deteriorating less rapidly than before.

been reached, that world attention was focused on their deliberations, and that they had to come to agreement over the weekend.

The U.S. position had been hammered out in lengthy, almost continuous meetings involving Secretary Fowler, Chairman Martin, and such senior officials as Treasury Under Secretary Fred Deming, Arthur Okun and James Duesenberry of the CEA, Anthony Solomon of the State Department, Edward Fried of the White House, and Dewey Daane and myself of the Federal Reserve, with Alfred Hayes and Charles Coombs down from New York for some of the meetings.

Before the March 16 meeting President Johnson sent personal messages to the Prime Ministers of the larger countries urging cooperation and asserting that the official price of gold would not be raised.[10]

The U.S. objectives by then were—if the gold pool were to be abandoned, as seemed inevitable—to assure that the Carli or "green stripe" plan contained safeguards that would prevent leakages of monetary gold into private hands or vice versa, to discourage central banks from asking the U.S. Treasury for gold in exchange for existing holdings of dollars, and to give a boost to the SDR (those negotiations were then near their climax) as being fully equivalent to gold. The major trump card the United States had was the possibility of suspending the convertibility of dollars into gold.

The objectives of the Europeans were less clear and more diverse. The British were extremely worried about the position of sterling, which had taken a battering as gold buyers moved out of currencies and into gold; British officials feared that a rise in the free market price of gold would lead to further pressure on the pound. Some of the central bank governors would have been pleased to resolve the problem by raising the official price of gold, but whether their governments agreed with this position was doubtful. All the European governors were concerned that, if the pound or another currency (perhaps the Canadian dollar) were forced to devalue or float, "chaos" would result, since one currency after another would be forced to follow. Thus they were anxious to put an end to the crisis atmosphere in general and to bolster the pound in particular (but without committing large amounts of additional funds to the United Kingdom). They saw the need for restrictive domestic policies in both Britain and the United States. It happened that Roy Jenkins' stringent budget was scheduled for presentation to the House of Commons on Tuesday, and hope for congressional enactment of President Johnson's tax surcharge was increasing.

Chairman Martin opened the meeting by making it clear that the United States was firm on holding the official gold price at $35 per ounce. He then outlined the various problems with which the group had to deal in the next two days. The first speaker was Governor Carli; in his usual manner, combining intensity, brevity, and clarity, he presented the case for a two-price system, and this led to discussion and ultimate agreement on the various features of such a system.

A considerable part of the meeting was devoted to the sterling problem. The other Europeans were calling on the British to limit or even block the use of sterling balances, which they regarded as constituting an almost endless threat to the viability of the pound, as a *quid pro quo* for additional financial support. In the end, the United Kingdom was given additional assistance, including an increase in the Federal Reserve swap line of $500 million, bringing the total of credits available to it to $4 billion. The pressure for a limitation on the use of sterling balances led to the negotiation of the guaranty arrangements described earlier.

The meeting was to last for two days. At the end of the first day, Martin, who chaired the meeting, privately asked Governor Carli and me to draft a communiqué. That night my wife and I were giving a long-planned dinner party; I managed to get home just as the first guests were arriving. After an evening during which the main topic of conversation was not the gold crisis but the war in Vietnam, I sat down and did what I could to put words on paper. When I got together with Carli the next morning, before the scheduled start of the formal meeting, another European central bank governor joined us, without invitation. It was one of the more difficult experiences of my career to try to get into the draft communiqué as much as possible of the U.S. viewpoint while maintaining the usual courtesies and the respect due to a central bank governor.

The meeting concluded on March 17 with agreement on the following communiqué:

> The Governors of the Central Banks of Belgium, Germany, Italy, the Netherlands, Switzerland, the United Kingdom, and the United States met in Washington on March 16 and 17, 1968, to examine operations of the gold pool, to which they are active contributors. The Managing Director of the International Monetary Fund and the General Manager of the Bank for International Settlements also attended the meeting.
>
> The Governors noted that it is the determined policy of the U.S. Government to defend the value of the dollar through appropriate fiscal and monetary measures and that substantial improvement of the U.S. balance of payments is a high-priority objective.
>
> They also noted that legislation approved by Congress makes the whole of

the gold stock of the nation available for defending the value of the dollar.

They noted that the U.S. Government will continue to buy and sell gold at the existing price of $35 an ounce in transactions with monetary authorities. The Governors support this policy and believe it contributes to the maintenance of exchange stability.

The Governors noted the determination of the U.K. authorities to do all that is necessary to eliminate the deficit in the U.K. balance of payments as soon as possible and to move to a position of large and sustained surplus.

Finally, they noted that the Governments of most European countries intend to pursue monetary and fiscal policies that encourage domestic expansion consistent with economic stability, avoid as far as possible increases in interest rates or a tightening of money markets, and thus contribute to conditions that will help all countries move toward payments equilibrium.

The Governors agreed to cooperate fully to maintain the existing parities as well as orderly conditions in their exchange markets in accordance with their obligations under the Articles of Agreement of the IMF. The Governors believe that henceforth officially-held gold should be used only to effect transfers among monetary authorities and, therefore, they decided no longer to supply gold to the London gold market or any other gold market. Moreover, as the existing stock of monetary gold is sufficient in view of the prospective establishment of the facility for Special Drawing Rights, they no longer feel it necessary to buy gold from the market. Finally, they agreed that henceforth they will not sell gold to monetary authorities to replace gold sold in private markets.

The Governors agreed to cooperate even more closely than in the past to minimize flows of funds contributing to instability in the exchange markets, and to offset as necessary any such flows that may arise.

In view of the importance of the pound sterling in the international monetary system, the Governors have agreed to provide further facilities which will bring the total of credits immediately available to the U.K. authorities (including the IMF standby) to $4 billion.

The Governors invite the cooperation of other central banks in the policies set forth above.[11]

The reader will note that the language on the termination of *sales* in the market is somewhat stronger than that on *purchases:* "they no longer feel it necessary to buy gold from the market." The Americans were unable to negotiate a stronger commitment from the European governors to refrain from market purchases. Astute observers must have taken note of the slight equivocation regarding future purchases from the market or, by implication, from gold-producing countries. This asymmetry reflected deep-seated views on gold that were and are held by some Europeans. In fact, within two months some European central bankers were privately expressing a dissatisfaction about the Washington agreement and a wish to buy gold from South Africa.[12]

It was agreed at the Washington meeting that the London gold market would remain closed through the end of March. This would carry beyond another major event, a meeting of the Ministers and Governors of the Group of Ten (scheduled for Stockholm on March 29–30) to settle some major issues in the SDR negotiations. The combination of the two high-level meetings in the second half of March was of historic importance. I put it this way to the FOMC on April 2:

> But the Washington meeting did much more than terminate pool sales. In my view, the most important sentence in the Washington communiqué is the one that says: "Moreover, as the existing stock of monetary gold is sufficient in view of the prospective establishment of the facility for Special Drawing Rights, [the Governors] no longer feel it necessary to buy gold from the market."
>
> That pronouncement, together with the Stockholm agreement on Special Drawing Rights, can be interpreted as constituting a demonetization of gold at the margin. In other words, what is being said is that the monetary authorities of the world—taken as a group—are not dependent on an increasing stock of gold. Their need for growing reserves in the future can be satisfied mainly by Special Drawing Rights.[13]

Immediately after the Washington meeting, the Federal Reserve sent the communiqué to central banks around the world and received, in most cases, responses indicating approval and cooperation. As far as I know, there were very few central bank purchases or sales of gold in the free market. France, which did not participate in the Washington meeting, conformed to its decisions even though, a few days after the Washington meeting, President de Gaulle made another attack on the dollar, calling the existing monetary system "unworkable." Six weeks later France was to be embroiled in troubles of its own that would lead it to borrow from the United States.

Over the years since 1968 a number of observers have mistakenly interpreted the Washington agreement as having put the world on a dollar standard. In fact, the agreement establishing the two-tier system did nothing to alter the U.S. commitment to buy and sell gold in transactions with monetary authorities.

In the days and weeks following the Washington agreement, numerous experts were quoted in the press as saying that the system was a temporary makeshift that was bound to break down. Others, including me, argued that the two-tier system was viable and consistent with the move to greater reliance on SDRs.[14]

When the London market reopened on April 1 the price was $38 per ounce, and it fluctuated within a narrow range until the turbulent events in France in May. Over the following year the price ranged between $38 and $43, but it began to fall in May 1969 and by the end of 1969 the market price was down to $35. The sharp drop in the price after mid-1969 is explained by an increase in supply from South Africa, whose balance of payments was in deficit, and by the liquidation of speculative holdings acquired before March 15, 1968.[15]

As the market price threatened to fall below the official price, some Europeans became concerned and pressed for a revision of the two-tier agreement that would permit official purchases of South African gold and establish a floor under the market price.

South African Gold and the Two-Tier System

Not long after the Washington meeting, European central bankers began to grow restive over their undertaking not to buy gold from South Africa. And the South African authorities were under pressure from their own gold-mining industry to come to an agreement on the marketing of gold. In both cases, the concern was that the market price might fall below the official price of $35 per ounce, though in mid-1968 the market price was around $39 (having dropped from about $42 in March).

In June 1968 South Africa pressed for action by offering to sell about $35 million of gold to the Fund; this led to an involved legal controversy over whether or not the Fund was obligated to accept gold offered to it by a member. The Fund's Article V, Section 6(a), stated: "Any member desiring to obtain, directly or indirectly, the currency of another member for gold shall, provided that it can do so with equal advantage, acquire it by the sale of gold to the Fund." The Fund deferred action on this request.

The issue was discussed actively at the monthly meetings of central bank governors at Basle in the summer of 1968, two of which I attended with Governor J.L. Robertson, Vice Chairman of the Federal Reserve Board. The U.S. position was that South Africa should be encouraged to continue selling gold in the market and to withdraw its application to sell to the Fund. If the market price were to fall *below* $35, South Africa might then offer to sell gold to the Fund.[16] (South Africa had stopped selling gold on the market and borrowed $62 million from the Fund when the IMF postponed a decision on its offer of gold.)

The bases for the U.S. position were these: It was undesirable to assure the market that the price could not fall below $35; this would only strengthen speculation and tend to keep the market price higher than it would otherwise be, thereby destabilizing exchange rates and possibly undermining the two-tier agreement. Second, it was undesirable to give South Africa an unlimited right to sell to the Fund at $35, since this would permit South Africa to apportion its sales between the market and the Fund in such a way as to maximize the market price and its own earnings (that is, in technical economic terms, to act as a discriminating monopolist). Finally, it was undesirable to have central banks buy directly from South Africa, since this would appear to contravene the two-tier agreement.

In the course of the discussions in Basle, it became evident that, despite the Washington agreement, some European central bank governors would have been pleased to acquire gold from South Africa at $35 per ounce. After the July Basle meeting, inaccurate reports from Europe began to appear in the press suggesting that agreement was close on central bank purchases of South African gold if the market price fell to $36 or $37 per ounce.[17]

It was agreed in Basle that Chairman Martin would look for an opportunity to discuss the matter with Governor de Jongh of the South African Reserve Bank. The only new element was that the United States was less insistent that the market price had to be *below* $35 before the Fund purchased from South Africa. But such Fund purchases would be *limited* to South Africa's balance-of-payments needs.[18] Thus there would be no firm floor under the market price.

During the IMF annual meeting in Washington in early October 1968, the Basle governors held a number of informal sessions and met with the South African authorities. Chairman Martin reported to the FOMC that "there appeared to be a greater degree of adherence to the position set forth in the March Washington Communiqué."[19] Perhaps the fact that the market price had stopped falling (it remained around $39) contributed to the improved atmosphere. The central bank governors of the Group of Ten, with France absent, issued a statement on October 4 saying that they had unanimously agreed on a common position, based on the March 17 declaration regarding the disposal of newly mined gold, but that it had not proved possible to reach agreement with South Africa at this meeting.[20] It appeared that the matter would drag on until after the American elections of November 1968, since it was a safe bet, from the South African viewpoint, that the views on gold of a Nixon Administration, if Nixon were to be elected, would not be tougher than those of the outgoing administration.

During 1969 Paul Volcker, Under Secretary of the Treasury for Monetary Affairs in the new administration, held a series of quiet discussions with the

South African authorities, but agreement was slow in coming. One of the obstacles was the fear on the part of the South African authorities that announcement of an agreement would be followed by a *fall* in the market price of gold—while U.S. officials were concerned that such an announcement would lead to an *increase* in the market price. When the market price fell rapidly in the autumn of 1969, to around $35 per ounce in December, this obstacle became less serious. The main substantive sticking-point throughout 1969 was a desire by the South African authorities to be able to sell some gold to monetary authorities (including the Fund) when the market price was above $35. The United States opposed this.

On November 13, 1969, *The Journal of Commerce* ran an editorial that began: "By the beginning of this week one thing was clear: former Treasury Secretary Fowler was right and those—who, like this newspaper, maintained that the two-tier gold price system wouldn't work—were wrong."

In this atmosphere Under Secretary Volcker met with the South African authorities in Rome in mid-December. Federal Reserve Governor Dewey Daane, U.S. Executive Director at the IMF William Dale, and (representing the European view) Jelle Zijlstra, President of the BIS, were present. They hammered out an agreement. The implementation of this agreement was left to the IMF, which, on January 13, 1970, released letters from South Africa and the United States to Pierre-Paul Schweitzer.[21] Essentially the agreement provided that when the market price was at $35 per ounce or below, South Africa could sell gold to the Fund in amounts necessary to meet its current foreign exchange needs. If South Africa had foreign exchange needs beyond what could be met by sales of newly mined gold, it might sell to the Fund additional amounts of gold out of its reserves regardless of the market price. In addition, South Africa had the right to sell gold to the Fund out of its reserves up to an amount of $35 million per quarter. In general, South Africa intended to sell its output of newly mined gold on the market in an orderly manner. A letter from Paul Volcker to Schweitzer accepted these arrangements, "assuming there is an understanding among Fund members generally that they do not intend to initiate gold purchases directly from South Africa."

The immediate significance of the agreement between the Fund and South Africa was that it strengthened the two-tier system and with it the expectation that the official price of gold would remain fixed at $35 per ounce. But the numerous discussions among central bank governors also revealed a lingering nostalgia for gold which we shall encounter again in later chapters.

In early 1970, the market price of gold remained around $35, occasionally dipping below. While some European central bank governors found this disquieting and would have preferred to see some central bank purchases in the market, the two-tier agreement held until November 1973, when it was terminated by agreement of the countries that had established it. At that time, the market price of gold was close to $100 per ounce and the official price was $42.22. Insofar as countries were prepared to abide by the IMF Articles, termination of the two-tier system in November 1973 opened the way for official sales, but not official purchases, in the market.

VIII

Gestation and Birth of the SDR, 1965–1969

While the international monetary system lurched from one crisis to another in the second half of the 1960's, the process of negotiation over a new reserve asset continued. The Deputies of the Group of Ten had been requested by their Ministers in September 1965 to intensify their studies and to determine what basis of agreement could be reached for improvements in the international monetary system, including the future creation of reserve assets. Under the chairmanship of Otmar Emminger of the German Bundesbank, the deputies were embarked on what was more a negotiation than the "study" of the Ossola group. Furthermore, their mandate went beyond the creation of a new reserve asset; they were asked to consider "improvements" in general, and this opened up the potential agenda.

After two exploratory meetings, in November and December 1965, the deputies got down to examining specific proposals in January.

The U.S. Approach

Within the U.S. government, which was being advised by the Dillon Committee (see page 82), a "dual approach" to reserve creation was developed in the months prior to the January 1966 meeting. In July 1965 I had circulated a proposal for a drawing rights scheme that was an elaboration of a plan we had presented to the Ossola group. Each member of the Fund would receive an extension of its existing automatic drawing rights—say by 5 percent—and its right to draw on its credit tranches in the Fund would be increased by an equal amount. The new reserve asset, in the form of increased automatic drawing rights comparable to the gold tranche, would be "wedged" into a country's Fund quota between its existing gold tranche and its credit tranches. Each Fund member would also extend to the IMF a line of credit at least as large as the increase in its reserve assets. This would provide the means for transferring the new asset. A country that had already used its Fund quota beyond the gold tranche would receive only potential reserve assets; this feature, as noted earlier, was a "self qualifying principle." An advantage of the scheme was that it could be established without amending the Fund's Articles of Agreement.

This proposal (another Solomon plan) was adopted as one prong of the U.S. dual approach. The other prong would involve the creation of a new "unit" by a limited group of countries, but a share of these units would be made available to the IMF for the benefit of countries not in the limited group.

In this way the United States attempted to reconcile the European desire for a limited group approach with the obvious desire of the rest of the world to be included on a nondiscriminatory basis in the process of reserve creation. At the same time, a number of American officials believed that a unit was a more credible substitute for gold than IMF drawing rights. But the approach was necessarily cumbersome and did not command universal enthusiasm among American officials; some of us were advocating a single type of reserve asset created for all Fund members. The Europeans, one of whom privately characterized the U.S. proposal as a "monstrosity," would have been satisfied with a simpler scheme: units for the limited group and drawing rights for the rest of the world. It was a desire to avoid this "separate but equal" approach that led to the complexity of the American proposal.

The European Approach

At the January meeting of deputies, Chairman Emminger presented a proposal that apparently represented the position of his country, Italy, and the Netherlands, but not France. Belgium's position was unclear. The Emminger proposal, which was leaked to *Le Monde* a few days before the meeting, called for a new reserve unit to be created and used by a limited group of countries. It would be transferred in a one-to-one ratio with gold. At the same time, the limited group would extend lines of credit to the Fund in some ratio to the reserves it created—these lines of credit to be used for lending by the Fund to other countries. There were two other elements: It would be agreed, and assured via multilateral surveillance, that the combined dollar holdings of the limited group would not rise appreciably above existing levels. And the decisions to set up and to activate the contingency plan would have to be unanimous.[1]

This proposal provoked a number of criticisms from both the American representatives and other deputies. The gold transfer ratio was strongly opposed by the United States on the ground that it would lead countries with relatively low gold holdings to convert dollars into gold (from the U.S. Treasury) in order to have sufficient gold to use with units. This in turn might lead countries outside the limited group to convert dollars into gold, if only to make themselves eligible for later participation in the limited group. The European counter-argument was that linking the use of the new unit to gold would be a clear demonstration that a substitute for gold was being created.

Another major objection concerned the provision for limiting the group's dollar holdings. While the United States was determined to eliminate its balance-of-payments deficit, there were other ways in which the group's official dollar holdings could increase—as the result of deficits in non-group countries, for example. A decision to convert into gold any dollar accruals above a given limit could thus reduce U.S. gold reserves even if the American balance of payments was not in deficit.

Finally, the proposal for unanimous decision-making was unacceptable to the United States and to others.

The Emminger proposal, clearly designed to keep France in the liquidity exercise, did not succeed. President de Gaulle met with his senior monetary officials on February 25, 1966, and a French position was formulated, much of which showed up in *Le Monde* in early March. The French deputy, Maurice Perouse, was instructed to make clear that his government saw no need for any scheme for reserve creation even on a contingency planning basis, given the "massive disequilibrium" in the balance of payments of both Britain and the United States. It was the French view that the deputies should confine themselves to "study and reflection." Furthermore, the French were dissatisfied with the drift of the deputies' discussions, which were moving away from the CRU proposal for an asset closely linked to gold, designed to substitute for reserve currencies and to be used outside the IMF by a limited group of countries. Contrary to press reports, the French did not withdraw from the deputies' deliberations.[2]

With the adoption of this stance, France and the United States had switched positions—a reversal much remarked upon and little understood. When the French began the discussion of a new reserve (their CRU proposal), the United States was in opposition, defending the status quo. By the spring of 1966, it was the United States that was pushing hard for contingency planning for a new asset while the French had retreated to the position that such planning was unnecessary.

The major objective of the original French proposal for a CRU "derived from gold," as the French liked to put it, was to create a substitute for *dollars* and thus to end the special privileges that the United States supposedly enjoyed as a reserve currency country. By 1966, however, the major impetus for creating a new reserve asset was to provide a substitute or supplement for *gold*. The prospects for a further decrease, if not a reversal, of the already small trickle of gold into monetary gold stocks was becoming an increasingly important influence on the willingness of Europeans (other than the French) to move ahead with the Americans so as to be in a position to create a new reserve asset. The other Europeans wanted to slow down or put an end to the *expansion* of the dollar's role as a reserve currency. Their objective was to provide for growth of reserves in the absence of adequate supplies of the traditional sources, gold and dollars.[3] The French were mainly preoccupied with reducing or ending the special role of the dollar.

The French position was not accepted by the deputies, who felt that their mandate from the ministers remained in force and they had to push ahead. As if to underline this rebuff of the French position, the deputies scheduled their May 1966 meeting for Rome after having met several times in Paris.

IMF Initiative

Meanwhile the Managing Director of the Fund had put forward two proposals for reserve creation. The first, a drawing rights scheme, was almost identical with my own proposal. The second would involve the creation of units and would include all members of the Fund, actually or potentially, in contrast with the proposals for a unit that had been put forward in the Group of Ten.[4]

Those of us in the U.S. government who had been pressing for a universal scheme warmly welcomed Schweitzer's initiative.[5] I had, in fact, done some analysis that demonstrated that developing countries had been accumulating reserves over the past five years; in terms of numbers, many more had accumulated reserves than had lost reserves. Thus there was no economic reason why developing countries could not participate fully in a reserve creation scheme. Not all would be net users of the new reserve asset.

In April and May, Schweitzer made a series of public speeches in which he (1) stressed the reduced flow of gold into monetary reserves and the consequent need for completing contingency planning, (2) expressed misgivings about a "separate but equal" dual approach as contrasted with a universal approach, and (3) summarized the Fund's two proposals for reserve creation. In an extemporaneous talk in Minneapolis, Schweitzer was quoted as having accused the Group of Ten of "dragging their feet" and of advocating "separate but equal" facilities for other countries.[6] This led Emminger, on May 12, to reply publicly, defending both the pace and the substance of the work of the Group of Ten.[7]

Schweitzer's public stance was having some effect. At the May, June, and July meetings of deputies, at which the report to ministers was negotiated, increasing lip service was paid to the principle of universality. But the major unspoken concern of the Europeans was that at the next stage of the negotiations or after agreement on contingency planning, the United States and the developing countries would combine forces and push through decisions that would be against Europe's interests. This fear showed up in the insistence on the concept of a limited group with respect to the form of reserves (units for the limited group only, drawing rights for the rest of world) and as regards decision-making to create the new assets, initially and over time.

Deputies Report

The deputies finally agreed on a report in early July, in time for the scheduled meeting of Ministers and Governors of the Group of Ten on July 25–26, 1966. This report first discussed possible improvements in the system other than reserve creation, then described various approaches to deliberate reserve creation, and concluded with a statement of what had and what had not been agreed by the deputies.

In discussing the balance-of-payments adjustment process, the report recognized, with insufficient explanation, that "the supply of international reserves has a bearing on the functioning of the adjustment process." A fuller explanation would have pointed out that, if the U.S. deficit was to be ended, an alternative supply of reserves had to be available, since countries in general regarded it as normal to experience growth in their reserves.

Possible improvements in the system included the strengthening of multilateral surveillance; there was no mention of a ceiling on dollar holdings. Proposals for "harmonizing" the composition of countries' reserves between gold and foreign exchange and for giving the IMF gold tranche a more certain status as a reserve asset were also discussed in the report.

It was agreed by all but "one member" that the supply of reserves from traditional sources—gold and reserve currencies—"is unlikely to keep pace with legitimate demands, at any rate in the long run. Supplementary means are therefore likely to be needed in order to provide for an adequate secular growth in world reserves." The "one member" was willing to accept this proposition "only as a legitimate working hypothesis."

The difficulties of assessing the optimum rate of growth of reserves were stressed, and the inadequacy of accretions of gold was recognized. The reasons for establishing a contingency plan, despite the fact that no immediate action to create reserves was called for, were: (1) to assure the world that a shortage of reserves will not be permitted to disrupt the world economy, (2) to take account of the time lag in securing legislative approval, and (3) to avoid hasty and ill-considered measures in the future.

The "one" dissenting deputy set forth his arguments against contingency planning. In his view, an international agreement for deliberate reserve creation "would, in present circumstances, give rise to an irresistible temptation to activate the agreement prematurely. He feels that the prevailing tendencies in both reserve currency countries and developing countries make it unlikely that the activation of an agreed scheme could in practice be deferred until a real need for additional reserves arose." That member therefore refrained from participation in the discussion and drafting of the rest of the report.

The report went on to compare units and drawing rights and included the argument that units would be more readily seen as a supplement to gold.

The cases for and against a limited group approach—"a coherent group of countries"—were presented. It was pointed out that one member (this time the United States, though it was not identified) favors both approaches.

Finally, provisions for the holding and use of a new asset were discussed, including holding limits for individual countries and a gold transfer ratio. Those who favored a gold transfer ratio argued, on the one hand, that it would make units more convincing as a supplement to gold but, on the other, that it would strengthen balance-of-payments discipline for deficit countries. It was not explained how these two propositions could be reconciled, since the second one implied that the loss of gold by a country in deficit has a greater effect on its policies than the loss of other reserves.

In the concluding section the deputies expressed their agreement on the need for contingency planning, with one dissent, but did not try to choose between units and drawing rights, except to say that "most of us" favor creation of a unit by the limited group. The assets to be created for other Fund members would be discussed in a wider forum at the second stage envisaged by the ministerial communiqué of September 1965. No agreement was reached on voting procedures (decision-making) nor on "holding and use" (whether there should be a gold transfer ratio or holding limits).

An annex to the report described, without identifying their sources, five schemes: (1) the continental European proposal put forth by Emminger in January, (2) the U.S. dual approach, (3) a scheme for creation of units by the limited group but worldwide distribution of these units, (4) the Fund's drawing rights scheme, and (5) the Fund's unit scheme. The use of the word "whilst" in the description of the third proposal identified it as being of British origin.[8]

Ministerial Meeting, July 1966

The Ministers and Governors of the Group of Ten met in the pleasant surroundings of the Parliament buildings in The Hague on July 25–26, 1966. They focused on two issues, decision-making and whether or not to proceed to a second stage of deliberation that would include other Fund members. French Finance Minister Michel Debré provided considerable color by arguing the basic French position in the manner of a courtroom lawyer trying to impress a jury. In lengthy and impassioned discourses, he stressed well-known French themes: that the basic problems of the system stemmed from the reserve currency role of the dollar, that the U.S. deficit showed no sign of disappearing and that it was causing inflation in other countries, and that there was a danger that control of the international monetary system would be wrenched away from the Group of Ten into the hands of the developing countries, whose need was for aid rather than reserves. From time to time, Debré got carried away with his own fervor, and smiles appeared on the faces of other participants around the room. Both his manner and his occasional hint that an increase in the price of gold should not be excluded weakened his influence on the other ministers and governors, including his EEC partners.

Treasury Secretary Henry Fowler represented the United States coolly and firmly and, where possible, avoided debating with the French Minister. He refused to agree to the concept of a Group of Ten veto on activation of a contingency plan and argued strongly for moving on to the second stage. When it came to a showdown vote, the other members of the Common Market abandoned Debré and a communiqué was issued based on the deputies' report. The decision-making issue was resolved in a paragraph that first stated the prerequisites for activation of a contingency plan: "attainment of a better balance-of-payments equilibrium between members and the likelihood of a better working of the adjustment process in the future"; it went on to say that decision-making arrangements should reflect the interests of all countries and "the particular responsibilities of a limited group of major countries with a key role in the functioning of the international monetary system and which in fact must provide a substantial part of the financial strength behind any new asset." The communiqué noted that one delegation disagreed and everyone knew it was France.

Finally, while instructing their deputies to continue their studies on unresolved questions, the ministers stated that it was appropriate to look for a wider framework in which to consider questions that affect the world economy as a whole. They recommended a series of joint meetings between the Group of Ten deputies and the Executive Directors of the IMF. Again one delegation dissented.[9]

Joint Meetings of Deputies and IMF Executive Board

The Deputies of the Group of Ten and the Executive Directors of the IMF held four joint meetings in 1966–67, two in Washington, one in London, and one in Paris. The grouping was rather awkward, since half of the twenty Fund Directors were from countries that were members of the Group of Ten. But it worked in practice since the dialogue (more accurately, multilogue) was conducted mainly among the ten deputies and the ten Executive Directors from countries other than the Group of Ten.

The members of the two groups initially approached each other in a gingerly fashion. There was distrust and resentment among the non-Ten Fund Directors over the role the Group of Ten had assumed and in particular over the known objective of some Group of Ten deputies to establish a two-tier voting procedure that would give a first crack at important decision-making to the Group of Ten. Some of the deputies, in turn, expected to find the Fund representatives from developing countries putting forward unacceptable proposals for what would in fact amount to development assistance in the guise of reserve creation. And European deputies feared a ganging up by the United States and developing countries.

In consequence, an atmosphere of tension and uncertainty prevailed when the large group assembled in the Fund's Board Room in Washington on November 28, 1966. More than 40 persons were seated at the table and an equal number behind them. Pierre-Paul Schweitzer chaired the meeting, with the understanding that Otmar Emminger would chair the two meetings to be held in Europe. Formally, they were designated co-chairmen.

As it turned out, the meeting was harmonious and revealed much common ground between the Fund Directors and the deputies. Emminger and

Schweitzer were quoted in the press as saying that the results exceeded "our most hopeful expectations." The deputies learned that the representatives of developing countries were responsible individuals and the Fund directors learned that the deputies were willing to be open-minded.

The French deputy, Maurice Perouse, presented the standard position of his country but added new elements, some of which had been alluded to by Minister Debré in his address to the annual meeting of the IMF in September 1966. Presumably because its earlier stress on a limited group approach outside the IMF was bound to displease developing countries, the French approach now included proposals to "organize" commodity markets so as to stabilize the prices of raw materials produced by developing countries. The French deputy also emphasized the need to increase development assistance. Another new element—one not particularly aimed at pleasing developing countries— was a proposal that the problems of gold in the international monetary system should be added to the agenda of the joint meetings.

Headlines appeared the next day in Paris newspapers about the possibility of an increase in the price of gold. The French Finance Ministry, in order to prevent turmoil in the gold markets, found it necessary to issue a statement denying that the French Government had requested an increase in the price of gold but simply wanted a study of the problem of gold, including its price. At a press conference on the last day of the first joint meeting, Schweitzer stated emphatically that the price of gold was not, and would not be, on the agenda. Further stories appeared in the French press questioning Schweitzer's authority to preclude such a discussion and, more generally, contrasting the positions of France and the "Anglo-Saxon" countries. According to these articles, while France saw no need now to increase world reserves, when such a need should appear, a rise in the price of gold was a way to do it and, in the process, to reestablish the rightfully dominant position of gold as a "neutral currency" without the stamp of any one country's national identity. It is impossible to believe that these news stories were not officially inspired.

The joint meeting brought out clearly that, apart from France, there was broad agreement on the need for contingency planning. On the form of the new reserve asset, no convergence on a unit or drawing rights emerged. The representatives of developing countries insisted, however, that all countries should participate on the same basis in the distribution of new reserve assets; they could not accept a separate but equal approach. In the course of the discussion, Under Secretary Deming appeared to move away from the U.S. dual approach.[10] Concerning the question of transfer and use of the new asset, considerable opposition to the gold transfer ratio was expressed and Emminger acknowledged the existence of this opposition.[11]

Shortly before the second joint meeting, French Finance Minister Debré created a small furor by granting an interview to *Le Monde* in which he made public, in more explicit terms, the position Perouse had taken in November on gold. While France was opposed to contingency planning, if the question of increasing reserves was to be examined, attention should also be given to the pros and cons of a gold price increase. The interview was generally interpreted, rightly or wrongly, as a French call for an increase in the price of gold.[12]

The second joint meeting, held in London on January 25–26, 1967, maintained the constructive spirit and momentum toward convergence of views that had been exhibited in November. On the question of the prerequisites for activation of a contingency plan, the formulation agreed to by the Group of Ten Ministers at The Hague was seen as not being susceptible to rigid interpretation. For example, the need for reserve creation could arise even if a moderate deficit in the U.S. balance of payments continued to exist. Secondly, the two-tier decision-making preference of European countries was strongly opposed by non-Ten representatives, who preferred to use the Fund's weighted majority voting procedure; this already gave large influence to the Group of Ten countries.[13] But, as one of the European deputies pointed out, the parliaments of the EEC countries might be regarded, at this stage, as being in a position similar to that of the U.S. Congress in 1945, when the Bretton Woods Agreements Act was passed; the Bretton Woods agreement gave the United States a veto on Fund decisions. Since the EEC did not have sufficient voting power to block action in the Fund, there was a case for a unit vote for a limited group plus a weighted majority vote.

As the discussion developed, considerable emphasis was given to the consultation procedure prior to voting on activation of a reserve creation scheme. But there was still to be a considerable amount of debate on decision-making.

EEC Formulates a Position

Between the second and third joint meetings, the Finance Ministers of the EEC convened in Munich on April 17–18, 1967. Evidently there had been intense prior consultations between the French and the German governments. The French had clearly been unsuccessful in swaying the joint meetings and had been isolated. The Germans felt the need for Common Market unity if Europe was to exert influence against a combined position of the United States and developing countries. Thus both France and Germany were motivated to forge a common EEC position. With prior German-French agreement, there was little the other EEC ministers could do but go along.

The Ministers of the Six, asserting that the EEC member countries ought to occupy a place in international monetary institutions more in accordance with their actual "responsibilities, their growing economic solidarity, expanding trade and economic and financial role in the world," decided to seek a common position in the reform discussions and to act together in the future so as to safeguard their "legitimate" interests. On this basis they agreed that:

1. The fact that there is currently no shortage of international liquidity does not preclude consideration ("reflexions") on the measures to be taken in case of a need for supplementary reserves in the future.
2. Measures to create additional reserves, including alternative solutions, should depend on a common judgment that a shortage exists, on a better functioning of the adjustment process, and on achievement of a better balance in international transactions. They should not be based on the balance-of-payments needs of "certain countries" nor should they favor any single country or group of countries.
3. These measures should be based on long-term needs, not cyclical phenomena.
4. The present strength of the Six must ensure that they have a sufficient influence in the IMF, particularly in voting procedures. To this end, decisions to create additional "facilities" should require an 85 percent vote and should include at least half of the major creditor countries (those whose currencies have been used in Fund drawings over the past five years).
5. On these conditions, it would be possible to envisage, in the event of an agreed shortage of liquidity, the creation of both conditional and unconditional drawing rights in the IMF.
6. It might be opportune, for this purpose, to establish a separate account and separate financing in the IMF.
7. Automatic drawing rights that are fully used or partially used over a long period, ought to carry a repayment obligation (a concept that came to be called "reconstitution").
8. Voluntary bilateral transferability of automatic drawing rights requires further study.[14]

This agreement brought France back into the liquidity exercise but (at least nominally) pushed the other EEC countries to support drawing rights rather than units. Whether this concession was of substantive importance was unclear at the time; it made it possible for the French to assert that what was to be created was another form of credit, whereas many of the participants in the joint meetings, including some from the Six, had been seeking an asset—a form of international money—that was "gold-like."

The United States and others were hardly pleased with this "new Munich," but its precise implications were difficult to interpret. Apart from the substantive consequences for the outcome of the negotiations, there was resentment at what appeared to be a "take it or leave it" pronouncement from the Six. The EEC was trying to swing its political weight. But, tactically, it would have been a mistake for the United States to raise a big fuss. Nothing would have pleased Debré more than a reaction by the United States that caused the negotiations to bog down.

Third and Fourth Joint Meetings

Thus the third joint meeting in Washington on April 24–26, 1967, took the EEC statement in stride and moved forward.

It discussed the question of the need for reserves and how to assess it. And it went on to examine the two IMF schemes for reserve creation. Although some major specific issues remained unresolved—whether the new asset should be directly transferable among Fund members, whether some reconstitution should be built into the scheme, and whether voting procedures should give the EEC a veto by requiring an 85 percent weighted majority for decisions to create a new asset—there seemed to be agreement that a broad outline of a plan for reserve creation could be presented to the IMF Annual Meeting in September.[15]

The fourth joint meeting, held in Paris on June 19–21, had before it revised IMF plans for the creation of drawing rights and units. At the end of the meeting, the group had produced a sketch of an agreed scheme, based on automatic drawing rights. But the sketch embodied a number of unresolved issues which would have to be decided at the ministerial level. Among these were the questions of decision-making and reconstitution "after unduly long or large utilization" by countries in deficit.[16] The new asset was being referred to as "reserve drawing rights" in the sketch but the French deputy objected to the word "reserve" and suggested "special" in its stead. At that stage, the word "reserve" was bracketed for future decision.

A meeting of the Finance Ministers of the EEC on July 4 failed to resolve any of the open issues. The Ministers did, however, reaffirm their determination to insist on an 85 percent vote for all major decisions in the Fund.[17]

Group of Ten Meetings, July and August 1967

The Ministers and Governors of the Group of Ten met in London on July 17–18, at stately Lancaster House, near St. James's Palace. British Chancellor of the Exchequer James Callaghan was chairman. From time to time the proceedings were interrupted as a military band passed by outside playing a sprightly march. There was less harmony inside the building.

Most of the meeting focused on two issues, voting and reconstitution. French Minister Debré insisted on some form of reconstitution, which he preferred to call "repayment," in order to support his contention that what was being agreed to was a form of credit. He was backed, in principle, by the other members of the Six though they did not agree that it was credit they were preparing to create. Debré's conduct was relatively low-key, and he went along with the idea of completing a plan in time for the September meeting of the IMF. The desire to avoid confrontation became evident early in the meeting, after Emminger summarized the open issues and Callaghan, in his capacity as chairman, suggested that the two major questions—decision-making and reconstitution—be taken up together. A long silence ensued. It was finally broken by a request from Callaghan that Schweitzer open the discussion on voting. Debré then stepped in with a discourse on the importance of these two issues if the group was to agree on a new form of international credit.

Italian Minister Columbo put forward a proposal for harmonization of the composition of countries' reserves, which would have effects similar to reconstitution, since it would have required a country that used the new asset disproportionately to restore its holdings in order to preserve the proposed harmonized composition of reserves.

Secretary Fowler stressed the need for a supplementary reserve asset that central banks would treat as they treat other reserves. While he accepted the principle of reconstitution to assure the liquidity of the scheme for reserve creation, he opposed specific rules that would impair the quality of the asset as a first-line reserve. His opposition to an 85 percent vote was based on the concern that, if the EEC maintained unity, a single member of that group could block action by the IMF. He argued that an increase in EEC influence in the IMF should come about as the result of increased quotas for these countries. What was not stated was that agreement by the United States to an 85 percent vote would be a major concession and would therefore not come until late in the negotiations, if it were to come at all.

The meeting ended with instructions to the deputies to try to resolve the issues and with agreement on another ministerial meeting in late August if necessary. The communiqué stated that it was expected that agreement would be reached on an outline plan in time for the annual meeting of the IMF. It did not mention the possibility of another meeting of ministers in August.

The deputies managed to resolve some issues and remove some brackets from the draft outline, but the two major issues remained. The French were insisting on both a harmonization formula—requiring that countries use drawing rights no more heavily than other reserves over a given time period—plus a specific limitation on the amount of drawing rights countries could use in a given period. On voting, some of the EEC members were no longer insisting on a majority unit vote of creditor countries (as proposed at Munich) in addition to the 85 percent voting requirement.

The ministers and governors reassembled in Lancaster House on August 26. Emminger reported on the progress the deputies had made regarding reconstitution. He stated that a majority now seemed to favor, instead of the complex harmonization formula, a requirement of "average net use" of drawing rights over a period of time, though there was still disagreement on the precise requirement. A proposal for 75 percent average net use over a six-year period was put forward by two of the EEC ministers: a country would be expected to hold rather than use, on average over six years, 25 percent of the drawing rights allocated to it.

This position was accepted by a sizable number of ministers, including Secretary Fowler, who also conceded the 85 percent decision-making rule on the condition that everything else in the Outline was agreed in an acceptable way. But Minister Debré was unable to go along, nor could Italian Minister Columbo.

Minister Debré and Secretary Fowler from time to time recounted the large number of concessions each had made from his initial position. One of the American concessions was to agree to drop the word "reserve" from the name of the new asset, which Minister Debré was still referring to as a form of credit.

The meeting recessed for an hour during the afternoon while various private caucuses were held. When it resumed the Italian Minister was still insisting on reserve harmonization and Debré could not accept a 75 percent average use rule even over a five-year period.

After another break,* possibly to permit Columbo to telephone Rome, the meeting reassembled at 10:45 P.M. The Italian Minister, who was the last EEC

---

*At one point late in the long day, the chairman stated that he had a sturdy "bottom" and was prepared to sit on it until agreement was reached.

member to hold out with Debré, reentered the room with his usual dignity and grace, accompanied by Governor Carli and an entourage of Italian officials. A mood of tension and drama pervaded the chamber as the participants waited for Minister Columbo to speak. He announced that he was prepared to accept a compromise—put forward earlier—for 70 percent average use over five years. Without delay Debré agreed but with a request that the record of the meeting show that to him the new facility was a form of credit.

The ministers and governors issued a communiqué stating that they had agreed on an Outline of a contingency plan which they would be prepared to support at the forthcoming annual meeting of the IMF at Rio de Janeiro. They specified the terms of their agreement on the two main issues.

It seems clear that Debré was under instruction to achieve two incompatible goals: to prevent the isolation of France, as had happened a year earlier at The Hague when the other members of the Six lined up with the United States, and to prevent agreement on a true reserve asset that the world might regard as a substitute for gold. While the other members of the EEC wished to preserve Common Market unity, they were not prepared to go very far with France on the substantive issues. The French ended up with some semantic victories and with reconstitution, neither of which justified Minister Debré's statement to the press that the agreement was "a success for the French thesis" and that "the question of creating new money was discarded."[18]

In the course of public discussion of whether the SDR was international money or credit, Otmar Emminger, always the mediator, characterized the SDR as being like a zebra: one could regard it as a black animal with white stripes or as a white animal with black stripes. In fact, Emminger himself referred to the SDR as "something like an interest-bearing gold certificate."[19]

Reporting to the FOMC, I analyzed the results of the London meeting:

In some respects the language of the agreement had an "Emperor's new clothes" quality. The outline provided for a facility to create "special drawing rights"— rather than a "reserve unit." And that it was called a drawing right rather than a unit had been characterized as a concession by the United States and a victory for France. . . .

The fact was that the new reserve facility was a drawing right in name and a unit in substance. It differed from existing IMF drawing rights in that it was directly transferable, whereas one used existing drawing rights in the Fund by purchasing other currencies with one's own currency. In the case of the SDR, one transferred it just as one transferred gold—in exchange for the currency of the country to which it was transferred. It was difficult to imagine what characteristics of the SDR would be changed in order to transform it into a unit.[20]

President de Gaulle was reported to have dismissed the London agreement as of no importance,[21] but President Johnson held a little ceremony at the White House on August 28 to commend Secretary Fowler and his associates for helping to achieve "the greatest forward step in world financial cooperation in the 20 years since creation of the IMF."[22]

Final Hurdle: The Stockholm Meeting of March 1968

The "Outline of a Facility Based on Special Drawing Rights in the Fund" was released by the IMF on September 11, 1967. Its first sentence stated that the facility "is intended to meet the need, as and when it arises, for a supplement to existing reserve assets."[23]

The Outline was formally approved by the Board of Governors of the IMF in Rio in late September, and the Executive Directors were asked to prepare the necessary amendments to the Articles of Agreement by March 31, 1968. They were also asked to prepare amendments relating to "improvements in the present rules and practices of the Fund" as had been agreed in principle but not in substance at the London meeting of the Group of Ten.

There was one further hurdle before the agreement on SDRs could become effective. As the Executive Directors of the IMF worked at transforming the Rio Outline into a set of amendments to the Fund Articles, a number of issues arose stemming from the basic difference in approach between the French and the majority. Some of the semantic compromises in the Outline had to be unmasked if the new legal language was to be clear and operational. In some instances the Executive Directors had found it necessary to go beyond the Outline. And some of the EEC proposals for "improvements" in the Fund's rules and practices were turning out to be unacceptable to the United States and other non-EEC countries.

The Group of Ten Deputies, now chaired by Rinaldo Ossola of the Bank of Italy, were unable to resolve these disagreements in a series of meetings in the fall and winter of 1967. At the request of Minister Debré, the Group of Ten Ministers and Governors were called to a meeting in Stockholm at the end of March 1968.

It will be recalled that the international monetary system had been in turmoil in the months leading up to this ministerial meeting. Just two weeks earlier the Washington gold meeting, to which France had not been invited since it was no longer an "active" member of the gold pool, had established the two-tier system and the communiqué had anticipated the establishment of the SDR facility. Thus, contrary to the French approach, the SDR was being regarded as a substitute for gold. Meanwhile, in Vietnam, the Tet offensive had occurred—a military advance for North Vietnam and the Vietcong that had a substantial impact on public opinion in the United States and elsewhere. A sense of the hopelessness of the U.S. venture in Vietnam was becoming more widespread.

All of this revived President de Gaulle's interest in international monetary matters. He repeated his views on the role of gold in the system, and stories came out of Paris about the need for a new international monetary conference comparable to Bretton Woods.[24] It seems likely that some French officials believed the long-expected ultimate crisis of the gold exchange standard was at hand. They saw at last the chance to achieve de Gaulle's goal of reducing or eliminating the American "hegemony" in the international monetary field, particularly at a time when its position in Vietnam was weakening. But, once again, France faced the problem of isolation from its Common Market partners, who had accepted the two-tier gold system on the assumption that the SDR would be established and who feared that the gold and foreign exchange markets would be disrupted if the Stockholm meeting displayed a breakdown of international cooperation.

The Economist interpreted the reversion to a hard line by France, after Debré's relatively benign stance in London in August, as reflecting a realization by de Gaulle that SDRs were not, after all, just another form of credit but rather "a true monetary instrument which would gradually replace gold as the principal element in international reserves." According to this view, the French Government asked for the Stockholm meeting in order to disown the London and Rio agreements in a "resounding" way.[25]

The major issues before the Ministers and Governors of the Group of Ten, when they sat down together in Stockholm on March 29, 1968, were: (1) Should "other holders" than central banks of IMF members be permitted to accept and use SDRs? (2) What conditions (not specified in the Rio Outline but spelled out in the July 1966 Communiqué of the Group of Ten at The Hague) should be met before the initial activation of SDRs? (3) Under what conditions should a participant in the SDR scheme be able to "opt out" of an allocation and the relation of this provision to voting? (4) Should the Fund itself be able to hold and use SDRs and, in particular, could it accept them in lieu of gold from members when quotas were increased?

Under the heading of "improvements" in the rules and practices of the Fund there were two major issues: (1) whether required majorities for Fund decisions on matters other than SDRs should be raised to 85 percent, and (2) in case of disagreement between a member country and the Fund on a legal matter, whether an outside tribunal should be established (as France had proposed).

Before the Ministers began to debate these issues, Debré made a general statement on the international monetary system. After congratulating Britain on its courageous actions to make the devaluation successful and denouncing the Washington gold agreement, he repeated the familiar French view on the special privileges of the United States. Then, arguing that the IMF could not be expected to create a replacement for gold, he tried to put the question of the price of gold on the agenda. A rise in its price was inevitable and had to be faced up to; negotiations, possibly in secrecy, had to begin.

This proposal was immediately rejected by the other EEC members. Some of them argued that even in Debré's vision of the future international monetary system an SDR facility would be needed, since most of the world's gold was held by a small fraction of the IMF membership.

What Debré apparently had in mind was the Rueff proposal that the profits the United States would realize from an increase in the gold price would be used to redeem official dollar reserves held by other countries. He did not claim that raising the price of gold was all that was needed, but in his view it was necessary and inevitable.

Secretary Fowler stressed the determination of the United States to improve its balance of payments and gave an optimistic forecast of Congressional action on the President's fiscal policy proposals. He pointed out that the U.S. share of any SDRs created would cover only a small part of the existing U.S. deficit. In any event, the United States would be pleased to see its reserves increase as a result of the creation of SDRs.

When the ministers and governors turned to the specific questions regarding SDRs, easy agreement was reached on "other holders"—to authorize the IMF to agree to holdings by institutions that perform functions of a central bank for more than one member. This language was designed to make it possible for the BIS to hold SDRs. On the conditions for activation, nine out of ten delegations agreed to language based on the July 1966 agreement. But there was greater disagreement on "opting out" and on permitting the Fund to accept and use SDRs.

Concerning "improvements" of the Fund, a split developed between EEC members and the others on changing required voting majorities to 85 percent for major decisions. On an outside tribunal to decide on legal issues, Schweitzer argued strongly against such a change on the ground that it would impair the efficient functioning of the Fund. He was supported by Secretary Fowler.

The Chairman of the meeting, Minister of Economic Affairs Krister Wickman of Sweden, proposed a package of compromise proposals. This was followed by a lengthy recess during which the EEC Ministers caucused. Their purpose was to make the final agreement as palatable to France as possible even though they were reasonably certain that France would not agree at this meeting. They wanted to keep the SDR door open for subsequent entry by France, not only for reasons of EEC unity but because the EEC veto (15 percent of the total weighted votes in the IMF) depended on French participation.

While the EEC caucus dragged on, each of the other delegations conferred among themselves. Secretary Fowler had to wrestle with the problem of keeping the door open to France while not giving up too much. Probably the major question was whether or not the Fund should be empowered to accept SDRs as well as gold in payment of quota increases. If the SDR was to be a full substitute for gold, it seemed important to include this provision. For this very reason, it was one of Debré's major sticking points. I was among those who tried to persuade Secretary Fowler to put up a fight on this issue. But he faced a formidable political problem if the rest of the EEC accepted the French position.

When the meeting finally resumed, Minister Columbo presented a revised package on behalf of a "majority" of the EEC countries. This included acceptance of a French proposal on opting out, which permitted a country that had voted against an issue of new SDRs not to accept its share once it had been allocated SDRs equal to one-half its IMF quota. It was also proposed that the draft proposal to permit use of SDRs in payment of quota increases be eliminated. Secretary Fowler accepted this. On interpretation of legal disputes, it was agreed that a standing committee of Fund Governors would be established rather than an outside tribunal.

This final package was accepted by all the delegations except France. Debré, in a lengthy, sorrowful statement, expressed the belief that the agreement to establish a credit facility had been abandoned. He also regretted the unwillingness of his colleagues to consider the more fundamental problems to which he had alluded at the outset of the meeting. But he stressed that France was under no illusion that its economy was independent of the world economy. He hoped there would be a readiness in the future to tackle the real problems, including the gold price. As irony would have it, within two months France was to be caught up in a monetary crisis that was in no way related to the weaknesses of the international monetary system about which Debré was complaining so insistently.

The communiqué, which did not present the substance of the agreements —these were to be communicated to the Executive Directors of the members of the Group of Ten, many of whom were in fact in Stockholm—reaffirmed the determination of the Ministers and Governors to cooperate to maintain exchange stability and orderly exchange arrangements in the world, "based on the present official price of gold." One delegation did not associate itself with several paragraphs of the communiqué and "fully reserves its position and will wait until it is in possession of the final texts before reporting to its government."

After participating in a background press briefing held by Under Secretary Deming at the U.S. Embassy, I was asked by Ed Fried, of the White House staff, to sit down with him in an office in the Embassy to help compose a paragraph to be cabled to Washington on the historic results of the Stockholm meeting. President Johnson was going to make a speech on March 31 and wanted to mention the progress on SDRs. Our paragraph ended up in the speech in this form: "Last week, at the monetary conference in Stockholm, the major industrial countries decided to take a big step toward creating a new international monetary asset that will strengthen the international monetary system. I am very proud of the very able work done by Secretary Fowler and Chairman Martin of the Federal Reserve Board."[26] Little did we know that this was to be the speech in which the President would announce his intention not to seek reelection.

The Stockholm results, taken together with the Washington meeting two weeks earlier, was felt by most of us to be of historic importance. My report to the Federal Open Market Committee interpreted the combination of the two meetings as constituting a demonetization of gold at the margin. (See page 123.) Chairman Martin confirmed this view, adding that the Stockholm meeting was dramatic, significant, and one of the most interesting meetings he had ever attended, "partly because of the obvious under-currents of feeling that the end of an era was at hand, and that it would now be seen whether it was possible to demonetize gold at the margin and to make it a supplementary rather than a central element in the system of international payments."[27]

The next steps were procedural. The Fund Executive Directors completed the preparation of the amendments in mid-April, and they were approved by the Governors of the Fund, by mail vote, at the end of May 1968. Then came the process of legislative ratification. In July 1969 sufficient approval had been received (three-fifths of the members of the Fund having four-fifths of the total voting power) and the amendments went into force. The SDR facility existed, and for the first time in world monetary history it was possible to create reserves deliberately and by multilateral decision. In fact, discussion was already under way of activating the SDR facility.

At the IMF annual meeting in Washington in the early autumn of 1969, Valéry Giscard d'Estaing, who was by then back in the Finance Ministry under President Georges Pompidou and had recently devalued the franc, announced in his formal address that France had decided "to participate in the activation of the SDR system." He went on to say that "we have ourselves always considered that alongside conditional liquidities there was room in the modern world for a new reserve asset of an unconditional type, designed to supplement gold and foreign exchange in the holdings of central banks."[28] The "we" could only be interpreted as a royal or editorial usage; neither de Gaulle nor Debré could have accepted a statement which not only blessed SDRs but mentioned foreign exchange as a reserve asset without derision. But much had happened to France between March 1968, when Debré dolefully lectured his fellow ministers on their failure to deal with what he regarded as the fundamental problems of the system, and the autumn of 1969. Thus ended France's on-again, off-again flirtation with the SDR. It had finally succumbed, and in a graceful way Minister Giscard d'Estaing announced the marriage.

Activation of SDRs

In both the Fund and OECD's Working Party 3, a realization was developing in 1969 that the achievement of balance in international payments might require early creation of SDRs. Paul Volcker pressed the idea on officials of other countries in his first meetings with them after he took office as Under Secretary of the Treasury for Monetary Affairs in early 1969. Initial reactions were unenthusiastic but opinions changed in the course of 1969.

In its *Annual Report* for 1969, the Fund included a chapter on the growth of reserves. It showed that during the four years 1964–1968, countries' holdings of traditional reserves—gold and foreign exchange—had *declined* by more than $4 billion as the result of two factors: the sales of gold by the gold pool up to mid-March 1968 and the surpluses on official settlements in the U.S. balance of payments in 1966 and 1968. The growth in reserves that did occur over the four-year period was the result in part of heavy borrowing from the Fund and from other countries by Britain and could hardly be counted on to continue.[29]

Discussion in Working Party 3 of the compatibility of the balance-of-payments aims of various countries was leading to a shift of opinion about the creation of reserves. Earlier it was commonplace to say, as Robert Triffin had said in 1960, that elimination of the U.S. deficit would deprive the rest of the world of a source of reserves. Now it was beginning to be seen that effective and lasting elimination of the U.S. deficit might not be possible *unless* an alternative source of reserve creation was first brought into play.

In 1968 and 1969 the U.S. balance of payments was in official settlements surplus (though the structure of the balance of payments was unsatisfactory, since it consisted of too small a current surplus and unsustainable capital inflows). The implications of the U.S. surplus were instructive. Everyone agreed that the United Kingdom should develop a sizable surplus, so that it could repay debt and rebuild its reserves. The same was true for France, though on a smaller scale. But if the combined position of the United States, Britain, and France was to be a surplus, which countries would incur the corresponding deficits and losses of reserves? The developing countries as a whole were accumulating reserves. Thus the only candidates for the deficits were Japan and the continental European countries other than France. Yet recent experience—the pull of funds to the United States via the Eurodollar market—showed that European countries reacted adversely to losses of re-serves. Belgium, the Netherlands, and Austria had drawn on Federal Reserve swap lines—that is, borrowed from the United States—rather than lose addi-tional reserves as the result of high interest rates in the Eurdollar market. And Japan still wished to increase its reserves.

What all this led to was the conclusion that reserve creation via SDRs was a necessary condition (certainly not a sufficient condition) for future balance in international payments. Only if countries' reserves were increased by SDR allocations would they be willing to permit their own balance-of-payments positions to reflect the improvements in the external positions of the United States, France, and Britain.[30]

This argument for reserve creation was a particular application of the more general proposition that countries in the aggregate tended to aim for overall balance-of-payments surpluses (increases in reserves) in a world of growing income and expanding international transactions. Yet for every surplus there had to be a corresponding deficit. As long as the United States was willing, or was permitted, to incur deficits, the reserve aims of other countries could be satisfied, as they were in the 1950's and early 1960's. If it was desired to end the era of U.S. deficits, countries would have to find another way to increase their reserves. And since new gold production could not fulfill this function, there was a case for creating SDRs.[31] (To some observers, the same arguments justified an increase in the price of gold.[32])

With this development of thought going on, the Deputies of the Group of

Ten began to consider the question of how much in the way of SDRs should be created.[33] Of course, work on this subject was proceeding in the Fund, since it was the responsibility of the Managing Director to make proposals for the allocation of SDRs, after consulting with others. It was this requirement of consultation that justified separate consideration of the matter by the Group of Ten Deputies.

By late June 1969, the view was beginning to emerge that Schweitzer might make a proposal for creating SDRs.[34] In July the Group of Ten Deputies reached agreement to recommend the creation of $9.5 billion of SDRs over a three-year period—$3.5 billion the first year and $3 billion in each of the next two years. This was a compromise between the EEC proposal for $2.5 billion per year for three years and the U.S. proposal for $4 billion per year for five years.[35] This amount of SDRs—$9.5 billion—would bring countries' SDR holdings to about one-fourth of their aggregate gold holdings in three years.

Mr. Schweitzer put forward a formal proposal on September 12 for the allocation of $9.5 billion of SDRs over a three-year period. His proposal assumed that the U.S. balance of payments would add $500 million to $1 billion per year to world reserves over the three years, which by itself would be insufficient to meet world reserve needs.[36]

The first allocation of SDRs was made on January 1, 1970. As it happened, the overall U.S. balance of payments moved from a surplus of almost $1 billion (not an annual rate) in the fourth quarter of 1969 to a deficit of almost $3 billion in the first quarter of 1970.

The SDR came along too late; the system needed other reforms, too—notably of its balance-of-payments adjustment process. We turn now to a dramatic instance of the deficiencies of that process, particularly of the exchange rate regime.

IX

The "Events of May" 1968 in France and the French–German Currency Crises

Following the resolution of the gold and SDR problems in March 1968, relative calm returned to the international financial scene. Sterling was still a big question mark. The struggle to get a tax bill through the American Congress was proceeding. (Though it became known only later, the U.S. balance of payments had moved into surplus in the second quarter of 1968 largely in response to tightening monetary policy.) Some were beginning to ask questions about the mark. But, on the whole, April and early May were quiet enough to permit monetary officials to catch their breath. I was able to enjoy a leisurely trip to South America, accompanying Federal Reserve Governor George Mitchell to a meeting of the Central Banks of the American Continent in Argentina and then visiting Brazil and Venezuela on the way back. This was a welcome relief from the frenetic pace of the previous six months. Then, suddenly, a political crisis in France, with economic and financial repercussions, broke this quiet in early May.

France in Crisis

While the United States and Germany had experienced recessions in 1967, in France the growth of output had only tapered off. But this was enough to produce an increase in French unemployment to the highest levels since the early postwar years. The relatively poor prospects for employment of university graduates was one of many factors that created the atmosphere in which student demonstrations at the suburban Nanterre campus of the University of Paris in early 1968 evolved into a generalized and violent student revolt and then to a general strike of French workers and a near-revolution. That it was all abrupt and unexpected is illustrated by the absence of any mention of France in a *Time* essay of May 3, 1968, "Why Those Students Are Protesting," which took note of student demonstrations in fifteen countries.

It would take us far beyond the scope of this book to attempt to describe or explain the "events of May" 1968, particularly the spontaneous reaction of workers in joining the revolt initiated by students.[1] What has to be recorded here is that the events of May profoundly shook French society and exposed the fragile nature of the stability over which President de Gaulle had reigned since 1958.

In his quest for *grandeur*—a goal of French policy that can be traced back to Louis XIV[2]—de Gaulle had, indeed, done much to restore self-respect to France. He had facilitated France's entry into the group of fortunate countries that enjoyed economic growth and rising living standards without the constraint of a balance-of-payments problem. But, however satisfactory had been France's performance, and however smug or even arrogant a few French officials had become as they viewed the disarray in the internal and external economic positions of the "Anglo-Saxon" countries, France's self-confidence was struck a violent blow in 1968.

Sparked by the events at Nanterre, a clash occurred between students and police at the Sorbonne in Paris on May 6 (shortly after American students shocked their nation by occupying and defiling the office of the president of Columbia University). Day after day saw student demonstrations in Paris, lengthy lines of march through the city, the erection of barricades in the Latin Quarter, and the use of tear gas by the police.[3] On May 10, Prime Minister Pompidou announced a program of university reforms—but it was too late. A general sit-in strike of students throughout France was called; in many cases students were joined by their professors. Surprisingly, young workers began to emulate the students by taking over factories; this activity spread to the important Renault automobile plants as older workers followed the example of their colleagues. Soon the country was gripped by a general strike which closed down even the Bank of France. At that institution, as elsewhere, the action of strikers prevented many who would have continued working from doing so.

In these chaotic conditions, Frenchmen tried to take their capital out of the country but, with the banks closed, this was not easy. (The BIS and the Federal Reserve were acting for the Bank of France to support the franc on foreign exchange markets.) There were reports of French citizens crossing the Swiss and Belgian borders with trunkloads of currency. On May 30, the Bank of France announced the imposition of exchange controls forbidding all exports of capital and temporarily requesting other monetary authorities to cease transactions in franc banknotes. This in turn led shopkeepers and gasoline station operators along the border of France's neighbors to stop accepting francs or to restrict the amounts they would accept.[4] The value of French hand-to-hand currency in neighboring countries went to a discount.

The Government offered workers a 10 percent wage increase and a 36 percent rise in the minimum wage, plus a gradual reduction in the work week. The offer was turned down, but some workers drifted back to their jobs and the paralysis of the economy began to ease in early June.

After a mysterious disappearance from Paris, during which, it was learned, he conferred with French Army leaders in Germany, President de Gaulle made a nationwide broadcast on May 30, blaming all the troubles on "totalitarian communism," dissolving the National Assembly, and calling new elections for June 23. The Cabinet was reshuffled and Michel Debré and Maurice Couve de Murville traded places: the latter moved from the Foreign Affairs Ministry to the Ministry of Finance, and Debré moved to the Quai d'Orsay. Couve de Murville was known as a long-time disciple of Jacques Rueff.

The de Gaulle speech on May 30 was followed the same day by a march in Paris of supporters of the President and of the status quo, in answer to the students and workers' march of mid-May.

Meanwhile, France was losing reserves as the result not only of capital flight in fear of political upheaval and speculation in anticipation of devaluation but also of the absence of foreign tourists. The Finance Ministry announced that French reserves had fallen by more than $300 million in May.

On June 5, the Bank of France drew the entire $100 million of its swap line with the Federal Reserve, the first use of that reciprocal credit in several years. On July 2, the swap line was increased to $700 million as part of an international credit package and in November it was expanded again to $1 billion. While French officials had been critical in the past of the Federal Reserve swap network, regarding it as one of the means of maintaining the special privileges the United States enjoyed by virtue of the reserve currency status of its currency, the credit facility turned out to be useful to France. And the Federal Reserve was able to act more quickly than France's Common Market partners in making credit available.[5]

At the same time, France drew $745 million from the IMF, its gold tranche drawing rights. This required activation of the GAB. France also transferred to four other countries its $140 million claim on the Fund representing earlier French loans under the GAB to finance Fund borrowings by the United

Kingdom.[6] This was the first occasion on which a GAB claim on the Fund was transferred from one country to another (which made it clear that such claims on the Fund were reserve assets). Along with the GAB claim, France sold to the same four countries about $93 million of gold—the amount it had received from the Fund when it made the GAB loan for the use of Britain in 1965. A French official was quoted as saying that it would have been "inelegant" not to transfer the gold along with the GAB claim with which it had been associated.

A fresh outbreak of violence occurred in mid-June and the Bank of France had to pay out $500 million in one week to support the franc.[7] This led on June 18 to a sale of $400 million of gold by France to the United States, Germany, Italy, and Switzerland; the sale had been announced a few days earlier by Finance Minister Couve de Murville, along with a denial that France had any intention of devaluing the franc.

In the second half of June the strikes subsided and wage settlements were being made in excess of the original agreement (the so-called Grenelle accord). Wage increases of between 10 and 15 percent were most common.

The elections, on June 23 and June 30, demonstrated that the French middle classes had been deeply frightened by the behavior of students and workers. This showed itself in a large victory for de Gaulle's party and a significant loss of votes for the parties of the left. In a National Assembly of 485 members, about 100 seats shifted from the two leftist groups to the Gaullist party. The Communist Party's representation, though not its popular vote, was more than halved.

In July 1968 economic activity moved back to normal in France. The losses of output during the months of May and June are impossible to calculate with precision; the BIS estimated them at about 3 percent of a year's GNP.[8] Crude steel production fell about one-third from April to the average of May and June, and passenger car output fell by more than half.[9]

French economic policy faced the problems of absorbing the large increase that would ensue in wage costs and consumer spending while encouraging an expansion of economic activity so as to reduce unemployment and weaken the causes of unrest. At the same time, the Government was obviously anxious to safeguard the exchange rate. In the face of these conflicting objectives, the decision seems to have been to give priority to a rapid increase in output. Thus, in the twelve months from July 1968, industrial production rose more than 8 percent and unemployment declined. From April 1968 to April 1969 hourly wage rates in manufacturing rose almost 17 percent, while consumer prices increased about 6 percent. Wholesale prices increased somewhat more.[10]

There were bound to be balance-of-payments impacts. The trade balance, which was showing a deficit at an annual rate of less than $700 million in the first quarter of 1968, became a deficit of $2.2 billion a year later and $2.7 billion, annual rate, in the second quarter of 1969.

While the rate at which France was losing reserves tapered off, the losses continued and France sold an additional $900 million of gold in 1968. As the franc became embroiled in a speculative crisis that also involved the mark, the Bank of France drew heavily on its credit lines with other central banks and also used its reserves. By the end of November 1968, France's total reserves were down to just under $4 billion, compared with $6.9 billion in April.

The words and actions of President de Gaulle's government in the years preceding the events of May had embittered some Americans and had not contributed to great warmth in official relations between the two countries. But former President Johnson, writing in 1971, said: "I made it a rule for myself and for the U.S. Government simply to ignore General de Gaulle's attacks on our policies and the doubts he had raised about the value of our pledges. Nothing he could say would, in my judgment, divert the French people from their friendship with the American people, a friendship firmly rooted in history."[11]

In this spirit, the United States acted in a normally cooperative manner to help France during the chaos of May and June 1968. The help consisted mainly of Federal Reserve credits and a withholding of snide commentary. The United States accepted, but did not demand, gold sales from France.

Of course, it was very much in the interest of the United States to prevent a devaluation of the French franc (or at least an excessive devaluation). This led to some contingency planning in the summer of 1968 by an interagency group under my chairmanship. While it was recognized that a modest devaluation might come to be justified, it was important to prevent a devaluation large enough to restore to France an excessive surplus or to kick off a series of devaluations by other countries, thereby putting intolerable pressure on the dollar price of gold. We assembled a list of political and technical measures that might be used, in our relations with France and with other European countries, to try to ensure that the undesirable contingencies did not come to pass.

The Franc and the Mark: *Après vous, mein Herr*

By the summer of 1968 Germany's currency was coming to be regarded as a candidate for (upward) revaluation while the viability of the French franc was in question as the large increase in real wages was working its way through the economy and being reflected in the balance of payments.

German monetary policy in 1968 had been keeping interest rates low so as to encourage capital outflows, both long-term and short-term. Such outflows were expected to finance the very large current surplus that persisted despite the renewed expansion of the German economy in 1968. But as output and employment increased, questions were bound to arise as to how long the Bundesbank would be prepared to maintain monetary ease, and these questions in turn led to uncertainty about the exchange rate. On May 10, President Blessing of the Bundesbank issued the first of what would turn out to be a series of official denials that Germany had any intention of revaluing the mark. (The French Finance Minister also denied that the franc would be devalued.)

One of several apprehensions of German officials was that, following a German revaluation, France might devalue by a large amount, thereby weakening the German competitive position excessively. Thus those Germans who were prepared to see the mark revalued preferred to have the French act first. The French, on the other hand, could only gain from a German revaluation, since such a move would improve their competitive position without requiring France to take an action that, in their view, would undermine French prestige. Thus an Alphonse-Gaston act was being played out.

A flurry of speculation on a mark revaluation occurred in late August 1968, and the Bundesbank purchased $1.7 billion of foreign exchange to keep the exchange rate from exceeding its upper margin. The Bundesbank, by offering to repurchase dollars in the future on attractive terms, induced German banks to borrow most of this sum from it and relend it in the Eurodollar market. After a quiet October, speculation was renewed and became cumulative. In the period November 1–19 (after which markets were closed), the German central bank took in $2.8 billion,[12] most of it coming from France and Britain as they sold dollars in an endeavor to support their currencies.

We can be sure that a spirited debate raged within the German coalition government between Ministers Schiller and Strauss, and within the Bundesbank, on whether or not to revalue. In fact, quite a debate must have raged between Schiller the economist and Schiller the politician. German farmers opposed an appreciation of the mark because it would, under the rules of the EEC agricultural arrangements, reduce farm prices in Germany. German exporters were opposed for obvious reasons, and their view was echoed by leading German bankers. More broadly, a widespread belief existed among Germans that, having followed successful policies, they should not be "penalized," whatever that meant. In some circles there was the additional view that, though it was an economic "giant," Germany had been a political "dwarf" and now wished to assert itself instead of being pushed around.

On November 12, the Bank of France raised its discount rate from 5 to 6 percent and took other measures to tighten credit. The next day President de Gaulle told his Cabinet that the franc would not be devalued and authorized his Information Minister to announce that devaluation "would be the worst form of absurdity." But the speculative drain on French reserves continued and the Bank of France drew on its credit lines.

Newspaper commentary, at least in the United States, seemed to focus more on the vulnerability of the franc than on the potential appreciation of the mark. Concern that the problem would be resolved by devaluations of the franc and sterling rather than by revaluation of the mark was no doubt a major reason why Secretary Fowler, who happened to be in Europe on a "farewell tour" before leaving office, pressed for a meeting of the Ministers and Governors of the Group of Ten. The U.S. position was that the mark should be revalued and that the franc should stand where it was.

Meanwhile, the central bank governors held their regular monthly meeting at Basle on November 17. They expressed opposition to a ministerial conference to consider changes in currency parities, presumably on the ground that the calling of such a meeting would exacerbate speculation. They forged a consensus among themselves in favor of a German revaluation, the figure most frequently mentioned being 7.5 percent. By this time it was clear that at least some of the directors of the Bundesbank and probably its President also favored revaluation. Although it was agreed that France was not in "fundamental disequilibrium"—the French shared this view at the Basle meeting—the "realities" of the situation seemed to the governors to call for a combined move by France and Germany.[13] These "realities" presumably were that the German Government, facing an election in 1969, was reluctant to move alone, not wanting to give the impression to German citizens that it was imposing "sacrifices" on them in order to solve the problems of other countries.

The next day, November 18, French Prime Minister Couve de Murville, whom de Gaulle had by then installed in place of Pompidou, gave a television interview in which he stated that he would go before the National Assembly the next day to request cuts in government expenditures and other restrictive measures. He said: "This is not, properly speaking, a French crisis. It is an international crisis, it is one of those monetary crises of which we have known many for several years. . . . It was set off by a frantic, I would say phenomenal, speculation in German money, which some claim should be revalued."[14]

Thus Couve threw the ball back to the Germans.

One of the ironies of the situation was that this particular crisis, in which France was so deeply caught up, did not involve the dollar and could not be attributed to the faults of the reserve currency system—the gold exchange standard—of which French officials had been so critical over the years. This crisis could even have occurred in the sort of monetary system that Jacques Rueff advocated.[15]

On November 19 the German and French governments both announced actions. In Germany, there would be emergency legislation to increase taxes on exports and reduce them on imports. This was equivalent to a revaluation for those transactions affected by the taxes—a partial revaluation. Furthermore, the government "will not revalue the DM." Economics Minister Schiller told the press that he hoped the Group of Ten would meet in Bonn in the next few days; the invitations went out that same day. (By coincidence, Schiller was Chairman of the Group of Ten for that year, just as Secretary Connally would be chairman in 1971–72 during a dollar crisis.)

In France, a budget cut of $400 million was announced, but its timing was not clear. Much of the reduction was in expenditures for France's nuclear strike force. The German border tax measures having been made known, there was no further suggestion from the French Prime Minister that the mark be revalued.

The Bonn Meeting of the Group of Ten, November 1968

The Group of Ten Ministers and Governors, with their senior advisers, assembled at the Economics Ministry in Bonn at 4:00 P.M. on Wednesday, November 20. The purpose of the meeting at that stage was unclear, since the German Government had acted on taxes—a partial revaluation—and the French President and Prime Minister had strongly rejected devaluation of the franc. In Harold Wilson's words, "inspired lunacy could go no further; if action were ruled out talk could only do harm, since foreign exchange markets would be driven crazy with rumours; rumours bad for the dollar and worse for sterling."[16]

This was one of the few major international monetary meetings of the period that I did not attend,* but I learned from all reports that it was, again

---

*I had arrived in New York on the evening of November 18 from Stillwater, Oklahoma, and was to leave the next morning for Paris to attend a routine OECD meeting. There was much telephoning to and from my hotel room that night and the next morning over whether I should go to Bonn, go back to Washington, or go on to Paris as planned. After I had checked in at the airport on a flight to Paris, I was phoned by Chairman Martin and asked to return to Washington. He wanted me there, since he was going off to Bonn.

in Wilson's words, "a shambles." It accomplished little and it apparently displayed, in the case of some of the participants, behavior that was less than admirable. The meeting has been described in terms of "acrimony" and "rudeness."

Minister Schiller opened the meeting with a statement affirming that the mark would not be revalued under any circumstances. After this was finally accepted, others tried to persuade the Germans to increase their border taxes and rebates to 7.5 percent or more rather than the 4 percent that the German Government had decided on. This proposal was firmly rejected.

Discussion of France was interrupted to allow Finance Minister François-Xavier Ortoli to phone Paris from time to time. As it was described to me, Prime Minister Couve de Murville had a telephone at each ear, with Ortoli in Bonn on one and President de Gaulle in the Elysée on the other. At one point the issue seemed to involve two alternatives: a 15 percent devaluation or none. The French were finally persuaded, in the early hours of Friday morning, November 22, to limit themselves to 11.1 percent, if they devalued at all.* Newspaper headlines that day announced a 10 percent devaluation of the franc.

Secretary Fowler, speaking for the United States, pressed for a German revaluation, then for a larger border tax adjustment. Fowler finally agreed to a French devaluation if it did not exceed 11.1 percent, on the condition that all other Group of Ten countries would hold their existing exchange rates.[17] Among the papers with which Secretary Fowler and Chairman Martin were armed were two Federal Reserve staff analyses: one pointed to the need for a German revaluation of up to 10 percent, and the other (the contingency planning paper referred to earlier) found that the maximum franc devaluation that could be justified was one of 5 percent.

Much of the discussion took place among finance ministers alone, their central bank colleagues having been asked to step out to discuss credit facilities. It was a long time before they were invited back in. The central bank governors and others amused themselves by playing ping pong and, for those fortunate enough to obtain cards, bridge.

At each break in the meeting, Ministers Schiller and Strauss, apparently competing for domestic political favor, engaged in a race to be the first to reach the German television cameras and the press. In one of his press interviews Strauss was quoted as saying, "My impression is that there will be a French

---

*This odd percentage was chosen to bring the devaluation of the franc to a round number in terms of grams of fine gold—from .18 grams to .16 grams, or from 20.255 U.S. cents to 18.004 cents.

decision to devalue, and very soon."[18] This statement is said to have enraged President de Gaulle. Here was a German minister telling the world about a decision that involved the sovereign prerogatives of the French government!

Faced with the German refusal to revalue or to adjust border taxes by more than 4 percent, the ministers' problem was to conclude the meeting with definitive steps to end the crisis in the foreign exchange markets (which had been closed during the meeting). Thus a French devaluation was considered, even by those who felt that the French economic situation did not warrant it.

We do not know what the views were, either of President de Gaulle himself or of his Prime Minister and Finance Minister. We do know that at one point the draft of the communiqué explicitly referred to a devaluation of the franc, but this reference was stricken after one of Minister Ortoli's phone calls to Paris.[19] On the one hand the French did not want to repeat Britain's cliff-hanging trauma of 1964–1967. If they had to devalue, they would want to do so by an amount large enough to be credible to the markets, which to them apparently meant at least 15 percent. Other countries regarded this as excessive. On the other hand, a franc devaluation would be a blow both to French prestige and to President de Gaulle's prestige, a distinction he was not in the habit of making. Devaluation would, in particular, weaken French leadership in Europe vis-à-vis Germany.

The communiqué that finally emerged added little of substance to the situation at the start of the meeting. In addition to the 4 percent border tax adjustments, the German Government announced its intention to restrict certain short-term capital inflows and to raise to 100 percent the reserve requirement on banks' liabilities to foreigners. In what must have been a difficult pill for many of them to swallow, the Ministers and Governors "endorsed the decision by the Federal Government to maintain the parity of the D-Mark."

The communiqué further stated that the French Finance Minister "explained the situation of the French currency, the measures already taken toward a restoration of internal and external equilibrium, and the problems still to be solved." This latter phrase was generally interpreted to mean devaluation.

Central bank credits of $2 billion to France were announced, and it was stated that the central bank governors would examine new arrangements to alleviate the impact on reserves of speculative movements. Thus the meeting ended on Friday, November 22.

Most of those who attended the meeting left Bonn fully expecting the

French Government to announce a devaluation of the franc. I remember going to the airport to meet Chairman Martin on his return from Bonn. Riding into Washington with him and Charles Coombs, I asked whether they were so sure that the French would act. Coombs' response was vehemently affirmative!

But on Sunday, November 24, President de Gaulle, in a radio address to the French nation, said *Non*. He attributed the French monetary crisis to the events of May and June, which required recovery measures and in the meantime gave rise to "odious speculation." With recovery well on the way, with foreign credits available to supplement French reserves, there was no need to have recourse to devaluation. To back up this decision, it was necessary, without reversing the wage increases of the summer, to moderate additional wage claims, to hold down prices, to encourage exports through tax relief, to cut the budget deficit for 1969 almost in half, and to apply strict exchange controls.[20]

President Johnson sent off a message to the General, pledging American cooperation. De Gaulle requested that this message be made public, saying that it was particularly valuable to him.[21] In a press conference in Washington on Monday, Secretary Fowler also applauded the French decision.

Sequels to the Bonn Meeting

The apparently unanimous determination of the German Government not to revalue, plus General de Gaulle's measures (and additional restrictive actions announced by the British Government on Friday, November 22), apparently persuaded the foreign exchange markets that existing parities would hold, at least for a while. The speculative funds that moved into Germany flowed out, encouraged at first by favorable offerings of forward marks by the Bundesbank. In addition, the Bundesbank maintained a policy of monetary ease, and this encouraged sizable borrowings by foreigners in Germany. By the end of March 1969, German reserves had fallen $2.5 billion, to about where they had been at the end of 1967.

In the case of France, the reversal of market expectations was less evident. France did recover the reserves lost in November but largely as a result of very stringent exchange controls that required French residents and banks to repatriate balances held abroad, attempted to reverse leads and lags by restricting the freedom of importers and exporters to delay receipts or accelerate payments abroad, and limited foreign funds available to French travelers.

But beginning in March 1969, France began to lose reserves again as its trade balance worsened and as capital outflows revived. The approach of a referendum (on regional policy and reform of the French Senate, among other issues) created additional exchange market uncertainties after de Gaulle announced on April 10 that he would resign if the referendum did not yield positive results. It did not, and the General resigned on April 28. He was succeeded in June by Georges Pompidou. Valéry Giscard d'Estaing rejoined the Cabinet as Finance Minister.

Sterling had also been buffeted by the speculative flow into marks. The large outflow of funds from Germany after the Bonn meeting did not immediately strengthen sterling, which required further support and swap drawings by the Bank of England in December 1968. In the early months of 1969, sterling's position improved, and this trend continued sporadically until both the franc and the pound were affected in May by another foreign exchange crisis based on expectations of a revaluation of the mark. Until the autumn of 1969, the possibility that sterling would be forced into another devaluation was a frequent cause of concern.

In Germany output continued to surge ahead in early 1969. Industrial production increased at an annual rate of almost 9 percent in the first half of the year, and unemployment declined further while job vacancies increased. Some restraining fiscal actions were adopted by the government, and the Bundesbank began to modify its policy of ease in a series of measures that included an increase in the discount rate from 3 to 4 percent in April. The trade surplus fell off in the first quarter but increased again for the rest of 1969, despite the November 1968 measures. Thus an indication that the easy money policy was being reversed, even though interest rates were rising elsewhere, was one factor in the revival of the belief that Germany's large trade surplus would soon lead to a sizable increase in reserves.

A speech by Finance Minister Strauss on April 29, 1969, suggesting that Germany might revalue as part of a multilateral realignment of currencies, set off a rush of funds into marks. Over the next 10 days, the exchange markets "witnessed the heaviest flow in international financial history." Germany's reserves increased by $4.1 billion, with funds coming from most European countries. On Friday, May 9, the coalition cabinet met for three hours of "intense debate" and decided against revaluation. An official spokesman told a news conference that the decision was "final, unequivocal and for eternity."[22] After the weekend new measures were introduced, including authority for the Bundesbank to impose minimum reserve requirements on foreign-owned deposits in German banks and an extension beyond March 1970 of the border tax adjustments that had been introduced in November 1968. Once again funds flowed out of marks, to the extent of $3 billion by early July.

After the mark crisis subsided and President Pompidou did well in the June elections, exchange markets quieted, though France continued to lose reserves. It was thus a complete surprise to the world to hear on Friday, August 8, that the French Government was devaluing the franc by 11.1 percent—the amount discussed at the Bonn meeting. The measure was well planned and cleanly carried out—so cleanly that, despite the rules of the Common Market, France did not consult its EEC partners.

Again the U.S. concern was to confine the devaluation—to keep other currencies from following the franc down. This effort was successful. The only nations that devalued with France were members of the franc area, mostly African countries.

Whether the French devaluation was necessary at all or in the magnitude undertaken is a legitimate question. French prices had risen over the past year, but by little more than in other countries. The deterioration of France's trade balance in the first half of 1969 appears to have reflected in large degree hedge buying of imports in anticipation of rising prices or devaluation or both. Import growth was abruptly reduced in the second half of 1969,[23] though industrial output continued to increase. The quick improvement in France's external position so soon after devaluation seems to fly in the face of all the economic analysis that suggests significant lags in the adjustment of trade to exchange rate changes. One is tempted to conclude that the French authorities were driven to devaluation not by the facts of their economic position but because they felt it imperative to put an end to the expectation that they would devalue.

According to *The Economist,* in a survey of France in 1972, "France devalued [in 1969] when the franc, if overvalued in terms of confidence, was not seriously overvalued in terms of trade. France thus emerged once again with an undervalued currency, an old recipe for success."[24]

The final act in the franc-mark drama of 1968–69 occurred immediately after the German election of September 28, 1969. In the weeks before the election, a speculative flow into Germany had commenced again, amounting to $1.5 billion, until the Bundesbank suspended foreign exchange operations on the Wednesday before the election weekend. The election results were not conclusive and when the Bundesbank resumed foreign exchange operations on Monday morning, September 29, it took in $245 million in the first hour and a half. It recommended, and the government agreed, that the mark be permitted to float. The market rate moved up but not in a spectacular fashion; presumably speculators were taking their profits rather than waiting for a sure peaking of the rate. The Bundesbank sold dollars (bought marks) each day, thereby "placing a floor just below each successive advance of the rate."[25]

When the Social Democrats and Free Democrats formed a coalition, there was little doubt that the government would acquiesce in revaluation. On October 24, a new parity was established at a level 9.3 percent above the previous parity. At the same time, the border tax measures and the special reserve requirement on deposits of foreigners in German banks were eliminated.

One may question whether the revaluation was sufficient, given the facts of the German position and the elimination of the border tax and rebate. For trade transactions, the additional revaluation amounted to 4.3 percent. But, as events were to show, the revaluation had a marked effect on Germany's non-trade transactions.

Participants in foreign exchange markets apparently had no question about the adequacy of the revaluation. Between the end of September and the end of December, funds flooded out of Germany in an amount that required the Bundesbank to sell $6.5 billion to support the new exchange rate. This reserve loss was partly offset by the maturing of earlier forward purchases of dollars by the Bundesbank so that the net reserve loss was somewhat over $5 billion. To finance this outflow the Bundesbank encashed U.S. Treasury notes it had earlier purchased, drew $540 million—its super gold tranche—from the IMF, cashed in or transferred a total of $550 million representing its GAB claim on the Fund, and sold $500 million of gold to the United States. In early January, the Bundesbank encashed, in advance of maturity, $540 million of U.S. securities it had bought in connection with military "offset" agreements in 1967 and 1968.[26]

The outflows from Germany, which came to an abrupt halt at the end of 1969, left German reserves at $7.1 billion, lower than at any time since early 1963. But over the next year, Germany's reserves increased again, by $6.5 billion, as the Bundesbank attempted to combat inflation and German companies borrowed heavily abroad while American banks were repaying debt to the Eurodollar market.

The expansion of the German economy continued rapidly in 1969–70. But the price stability of 1967–68 gave way in 1969–70. Wage advances had lagged during the recession and Germany had experienced a significant decline in unit labor costs, which enhanced its competitive position and, along with an adjustment of its tax system when it adopted a value-added tax in conformity with Common Market policy, helped to generate its very large trade surplus. German workers reacted to the lag in their wages in late 1969. From the third to the fourth quarters of that year, hourly wage rates in manufacturing industries jumped 5 percent and over the next four quarters they rose almost 16 percent.[27] As a result of rising wage costs and strong demands at home and abroad, German prices began to accelerate. This was the background for the Bundesbank's tight money policy in 1970–71 and for a series of fiscal policy measures designed to dampen the boom.

Meanwhile, the United States entered a recession in late 1969. The contrasting condition of the two economies helps to explain the contrasting policies, which in turn led to the flood of funds back into Germany and the decision in May 1971 to let the mark float again.

X

The Exchange Rate System:
A Reform That Failed

In the mid-1960's, the prevailing view among Treasury and central bank officials had been that the exchange rates of industrialized countries should remain fixed. The series of crises that began with the devaluation of sterling in November 1967 revealed how mistaken this view was.

Marius Holtrop, President of the Netherlands Bank, was more perceptive than most of his colleagues on this question. In a lecture in Frankfurt in November 1965, Holtrop discussed, among other subjects, the imbalance in payments between the United States and Europe. He examined, as one of four methods of correcting this imbalance, the possibility of "changes in parities." Admittedly with hindsight, he regretted that the German and Dutch revaluations of 1961 had not been larger. Acknowledging that "a reserve-currency country, even when fundamental disequilibrium vis-à-vis the rest of the world is manifest, does not have a free choice in the matter of changing the parity," partly because "a heavy loss would be inflicted on holders of reserves in the currency in question," he said that "the rest of the world is also unable to take the initiative for any change of parity in relation to the reserve-currency country, because coordination of such action is virtually impossible." He rejected floating exchange rates, "unless a large-scale unified European economic area had been created beforehand" and suggested that "the question should be studied whether it would not after all be possible to introduce greater flexibility into the rigid system of fixed parities." It was his belief that "agreement on the principles of the international adjustment process should precede the creation of new reserve media."[1]

It is a nice question whether monetary officials had their priorities right in the second half of the 1960's, when they devoted so much time and energy to the "liquidity problem" and so little to the "adjustment problem." It may well be that the American deficit could not have been eliminated—or reduced to tolerable size—until a new source of reserves was put in place. Observation of the reaction of a number of European countries to reductions in their reserves in 1969 strengthened this view. But even if establishment of a reserve-creating mechanism was a necessary condition for international payments balance— specifically the elimination or reversal of the U.S. deficit and the European surplus—earlier attention should have been given to introducing greater flexibility of exchange rates.

There were no echoes among officials in 1965–1967 of Marius Holtrop's farsighted statement. In the United States, the Joint Economic Committee's Subcommittee on International Exchange and Payments, under the chairmanship of Congressman Henry Reuss, had proposed in 1964 and 1965 an examination of the "advantages and disadvantages of widening the permissible limits of exchange rate variation" but did not question the "impressive record of exchange rate stability among major currencies." What the Subcommittee seemed to wish to have studied was a widening of margins around "pegged exchange rates."[2]

It was only in late 1968 that talk of greater exchange rate flexibility began to be heard. Even in early October, when the Fund and Bank held their annual meetings, there was not enough corridor discussion of exchange rates to be picked up by *The Economist*'s alert reporters.

After the November 1968 Bonn meeting, Chancellor of the Exchequer Roy Jenkins was reported to believe that it was high time to begin considering fundamental reforms of the international monetary system.[3] Since the SDR was already agreed to, he could only have been referring to the exchange rate system. At about the same time the editorial policy of *The Wall Street Journal* began to favor more flexible exchange rates (it has more recently reversed its position). Even I was quoted in *The New York Times* on December 26 as "not being against" consideration of techniques for limited flexibility of exchange rates. What I stressed was that the obstacles to greater flexibility could not be ascribed to a fetish for fixed rates but rather to political inhibitions, such as the German Government's concern about farmers.[4]

The Case for Greater Flexibility

Why was it that serious consideration of a more flexible exchange rate system did not begin until 1968? Among American officials, it was only in 1968 that it became evident that the substantial reduction in the surplus on goods and services was being affected by more than cyclical—and therefore reversible —influences. U.S. prices were rising more rapidly than those elsewhere. While capital flows were favorable to the U.S. balance of payments in 1968—and again in 1969—it was doubtful that these capital flows could be sustained over time. It was beginning to dawn on many of us that a realignment of exchange rates would probably be necessary if the U.S. balance-of-payments deficit was to be kept to manageable proportions. Given the inability of the United States to change its own exchange rate, there was no alternative but to seek revaluations of other currencies against the dollar.

The case for greater flexibility in the exchange rate regime rested not only on the U.S. situation but on what was happening in Europe and Japan. Germany had an enormous trade surplus, but political forces inhibited the German Government from revaluing the mark. Italy also developed a substantial trade surplus in 1968, as did Japan. What was needed was a way for countries to change their exchange rates routinely, without endangering the prestige of their governments. For countries in deficit, like France after May 1968, the same case could be made. If devaluation was to be a major political question, it was likely to be delayed and then, when forced, to be excessive. For this reason too a de-politicized procedure for "small and frequent" changes in exchange rates seemed desirable.

Reactions to Apparent Need for Greater Flexibility

In these new conditions, the U.S. Government began to consider the desirability of an improvement in the exchange rate system as it operated under the IMF Articles. Thus, apart from consideration of the current need for exchange rate adjustment by individual countries, notably Germany, study was begun in the Deming Group of a possible change in the Fund's exchange rate regime.

In August 1968, I circulated to a few senior officials in Washington a paper prepared by the Board's staff analyzing three proposals for "limited exchange rate flexibility": (1) wider margins for exchange rate variation around parity, (2) variants of sliding parities or "crawling pegs," and (3) sliding parities with wider margins. All of these proposals had been put forward in the professional literature by academic economists.[5]

In September Fred Deming quietly distributed to senior colleagues of a number of countries an outline that would provide a basis for discussion of wider bands and crawling pegs.

The German action on border taxes in November 1968 led to discussion of the advisability of introducing variable border taxes and subsidies as a device for balance-of-payments adjustment.[6] Such a proposal had been advocated by Keynes as long ago as 1931 as a substitute for a devaluation of sterling.[7] One of the arguments in favor of this type of proposal was that it would induce less speculative movements of funds than greater flexibility of exchange rates. And such a system would be usable by the United States without altering the dollar price of gold. A major disadvantage was that the taxes and subsidies would apply only to a part of the balance of payments, probably only trade. The result would be equivalent to a system of multiple exchange rates with different rates for different types of transactions. It was difficult to justify such a system on economic grounds.

A task force report on balance-of-payments policies, prepared for President-elect Nixon by a group of economists under the chairmanship of Professor Gottfried Haberler, stressed the desirability of dismantling controls on capital outflows and of achieving a greater degree of flexibility in exchange rates via wider bands and crawling pegs. The possibility of suspension of convertibility of the dollar into gold was discussed as a first response to an international crisis involving the dollar or as a transitional measure designed to facilitate other improvements or even as a permanent policy. In April 1969, the new administration took a first step in the direction advocated by the task force when it relaxed somewhat the existing restraints on the outflow of U.S. capital.

In early 1969, a group of professors and bankers organized a conference on exchange rates. This group, which came to be called the Burgenstock group, published in 1970 a collection of 52 papers analyzing exchange rate flexibility.[8]

The Executive Directors of the IMF were also considering the subject— in the light of possible "undue rigidity" of parities and of the scope for short-term capital flows.[9] The result of the lengthy deliberations in the Fund was a report published in September 1970.

Meanwhile, in the spring of 1969, U.S. officials held a series of bilateral technical discussions with officials of a number of other countries, in which limited exchange rate flexibility was explored.

The American Dilemma

The United States faced the dilemma that while it was clear that the international monetary system needed an improved exchange rate regime, it was less clear that any of the specific proposals under consideration would lead, soon enough, to a strengthening of the U.S. balance of payments. In fact, a crawling peg system of "small and frequent" changes in parities would probably work well only if it were introduced at a time of general balance-of-payments equilibrium. What this suggested was that a significant realignment of exchange rates between the U.S. dollar and European currencies (plus the Japanese yen) was desirable as a first step. But how could this be brought about?

For reasons emphasized earlier, the United States could not devalue unilaterally even if it could assume—which it could not—that the other industrial countries would stand still. The alternative was to persuade the surplus countries to revalue. But what leverage did the United States have? Only a threat to suspend the convertibility of the dollar, which, if carried out, would confront countries in surplus with the option of accumulating inconvertible dollars or revaluing their currencies. Like the nuclear deterrent, this was a weapon that it was preferable not to use. As Francis Bator put it, "it would be a bad thing for the United States to do, unless absolutely forced to it by others. As long as there is a chance for a reasonable, cooperative solution by consensus, it is wrong for a great power to settle matters by *force majeure.*"[10]

Yet persuading countries in surplus to raise the value of their currencies was not easy. When Germany finally revalued in 1969, no other country accompanied it, even though Italy and Japan also had substantial surpluses on current account.

Part of the resistance to a general upward revaluation of other currencies against the dollar stemmed from a belief in Europe that such an action would too easily take the United States off the hook, as it were, of worrying about its balance of payments. Many European officials believed that if they were to relieve the U.S. balance of payments by appreciating their currencies, the United States would never be subject to "discipline," since it would always feel confident that it could count on other countries to adjust *their* exchange rates if an imbalance in the U.S. payments position developed. They believed, in other words, that a willingness by them to revalue their currencies would encourage what came to be called a U.S. attitude of "benign neglect" toward its balance of payments,[11] as well as a relaxed attitude toward inflation on the part of American policy makers.

Officials in a number of European countries, with the exception of Germany, believed that it was only the "discipline" of the balance of payments that made it possible for them to make restrictive fiscal and monetary policies palatable to their own citizens. They tended to impute a similar state of mind to the United States. It is true that the international financial situation was a significant influence on the willingness of Congress finally to adopt a restrictive policy in 1968. But there have been other occasions—in the late 1950's, in 1971, and in 1973–74—when inflation was an important political issue in its own right in the United States.

Attitudes Toward Flexibility

The discussion of exchange rate flexibility dragged on through 1969 and into 1970. The temporary floating of the mark in the autumn of 1969 led to an addition to the list of methods of flexibility—a "transitional float" to a new parity.

At the Fund's annual meeting in the autumn of 1969, during which the German authorities permitted the mark to float, there was considerable discussion of the exchange rate regime. In his opening speech, Schweitzer referred to the intention of the Executive Directors to investigate greater flexibility of exchange rates.

U.S. Secretary of the Treasury David Kennedy treated the proposals for greater flexibility with a good deal of reserve. He recognized that there had been too much rigidity in exchange rates but stressed the "formidable technical and policy problems that will require careful study over a considerable period by national authorities, as well as international monetary bodies, before any consensus is possible." He summarized his comments on this subject by saying, "we believe that proposals for limited flexibility offer no panacea for present problems." And, "the subtle and unsettled technical and policy questions" are "a long way from fruition, if, indeed, some variant proves practical at all in the end." Nevertheless, he welcomed the Fund's intention to study the matter.[12]

This was hardly a resounding expression of support for movement toward greater flexibility. The U.S. perception was that while work on greater flexibility should proceed actively, with American support, it would not be constructive for the United States to adopt a *public* posture of activism on this matter.

The preference for a low-key posture reflected the basic dilemma in which the United States found itself. While the international monetary system might be improved by the adoption of "limited flexibility" of exchange rates, the basic U.S. balance-of-payments deficit was too large to be corrected in a reasonable period of time by the types of flexibility proposals under consideration.

At the same IMF meeting, Minister Giscard d'Estaing announced that France was prepared to participate in the studies of limited flexibility but warned against abandoning the principle of "fixed rates" and stressed that EEC countries have a "need for maintaining the conditions for the working of the Common Market, which cannot, obviously, survive daily fluctuations or 'crawling' uncertainty."[13]

Italian Minister Columbo showed somewhat greater enthusiasm for increased flexibility while President Zijlstra of the Netherlands Bank supported the notion of an upward crawling peg as "a solution for the problems of countries that wished to protect themselves against inflationary developments in the rest of the world." But such a system could be introduced, in his view, "only after elimination of serious imbalances that might still exist."[14]

Most Ministers from developing countries expressed opposition to the notion of greater flexibility of exchange rates on the ground that this would introduce one more uncertainty into what was, for them, already too uncertain an economic environment.

At the end of 1969, I summed up for the FOMC the developments of that year. After discussing the establishment of SDRs and the success of the two-tier system, I turned to exchange rates:

> This brings me to the third major development of 1969—the change in attitude toward using the exchange rate as an economic policy instrument. It was in 1969 that the British devaluation belatedly bore fruit in a startling betterment in Britain's balance of payments. It has been shown that exchange rate adjustment, once it is coupled with effective domestic policies, can shift resources to or from the foreign sector. Hopefully, the French and German experience will provide further confirmation for this proposition.
>
> The very fact that three major countries adjusted their exchange rates in a two-year time span has dispelled the idea, which was current earlier in the 1960's, that exchange rates should remain absolutely fixed, at least for major countries. It is now rather widely accepted that, as long as sovereign nations have independent fiscal and monetary policies and differential rates of productivity growth, and as long as they are unwilling to extend unlimited credit to each other, exchange rates will need occasional adjustment.
>
> All this being quite generally accepted, the debate at the moment is over the less important question of how and when exchange rates should be changed when they need to be changed—whether in smaller and more frequent steps or, as in the past, in large occasional steps. As you know, this entire question is now under study in the International Monetary Fund.
>
> As far as the United States is concerned, the role played by the dollar forces us to be passive, though not necessarily silent, in exchange rate policy. Since there are many reasons why the gold value of the dollar should stay where it is, our exchange rate against other currencies can be changed only as a result of decisions by other countries to change their exchange rates against the dollar. The United States has an obvious interest in trying to assure itself that the accepted procedures

for exchange rate adjustment will not contain a bias toward devaluation of other currencies against the dollar. This point takes on particular significance in light of our need, to which I referred earlier, to control the U.S. balance of payments over time. For these reasons, the recent revaluation of the German mark was an event of great importance, not mainly because of its immediate benefits to the U.S. trade balance, which will not be large, but because it is an important precedent. Unless countries in structural surplus are willing to revalue early in the game, those in deficit will be forced to devalue, and this could leave the U.S. dollar high and dry in terms of competitiveness.

One of the delicate problems we face at the moment is to convince other countries that the U.S. interest in a better regime of exchange rate adjustment is not motivated by a wish to find an escape from the consequences of inflation in the United States. The best way to persuade them of this is to persevere with a sustainable program of fiscal and monetary restraint designed to stop the inflation.[15]

The Group of Ten Deputies took up the question of limited exchange rate flexibility in April and July 1970 but did not carry it very far. On the whole, they were somewhat more sympathetic to greater flexibility than were their Executive Directors in the Fund. Most of the deputies favored flexibility in the form of smaller changes in parities, and among these there was some sympathy for an asymmetrical system in which upward movements of the exchange rate were more favorably regarded than downward movements.

At the end of May 1970, in the face of a sharply improving current account position and an influx of capital, the Canadian authorities decided to let the Canadian dollar float. Having observed the German experience, they preferred to move before being overwhelmed by speculative capital movements.

The Fund Report

The report on exchange rates prepared by the IMF was released in mid-September 1970. It discussed the achievements that the world economy had recorded under the existing par value system and went on to identify the problems that had arisen: undue delay in changing exchange rates when such changes were justified and the development of large disequilibrating capital flows. After rejecting freely fluctuating rates, substantially wider margins, and an automatic crawling peg, the report examined three proposals for reform: (1) prompter and perhaps smaller adjustments in par values, (2) somewhat wider margins, and (3) transitional floating rates to facilitate the establishment of a new par value.

In a guarded way, the report pronounced a favorable verdict on prompter

—and possibly smaller and recurring—adjustments in par values. The Executive Directors left for further study proposals that member countries be given a certain degree of leeway to adjust their exchange rates without prior Fund approval. They did not reach a consensus on a widening of margins. While the Directors did "not come to a final view on the various issues raised" by transitional floating, the report treats the matter with some sympathy.[16]

Given the wide basic differences of opinion among the members of the IMF, the report was hardly a revolutionary document. (In the course of lengthy deliberations in the IMF Board, it was mainly the Directors from Germany, Italy, and the United States who pressed for a form of the crawling peg.) While cautious, the document made its contribution (perhaps too little and too late) to the emerging view that the monetary system was in need of greater flexibility of exchange rates. The notion that the exchange rates of industrial countries should remain fixed was now dead.

End of the Flexibility Exercise

Meanwhile, the EEC countries, in pursuit of their aspiration to form a complete economic and monetary union by 1980, began to discuss a narrowing among their currencies of the margin for fluctuation of market exchange rates. At the annual meeting of the IMF in Copenhagen in September 1970 this subject was very much in the air alongside the broader question of increased exchange rate flexibility as discussed in the Executive Directors' report. From a global perspective, this effort of the EEC seemed to many of us to be ill-timed. When the world needed greater exchange rate flexibility, the EEC countries were talking about moving in the opposite direction in their relations with each other. But the impulse to narrow EEC margins was basically a political one. When it was implemented in April 1972, the decision was made by Prime Ministers while many EEC technical experts shook their heads in doubt.

In these circumstances the 1970 annual meetings of the Fund and World Bank were uneventful, except for a few demonstrations and some window-breaking by young Scandinavians who regarded the World Bank as a tool of imperialism even though, inside the meeting hall, Robert McNamara, President of the World Bank, was criticizing the United States for devoting too little of its national product to development aid.

Lukewarm support for greater flexibility was expressed by Secretary Kennedy and Ministers Schiller and Ferrari-Aggradi (Italy), while Minister Giscard d'Estaing was skeptical. Anthony Barber, Chancellor of the Exchequer in the new Conservative government in Britain, delivered a strong attack on floating exchange rates. Such a lecture to an audience of finance ministers and central bank governors in 1970 was like a sermon against atheism before a convocation of bishops.

The effort to introduce into the Fund a more systematic approach to flexible exchange rates did not come to a definitive conclusion. It was swamped by the speculative storm of 1971, and in any case there were significant political obstacles in other countries to a system of greater flexibility in which the dollar would not flex.

XI

The Road to Camp David

An abrupt reversal of the U.S. balance-of-payments position occurred in early 1970 as U.S. banks stopped borrowing from the Eurodollar market and investors abroad found U.S. stocks less attractive when prices on the New York Stock Exchange were falling. This change in the U.S. balance of payments did not at first create very much concern abroad. Britain and France absorbed a substantial amount of dollars and used them to repay debts and to restore their depleted reserves. And Germany was pleased to recoup the reserves it had lost after the mark revaluation in October 1969.

As late as September 1970, at the central bank governors' meeting in Basle and at the IMF annual meeting in Copenhagen, remarkably little attention was paid to the American payments balance. Part of the explanation lay in the increase in the U.S. trade surplus that resulted from the recession-induced slackening in import growth in the first nine months of 1970. That and the assumption that the runoff of Eurodollars by American banks was temporary (based on temporary interest rate differentials), led to the view that the large deficits would not last. This complacency soon gave way to a somber, more realistic view.

From Complacency to Concern About the Dollar

Pierre-Paul Schweitzer caused a stir at the Copenhagen meeting by suggesting in his opening address that the United States should be financing its deficit "by the use of U.S. reserve assets to the extent necessary to avoid an excessive expansion of official holdings of dollars by other countries."[1] American officials reacted with some ire to what they interpreted as an invitation to holders of dollars to ask the United States to convert them into gold, SDRs, or Fund positions. Schweitzer was only doing his duty; it was he who had, with enthusiastic American support, proposed the initial allocation of SDRs, which took place in January 1970. His proposal was based on the assumption that the U.S. dollar reserves of the rest of the world would rise only moderately. Yet in the first three quarters of 1970, the dollar liabilities of the United States to foreign monetary authorities increased by more than $5 billion.

In the fourth quarter of 1970, the U.S. export surplus declined, partly reflecting a strike in the automobile industry. At the same time, American banks accelerated repayments of earlier borrowings to their branches abroad. The overall deficit came to more than $3 billion in that quarter, bringing the total for the year to $9.8 billion. About two-thirds of this deficit was reflected in an increase in Germany's reserves as German companies borrowed heavily in the Euro-currency markets to avoid the Bundesbank's stringent monetary policy at home. Germany once again found itself in the position of trying to conduct a restrictive monetary policy while at the same time purchasing dollars in order to hold its exchange rate at parity. (Under the terms of the Blessing letter, Germany had little choice but to hold the dollars.)

As the reserves of other countries increased, some of them—notably Belgium, the Netherlands, and Switzerland—requested the Federal Reserve to use its swap facilities to provide them with an exchange value guaranty. Federal Reserve swap drawings on these three countries came to almost $600 million in the second half of 1970. In early 1971, these Federal Reserve obligations were reduced by sales of SDRs, gold, U.S. drawings on the IMF, and other means.[2] But U.S. swap obligations mounted again in the course of 1971.

Growth of world reserves in 1970 was abetted and complicated by the decision of a number of central banks to deposit dollars with the BIS, which in turn invested them in the Eurodollar market. As these amounts were loaned out by Eurodollar banks and spent by the borrowers in countries other than the United States, they ended up in the reserves of central banks. Thus a multiplication of world reserves occurred and the rest of the world's dollar holdings increased much more in 1970 than could be accounted for by the deficit in the U.S. balance of payments.[3]

At a meeting of central bank governors at the BIS in April 1971, attended by Chairman Burns, a holding operation on such central bank placements was agreed to in principle; a month later there was agreement in practice. The episode was strange. Here were central banks, already receiving what they regarded as excessive dollar inflows, managing their reserves in a way that aggravated their dollar inflow problem. But as so often happens, they may have focused on the specific effects of their actions rather than the general ones (that is, on the micro rather than the macro effects). From the viewpoint of the individual central banker, placing his reserves in the Eurodollar market permitted him to increase his interest earnings by as much as 1.5 percentage points, which in his eyes may have compensated for what was coming to be regarded as an increasing risk in holding dollars. But such placements simply magnified the dollar receipts of central banks as a whole. In any event, these official placements by central banks of Group of Ten countries stopped in the spring of 1971. And the agreement was carried forward in spirit even after August 1971.

The American payments deficit grew still larger in early 1971 as the differential in interest rates between the United States and European countries widened further. In the first quarter of 1971, American banks repaid more than $3 billion to their branches abroad and the official settlements deficit was recorded at $5.8 billion for the three-month period. German companies continued to borrow heavily—in fact they borrowed an amount almost equal to the repayments by American banks. Thus Germany's reserves increased by more than $2 billion in the first quarter.

At a Working Party 3 meeting in late March 1971, European officials expressed considerable dissatisfaction with the low level of short-term interest rates in the United States. They acknowledged the need to stimulate recovery from the recession but wondered whether more reliance should not be placed on fiscal policy. At the same time, the possibility of some reduction in European interest rates was discussed.

In early April, the Bundesbank and four other European central banks reduced their discount rates. American short-term rates began to rise in April and a convergence of interest rates seemed to be on the way. But by then speculative motives had become paramount and funds flowed massively to Germany.

Pressure on the Mark

In early April 1971, "authoritative Treasury officials" (Paul Volcker) spoke to a few journalists and conveyed the message that the United States expected no change in the exchange rate of any foreign currency.[4] Despite this statement and the narrowing of interest rate differentials, the Bundesbank had to buy dollars in large amounts, either spot or forward, during April. For the month as a whole such purchases came to $3 billion.[5]

At a meeting of EEC finance ministers in Hamburg on April 26, Minister Schiller apparently proposed that the European currencies should float or revalue together against the dollar. Minister Giscard d'Estaing responded by suggesting a devaluation of the dollar. Some of this leaked to the press[6] and stimulated further speculation in both the foreign exchange and gold markets. On April 28, the Bundesbank suspended its purchases of dollars in the forward market, permitting the forward rate of the mark in terms of dollars to rise to a premium over the spot rate. With German interest rates still above U.S. rates, the mark would have been at a discount in the forward market in the absence of speculation.

On May 3, four German economic research institutes recommended that the mark be permitted to float and a fifth one proposed an outright revaluation. The Economics Ministry was reported to have characterized these recommendations as a "useful contribution."[7]

On the following day the Bundesbank took in $1 billion in holding the mark at its upper margin. Some of the speculative funds were coming from other European countries. Also on May 4, Secretary of the Treasury John Connally issued a statement saying that "no change in the structure of exchange parities is necessary or anticipated." Both this statement and the Volcker statement a month earlier reflected the tactic that it would be unwise for the United States to appear enthusiastic about a German revaluation. A revaluation of the mark by itself, unaccompanied by other currencies, would be of only minor benefit to the U.S. balance of payments. It would, however, accentuate speculation against the dollar and encourage foreign official purchases of gold from the United States. The United States did not yet have a coherent plan for bringing about a broad and sufficiently large realignment of currencies. Piecemeal revaluations, while in the right direction, were unlikely to solve the fundamental problem. In any event, if Germany and possibly other countries did decide to float, the U.S. Government did not want to be seen to have urged them to take this action.

In the first hour of foreign exchange trading on Wednesday, May 5, 1971, the Bundesbank took in more than $1 billion. It then announced that it was suspending official operations. Austria, Belgium, the Netherlands, and Switzerland made similar announcements; these countries were uncertain what the next official steps might be.

A debate was raging within the German Government between those, led by Schiller, who favored floating and those who preferred to see Germany impose stringent controls on inflows of funds from abroad. I was deeply impressed then by a comment of a German friend who said to me that if his country started down the road of using foreign exchange controls, German "thoroughness" would assert itself. Those aging Germans who had carried out Shachtian policies in the 1930's would "come out of the woodwork," and the results might be an excessive and highly undesirable shift in Germany's basic stance away from freedom of international transactions. (American officials debated the desirability of a German or European float, but there was little action the United States could take to influence the decision.)

The EEC Finance Ministers met in Brussels on May 8 and 9. Schiller was calling for a concerted float of EEC currencies, but this was rejected by both the French and the Italian Ministers. Giscard was quoted as saying that a concerted float was "not plausible" because it would not be possible for the currencies of the Six to return to their old parities after a temporary float. Apparently France was not yet prepared to face up to a change in the exchange rate between the franc and the dollar, or at least not unless the United States made a move to devalue the dollar in terms of gold. Even if that were to happen, it was not then clear how much of a change in the franc-dollar rate France would tolerate.

In these circumstances, the Ministers adopted and issued a resolution acknowledging that some EEC members, in the face of excessive capital inflows, might for a limited period widen the margins for fluctuation of their currencies around present parities, which the member governments were determined to maintain. They also announced their intention to take measures to discourage excessive capital inflows.[8] With this vague announcement, the Germans and the Dutch received a reluctant blessing to let their currencies float, joining the Canadian dollar which had been floating for a year. The Belgian government did not join them but adapted its dual exchange market so as to curb capital inflows by letting the exchange rate for capital transactions move above the official parity. Also on May 9, Austria announced a revaluation of its currency by 5 percent and Switzerland revalued by 7.1 percent.

Thus ended the crisis of May 1971. Germany was enabled to gain better control over its domestic monetary situation once it was not obligated to purchase foreign currency in order to preserve its foreign exchange parity. (Otmar Emminger, referring to the problem of the coexistence of European currencies with the dollar, likened Europe's vulnerability to massive capital inflows from the United States to "being in the same boat with an elephant."[9])

Approaching the Climax

The German mark and the Dutch guilder did not float very far; after two weeks, the mark was 3.7 percent above its previous ceiling. Then the Bundesbank began to sell dollars in order to reduce liquidity in the German economy, and this action pushed the mark up by the end of July to a premium of about 5 percent. The German Government found the float useful as leverage over wage bargaining between labor and industry—which would be concerned, it was hoped, that too large an increase in wages and prices, together with a higher exchange rate, would reduce prospects for sales abroad.

Meanwhile, U.S. trade figures for April, announced toward the end of May, showed that the now small export surplus had given way to an import surplus as exports fell off and imports increased. The trade balance continued in deficit throughout 1971, 1972, and into the first half of 1973.

The deficit on official settlements increased from $5.8 billion in the first quarter of 1971 to $6.3 billion in the second quarter; of this latter amount more than one-third was accounted for by "errors and omissions"—unrecorded and presumably speculative outflows of dollars.

In late May 1971, Secretary of the Treasury Connally, who had formally assumed office in February, made his first appearance on the world stage when he addressed the International Banking Conference of the American Bankers Association in Munich. It was a luncheon speech, and it was delivered a few decibels too loudly. John Connally made it clear to the audience of central bankers, Treasury officials, and commercial bankers that he was a force not to be overlooked. While making a bow to international cooperation, he called attention to the shift in relative economic power from the United States to Europe and Japan. He complained specifically about restrictions on industrial and agricultural imports in other countries and about the failure of Europe to share defense burdens adequately. And he specified certain "unalterable positions" of the United States: "We are not going to devalue. We are not going to change the price of gold."[10]

The month of June saw some temporary easing of the speculative pressure against the dollar. The Bundesbank was selling dollars as a domestic monetary policy measure, and the exchange rate for the guilder tended to decline. But the reserves of Japan and Switzerland continued to increase substantially.

In the latter part of June, the Subcommittee on International Exchange and Payments of the Joint Economic Committee held a series of hearings on "The Balance of Payments Mess." Congressman Henry Reuss, Chairman of the subcommittee, supported by Senator Javits, was recommending an international conference or, in its absence, a severing of the dollar's link to gold, which would permit the dollar to float temporarily until an appropriate realignment of exchange rates had occurred.[11]

Paul Volcker, testifying for the administration, argued that it was necessary to distinguish between the basic or underlying deficit, which he put at $2.5 to $3 billion, and short-term capital flows responding to differences in interest rates among countries. "Solution of this balance-of-payments problem requires fundamental improvements in both our domestic economy and the international setting that will permit restoration of a stronger competitive position internationally." He stressed the need to overcome inflation at home and to secure a "fairer sharing of responsibilities in trade and defense." But, "we don't want to destroy the system of integrated capital markets, generally free convertibility, wide freedom of trade and payments, and reasonably stable exchange rates."[12]

In June and July 1971 interest rates continued to converge. In fact, the Federal Reserve faced the problem of U.S. interest rates rising rapidly at an early stage of recovery from the recession while the money supply was expanding at a substantial pace. Nevertheless, speculative movements of funds accelerated. The worsening U.S. trade statistics contributed to the speculation, as did discussion in Europe of a possible widening of margins around parities. The latter factor stimulated a heavy speculative flow to France in July. Some countries, notably Japan and Italy, managed to hold down their reserve increases by inducing their commercial banks to buy dollars and invest them in the Eurodollar market.

The problem was being seen more and more as a dollar crisis, in contrast with the view in 1968–69 when European currencies were under pressure. When news stories announced purchases of dollars by foreign central banks, as they did almost daily, these purchases were described as being intended to "support the dollar" rather than to prevent the purchasing country's currency from appreciating.

In late June President Nixon, concerned about the slow recovery from the recession as well as the persistence of inflation, met with his chief economic advisers at Camp David. It was decided to stick to the status quo for the time being. Secretary Connally, by now chief economic spokesman for the administration, announced the decision in terms of "four no's": no wage and price controls, no wage and price review board, no tax cuts, and no spending increases.

A Working Party 3 meeting in early July examined balance-of-payments positions on a "cyclically-adjusted" basis—that is, taking account of the effects of the recession in the United States and the excess demand in Europe. This analysis revealed that the basic disequilibrium in international balances in 1970 was considerably greater than what was shown by the actual figures. The U.S. current balance would have been about $3 billion worse and the current surplus of the EEC countries and Japan about $3 billion larger. This result clashed with the view then prevalent in Europe that the balance-of-payments crisis was mainly a matter of divergent monetary policies and short-term capital flows. This view had led many Europeans to believe that Germany's exchange rate could and should return to the May parity and that no other European currency needed to be revalued.

Throughout July 1971, official dollar reserves of other countries increased rapidly as speculation mounted. Early in the month, 36 Japanese economists proposed that Japan adopt a crawling peg in order to revalue the yen. The Finance Ministry announced that it had no such intention.[13] On July 13, for the second time in two weeks, Finance Minister Giscard d'Estaing publicly denied that the franc needed to be revalued, stating that a revaluation of the franc would hurt French exports at a time when the currency was in "equilibrium."[14]

A Gallup poll survey published on July 15 indicated that 50 percent of the American public favored a wage-price freeze.[15] At about the same time an AFL-CIO Conference on Jobs revealed that the American labor movement was becoming more sympathetic to import restrictions in order to protect employment in the face of rising imports.[16]

On July 18 the GNP figures for the second quarter were released, showing that, in real terms, output had advanced at an annual rate of only 3.6 percent while unemployment remained close to 6 percent.

Chairman Burns told the Joint Economic Committee on July 23 that there had been "very little progress in checking inflation" and that this constituted "a grave obstacle" to a rapid recovery in production and employment. Once again he urged a wage-price review board.[17]

In late July, I put on paper for Chairman Burns and Under Secretary Volcker a proposal for an American initiative at the September IMF meeting. The proposal was based on the belief that it was necessary to try to engineer a concerted revaluation by the industrial countries—not only because this was necessary to improve the U.S. payments balance but because a *joint* revaluation would reduce each individual country's resistance to up-valuing its own currency. To this end, I recommended that the United States propose serious immediate study of reform of the international monetary system in which all international reserve assets would be consolidated into a single new asset, a "super SDR." In essence the United States would be offering to give up the reserve currency role of the dollar; in exchange we could expect greater cooperation from other countries in revaluing their currencies and in agreeing to arrangements on trade and defense matters. Once the reform had been carried out, the United States would no longer be constrained from devaluing the dollar. Thus European objections to revaluation should be weakened, since the revaluation would be a one-time affair. This proposal, which might not have had much appeal to Secretary Connally in any case, was overtaken by the decisions of August 15.

On August 5, *The Wall Street Journal* carried a front-page story headlined "Monetary Troubles Erupt Anew, Prompt Talk of Devaluation." The dollar had come under increased pressure in the exchange markets in Europe, and both the French and Swiss authorities were reported to be taking actions to keep out speculative funds.

On the same day, the press reported a Presidential news conference at which Mr. Nixon stated that he would "consider" with an "open mind" such ideas as a wage-price board. This was a shift in attitude. It is likely that by that time President Nixon and Secretary Connally had had their "long conversation" in the Oval Office, at which the basic decisions of August 15 were adumbrated.[18] Apparently Nixon, Connally, and George Shultz (then head of the Office of Management and Budget) decided on August 2 to abandon the "game plan of gradualism" after the steel companies announced a price increase of 8 percent following a wage agreement granting a 30 percent rise over three years.[19]

The press of August 8 carried stories that France intended to purchase $191 million of gold from the United States in order to make a repayment to the IMF. What should have been noted was that foreign central banks had been extremely circumspect about buying gold, despite the enormous increase in their dollar holdings. As Peter Kenen has said, "No one country was large enough to blackmail Washington by demanding gold for dollars, but each was large enough to fear that its actions could undermine the monetary system."[20] In the first nine months of 1971, while U.S. liabilities to foreign monetary authorities increased by more than $21 billion, total foreign gold purchases from the United States came to only $840 million, of which more than half was by France to effect repayments to the IMF. Nevertheless, news of the gold purchase added further tension to markets already in turmoil.

At about the same time, the Reuss subcommittee issued a report stating that the dollar was overvalued and should be devalued. Its preferred method was for the IMF to exert pressure on other countries to revalue. If this failed, it favored unilateral action by the United States "perhaps by floating the dollar within specified limits." A number of members of the subcommittee dissented.[21] The Treasury issued a statement to the effect that the report of the Reuss subcommittee did not reflect a wide body of Congressional opinion; while referring to Secretary Connally's Munich speech, the Treasury did not explicitly reject the course proposed by the subcommittee.[22] The mark rose in value and the market price of gold increased to almost $44 per ounce, the highest level since the two-tier system was established.

Over the next few days, the outflow of dollars reached enormous proportions and the effects on foreign exchange markets drew daily headlines. But the press of August 12 reported that the dollar had recovered some strength in Europe following action by various countries to discourage speculative inflows. However, on both Thursday and Friday, major foreign central banks purchased about $1 billion. Some time during the week Paul Volcker made it known to senior officials in Washington that the crisis had reached its climax and something had to be done. This led to the Presidential decision to activate what had been agreed on August 2.

Camp David, August 13–15, 1971

On Friday, August 13, President Nixon and his top economic officials went off to Camp David for the weekend.

Some observers have said that the weekend meeting was triggered by a British request for coverage of its dollar holdings by means of a Federal Reserve swap drawing on the Bank of England.[23] It is true that such a drawing was agreed to on August 13, in the amount of $750 million. There was confusion in the communications between the British and American authorities as to just how large a drawing was being requested; the swap line would have permitted a drawing of $2 billion. The amount of $750 million, agreed to on Friday, August 13, was about equal to the Bank of England's dollar accruals in August. But, as Henry Brandon points out, the British request was no more than an irritant.[24] The decisions of August 15 were already well on their way.

At Camp David, Secretary Connally took the lead in setting forth the reasons for a change in the strategy of economic policy, domestic and international, and the possible elements of a new program. The economy was expanding too slowly, inflation was not subsiding, the trade balance was negative, and the overall balance of payments was in mammoth deficit. Included in the proposed program were: a 90-day freeze on wages and prices designed to break the inflation psychology, to be followed by a program of price and wage restraint; an investment tax credit of 10 percent to spur business investment spending; an import surcharge of 10 percent; and suspension of the convertibility of the dollar into gold and other reserve assets for foreign monetary authorities (closing the "gold window").[25]

The only major controversy in the program worked out during the weekend was the question whether or not to close the gold window. Chairman Burns argued that the rest of the program might be sufficient to convince the world that the U.S. payments position would improve. If that proved wrong and large conversions of dollars into gold were to take place, the gold window could later be closed. What Burns feared was widespread floating of currencies and consequent disruption of trade and investment. Volcker and Paul McCracken, Chairman of the Council of Economic Advisers, were somewhat concerned that the 10 percent surcharge plus suspension of convertibility might constitute "overkill." In the end, the decision was made to close the gold window and impose the surcharge too.

With the major elements of the program agreed, the rest of the weekend was spent working out the operational details.

On Sunday evening, August 15, President Nixon addressed the nation. He announced a 10 percent Job Development Credit (a tax credit to businesses that invested in new American-made equipment, to be cut to 5 percent after a year); he proposed repeal of the 7 percent Federal excise tax on automobile purchases and a speedup of the scheduled increase in personal income tax exemptions; he ordered a $4.7 billion cut in Federal spending and in foreign economic aid. A 90-day wage-price freeze was announced and a Cost of Living Council was established to set up a mechanism "for achieving continued 'price and wage stability' after the 90-day freeze is over."

On the international side, the President, referring to the many monetary crises and to the fact that "the speculators have been waging an all-out war on the American dollar," announced that he had directed Secretary Connally

> to suspend temporarily the convertibility of the dollar into gold or other reserve assets, except in amounts and conditions determined to be in the interest of monetary stability and in the best interests of the United States. . . . This action will not win us any friends among the international money traders. But our primary concern is with the American workers, and with fair competition around the world.

That last sentence sounded like pure Connally.

Further, after assuring "our friends abroad" about American intentions to continue to act as a "forward-looking and trustworthy trading partner," and to cooperate fully with the IMF to press for "the necessary reforms to set up an urgently needed new international monetary system," he announced a 10 percent "additional tax" on imports, which he characterized as a "temporary action" to make certain "that American products will not be at a disadvantage because of unfair exchange rates. When the unfair treatment is ended, the import tax will end as well." And further, "The time has come for exchange rates to be set straight and for the major nations to compete as equals. There is no longer any need for the United States to compete with one hand tied behind her back."

Finally, before the peroration, the President referred to the program he had just announced as "the most comprehensive new economic policy to be under-taken by this nation in four decades."[26] (In the text distributed by the White House on August 15, the words "new economic policy" began with capital letters. One wonders why none of Nixon's advisers remembered that Lenin had instituted an NEP in the early 1920's.)

Observers in England noted the similarity in word and tone of the Nixon speech to Prime Minister Wilson's devaluation announcement of November 1967. Both used the "speculators" as scapegoats and both assured their citizens that the actions would not affect them significantly.

President Pompidou commented that Nixon had succeeded in "the most difficult of all things, in making a virtue of necessity."[27]

Thus began a period of turmoil that was to last four months, until December. And, more significant, thus ended the old monetary system of par values and convertibility of the dollar. Whether the old system was worth preserving or whether the timing of its demise was appropriate we need not consider. The combination of circumstances—especially the inability of the United States to devalue its currency and the unwillingness of other countries to revalue their currencies—made the crisis inevitable. As is true of most crises, this one presented both dangers and opportunities.

XII

From Camp David to the Smithsonian:
August–December 1971

The measures announced on August 15, 1971, ushered in a four-month period of turmoil both in financial markets and in the political and economic relations among countries. This chapter traces these developments and the negotiations that culminated in the Smithsonian realignment of exchange rates in December and then examines the lessons of the events of 1971.

The Aftermath of August 15

Monday, August 16, happened to be a holiday in continental Europe, and foreign exchange markets were closed for the rest of the week in most countries. In Japan, the August 15 announcement was dubbed the "Nixon shock" and the stock market nosedived; the foreign exchange market stayed open and the Bank of Japan took in well over $2 billion in one week in an effort to hold the yen at its parity with the dollar.

On the evening of August 15, Paul Volcker and Dewey Daane had left for London in a special Air Force plane. There they conferred on August 16 with a hastily assembled group of their counterparts from Britain and some of the Continental countries and Japan. Concern was expressed to them about the impact of the surcharge in combination with what would happen in exchange markets when they were reopened.

Before returning to Washington, Volcker and Daane visited Minister Giscard d'Estaing in Paris and found him "relaxed."

The combination of the import surcharge and the suspension of dollar convertibility confronted many countries—those in surplus or those whose currencies were expected to rise in value relative to the dollar—with the option of continuing to add dollars to their official reserves or letting their currencies appreciate. The EEC Finance Ministers met on August 19 and France turned down a German proposal for a concerted European float, preferring instead to use exchange controls in order to hold its old parity against the dollar for trade transactions while establishing a floating exchange rate for capital trans-actions. Belgium had a similar two-tier foreign exchange market. The Bank of Japan, after taking in nearly another $2 billion in the second week after August 15, decided to let the yen float but continued to purchase dollars to dampen the yen's upward movement. Many countries imposed restrictions on the inflow of capital. By the end of August, all major currencies except the French franc were floating, but exchange controls were in widespread use and central bank intervention was substantial. Most developing countries continued to peg their currencies to the dollar.

Meanwhile the American import surcharge came under sharp attack. The EEC lodged a formal complaint under the GATT. An emergency meeting of Latin American officials in Buenos Aires issued a "manifesto" condemning the unilateral actions of the United States and asking that developing countries be exempt from the surcharge.[1] Some Europeans argued that the surcharge was distorting exchange rate relationships, making it more difficult for monetary authorities to judge "realistic parities" for their currencies.[2] As it happened, the surcharge applied to only 4 percent of France's total exports, compared with 9 percent for Germany, 16 percent for Canada, 29 percent for Japan, and more than 50 percent for Mexico.

The Job Development Credit was also criticized, since it was available to companies only if they purchased American-made equipment and therefore discriminated against imports.

Pierre-Paul Schweitzer, the Fund's Managing Director—who had been informed of the August 15 announcement only shortly before it was made and then viewed the President's speech on a television set in Secretary Connally's office—sent a message to all Fund members on August 19, rejecting "piece-meal approaches" and calling for prompt, collective, and collaborative action to reach agreement on exchange rates and other measures to "restore the system to effective and lasting operation." He expressed concern that, unless prompt action were taken, "the prospect before us is one of disorder and discrimination in currency and trade relationships."[3]

On the morning of August 23 Schweitzer, interviewed on the "Today" television program, stated that devaluation of the dollar in terms of gold was one "contribution" the United States could make toward restoring monetary stability. This contrasted with Secretary Connally's response, at a press briefing on August 15, to a question about the effect of the program on the price of gold: "We continue to anticipate that this will not change one iota."

At about the time of Schweitzer's television appearance, calculations of possible exchange rate changes prepared by the IMF staff leaked to the press. These included a 15 percent revaluation for Japan, slightly less for Germany, and 7 percent for France and Britain.[4] These developments did nothing to improve the relationship between Connally and Schweitzer; the freewheeling Texan and the sophisticated and occasionally sarcastic Frenchman had not hit it off well even before August 15. And the leaking of the Fund staff's exchange rate proposals caused unhappiness among officials of other countries, to whom the revaluations appeared to be too large.

John Connally

As Secretary of the Treasury, John Connally was the principal American spokesman and bargainer in the international negotiations that followed the announcements of August 15. Like most successful political figures, Connally is a consummate actor. As the saying goes, he "comes on strong," exuding self-confidence, never ruffled, physically impressive. Tall and handsome, immaculately and expensively tailored, his prematurely white hair carefully groomed, Connally makes his presence felt. He speaks articulately, forcefully, and assuredly. Yet, I've been told, he often appears exhausted after a public speech or press conference. Acting is apparently a strain.

Connally's Texas drawl and his physical appearance create an eerie reminder of Lyndon B. Johnson. Someone has called him an LBJ with "couth." In fact he had been a protegé of Johnson, had managed Johnson's election to the Senate in 1948, and had served briefly as administrative assistant to Senator Johnson in 1949 before returning to Texas to make his fortune.[5] He returned to Washington as President Kennedy's Secretary of the Navy in 1961 but left before the end of the year to run for Governor of Texas. James Reston noted in 1975 that Mr. Connally has always used Washington "like a swinging door: a rush of wind, a whirling sense of something important about to happen, a big smile, and there he is or there he goes, always in a hell of a hurry."[6] John Connally made a strong impact on President Nixon—perhaps because, as has often been said, Connally had many qualities that Nixon lacked.

Despite the nationalistic overtones in his Munich speech of May 1971, Connally seemed to have made an early positive impression on European officials. In September 1971 it was the turn of the United States to take the chairmanship of the Group of Ten. When, during the IMF annual meeting in September 1971, I discreetly asked a European friend why I had heard no complaints about the fact that Secretary Connally would be chairing a series of meetings in which the United States was endeavoring to negotiate concessions from European countries and Japan, I was told that Connally had "charmed" the European finance ministers and central bank governors.

Connally appears to be a strong nationalist but not an isolationist. Yet as Governor of Texas in 1963 he followed the recommendation of the Dallas National Indignation Convention by issuing a proclamation blessing the establishment of a "United States Day" as a counterpoise to United Nations Day.[7] In the economic sphere, he believed that foreign countries had been exploiting the United States for years by discriminating against American exports. It was time to change the rules of the game and to provide "fair access to world markets for U.S. products." This view was not groundless, especially as regards Japan, but it was certainly exaggerated. What it overlooked was that we too had taken actions to restrict imports, in part by getting other countries to limit their exports of steel and textiles to the United States.

Another indication of Connally's nationalism is revealed in the report that he proposed to President Nixon the formation of a dollar bloc as a counterweight to the power of the EEC. (This was rejected on advice of Henry Kissinger.[8])

Connally also believed that the United States had borne too large a share of the NATO defense burden. Thus he began the post-August negotiations with three objectives: realignment of exchange rates, reduction of foreign trade barriers, and better sharing of defense burdens. Somewhere along the way between August 15 and the Smithsonian meeting of December 17–18, the defense-sharing objective was dropped and the request for reduced trade barriers abroad was watered down to a few trivial demands that appeared to be related to President Nixon's election campaign of 1972. But these changes in negotiating demands came later. In the period immediately after August 15, the American position forcefully included this triple objective, with the added and more long-run aim of reforming the international monetary system.

Apart from the various facets of John Connally's nationalism, it is difficult to discover what principles motivated him as Secretary of the Treasury. One close observer characterized him to me as a man with "no idealism." As Secretary of the Treasury, he was, in my view, every inch the politician. While his keen intelligence enabled him to grasp the substance of the economic problems he was forced to deal with, he brought to the job no broad vision of how to improve the economic welfare of his own country or the world.

The Issues Identified: Deputies Meeting of September 3–4

Canadian Minister of Finance Edgar Benson called a meeting of the Ministers and Governors of the Group of Ten for September 15–16, 1971. This was preceded by a deputies' meeting in Paris on September 3–4. At this meeting Under Secretary Volcker unveiled the American balance-of-payments objective. What was called for, he said, was a swing in the current account of the U.S. balance of payments of $13 billion from what it would be in 1972. Virtually all of this swing would have to be in the trade balance. Volcker argued that with high employment in both the United States and its trading partners, the United States would have a deficit on current transactions of about $4 billion in 1972. Yet the United States should be a net supplier of capital to developing countries to the extent of about $6 billion per year. Furthermore, unrecorded outflows in the balance of payments would be at least $1 billion. Finally, for several years to come, the aim should be for an overall surplus (on official settlements) of $1 to $2 billion so as to restore confidence in the dollar. These estimates assumed that there would be no *net* flow of recorded capital from the United States to developed countries even in the absence of capital controls, which the United States had been employing over the previous eight years and wished to dismantle.

To achieve all this, the U.S. current surplus would have to reach about $9 billion, as compared with the projected deficit of $4 billion. This shift could be brought about by a combination of exchange rate changes, trade liberalization by other countries, and greater sharing of defense burdens.

These aims were not discussed in detail on September 3–4, but their presentation was a shock to the other deputies. A swing of $13 billion in the U.S. trade balance implied an equal reduction in the combined trade balance of other industrial countries. That struck them as a very large adjustment.

The magnitude of the needed exchange rate realignment was not discussed by the deputies, but the method of bringing it about raised the question of the gold price. Volcker and Dewey Daane restated the U.S. position against changing the price of gold. Most other deputies argued that, for both economic and political reasons, a small devaluation of the dollar in terms of gold was a necessary element in an agreement on a new set of exchange rates. Their case was based on the assertion that countries would find it politically difficult to make an adjustment of their exchange rates while the United States did nothing, apart from removing the surcharge. Furthermore, it was said, willingness by the United States to participate in the realignment by devaluing the dollar in terms of gold would facilitate an early agreement. It was also argued that as some countries revalued against gold while the United States devalued, the average price of gold in terms of currencies would not change significantly.

Two additional, but unstated, European arguments for an American devaluation were (1) that France would refuse to go along with a revaluation against the dollar, an action that would reduce the franc price of gold and cause domestic political dissatisfaction among French citizens, many of whom held gold in their mattresses or buried in their gardens, and (2) that those countries that had consistently held their reserves mainly in gold rather than interest-earning dollar balances would be revealed to have pursued an unprofitable policy if the dollar price of gold remained unchanged.

Another consideration, put forward explicitly, was that uncertainty about the future gold price would immobilize the use of IMF credit and the SDR, the value of each of which was tied to gold. Countries would be reluctant to assume debts to the Fund or to give up SDRs if there were a possibility that the dollar price of gold might rise. To this Volcker responded that the United States had tried to stabilize such expectations by asserting that the gold price would not change.

Ministerial Meeting, September 15–16

The Ministers and Governors of the Group of Ten met at Lancaster House in London for their first confrontation after the U.S. actions of August 15. They did not get to the point of negotiating but merely set forth their positions, much as had been done by their deputies in Paris earlier in the month.

The major differences that appeared in the positions taken by ministers concerned: (1) the size of the improvement to be sought in the U.S. balance of payments, (2) whether or not the United States should "contribute" to the realignment by a small devaluation of the dollar in terms of gold, and (3) whether or not the United States should continue to use capital controls in the future. No one questioned the desirability of a return to a system of "fixed parities."

Schweitzer stressed the urgency of agreement on a new pattern of exchange rates, arguing that because of restrictions on capital flows and the U.S. surcharge, floating rates by themselves would not bring forth an adequate and properly distributed realignment. He proposed a three-stage program of work: the first stage would include agreement on a new pattern of exchange rates and on the gold price, the adoption of wider margins, and abolition of the surcharge; the second stage would focus on other measures to improve the U.S.

balance of payments and new understandings about convertibility of the dollar; and a third stage would consist of negotiations on fundamental reform of the system, including the role of reserve currencies.

Italian Minister Mario Ferrari-Aggradi, speaking for the EEC, stated that the size of the balance-of-payments improvement sought by the United States was too large to be adjusted to by the rest of the world in a short period of time. While accepting the need for a realignment of currencies, he stressed that all countries should share in the adjustment in a way that would leave the average price of gold unchanged. Early removal of the surcharge was desirable. Finally, the principles of the reform of the system should include "fixed parities" subject to modification when they are no longer realistic, wider margins and "other means" of limiting short-term capital flows, reduction of the role of the dollar as a reserve currency, and a new form of convertibility.

Secretary Connally, forcefully presenting the case for the three U.S. objectives, had little to say about reform of the system.

Minister Giscard d'Estaing, absent on the first day because of a Cabinet meeting in Paris, came to Secretary Connally's assistance at a late stage of the meeting when Connally was resisting inclusion in the communiqué of Schweitzer's proposed "work program." That France was not in a hurry to reach an agreement was revealed by President Pompidou in a press conference on September 23: "But I am convinced that the desire to reach a conclusion at any cost in the near future would lead the partners of the United States to exorbitant concessions that in the end would finally make a balanced solution impossible."[9]

The Group of Ten communiqué simply identified the problems and set forth procedures for dealing with them. It requested the deputies to prepare a work program and to collaborate with the IMF in exploring ways and means of reforming international monetary arrangements. The ministers and governors noted that OECD's Working Party 3 would be assessing the scale of the balance-of-payments adjustment required for the United States and the implications for other countries.

In general, the meeting ended in a spirit of greater antagonism than it had begun with.

Annual Meeting of the IMF

The Ministers and Governors of the Group of Ten met again on September 26, the day before the opening of the 1971 IMF annual meeting. They agreed on a work program for the more immediate issues that included "the magnitude and the method of a realignment of currencies, the temporary adoption of somewhat wider margins around par, the abolition of the surcharge and some other measures, outside the exchange field, designed to improve the United States balance of payments."

The use of the word "method" in connection with realignment was inevitably interpreted by the press as a concession by the United States, since it implied the possibility of a devaluation of the dollar in relation to gold.

Karl Schiller who, with Bundesbank President Klasen, was co-chairman of the Board of Governors of the Fund and World Bank, stressed in his opening address the opportunities for reform presented by the "jolt" of the American actions. "Ideas that some time ago appeared overly ambitious are today examined as possible steps in a program of realistic reforms."[10] In his address as German representative, Schiller was more explicit. He condemned the use of "physical controls" on international payments, called for prompt adjustment of "unrealistic parities," and endorsed greater flexibility in the future system. He also called for control of international liquidity and "consolidation" of reserve currency balances.[11]

Secretary Connally's speech included the following offer: "If other governments will make tangible progress toward dismantling specific barriers to trade over coming weeks and will be prepared to allow market realities freely to determine exchange rates for their currencies for a transitional period, we, for our part, would be prepared to remove the surcharge."[12] While this offer attracted newspaper headlines and signalled a conciliatory attitude on the part of the United States, it elicited no discernible response from other countries. Connally's speech also included a reference to the need for adequate exchange rate flexibility in the future.

Most European ministers repeated the stance they had adopted at the two Group of Ten meetings; ministers from developing countries complained strongly about the surcharge, about floating rates, and about their exclusion from the negotiations.

One theme sounded by a number of officials was that Europe seemed to be heading for a slowdown in economic activity. If a recession should develop, it would be more unpalatable to accept a revaluation of currencies, which would tend to reduce the exports of European countries; therefore an agreement ought to be arrived at as soon as possible.

German officials were becoming increasingly concerned about the disparity between the mark and the French franc. By early October the mark had floated 9.5 percent above its upper limit in May, while the commercial franc was unchanged. On top of this, Germany was more affected by the U.S. import surcharge and the discriminatory tax credit on capital equipment. In early October, Schiller publicly accused France of adopting a mercantilist stand reminiscent of the policies of Colbert in the seventeenth century.[13] Among other currencies, the yen was 7.5 percent above its earlier upper limit, the Dutch guilder 7 percent, and sterling about 3 percent. The French commercial franc was slightly below the upper margin, while the financial franc was up 1.7 percent.[14]

During the IMF meeting Chairman Burns took an initiative designed to facilitate an agreement at the following Group of Ten meeting, scheduled for November. He asked Jelle Zijlstra, President of both the Netherlands Bank and the BIS, to take on the role of "honest broker" among the Group of Ten countries. Zijlstra was to meet with officials of each of the countries and to explore "the area of settlement." No one was to be committed to what Zijlstra came up with, but the hope was that the exercise would provide a basis for agreement. Though consulted by Burns, Secretary Connally was not particularly pleased with the Zijlstra mission.

The IMF meeting produced a resolution, which, among other things, called on the Executive Directors of the Fund to undertake a study of all aspects of the international monetary system and to report on measures that were necessary or desirable for its improvement.

The Gold Price Question

In his speech at the IMF meeting, Secretary Connally had said: "A change in the gold price is of no economic significance and would be patently a retrogressive step in terms of our objective to reduce, if not eliminate, the role of gold in any new monetary system." The first part of this sentence was seized upon, together with the language in the Group of Ten communiqué, as evidence that the United States would ultimately agree to an increase in the dollar price of gold as part of a realignment of exchange rates.

Senator Javits and Congressman Reuss introduced a concurrent resolution expressing the sense of Congress that "it would be fair to agree to some kind of change in the dollar-gold parity, but in a manner that is consistent with the articles of agreement of the International Monetary Fund and which will in due course be authorized by the Congress." The introduction of the resolution was intended, Senator Javits said, to determine just how Congress felt about the question, "because the general impression abroad is that Congress had a rather strong bias against doing anything" about the gold price.[15]

Even before the IMF meeting, Henry Reuss had spoken on the House floor to say that he had shifted his position on the price of gold. He now favored a dollar devaluation as part of a realignment—on the condition, among others, that "at no time in the future will free convertibility between the dollar and gold be re-established. The Treasury's gold window will remain closed."[16]

Was it correct to say that an increase in the gold price had no economic significance? The answer to the question depended on the features of the future monetary system; this was illustrated by the fact that Henry Reuss conditioned his proposal on the continued inconvertibility of the dollar into gold. Yet it seemed unlikely then that the rest of the world would be willing to live forever with an inconvertible dollar.

At the Camp David meeting of August 13–15 the gold price had been touched upon only lightly, and the shape of the future monetary system was not seriously considered despite Paul Volcker's efforts to introduce the subject. It was apparently agreed that the President himself would avoid the gold price question in public statements, while Secretary Connally and other officials would maintain the traditional U.S. position without involving the prestige of the Presidency.

Those of us who believed that a change in the dollar price of gold was more than a political matter—that it would have economic repercussions—had this consideration in mind: Any initial realignment of exchange rates that could be negotiated, even if it involved a U.S. "contribution" in the form of a dollar devaluation against gold, would probably not be large enough to restore a strong balance of payments to the United States. This was so not only because other countries would be reluctant to see their exchange rates rise very far against the dollar but because a decision by the U.S. Government to devalue would almost inevitably, for political reasons, have to be accompanied by a decision to phase out the existing controls on capital outflows. It was therefore likely that more than one realignment of exchange rates would be necessary.

Thus, if the United States were to raise the price of gold as part of the first realignment, the expectation of one or more additional gold price increases would be established. The initial devaluation would reduce the relative value of that portion of their reserves that countries held in dollars. The expectation of future devaluations would lead the many countries that held their reserves in dollars to try to protect these reserves from further loss in value. In the absence of a U.S. arrangement to compensate them for the reduction in the value of their dollar reserves, such countries would look for other means of safeguarding their reserves. This could involve purchasing gold in the market (the price was between $42 and $43 in the autumn of 1971), or diversifying their reserves by switching them into currencies (like the mark and the yen) that were expected to revalue against the dollar. A related point was that the effects of an increase in the price of gold would be distributed inequitably, since it was the poorer countries that held large proportions of their total reserves in dollars.*

A further element in the case against a gold price increase was the belief that it would strengthen the role of gold in the international monetary system. Those who, like Schweitzer, argued for a dollar devaluation often cited the desirability of maintaining the attractiveness of the SDR relative to the dollar, but since the value of the SDR was at that time linked to gold they were also recommending, implicitly to be sure, that the value of gold be enhanced relative to dollars.

Many who favored a concerted revaluation of other currencies against the dollar without a change in the dollar price of gold were prepared to see other changes in the system that would be welcomed by the countries that would be revaluing. We favored broad reform of the system, including a reduced role for the dollar as well as gold, and enhancement of the role of the SDR. But such an overhaul would take time, and it could not be brought about in the crisis atmosphere of the autumn of 1971.

In the end, it was the ability of France to hold out while other countries felt a more urgent need to end the crisis that led most of us, rightly or wrongly and with varying degrees of distaste, to capitulate on the gold price question. We comforted ourselves with the knowledge that the continued inconvertibility of the dollar would give the United States considerable leverage in future negotiations over reform of the system.

Negotiations on Realignment, October–November 1971

Working Party 3 met in mid-October to examine the size of the underlying imbalance between the United States and the rest of the world, under the assumption that most of the counterpart of a shift in the U.S. current balance would fall on other OECD countries.

The OECD Secretariat had produced estimates of the starting positions—the assumed cyclically-adjusted surpluses and deficits of the major OECD countries in 1972—and the implied changes in these positions if the United States were to move to a current surplus of either $6 billion or $9 billion.

---

*A friend who read these two paragraphs in draft asked, "Were you really so prescient?" In fact, the essence of what is set forth above appears in a document, dated March 21, 1971, prepared by me as part of our contingency planning.

Considerable disagreement showed up in the examination of these estimates; it was a blend of technical differences among the various delegations, differences in the aims of their countries, and, in the background, a realization that this supposedly technical exercise was the beginning of a negotiation. The officials who agreed that a substantial reduction in their country's current surplus was to be expected, would be affecting the negotiating position of their minister when exchange rate changes were examined at the next Group of Ten meeting.

As a result, while the United States was claiming that its current balance had to shift by $13 billion from 1972, the other major countries of the OECD could envisage, when their individual estimates were summed, a reduction in their current balances of only $3 billion, even though the exchange rate changes that had already occurred implied a shift of more than $3 billion in the positions of these countries. Therefore the OECD countries as a group (including the United States) appeared to have forecasts and objectives for their current balances that were incompatible. While the total OECD surplus with the rest of the world was estimated at about $11 billion, the United States wanted a current surplus of $9 billion and the other members of the OECD seemed to have a combined objective of $7 to $8 billion, for a total of $16 to $17 billion. The combined estimates of all the countries, including the United States, of their 1972 positions, cyclically adjusted, came only to $5 to $6 billion. Thus countries underestimated the strength of their positions before the assumed realignment and set forth aims that were too large to be consistent with the total OECD position after the assumed realignment.

Events in October supported the widespread belief that, despite his conciliatory tone at the IMF meeting, Secretary Connally was in no hurry to come to an agreement. There were reports that he had offered to reduce the surcharge selectively against countries that let their currencies float up freely.[17] This in turn is said to have led the German Government, concerned about unity of the EEC, to consider abandoning Schiller's policy of cooperation with the United States and adopting a "joint European solution."[18] This would presumably have involved the imposition of controls and a two-tier exchange market in Germany (as existed in France) as well as a common EEC surcharge on imports from the United States.[19]

On October 19 Denmark announced its intention to apply a 10 percent surcharge on imports. The Danish Prime Minister was quoted as saying, "Let's do like Nixon; you know he is my great example."[20] While pressure was building both in the United States and abroad for a relaxation of the surcharge, Secretary Connally was reported to have said that it "is going to stay

on for awhile because it frankly is to our advantage to keep it on for awhile."[21]
On October 27, Congressman Reuss proposed that President Nixon replace
Connally with Federal Reserve Chairman Arthur Burns as the "U.S. monetary
realignment negotiator."[22]

During all this, Secretary Connally was deeply involved in the establishment of Phase 2 of the U.S. domestic price-wage control program announced
on October 7. (It turned out to be a more comprehensive program than might
have been expected from the Nixon announcement of August 15.)

Testifying before the House Banking and Currency Committee on November 1, Chairman Burns said he had "grave doubts" that "time is on our side"
in the international monetary negotiations. This was interpreted as a disagreement with the Connally view.[23]

The finance ministers of the Common Market countries met at Versailles
in early November and agreed that they would demand that the United States
devalue the dollar against gold as part of a realignment. French Minister
Giscard d'Estaing also hinted that France would "probably not follow the
dollar down if the dollar were devalued."[24] In private conversations between
American and French officials, the French had consistently been vague as to
how much of an American devaluation they would stand still for. Reports
reaching Washington from Europe indicated that France would agree to a
devaluation of the franc against the dollar of no more than 5 percent. For this
and other reasons, Connally delayed the next meeting of the Group of Ten
until the end of November.

During a visit to Japan, Secretary Connally (he was dubbed "Typhoon
Connally" in the Japanese press) was quoted as saying that the international
monetary crisis would not be solved in the near future. "I don't think we are
about to have a settlement, because I don't think the various countries are
ready to settle yet." Furthermore, he said, "I look forward to a very relaxed
series of meetings."[25] The Connally visit to Tokyo was interpreted by the
Japanese as an effort to reach an agreement on currency realignment with
Japan first and then to use that agreement as leverage with European countries.[26]

On November 16, Secretary Connally gave a hard-hitting speech before the
Economic Club of New York. He deliberately took on the role of "devil's
advocate" against those who were predicting a trade war, protectionism in the
United States, and world recession as a result of current U.S. policies. The
speech was mainly a defense of his stance since August 15, and he seemed to
be aiming the defense at fellow Americans, who, he probably thought, were
undermining his bargaining position. One fact cited in the speech drew wide

attention: he had found that "while a Ford Pinto sells for $2200 in the United States, it sells for more than $5000 in Japan because of high tariffs and discriminatory commodity taxes."[27] Thus there was some basis for the Secretary's complaints about foreign barriers to U.S. exports.

In these circumstances, it is reported, Henry Kissinger (at that time the National Security Adviser to the President) and Arthur Burns had become increasingly concerned about the economic and foreign policy effects of a continued tough stand by the United States, and they brought these concerns to the attention of President Nixon.[28] Nixon held a lengthy meeting, including a working lunch, with Connally and Burns on November 24. Evidently it was then that Nixon signalled to Connally that the time had come to reach a settlement or at least to lift the import surcharge. Connally is said to have gotten the message and without overt pressure swung around during that meeting to the position that an early settlement was desirable. The next day Arthur Burns issued a brief press statement saying that the President expects "definite progress" to be made at the Group of Ten meeting scheduled for the next week in Rome and that "the American delegation will do what it can to contribute to this result."[29] The word "contribute" had taken on a meaning of its own. If Burns used the word advisedly, he was signalling a readiness of the United States to devalue as part of a settlement.

It may be a coincidence but on the next day the President of the Bundesbank, Karl Klasen, was reported to believe that "reiterated American refusals to devalue the dollar should not be taken too seriously."[30]

The optimism about the upcoming Rome meeting turned out to be unrealistic. A Pompidou-Nixon meeting had been scheduled for mid-December and President Pompidou was unlikely to permit his finance minister and potential political rival to agree to a settlement at Rome; he would prefer to bring off such an agreement with the United States himself. As someone put it, the Rome meeting might turn out to be "an indispensable failure."

Meanwhile, Jelle Zijlstra had managed to complete his mission in complete secrecy and to circulate a "working paper" to the Ministers and Governors of the Group of Ten before their scheduled meeting at the end of November. He had visited all the capitals, but, as it happened, Secretary Connally was in Japan when Zijlstra went to Washington.

Zijlstra's paper, citing the various urgent reasons for a prompt settlement and the lack of agreement revealed at Working Party 3, proposed a swing in the U.S. current balance of somewhere between the $8 billion that had been put forward by the staffs of the OECD and IMF and the $13 billion figure proposed by the United States. The exchange rate changes he proposed, which included a modest devaluation of the dollar against gold and appreciations by the major surplus countries, appeared too small to Connally and Volcker (and to Federal Reserve analysts) to accomplish the trade balance swing that Zijlstra himself regarded as reasonable. While Connally and Volker thought that, on balance, Zijlstra's exercise hindered the achievement of a satisfactory settlement, Arthur Burns later characterized Zijlstra's effort as advancing the consensus by making it possible to think constructively and in concrete terms.[31] It provided, he believes, a base from which to start negotiating.

The Deputies and then the Ministers and Governors of the Group of Ten met in the Palazzo Corsini in Rome from November 29 to December 1, 1971. At the deputies' meeting, Under Secretary Volcker circulated a statement of U.S. proposals. After reaffirming the need for a substantial swing in the U.S. balance of payments, the statement noted that other countries apparently do not contemplate exchange rate and other actions large enough to bring about the needed balance-of-payments change. Given the desire for a prompt settlement and for removal of the surcharge, the statement proposed that the 10 percent surcharge and the discriminatory element of the investment tax credit be eliminated on these conditions: (1) an average appreciation of other OECD currencies of 11 percent in relation to dollar exchange rates of May 1971 (which would, Volcker stressed, fall well short of the needed revaluation), (2) early decisions on some trade concessions, especially in the agricultural area, (3) progress in sharing defense expenditures, (4) a widening of margins for exchange rates to 3 percent above and below the new exchange rates, and (5) abolition of two-tier exchange markets. All of this presumed no change in the official price of gold, no convertibility of the dollar into other reserve assets, and a relaxation of U.S. capital controls.

Volcker said the statement was offered in response to requests for a more precise presentation of the U.S. position and intended as a practical contribution toward a solution. He added that the statement would be given to the press that evening.

The remainder of the deputies' meeting was taken up with reactions to the U.S. intention to publish the statement. Almost all the other deputies tried to persuade Volcker not to publish it on the grounds that it would prejudice the ministers' negotiations beginning the next day and would disturb financial markets. After contacting Secretary Connally by phone, Volcker finally agreed to withhold the statement from the press. Nevertheless, the essense of the proposal appeared in the newspapers, attributed to "conference sources."[32] As far as I know, the source was not American.

The ministerial meeting began with some preliminary statements of position and then went into executive session. With Secretary Connally as chairman of the Group of Ten, Paul Volcker and Arthur Burns represented the United States.

At one point Volcker said to the group, since you've been pressing for a U.S. devaluation, let's talk about it. Let's take a hypothetical case. Suppose the United States agreed to devalue by 10 percent or 15 percent. What can we expect from other countries? Connally, as chairman, picked up the point, suggesting that the "hypothetical" discussion start with a U.S. devaluation of 10 percent (Volcker would have preferred that he begin with 15 percent). A lengthy silence ensued. Connally sat patiently, making no effort to break it. There was much private conferring.

Economics Minister Schiller finally ended the silence by stating the maximum revaluation against the dollar his government could accept. Others followed, and it became clear that once the United States had indicated a willingness to devalue, a number of the European ministers were trying to persuade the American officials to minimize the devaluation. After asking over a three-month period for a U.S. "contribution," they were now requesting that the contribution not be too large. While it would have been unacceptable at that time for any of the other members of the Group of Ten to follow the U.S. devaluation even part way, some of them wished to leave their parities in terms of gold unchanged when the U.S. devalued. Thus the larger the U.S. devaluation, the larger would be their appreciation against the dollar.

The two-day meeting was punctuated by frequent recesses during some of which the EEC ministers and governors caucused. A major question for them was the relationship among their own currencies, apart from what might be agreed on their collective movement against the dollar.

One of the EEC caucuses went on much longer than had been expected and Secretary Connally and Japanese Minister Mizuta sat waiting in lonely splendor at the large table. In frustration, Connally suddenly stood up and said, "Let's go to lunch." At another point the meeting was delayed while Minister Giscard d'Estaing went to the French Embassy to phone President Pompidou.

Although a number of participants believed it was possible to reach an agreement if the Rome meeting was extended another day, it seems quite certain that Giscard did not have, and could not get, the authority to settle. Since both the British and Italians were strongly resisting a large appreciation of their currencies relative to the dollar, he was able to be relatively passive.

The Americans, on the other hand, were prepared for an agreement on exchange rates and related trade matters in Rome. (The chief U.S. trade negotiator, William Eberle, was there, ready to talk to his EEC counterparts.

But few of them were in Rome.) Probably President Nixon would have preferred not to have to negotiate about the gold price with Pompidou in December. But because of the French stance and the inadequacy of the maximum realignment that seemed to be negotiable, the Rome meeting broke up without agreement. Another meeting was scheduled for December 17–18 in Washington, following the Nixon-Pompidou get-together.

At a press conference at Andrews Air Base upon our return to Washington, Secretary Connally refused to characterize the 10 percent devaluation as an "offer" by the United States but merely one of several "assumptions" that were made to encourage discussion.

December 1971: Azores and Smithsonian Meetings

News stories about the Rome meeting and the "hypothetical" 10 percent dollar devaluation led in early December to renewed upward pressure on European exchange rates and, in turn, to a further tightening of controls on inflows of funds, especially in France and Italy.

In the course of a visit to Washington, Prime Minister Pierre Trudeau of Canada announced publicly on December 6 that the Canadian dollar would continue to float even after an agreed realignment involving the U.S. dollar, the yen, and European currencies.[33] Meanwhile, Canada and a few other countries had been pressing for exemption from the surcharge.

On December 9, William Eberle began discussions in Brussels with EEC officials on trade concessions. The next day, newspapers reported that Common Market officials were "astounded" at the U.S. demands,[34] although in fact these demands were hardly news to them. A similar meeting between American and Japanese officials was taking place in Honolulu. Neither of these meetings produced tangible results.

The Secretary General of the United Nations Conference on Trade and Development (UNCTAD), Perez-Guerrero, sent a message to Schweitzer about the differential effects on countries' reserves of a 10 percent increase in the price of gold. Developing countries, which hold relatively little of the world's official gold reserves, would benefit much less from the "windfall gain" than industrial countries. Furthermore, he said, the increase in the value of gold reserves might jeopardize further issuance of SDRs.[35]

On December 13–14, Presidents Pompidou and Nixon met in the Azores, accompanied by their finance ministers and other officials, including Henry Kissinger and Paul Volcker. After the first day, Secretary Connally told the press: "In my judgment we can't keep on month after month after month holding these Group of Ten meetings without some specific results." Following a series of bilateral Presidential meetings scheduled with France, Germany, Britain, and Japan, "if we can't resolve it in a reasonable time thereafter, then I think we ought to agree that we can't agree."[36] The Secretary of the Treasury was not aching for an agreement.

But that evening and the next day, President Nixon settled the matter. He and Pompidou, after much private discussion of monetary matters—a subject that fascinated Pompidou but, it is said, made Nixon's eyes glaze over—agreed that the dollar would be devalued by raising the price of gold from $35 to $38 per ounce.[37]

A communiqué was issued the next day announcing "a broad area of agreement on measures necessary to achieve a settlement at the earliest possible date of the immediate problems of the international monetary system." The Presidents agreed, in cooperation with other nations, to work toward a realignment of exchange rates "through a devaluation of the dollar and revaluation of some other currencies." They also agreed on wider margins, and President Pompidou confirmed that France, together with other EEC countries, "was preparing the mandate which would permit the imminent opening of negotiations with the United States in order to settle the short-term problems currently pending and to establish the agenda for the examination of fundamental questions in the area of trade." That circumlocution apparently satisfied President Nixon on the trade issue.

The communiqué, after noting that President Nixon had underscored the contribution of U.S. measures to restore wage-price stability and productivity to international equilibrium "and the defense of the new dollar exchange rate," stated that the Presidents agreed that discussions should be undertaken promptly "in appropriate forums" to resolve fundamental and interrelated issues of monetary reform.[38]

What was not stated, though it was implied by Nixon's reference to defense of the dollar through wage-price stability, was agreement by Pompidou not to press for an early return to convertibility of the dollar. That was the *quid pro quo* for U.S. willingness to raise the price of gold. Not mentioned either was the U.S. intention to drop the surcharge when agreement was reached on realignment. The amount of the dollar devaluation agreed between France and the United States did not leak out before the Group of Ten Ministers and Governors convened in Washington on December 17.

On December 16 a joint meeting was held of the Executive Directors of the IMF and the Deputies of the Group of Ten. This provided an opportunity for the representatives of countries outside the Group of Ten to state their views. A number of them expressed opposition to an increase in the price of gold and to greater exchange rate flexibility. They stressed the desirability of conducting monetary reform discussions in a forum that would involve representation of all IMF members. Schweitzer reported their views to the Group of Ten.

The Ministers and Governors of the Group of Ten convened in the romanesque red sandstone Smithsonian Institution Building (the original Smithsonian structure, completed in 1855) on the Mall in Washington on Friday, December 17. Inside the meeting room, with its small ribbed windows, a modern lamp had been temporarily installed at each seat around the table, creating an anachronous clash with the decor of the room. Again the ministers and governors met in executive session, each country having three persons in the room. The United States had Burns, Volcker, and Daane—plus Connally as chairman of the meeting.

We deputies and advisers killed time by playing bridge or otherwise amusing ourselves between breaks in the meeting. On Saturday morning I was called out of a bridge game to work with two American colleagues on a draft communiqué that Secretary Connally hoped to distribute that afternoon.

The frequent comings and goings of ministers and governors from the meeting room—to confer with their advisers or to phone their capitals, in some of which cabinet meetings were being held—made it possible for those of us in the lounge to keep track of the bargaining positions.

The first order of business was to agree on procedures. It was clear that trade negotiations could not be completed at this meeting. If agreement could be reached on realignment of exchange rates, the United States would wish to withhold either the gold price increase or suspension of the import surcharge. It was accepted that removal of the surcharge would accompany an immediate realignment but that the U.S. administration would delay submission of the gold price increase to Congress until after the trade matters had been settled.

The remainder of the two-day meeting was devoted mainly to the realignment, with Connally, Burns, and Volcker skillfully wheedling the various ministers to maximize the appreciation of their currencies relative to the dollar. As a basis for discussion, Volcker distributed a table that assumed a 9 percent increase in the dollar price of gold and showed proposed changes in the exchange rates of other countries in relation to the dollar and to gold as well as the weighted average change in each exchange rate. The table revealed that, apart from the United States, Japan, Germany, and Switzerland, the effective or weighted average change proposed for other countries was minimal.* The appreciation of these other currencies relative to the dollar would simply prevent their effective exchange rates from depreciating as a result of the appreciations of the yen, the mark, and the Swiss franc.

At the suggestion of Minister Giscard d'Estaing, the proposed U.S. dollar devaluation was reduced slightly so that it came out precisely to the figure agreed by Nixon and Pompidou at the Azores. With that charade behind them, the negotiators spent their time on these major problems: (1) Canada's unwillingness to establish a new parity, its currency having floated from $0.925 to over $1 since May 1970 and its balance-of-payments prospects uncertain; (2) the desire of Japan to hold down its appreciation against the dollar and not to move up too much more than Germany; (3) the preoccupation of European ministers with the interrelationships among their own currencies, whatever the degree of appreciation against the dollar; and, related to the previous point, (4) the reluctance of the Italian and Swedish ministers to allow their currencies to stand still against a devaluation of the dollar by 7.9 percent.†

Whenever the ministers seemed to arrive at an impasse, Secretary Connally would remind them that continued generalized floating was always an alternative to an agreed realignment.

Minister Schiller, who had all along been the least recalcitrant man around the table, broke the logjam. After a phone conversation with Chancellor Brandt, he reentered the room to announce that a lengthy cabinet meeting in Bonn had authorized him to agree to a revaluation of the mark against the dollar by 13.57 percent (a new exchange rate of 3.22 marks per dollar). At the end of the phone conversation Brandt had said to Schiller, "Mr. Minister, God save you." Japanese Minister Mizuta then fell into line (following a telephone call to Tokyo), agreeing to a new yen-dollar rate of 308, implying a yen revaluation against the dollar by 16.9 percent.

After a brief adjournment, Secretary Connally announced that President Nixon was prepared to come over from the White House to congratulate the group on its accomplishment.

In the interim, the Italian delegation returned to the room to announce that

---

*The "effective" change in a country's exchange rate is the change, not in relation to a single currency—for example, the dollar—but in relation to the currencies of all its major trade partners.

†An increase in the price of gold from $35 to $38 per ounce, or 8.57 percent, implies a devaluation of the dollar in terms of gold, and of currencies whose exchange rates would remain unchanged in gold value, from 1/35 to 1/38 or 7.9 percent. In general, an increase in the dollar price of gold by r percent implies a devaluation of the dollar by $\frac{r}{1 + r}$ percent and an appreciation of other currencies by r percent. If another currency revalues in terms of gold by s percent while the dollar price of gold rises by r percent, the other currency appreciates against the dollar by $(1 + r)(1 + s) - 1$, which is slightly larger than $r + s$.

they could not stand still with France and Britain but would have to devalue the lira by 1 percent against gold, making their appreciation against the dollar 7.48 percent instead of 8.57 percent. Sweden did the same.

After some haggling, it had been agreed that new temporary margins of 2.25 percent above and below exchange rates would be established. Countries changing their parities in terms of gold might adopt "central rates" rather than new parities. Given the uncertainties, central rates, which had a less fixed connotation than parities, were appealing; they could be altered with less legal and political complications than par values. Among the Group of Ten countries, only France and Britain were retaining their old parities.

Before the ministers and governors had a chance to consider the draft communiqué, President Nixon arrived and spoke to the group, still in executive session. Then we all trooped over to the nearby Air and Space Museum, where the press had been incarcerated for two days amidst vintage aeroplanes and modern rockets. President Nixon, flanked by Connally, Burns, Volcker and Daane, was on a platform, in the glare of TV lights, while the finance ministers, central bank governors, and their associates stood to one side, separated by ropes from the crowd of reporters and cameramen.

President Nixon, exercising his penchant for hyperbole and repeating what he had said inside the meeting room, announced "the conclusion of the most significant monetary agreement in the history of the world." He gave no details of the agreement.[39] It would be left to each country to announce the change in its exchange rate.

The ministers and governors returned to complete their communiqué and the meeting adjourned shortly after 8:00 P.M. on Saturday, December 18.

The communiqué noted that agreement had been reached "on an interrelated set of measures designed to restore stability to international monetary arrangements and to provide for expanding international trade," including a pattern of exchange rate relationships. It reported that Canada would temporarily maintain a floating exchange rate "and intends to permit fundamental market forces to establish the exchange rate without intervention except as required to maintain orderly conditions." While Canada was treated as something of a pariah at that time, its decision to float appeared considerably more respectable later.

The communiqué announced agreement on exchange rate margins of 2.25 percent and urged countries outside the Group of Ten, in reaching decisions about their exchange rates, to avoid "seeking improper competitive advantages."

It was stated that trade negotiations were under way and that the United

States would propose a devaluation of the dollar in terms of gold to $38 per ounce "as soon as the related set of short-term measures is available for Congressional scrutiny." The 10 percent import surcharge and the related provision of the Job Development Credit would be suppressed immediately.

The communiqué concluded:

> Ministers and Governors agreed that discussions should be promptly undertaken, particularly in the framework of the IMF, to consider reform of the international monetary system in the longer run. It was agreed that attention should be directed to the appropriate monetary means and division of responsibilities for defending stable exchange rates and for insuring a proper degree of convertibility of the system; to the proper role of gold, of reserve currencies, and of Special Drawing Rights in the operation of the system; to the appropriate volume of liquidity; to reexamination of the permissible margins of fluctuation around established exchange rates and other means of establishing a suitable degree of flexibility; and to other measures dealing with movements of liquid capital. It is recognized that decisions in each of these areas are closely linked.[40]

Sequels to the Smithsonian Agreement

There is no single correct answer to the question of how much the dollar was devalued or how much other currencies were appreciated by the Smithsonian agreement. Compared with May 1971 parities, the yen went up 16.9 percent, the mark 13.6 percent, the Swiss franc 13.9 percent, the Dutch guilder and the Belgian franc 11.6 percent, the pound and the French franc 8.6 percent, and the Italian lira and the Swedish krona 7.5 percent, *all in terms of their dollar value.* But these percentages exaggerate the extent of the upvaluations of these currencies because they ignore the relationship of each currency to other non-dollar currencies. Various weighted average or effective exchange rates can be computed, but there is no obviously correct set of weights, and the results vary with the weighting system used.

Calculations by the Federal Reserve staff immediately after the Smithsonian meeting showed a devaluation of the dollar of between 6.5 percent and 7.75 percent (depending on the weights chosen) against all countries, many of which did not change their rates in relation to the dollar. Against Group of Ten currencies, the devaluation appeared to be about 10 percent; putting it the other way round, the currencies of Group of Ten countries appreciated by somewhat more than 11 percent.

We estimated that after the effects of the exchange rate changes had worked themselves through, which could take two or three years, the impact on the U.S. trade balance would be about $8 billion from 1972 levels.[41] Most of the counterpart would show up in reduced trade surpluses for Germany and Japan, for which the implied effective exchange rate appreciations came to about 4.75 percent and 11.25 percent respectively. For other countries the implied effective appreciation was: Switzerland, about 6 percent; Belgium, about 3.75 percent; the Netherlands, about 3.25 percent; Britain and Italy, about 1.75 percent; and France, about 0.25 percent.

Thus we estimated the trade balance results at considerably less than the $13 billion put forward initially as the U.S. objective. On the other hand, it was possible that the exchange rate realignment would affect elements of the balance of payments other than the trade balance. Non-trade transactions such as foreign travel and investment receipts could be influenced favorably, and so could capital flows.

Whatever the ultimate effects might be, the initial results of the realignment were expected to be perverse for two reasons. First, it was normal that a change in exchange rates would affect prices of goods traded internationally before it affected the quantity of trade. For a country that devalues, the prices of its exports fall, in terms of foreign currencies, and only later, in response to the price decline, do exports increase. In the interval export receipts decrease. Similar effects occur on the import side.[42] (This phenomenon is sometimes referred to as the J-curve.) In trying to estimate the lags involved, one had to remember that a number of currencies had begun to move up against the dollar before December—the Canadian dollar as long ago as May 1970.

The second reason why the initial impact of the realignment might be perverse, or at least delayed, was that the United States was in the process of emerging from a recession while European countries and Japan, where output growth had slowed in 1971, were expected to experience either further reductions or, at best, slower expansion than the American economy. Thus U.S. import demand was likely to increase more rapidly than foreign demand for U.S. exports, apart from the effects of the realignment. As it turned out, the American trade deficit, which had amounted to $2.7 billion in 1971, was almost $7 billion in 1972. It was only in early 1973 that the trade balance began to show the effects of the exchange rate realignment.

Another uncertainty had to do with the amount of capital that would return to the United States following the realignment. In 1971, the balance of payments showed an enormous deficit on official settlements—just under $30 billion. Of this amount, about one-third was unrecorded (that is, shown as errors and omissions), presumably reflecting mainly leads and lags in payments. Recorded outflows of short-term capital exceeded $10 billion. There was some hope or expectation that a large portion of these funds would move back to the United States, just as speculative flows had been unwound following the German revaluation of 1969. But this was not to be. There was undoubtedly some reflow; for example, errors and omissions, which were negative to the extent of almost $2 billion in the fourth quarter of 1971, were positive by $1.2 billion in the first quarter of 1972. And for 1972 as a whole, the deficit on official settlements ($10.4 billion) was smaller than the basic deficit (the deficit on current transactions plus long-term capital); thus there was a net inflow of short-term capital.

The failure of a more substantial reflow to develop was attributed to uncertainties as to whether the new exchange rates were durable. The estimated swing in the U.S. trade balance was considerably smaller than what American officials had been calling for in the autumn of 1971. Interest rates in the United States fell and remained lower than in Europe in early 1972, though the differential narrowed in the course of the year. Finally, the wider margins for exchange rate variation around parities or central rates may have acted as a deterrent to a reflow of short-term funds. When the dollar was near the upper end of the range, it appeared expensive to switch out of foreign currencies into dollars; when the dollar was near the lower edge of the 4.5 percent band, uncertainties developed as to whether further changes in parities or central rates might not be forthcoming. A considerable amount of speculation occurred in January and February 1972, requiring central banks in Germany, Japan, the Netherlands, and Belgium to purchase dollars heavily to prevent their currencies from appreciating.

It had to be remembered that it would take some time for the Smithsonian realignment to reverse the basic U.S. deficit and the corresponding surpluses of other countries. Therefore, in the absence of a substantial reflow of speculative capital, there was no alternative to further accumulations of dollars by foreign central banks.

Lessons of the 1971 Experience

The year 1971 provided a dramatic climax to a series of developments that reflected themselves in the American balance of payments. The drama did not end in 1971, but there were lessons to be learned from what happened in the period leading up to the Smithsonian meeting.

The Bretton Woods system, in which the United States played a unique role as the ultimate supplier or absorber of dollar reserves through its policy of buying or selling gold in transactions with foreign monetary authorities, required the United States to be passive with respect to its exchange rate. Under the Bretton Woods system the world experienced an unprecedented expansion of production and trade, and it worked reasonably well until the second half of the 1960's. Although there were complaints from some quarters in Europe about the lack of balance-of-payments discipline on the United States, the additions to world reserves stemming from U.S. deficits were hardly excessive. We could conclude that, had it not been for the Vietnam-caused inflation after 1965, the old system might have gone on for quite a while. It is ironical that Valéry Giscard d'Estaing, speaking as President of France in 1975, attributed the monetary crisis of the seventies not to the faulty structure of the system but to "the massive increase in the United States balance-of-payments deficit generated by the war in Vietnam; and secondly [to] the *oil crisis* in October 1973."[43]

For a while it was thought that the Triffin dilemma (see page 32) might lead to a breakdown of the Bretton Woods system, but the establishment of SDRs provided a way of dealing with the Triffin dilemma, since it made it possible for the countries of the world to satisfy their desire for growing reserves in the absence of a deficit in the U.S. balance of payments.

What brought the system down was the failure of the adjustment process. One might argue that, if only other nations—specifically the surplus countries of Europe and Japan—had been readier to adjust their exchange rates upward as the U.S. trade surplus eroded away in the second half of the 1960's, the system might have been preserved and it would not have been necessary for the United States to suspend convertibility in August 1971.

But there were many reasons—both political and economic—why other countries were reluctant to change their exchange rates. One of them was resentment against the special role of the United States in the system and a consequent reluctance to revalue their currencies so as to relieve the U.S. payments deficit, while the United States remained passive.

What actually happened was that the growing economic and political strength of Europe and Japan made the Bretton Woods system obsolete. A more symmetrical system, in which the role of the United States was more equal to that of other countries, was called for. This explains the failure of the efforts to reform the system further by introducing limited flexibility of exchange rates. Such flexibility could be envisaged for all currencies except the U.S. dollar—as long as the dollar was widely held in reserves and was convertible into gold and other reserve assets.

Thus the SDR reform succeeded because it appeared to be a step toward greater symmetry; it made further dollar deficits unnecessary. But the exchange rate flexibility exercise failed because it revealed and would have accentuated the asymmetry of the Bretton Woods system.

In the absence of a systematic means of adjustment, the U.S. trade surplus turned to a deficit and forced the actions of August 15, 1971. After four months of turmoil and dangers of international political dissension, a new set of exchange rates was agreed upon and the dollar remained inconvertible. Though many of the new exchange rates were designated as central rates rather than par values, and margins were wider, there was still no systematic procedure for adjusting exchange rates when they needed adjustment. That problem was reserved for discussions of the reform of the system "over the longer term" (as outlined in the last paragraph of the Smithsonian communiqué).

Following a second devaluation of the dollar in February 1973, the system of pegged exchange rates was abandoned fifteen months after the Smithsonian meeting. This raised the question whether Secretary Connally had not been right after all in resisting a return to a new set of exchange rates—if in fact that was his position. It appeared that he was less concerned with the issue of floating *versus* "fixed rates" than with what he called "fair" exchange rates.

The major problem in the autumn of 1971 was that Germany was placed in a highly disadvantageous position vis-à-vis France. Unwilling to adopt exchange controls on the French model and, by chance, more affected by the U.S. import surcharge, Germany could not be expected to tolerate for long the Connally policy. One possibility would have been for the United States to have suspended the surcharge. Whether France would then have let its currency float is not known, but it seems unlikely. As long as France was willing and able to hold its exchange rate with stringent controls, the floating option was bound to cause serious dissension in Europe. And some Germans were threatening to adopt the French methods.

One is tempted to conclude that the traumas of the period from August 1971 to March 1973 were unavoidable as part of a learning process. Yet most of what was learned in that period was already evident by 1971.

It had become abundantly clear that when markets think an exchange rate is untenable, enormous flows of speculative funds can move from one currency to another. The experiences of Britain in the years 1964–1967, of both Germany and France in 1968–69, and of the United States in 1971 provide the evidence. It would have required more than a simple and benign set of controls to suppress such capital movements. In 1971 the sum of American exports and imports amounted to about $7.5 billion per month. One month's delay in receipts for exports and one month's acceleration in payments for imports could result in a potential capital outflow of $7.5 billion. In the case of Germany, one month's total trade amounted to almost $6 billion; for Japan the figure was about $3.5 billion, equal to Japan's total reserves at the end of 1970. To prevent such potentially large leads and lags would have required stringent controls on the operations of companies—controls that would have interfered with efficient business practices and would have been politically unacceptable in the United States and many other countries.

Another lesson already evident in 1971 was that large-scale intervention by central banks to hold an exchange rate could undermine their monetary policies. Germany was the prime example of this dilemma—as early as 1961 and again in 1968–69 and in 1971.

Thus the need for a more supple exchange rate system was evident. But the Smithsonian agreement did little to create it.

Other, more cheering, lessons may also be drawn from the developments of 1971. In our contingency planning in 1970 and 1971 for a possible international crisis we tried to envisage the likely effects of a run on the dollar. It was possible to imagine that as individuals, businesses, financial institutions, and even central banks around the world tried to shift out of dollar assets in order to protect themselves against an expected dollar devaluation (relative to other currencies and possibly relative to gold), there would be severe disruptions of American financial markets and of the Eurodollar and Eurobond markets. It was also conceivable that, should the crisis lead to a suspension of convertibility and floating exchange rates, countries would impose trade restrictions in order to protect their industries against cheaper American products, even though such actions would weaken the dollar even more.

As it turned out, the worst fears did not materialize. While foreign investors were estimated to own almost $20 billion of U.S. corporate stock, in the first eleven months of 1971 they did no more on balance than reduce their new acquisitions of American shares to $250 million from about $625 million in 1970. (In late 1971, after the Smithsonian, foreign purchases must have been very large; for December as a whole they came to almost $500 million).[44]

Similarly, the withdrawal by foreigners of deposits in American banks was not massive. Nor did the Eurodollar market suffer a collapse. From late July to early September, the interest rate on three-month Eurodollar deposits increased from 6.25 percent to about 9 percent, but the market adjusted smoothly to the shifts in demands for dollars. By late September the rate fell back to 6 percent.[45]

Financial markets proved to be remarkably resilient to what was probably the most severe shock to the international monetary system since World War II.

Finally, although controls on capital movements were actively used by many countries in 1971, there was very little governmental interference with international trade apart from the import surcharges imposed by the United States and Denmark.

The prospect, and the fact, of revaluations of currencies in some European countries and Japan must have had a depressing effect on economic activity in these countries. But this would have tended to happen even in the absence of a crisis atmosphere. The expected reduction in the trade surpluses of Japan, Germany, and others as a result of currency realignment, even if it could have been engineered without crisis, would have depressed aggregate demand in those countries, which had come to rely too heavily on trade surpluses.

The Smithsonian realignment, while it appeared at the time a historic event, fell short of what the best estimates in the U.S. Government indicated was necessary to restore a sustainable balance to the external position of the United States. The next fifteen months were to be an adagio movement in a minor key, which ended with a repetition, in muted tones, of the Smithsonian theme.

XIII

The Crumbling of the Smithsonian Agreement, 1972–1973

In early 1972 there were widespread doubts concerning the strength of the economic recovery in the United States, the effects of Phase 2 of the price-wage control program, and the durability of the exchange rate structure established at the Smithsonian.[1] As it turned out, the economy displayed the largest rate of growth since 1966 and prices, as measured by the GNP deflator, rose less than in any year since 1966.[2] While wholesale prices of industrial products advanced 3.6 percent, varying little during the year from a monthly rise of 0.3 percent, the prices of farm products began to accelerate ominously in the second half of 1972; in that period food products in the wholesale price index rose at an annual rate of more than 10 percent. Exports of food commodities increased more than 17 percent in 1972 as Russia, China, and India purchased massive amounts of grain from the United States.

The expansion of the U.S. economy—by 6 percent in real terms—brought unemployment down to 5.1 percent at the end of 1972 from 6 percent a year earlier. Although the rate of utilization of total manufacturing capacity rose to only 82 percent in the fourth quarter of 1972, capacity utilization in the major materials industries had risen to more than 92 percent, higher than at any time in the postwar period.

The danger of excess demand and an "inflationary boom" was recognized, but the specific danger of a rapid commodity price inflation only became evident in the course of 1973.[3] In early 1973 the Council of Economic Advisers was projecting a further abatement of inflation.[4]

In other countries, economic conditions were diverse. Japan's economy rebounded from the recession of 1971 and by the second half of 1972 was

216]

expanding at an annual rate of 14 percent. France, aside from a mild slowdown in early 1972, maintained a steady rate of expansion. In Germany, economic activity levelled off in the second half of 1971 but picked up in 1972; nevertheless, the rate of wage advances decelerated. Britain and Italy both experienced a faster expansion of output in 1972 than in 1971, though Italy did not manage to restore the growth rate it had maintained in the 1960's.

The increased current deficit of the United States in 1972 had its reflection in the current balances of most other industrial countries, with the notable exception of the United Kingdom. These countries, as well as many developing countries, gained reserves in 1972.

Foreign exchange markets were disturbed in the early months of 1972. In late February, Germany introduced a 40 percent deposit requirement—the Bardepot—on business borrowing from abroad. Heavy purchases of dollars by the central banks in Germany and other countries became necessary again in March. Germany, the Netherlands, and Belgium all reduced their discount rates at the beginning of March, and U.S. short-term rates turned up from their low points at about the same time. The narrowing of interest rate differentials, passage by Congress of the devaluation measure (the Par Value Modification Act of 1972), and the demonstrated intention of foreign central banks to defend existing exchange rates all served to strengthen confidence in the Smithsonian pattern of rates. Speculative flows of funds abated. From mid-March to mid-June the dollar was relatively strong in foreign exchange markets.

European Attitudes

Two distinct attitudes were discernible in Europe in the early months following the Smithsonian agreement. One was a complaint about the failure of the United States to act to "defend" the new exchange rates; the entire "burden" of holding exchange rates was said to fall on European central banks. Just what the United States was expected to do was not clear. The slack in the U.S. economy made it unnecessary to follow the orthodox prescription of tightening fiscal and monetary policies in order to support the devaluation. On the other hand, U.S. short-term interest rates fell in early 1972, which no doubt aggravated European concerns. And though it was an irritant, the inconvertibility of the dollar was inevitable until the U.S. balance of payments improved and the international monetary system was reformed. More than anything else, it was probably the apparent lack of concern on the part of Americans that annoyed Europeans. It seemed to be necessary to find ways to reassure them from time to time that "we cared." In early March, Minister Giscard d'Estaing told a group of American and European businessmen meeting at Versailles that "indifference" by the United States Government to short-term capital outflows and the dollar's inconvertibility posed a threat to monetary truce in the West. He warned of the possibility of a maze of European controls that would severely restrict the dollar's use.[5]

A second European complaint concerned U.S. unwillingness to agree to what was called "mini-convertibility"—that is, sufficient convertibility of the dollar to facilitate the continued operations of the IMF. Since the Fund's holdings of dollars were above 75 percent of the U.S. quota, other countries could not use dollars to repay their obligations to the Fund. This issue became acute as the date—the end of April—approached for a large British repayment.

Another development in Europe was a revival of the move toward monetary union in the EEC. On March 7, 1972, the six members of the Common Market announced their intention to maintain their exchange rates within 2.25 percent of each other (the IMF rules permitted a range of 4.5 percent). The EEC countries were to implement this arrangement, which came to be known as "the snake in the tunnel," by purchases or sales of each other's currencies. Such acquisitions or loans of currencies were to be settled periodically by transfers from debtors to creditors of assets whose value was linked to gold (gold, SDRs, and Fund positions) on the one hand, and foreign exchange on the other, in proportion to the debtors' holdings of these two types of reserves. The EEC countries would intervene in dollars only when one of their currencies touched the lower or upper edge of the Smithsonian tunnel. On May 1 Britain, a prospective member of the EEC, decided to join the snake.

A French economic correspondent, Alain Vernay, wrote in *Le Figaro* that credit for the new EEC agreement should go to Secretary Connally,

> whose blunt frankness gave food for thought. The reaffirmation of inconvertibility of the dollar laid down as a dogma, the priority given American domestic affairs over international policies, the continued deficit of the balance of payments for two or three more years with increased facilities for direct investments abroad by American corporations—all these have been for the Common Market nations powerful incentives to tighten their ties.[6]

A consequence of the agreement on narrowing margins among EEC currencies was to reduce, at any given time, the scope for fluctuation of individual EEC currencies against the dollar as well. Although the entire EEC snake could move up and down in the tunnel, the decision to limit the movement of, say, the franc against the guilder also inevitably limited the franc's movement against the dollar unless the guilder moved with it.[7] In this way, some of the increased exchange rate flexibility agreed to at the Smithsonian was nullified.

Another irritant in U.S.-European relations was the apparent reluctance of American officials to move ahead with discussions of reform of the international monetary system. Secretary Connally had no desire to pursue such discussions in the Group of Ten, which he regarded as heavily stacked against the United States. And he felt that the Europeans and Japanese were not yet ready to come to grips with the fundamental issues of monetary reform.

U.S. Attitudes

On March 15 Secretary Connally, in a speech before the Council on Foreign Relations, answered some of the criticisms that had been levelled at the United States, and at him, while announcing that he had authorized Under Secretary Volcker to "begin conferring with officials of other countries" to solve the problem of the appropriate forum for negotiations on reform. One possible approach, he said, was a forum of 20 nations based on the existing representation in the IMF's Executive Board.[8] He also indicated a willingness to solve the IMF repayment problem by "truly cooperative efforts in which others participate in accordance with their strength." With a fine choice of words, the Secretary rejected the "accusation" that he was "a sort of bully boy on the manicured playing fields of international finance."[9]

In the weeks that followed Connally's speech, both Henry Reuss and the Atlantic Council (headed by former Treasury Secretary Fowler) added their voices to the call for a beginning of monetary reform discussions.

At the annual International Monetary Conference sponsored by the American Bankers Association, held in Montreal in May 1972, Chairman Burns set out ten "elements that one might reasonably expect to find in a reformed monetary system." Among these were "more prompt adjustment of parities," including internationally agreed guidelines and consultative machinery for determining when parities need to be changed; symmetrical responsibilities on surplus and deficit countries, instead of equating deficits to "sin" and surpluses to "virtue"; adequate reserves and, though "it seems doubtful to me that there is any broad support for eliminating the monetary role of gold in the near future," its role should diminish and that of SDRs should increase; "some form of dollar convertibility" but, Burns said, this issue "has received excessive emphasis in recent discussions"—it should be treated as one aspect of reform. In fact, "the various elements of a new monetary system are bound to be interrelated" and interdependent. Chairman Burns concluded that "it is an urgent necessity to start the rebuilding process quite promptly."[10]

This was the first comprehensive statement on a reformed monetary system to come from a high U.S. Government official, as the newspapers noted, and the Treasury Department was not especially pleased to have it emanate from the Federal Reserve. Connally and Volcker felt that Burns' speech created the impression that an early effort at reform could succeed, and they regarded this as an unrealistic illusion. Paul Volcker, who was also in Montreal, found it necessary to tell the press that Burns "is not speaking for the United States Government" though he added that there was much he could agree with in the Burns speech. Volcker went on to say that "we haven't any pre-packaged plan for reform to spring on the waiting world, nor frankly, have we found other nations yet ready to pronounce their considered judgments."[11]

Volcker was certainly correct about the absence of "pre-packaged plans." An interagency working group in the U.S. Government, chaired by Jack Bennett, Volcker's Deputy Under Secretary, had been meeting regularly since early March to examine a broad range of issues related to reform, but it was far from crystallizing a coherent plan. That was to come later.

Secretary Connally's absence from the Montreal Conference should have been a tipoff; on May 16, 1972, his resignation was abruptly announced. Simultaneously, the White House designated George Shultz to succeed him.

Shultz could not have been more different from Connally in demeanor. Where Connally was forcefully articulate and assertive, Shultz was soft-spoken and more a listener than a talker. A professional economist—the first in American history to occupy the post of Secretary of the Treasury, though Kermit Gordon had been offered the position by President Johnson and turned it down—Shultz had been a specialist in labor problems. He has a Ph.D. from and has taught at M.I.T., he was a staff member at the Council of Economic Advisers under Arthur Burns in the 1950's, and he was Dean of the Graduate School of Business at the University of Chicago when he was selected to be Secretary of Labor in the Nixon Administration in 1969. He later moved to head the Office of Management and Budget, which brought him closer to the center of economic policy-making.

Reputed to be somewhat of a monetarist, very much a "free market" man, with a leaning toward floating exchange rates, George Shultz had the confidence of the President. He was later to be given an office in the White House, in addition to his Treasury quarters, and to become a sort of "economic policy czar."

Midyear Foreign Exchange Crises

Britain's ability to remain in the EEC snake turned out to be of short duration. The sizable current surplus it had been earning in 1970 and 1971 declined substantially in 1972. And its wage and price inflation worsened. As these developments unfolded, the public was reminded of a passage in the March budget speech of the Chancellor of the Exchequer, Anthony Barber: "the lesson of the international balance-of-payments upsets of the last few years is that it is neither necessary nor desirable to distort domestic economies to an unacceptable extent in order to maintain unrealistic exchange rates, whether they are too high or too low."[12] Although an economist could not quarrel with one word in this statement, it was not the sort of thing that foreign exchange market operators expected to hear from a finance minister. It was interpreted to signify that, should sterling come under pressure, Barber would not wait long before changing its value.

Sterling did come under pressure in June, and heavy intervention became necessary both by the Bank of England and by the central banks of other countries in the EEC snake. Ironically, other countries' purchases of sterling with their own currencies and British sales of continental European currencies tended to weaken the snake against the dollar in foreign exchange markets, thus making continental currencies an attractive speculative bet in relation to the dollar.

The speculative flurry against sterling built up, encouraged by a statement by the shadow Chancellor, Denis Healey, to the effect that sterling might have to be devalued in the next two months.[13] It culminated in net British sales of foreign exchange in the amount of $2.6 billion in the six days leading up to June 23. On that day, the British authorities announced that the pound would float "for a temporary period."

With the cessation of central bank intervention to hold sterling in the snake, that serpent shifted upward in relation to the dollar. This movement, plus concern in the market that other Smithsonian rates might change in reaction to the downward float of sterling, led to heavy flows out of dollars and into European currencies and the yen. After large purchases of dollars by central banks, particularly the Bundesbank, foreign exchange markets were closed and a meeting of EEC Finance Ministers was called for June 26, 1972.

The EEC ministers quickly agreed that they would continue to support the Smithsonian exchange rates and then spent most of their time trying to hold the EEC snake together. Denmark decided to withdraw from the snake but to maintain its Smithsonian central rate. Governor Carli of Italy had apparently come to the meeting threatening to take the lira out of the snake, and with this threat he won approval of a "temporary" change in the intervention and settlement rules of the EEC: Italy would be permitted to intervene in dollars as well as in other snake currencies; to the extent that it did sell snake currencies or other EEC countries purchased lire, Italy would settle the debts in dollars only.

Markets in most countries were reopened on June 28. In Switzerland the market remained closed while the central bank pondered what action to take, thus signalling its fear of a heavy inflow of dollars.

The German Cabinet met on June 25 and debated a measure recommended by President Klasen of the Bundesbank. This measure would prohibit the sale of German securities to foreigners and would represent the first use by Germany of foreign exchange controls. (Previous restrictive measures had consisted of reserve requirements or other provisions that acted through the price system.) Minister Schiller strongly opposed this proposal.

Schiller apparently preferred to hold control measures in reserve as a last-resort bargaining tool to induce other EEC countries to float jointly with Germany in the event of a large inflow of dollars. He quoted the German Ambassador in Paris as saying that President Pompidou "appears to be ready to consider a joint floating of all currencies."[14] That this was Pompidou's position was denied by *The Economist.*[15]

The German Cabinet outvoted Schiller and on June 29 adopted a prohibition on sales of bonds to foreigners; out of deference to Schiller, the measure did not prohibit foreign purchases of German stocks. On July 2 Schiller submitted his resignation in a lengthy letter to Chancellor Brandt. This letter leaked to the press in July, to be followed by an article published by President Klasen, taking issue with some of Schiller's points.

The entire debate in the Cabinet was overshadowed by the fact that elections were scheduled before the end of the year. Klasen's argument that imposition of the curb on capital inflows would help Germany to hold the mark exchange rate through the elections must have had a powerful influence (though Klasen denies that he gave a "guaranty" of this outcome).

One issue between Schiller and Klasen was their differing notions regarding the American attitude toward the adoption by Germany of capital controls. Klasen quotes Chairman Burns as stating that he welcomed the German measures.[16] Schiller's letter of resignation cites a message from the German Ambassador in Washington reporting that the new German measure is "regretted." Both reports were probably correct, since they came from different sources.

Schiller's letter was somewhat ambiguous. He presented many arguments against a drift toward controls and "dirigisme" in Europe yet indicated that he might have been willing to use exchange control measures as leverage to persuade France and other European countries to adopt a common float. Nevertheless, one cannot help paying respect to Karl Schiller as he drops out of our narrative. He did much to introduce modern fiscal policy to Germany; in the period leading up to his resignation he had been trying to get governmental agreement to a more restrictive budget in the face of a strong rise of demand in the economy. His stance on international monetary questions was consistently oriented toward open economies and a one-world approach, and this led him to favor quite early the type of exchange rate regime that was ultimately adopted.

President Klasen, on the other hand, opposed a float, unilateral or joint, and was probably correct about the disposition of other EEC countries (notably France) not to join a common float.

Shortly after the markets reopened, and despite the imposition of additional capital controls by a number of countries, strong speculative pressures against the dollar led to massive flows of funds into various European countries and Japan. Between June 28 and July 14, the inflows came to $6 billion.[17]

In an attempt to clarify, for myself and others, the reasons for the massive flight from the dollar—after three months of net capital flow *to* the United States—I presented to the Federal Open Market Committee on July 18 several possible explanations:

One explanation was that market participants believed that the downward movement of sterling would erode some of the competitive advantage the United States had gained at the Smithsonian. But the devaluation of sterling was offset by rapidly rising prices in Britain, whose current account surplus had already been reduced substantially. Thus, although the downward float of sterling might reduce the arithmetic devaluation of the dollar, there was no reason to expect it to reduce the potential improvement in the U.S. balance of payments.

A second explanation was that U.S. trade figures thus far in 1972 were revealing that the 1972 deficit would be much larger than was assumed at the time of the Smithsonian meeting. Perhaps, therefore, the United States needed a larger balance-of-payments swing than was earlier thought. It was as though a mountain climber, having started his ascent, becomes aware that the valley from which he started is much deeper than he had realized and that he has a longer climb ahead of him. Whether he would make it is less certain than when he started.

A third explanation for the speculative activity may have been the alacrity with which other governments closed markets and imposed controls. This could have been interpreted to mean that foreign central banks were not prepared to absorb dollars in sizable quantity in order to preserve the Smithsonian exchange rates.

Finally, the apparent passivity of U.S. policies in the face of grave international uncertainties may have contributed to market expectations that the United States wished to see further appreciations of foreign currencies.

On that same day, July 18, the Federal Open Market Committee decided, with the approval of the new Secretary of the Treasury, to reactivate the swap network (use of which had been suspended on August 15, 1971) in order to permit operations by the Federal Reserve in the foreign exchange markets.

These operations began on July 19 and apparently had a remarkable effect on the markets. Although the Federal Reserve sold only a little more than $30 million of foreign currencies (while offering greater amounts) the speculative flows of funds came to a halt.[18] The U.S. official settlements deficit fell sharply in August and turned to a surplus in September.

Explaining the Federal Reserve's action, which was warmly welcomed abroad, Chairman Burns said that there wasn't any "commitment on anything" but "we want to do our part to restore order in the exchange markets."[19] One American banker, overcome with euphoria, was quoted as saying that the action put the United States "back in the human race."[20]

Progress on Reform

During the spring of 1972, the questions of the forum for negotiating international monetary reform and the content of the reform exercise had been actively debated. Agreement was finally reached on the establishment of a new Committee of the Board of Governors of the Fund on Reform of the International Monetary System and Related Issues (to be known as the "Committee of Twenty"). The "related issues" comprised trade and investment. The United States had been insisting that it made no sense to try to reform the international monetary system without assurance that international arrangements regarding trade and investment, including development assistance, would be consistent with the aims of monetary reform. The proposal for a Committee of Twenty was announced by the IMF on June 26 and was approved by mail vote on July 26 by the Board of Governors of the Fund.[21] (Its activity will be covered in the next chapter.)

In August the Fund's Executive Board completed a report on *Reform of the International Monetary System*, requested in September 1971. It was released to the public on September 6, 1972. The report, reflecting the diverse views of 20 Executive Directors from Europe, Asia, Africa, and North and South America, was inevitably somewhat bland in its recommendations, overt or implied. On the other hand, the report contained much useful analysis and clearly identified the issues relating to international monetary reform. That it did not resolve these issues was no surprise and certainly no criticism of the Fund. It was widely recognized that a fundamental reform of the international monetary system would require negotiation and decision at a high political level. Hence Committee of Twenty members were to be at ministerial level, and their deputies were to be senior treasury and central bank officials.

A week or so before the 1972 IMF annual meeting, the news leaked out, initially from Washington, that the United States would not support the reappointment of Pierre-Paul Schweitzer as Managing Director of the Fund when his term ended in September 1973. Why and by whom the decision was made has never been revealed. But in view of the antagonism that had developed between Schweitzer and Connally, it was widely surmised that the former Secretary of the Treasury had a hand in it. Many of us in the government were shocked. One knowledgeable associate said that it was senseless to get rid of Schweitzer without even knowing whom you want to replace him with. Surprisingly, the reaction from European capitals was mild.[22]

It was my judgment at the time that the French authorities were not displeased to see Schweitzer go—he had, after all, a long record of opposition to French positions—and were content to see the United States take the political onus in the matter. However, at the Fund's annual meeting, Minister Giscard d'Estaing, noting the support Schweitzer had received from previous speakers, said, "In an international organization governed by democratic principles, it would be inconceivable that the attitude thus taken by the great majority should ultimately be disregarded."[23] Officials of developing countries expressed greater resentment and some of them proposed that Schweitzer be reappointed. Schweitzer's immense popularity was revealed by the sustained applause that greeted him when he took the rostrum to make his traditional opening address at the IMF meeting.

An American Plan

At the same IMF meeting, the United States surprised the world by putting forward a plan for international monetary reform.

While the interagency group under Jack Bennett had been arguing and floundering, Paul Volcker sat in his office and pieced together an integrated proposal for a reformed monetary system. He had it in a form sufficiently complete to try out on others in the government in August, and I was called back from a Cape Cod vacation to work on the plan with a small group from other agencies. My files identify it as Plan X. We spent a lot of time on the technical details of the plan, both before and after the IMF annual meeting.

Apart from the substance of the U.S. proposal, there was the tactical problem of when and how to present it to the world. In the absence of American leadership, adequate reform proposals would not be forthcoming from others. On the other hand, there were dangers in a U.S. initiative. Publication of the proposals might disturb foreign exchange markets, since considerably greater flexibility of exchange rates was called for.[24] It was possible that other countries would accept only part of the proposal (U.S. officials regarded it as a complete package that could not be dismembered). And there might be political resistance to accepting a "made in America" plan even if other countries had no serious objections to it on substantive grounds. In the end, the decision was made to take the initiative. A general outline would be presented by the Secretary of the Treasury at the IMF meeting, and a detailed paper would be put to the Committee of Twenty later.

Secretary Shultz chose to speak early in the five-day IMF meeting in order to give other ministers an opportunity to react. President Nixon, greeting the gathering at its opening session on September 25, announced that Shultz would be outlining a number of proposals which he commended for careful consideration.

Shultz's speech acknowledged that "most countries want to maintain a fixed point of reference for their currencies—in other words, a 'central' or 'par' value," but he also suggested that provision "needs to be made for countries which decide to float their currencies." He called for wider margins than existed at the time. With respect to reserves, he stressed the importance of the SDR and the need to increase the amount over time to meet the aggregate need for reserves.

> At the same time, official foreign currency holdings need be neither generally banned nor encouraged. Some countries may find holdings of foreign currencies provide a useful margin of flexibility in reserve management, and fluctuations in such holdings can provide some elasticity for the system as a whole in meeting sudden flows of volatile capital. However, careful study should be given to proposals for exchanging part of existing reserve currency holdings into a special issue of SDRs, at the option of the holder.

Regarding the adjustment process, he pointed to the asymmetry in the existing system, under which countries in surplus are under less pressure to revalue their currencies—or to take other actions with similar effect—than are countries in deficit. He therefore proposed—and this was the heart of the U.S. approach to reform—that "a surfeit of reserves" would indicate, and produce pressures for, adjustment on the surplus side "as losses of reserves already do for the deficit side." Thus, "disproportionate gains or losses in reserves may be the most equitable and effective single indicator we have to guide the adjustment process."

Further, "a country permitting its reserves to rise disproportionately could lose its right to demand conversion, unless it undertook at least limited revaluation or other acceptable measures of adjustment." Finally, the Fund's scarce currency clause should be available for use.

On controls, Secretary Shultz argued that capital controls (on inflows) should not be a means of maintaining a chronically undervalued currency, and no "country should be forced to use controls in lieu of other, more basic, adjustment measures." He also called for related negotiations on trade and investment arrangements.

Finally, recognizing that the United States and others could not leap into new monetary and trading arrangements without a transition period, he said that after such a period, "the United States would be prepared to undertake an obligation to convert official foreign dollar holdings into other reserve assets as a part of a satisfactory system such as I have suggested—a system assuring effective and equitable operation of the adjustment process."[25]

Reactions to the U.S. Proposal

The Shultz address was generally praised by other ministers. Helmut Schmidt, Germany's new Economics Minister, while expressing concern about the explosion of international liquidity of the past two years, stressed the need to begin reform negotiations immediately. Otherwise, he said, "we are like the chain-smoker who decided to give up smoking—but only after his next heart attack."[26]

Minister Giscard d'Estaing also welcomed Secretary Shultz's presentation and stressed the need for a more symmetrical system. He proposed a three-stage program for the reform exercise. In the first year, there should be agreement on the exchange rate mechanism and on specific arrangements in favor of developing countries. In his view, the exchange rate regime should involve "fixed" but "adjustable" par values, but such adjustments "must not be governed by automatically applicable criteria." (Thus began a debate that was to continue for two years.)

A second stage would involve the restoration of convertibility. Giscard d'Estaing took issue with Shultz's "apparent neutrality" regarding reserve currency holdings. Here was a second major issue. A third had to do with capital controls. While accepting the objective of the "greatest possible freedom" of capital flows, Giscard saw a need for "harmonized restrictions."

In the third stage of negotiations, "the fundamental problems of the *numeraire* and of supplying the new system with liquidity should be dealt with."[27] The question of the *numeraire* in which to define parities greatly preoccupied the French at that time but they later dropped the matter. It did serve as a means of focusing attention on the role of gold, which the finance minister of a government presided over by the heir of Charles de Gaulle could not avoid.

The Governor for El Salvador, Edgardo Suarez, speaking for the "Latin American bloc," called for further allocations of SDRs on the grounds that the recent large increase in international reserves had been concentrated in a few countries. (The IMF *Annual Report* showed that, in 1971, $27.3 billion of the $29.4 billion of growth of world reserves was accounted for by eleven countries.[28]) With respect to reform, he stressed the need to encourage the flow of real resources to developing countries. Finally, he put forward the familiar case for linking SDR creation and development assistance as one means of achieving this objective.[29]

These and other addresses identified the major issues with which the Committee of Twenty was to be concerned.

The annual meeting was thus a hopeful one, in the sense that a needed reform effort was launched and the United States had assumed a more cooperative international stance. Minister Schmidt said at a press conference that the "religious war" over monetary reform had ended.[30]

The dollar was relatively strong in September and the U.S. trade deficit had declined a little in July and August. The dollar strengthened further after the IMF meeting. Schweitzer was quoted as telling a press luncheon that he was "more convinced than ever" that the basic pattern of exchange rates negotiated at the Smithsonian would stand up.[31] Famous last words!

The Calm Before the Monetary Storm

In the last quarter of 1972, the rate of economic activity in the United States accelerated; GNP in real terms advanced at an annual rate of 9 percent and the unemployment rate fell to 5.1 percent in December from 5.5 percent in September. Consumer prices, under Phase 2 controls, rose at an annual rate of about 3.5 percent and wholesale industrial commodity prices advanced at an annual rate of just over 2 percent.

In Europe and Japan output also accelerated, but so did the rate of inflation, partly as a reflection of soaring prices of raw materials and foods on world markets.

Interest rates rose on both sides of the Atlantic but more rapidly in Europe than in the United States. Once again action in Europe to restrain demand was primarily focused on monetary policy.

Nevertheless, calm prevailed at year's end. The reserves of most European countries had actually fallen in the fourth quarter of 1972 despite the continued though much-reduced U.S. deficit. On the other hand, Japan's reserves increased almost $2 billion in the same period. The U.S. trade deficit, which had contracted a little in the autumn, increased again, temporarily as it turned out, in November. The strong improvement in the U.S. trade position did not become evident until the spring of 1973. Foreigners were purchasing American stocks in large volume and the dollar was relatively strong as the year ended.

Foreign Exchange Crisis and Resolution

On January 11, 1973, the Nixon Administration abruptly announced the end of Phase 2 of the wage-price controls. The mandatory program was replaced in Phase 3 by a looser, more voluntary approach.

On January 20 Italy announced the establishment of a two-tier foreign exchange market as a means of discouraging capital outflows. This led to an immediate flow of funds into Switzerland, and "the Swiss panicked."[32] On January 23 the Swiss authorities decided to let the franc float.

Foreign exchange markets were soon being described as "jittery," and they were not made less so when Minister Schmidt denied that the mark would be revalued.[33] Understandably, participants in foreign exchange markets had come to look upon such denials with cynicism. By early February it was clear that another crisis was under way. On February 1 and 2 the Bundesbank purchased $1 billion while the Federal Reserve sold marks in New York. Over the weekend of February 3–4 the German Cabinet decided to impose additional exchange controls on capital inflows. Foreign purchases of stock, which had been exempt from the exchange controls applied in June 1972, were now also made subject to permit, as were foreign loans to companies, subsidiaries, and plants in Germany.[34]

Further fuel was added to the speculative fire by newspaper reports on

February 6 that when Minister Schmidt phoned George Shultz over the weekend, Shultz was sympathetic to permitting the mark to float.[35]

During the week of February 5–9, the Bundesbank purchased an additional $4.9 billion in an effort to keep the mark from piercing its ceiling. The central banks of Belgium and the Netherlands took in $250 million and $400 million respectively. In the first 9 days of February the Bank of Japan purchased $1.1 billion and then closed its foreign exchange market. On February 12, European exchange markets were closed.[36]

While all this was going on, and on the basis of a conference among President Nixon, Secretary Shultz, and Chairman Burns on February 6, Paul Volcker secretly took off in an Air Force plane for Tokyo on Wednesday, February 7, where he conferred briefly with the finance minister and other officials. From Tokyo he flew over the pole to Bonn, then to London, Paris, Rome, and back to Paris, taking Italian Finance Minister Malagodi with him for a meeting with several ministers in the residence of Giscard d'Estaing. After a second visit to Bonn, Volcker returned to Washington on Monday, February 12. He had covered more than 31,000 miles, had run out of cigars and clean shirts, and had lost his hat in Tokyo.

On the evening of Volcker's return, Secretary Shultz announced a 10 percent devaluation of the dollar.

Shultz issued a formal statement which (1) referred to the U.S. proposals for monetary reform and asserted that progress in the work of the Committee of Twenty had been "too slow" and needed "renewed impetus"; (2) noted that the further increase in the dollar price of gold (to $42.22) "has no practical significance" (in fact, he pointedly defined the 10 percent reduction in the dollar's value in terms of SDRs rather than gold); (3) reported that consultations with "our leading trade partners in Europe assure me that the proposed change in the par value of the dollar is acceptable to them"; (4) announced that the Japanese authorities would let the yen float; (5) noted that the United States had "undertaken no obligations" to intervene in foreign exchange markets; (6) announced that the President would shortly send to Congress proposals for comprehensive trade legislation, and (7) reported the intention to phase out by December 31, 1974, the existing controls of capital outflows (the interest equalization tax, the Commerce Department program limiting corporate capital outflows, and the Federal Reserve "voluntary" program restraining lending abroad by American financial institutions).[37]

Thus the second American devaluation supplemented the inadequate Smithsonian realignment. The IMF estimated that the new realignment was of the same order of magnitude as the Smithsonian settlement.[38] But now the yen, the Swiss franc, and, as it turned out, the Italian lira, in addition to sterling and the Canadian dollar, were floating.

When Volcker set out on his whirlwind trip, the United States would have been prepared to end up with a float of the currencies of Europe and Japan instead of an overt U.S. devaluation. Volcker's brief also included a proposal that the United States and other countries sell gold in the market in order to dampen speculative activity. This proposal was rejected by the French. A joint float was discussed actively in Europe, but the willingness of the United States to devalue unilaterally provided an easier option to the Europeans.

American authorities were concerned about the possible acrimony that would develop, as well as about the imposition of additional controls in Europe, were a float adopted at that time. It is significant and somewhat startling that on February 15, following a post-devaluation meeting of EEC Finance Ministers, Minister Schmidt stated at a press conference that a new international monetary crisis would lead the Common Market countries to float their currencies jointly in relation to the dollar. "The move is being held in reserve," he said.[39]

It didn't have to be held in reserve for long.

In the first week or so after exchange markets reopened on February 14, the dollar rose to its ceiling against foreign currencies and the Bundesbank was able to sell $1 billion, a small part of what it had taken in before the devaluation. But the market price of gold rose sharply, reaching $89 on February 23.[40] By then the dollar had weakened in European exchange markets, and central banks had to purchase dollars. That Friday, February 23, the Commerce Department issued, in advance of the scheduled publication date, the U.S. trade figures for January. They showed a significant reduction in the deficit, to about $300 million—the smallest monthly trade deficit in over a year. Nevertheless, the following week saw a swelling of speculation, and on Thursday, March 1, European central banks, having absorbed more than $3.6 billion during the day, ordered their exchange markets officially closed. They were to stay closed—in the sense that central banks stayed out of the markets and trading was very light—until March 19, while a series of international consultations took place.

The Finance Ministers of the EEC countries met in Brussels on Sunday, March 4, and considered, at the urging of Germany, a joint float of all their currencies. Apparently neither Italy nor Britain was prepared to tie its currency to the stronger Common Market currencies. It is reported that Chancellor of the Exchequer Anthony Barber laid down certain "essential conditions" for Britain's participation in the common float, including unconditional mutual financial support without limits of amount, without guaranties, and without specific obligation to repay.[41] It seems unlikely that this was a serious demand; to say that it lacked subtlety is to treat it kindly. The meeting ended with an invitation, proposed by Giscard d'Estaing, to the United States, Japan, Canada, Sweden, and Switzerland to join the nine Common Market countries in a meeting on March 9. (Britain, Ireland, and Denmark had formally joined the EEC on January 1, 1973.)

In another meeting in Brussels on March 8, the EEC Finance Ministers prepared a "shopping list" of requests to be made to the United States. The list reportedly included intervention in the exchange markets by the United States on the basis of an IMF drawing or credits from other countries or the use of reserve assets; the issuance of long-term bonds by the U.S. Treasury, with an exchange-value guaranty, to absorb dollars held abroad; restrictions on outflows of capital; and increases in U.S. interest rates.[42]

At the fourteen-nation meeting in Paris on March 9, Secretary Shultz politely rejected these proposals but stressed the willingness of the United States to be cooperative.[43] Both he and Chairman Burns underlined the importance of accelerating the efforts of the Committee of Twenty to agree on a reform of the international monetary system. The meeting ended in some uncertainty with the issuance of a communiqué that said the group would reconvene in one week, during which the deputies of finance ministers would undertake a technical study of "a set of measures" designed "to insure jointly an orderly exchange rate system." The communiqué stated that the ministers and central bank governors agreed that "the crisis was due to speculative movements of funds. They also agreed that the existing relationships between parities and central rates, following the recent realignment, correspond, in their view, to the economic requirements and that these relationships will make an effective monetary contribution to a better balance of international payments." Finally, they agreed on the urgent need for an effective reform of the system and "decided to take the necessary steps to accelerate the work of the Committee of Twenty of the International Monetary Fund."[44]

Before the scheduled meeting of the larger group a week later, the EEC Ministers met in Brussels on Sunday, March 11. This happened to be an election day in France; President Pompidou's Gaullist party lost a considerable number of seats in the Parliament, making him more dependent on Giscard's Independent Republican Party to form a majority. Thus Giscard was probably less hobbled by Paris than he might have been at earlier meetings. In any event, Giscard agreed to a joint float among six EEC currencies and, in return, the German Government revalued the mark by 3 percent. The six countries whose currencies would float jointly—as a 2.25 percent snake without a tunnel—were Germany, France, Belgium, the Netherlands, Denmark, and Luxembourg. (Since Luxembourg does not have a currency independent of the Belgian franc for international transactions, the announcement that "six" currencies would jointly float was somewhat exaggerated.) Within the snake, Belgium and the Netherlands arranged to keep their currencies within 1.5 percent of each other; this was called the "worm" in the "snake." Although the decision to float was announced on March 11, it was not to take effect until after the March 16 meeting of the fourteen countries.[45]

It is worth observing, in light of the further revaluation of the mark, that new orders for German exports had increased 27 percent from the second quarter of 1972 to the same period of 1973 and that this was soon to show up in the trade surplus, which increased more than 60 percent from 1972 to 1973. Thus the continued upward pressure on the mark appeared to have some economic justification.[46]

Why, one may ask, did the European governments decide on the common float in advance of the March 16 meeting with the United States and other non-European countries? The answer seems to be that they wished to take an initiative that expressed their aspirations for European unity instead of appearing, once again, to be reacting to American decisions or lack of them. As one symbol of this posture, Germany announced its new exchange rate in terms of SDRs rather than dollars (or gold).

The March 16 meeting was an amicable one; it resulted in a communiqué announcing agreement

> in principle that official intervention in exchange markets may be useful at appropriate times, to facilitate the maintenance of orderly conditions, keeping in mind also the desirability of encouraging reflows of speculative movements of funds. Each nation stated that it will be prepared to intervene at its initiative in its own market, when necessary and desirable, acting in a flexible manner in the light of market conditions and in close consultation with the authorities of the nation whose currency may be bought or sold.

While the intention of the U.S. authorities to phase out its capital controls by the end of 1974 was noted, it was stated that any interim actions in this direction would "take due account of exchange market conditions and the balance of payments trends." The United States also agreed to consider actions to remove inhibitions on capital inflows (such as the withholding tax on foreign income earned on U.S. securities and the reserve requirement on Eurodollar borrowings by U.S. banks).

The communiqué stressed the importance of dampening speculative capital movements and promised to have studies undertaken to this end, including examination of the Euro-currency markets. Meanwhile European central banks would take steps, "gradually and prudently," to withdraw reserves earlier placed in the Eurodollar market.

Finally, the ministers and governors reiterated their desire to expedite and conclude the work on reform in the Committee of Twenty.[47]

A historic development thus came to pass. Most continental European currencies (Sweden and Norway had joined the snake) and the Japanese yen were now floating. It was a philosophical, as well as a political, question whether the dollar was also floating. Although additional severe controls or penalties on capital inflows were imposed in a number of countries, the crisis-prone par value system had been abandoned, except by the countries in the snake in relation to each other.

Initially the move to floating exchange rates was widely viewed as a means of coping with speculation rather than as a new method of adjusting balance-of-payments positions. (As we shall observe in the next chapter, the reform discussions continued to envisage a par value system as the normal exchange rate regime.) But the hard realities had in fact forced a reform on the system. It would take some time for the thinking of treasury and central bank officials, businessmen, and bankers to adjust to the new regime.

XIV

International Monetary Reform:
The Committee of Twenty, 1972–1974

In the autumn of 1972, the Committee of Twenty made a start on what was expected to be a two-year effort to forge agreement on a reformed world monetary system. At the outset, those of us involved had the sense that we were engaged in an undertaking of historic importance—to redesign the monetary system to make it conform more with the economic and political realities of the last quarter of the twentieth century. The task of monetary reform was regarded as one of improving on the Bretton Woods system so that it would operate, without frequent crises, to facilitate the continued expansion of international trade and productive capital flows, and in a more symmetrical way than the system had functioned in the quarter century after the Bretton Woods agreement.

Organization and Procedures

During the IMF annual meeting in Washington, September 25–29, 1972, the Committee of Twenty held its first session for the purpose of organizing itself. The Committee's activity was to be carried on at two levels: the ministerial (or central bank governor) level, where ultimate political responsibility lay, and the level of deputies to finance ministers and central bank governors, where the major work at the "technical level" would be done. Although the distinction between the technical and the political is not always clear-cut, it was impractical to expect ministers to meet sufficiently often or—to put it bluntly—to expect most of them to comprehend the technicalities well enough to do the job themselves. Bretton Woods, it will be remembered, was designed by two master technicians, Keynes and White.

At the top level—the Committee itself—the arrangement was that each of the twenty IMF constituencies would be represented by a "member." In most cases the member was the minister of finance of the largest country in the constituency; in a few cases, the "member" was a central bank governor. Each member could be accompanied by two "associates" who, though they sat behind the member, were entitled to speak. This permitted each of the five largest countries to designate its central bank governor as well as its deputy to the finance minister as associates, and it permitted the other fifteen delegations to include as associates ministers of finance or central bank governors from other countries in the constituencies. Ali Wardhana, Indonesia's Minister of Finance, was chosen chairman of the Committee.

The deputies were organized in a way that allowed two deputies from each of the Fund's twenty constituencies to be accompanied by their IMF Executive Directors and by advisers. The deputies were senior officials of finance ministries and central banks (in some cases, they were governors of central banks). The Committee itself chose Jeremy Morse (now Sir Jeremy) of the Bank of England as chairman of the deputies.

The deputies were men of high responsibility in their capitals.* Being intimately attuned to and involved in the monetary affairs of their countries, they were sensitive to what was and what was not acceptable to their finance ministers and central bank governors. This was essential because meaningful reform would necessarily involve changes in countries' policies.

The number of people in the room, when either the ministers or the deputies met in plenary session, was over 150, and this gave rise to occasional jocular criticism in the press and even among some of the participants. But most of those present were observers, not speakers. That the group was cumbersome is undeniable. It had to be, for it represented a cumbersome world: 124 member nations of the International Monetary Fund. The size of the group was not, in my view, an insuperable obstacle to a successful outcome. Various means were used—executive sessions, division into smaller groups, and working parties—to transform what Adolfo Diz of Argentina termed "multilateral monologue" into give-and-take debate and negotiation.

The deputies' work was organized, presided over, and generally led by the "bureau," which consisted of the chairman (Jeremy Morse) and four vice chairmen, who were regarded not as country representatives but as international civil servants. The vice chairmen, selected by the deputies, were Jonathan Frimpong-Ansah, former Governor of the central bank of Ghana; Alex-

---

*Although "person" is the preferred term nowadays, the fact is that all the deputies were male.

andre Kafka, Executive Director of the IMF for Brazil and associated countries; Hideo Suzuki, former Executive Director of the IMF for Japan; and myself. We were most ably assisted by Edward George of the staff of the Bank of England. The six of us performed virtually all of the professional functions of a "secretariat" during the two-year life of the Committee of Twenty.

In a way the bureau was a microcosm of the Committee and its deputies. Our nationalities encompassed Europe, Asia, Latin America, Africa, and North America. While we all regarded ourselves as international officials rather than national representatives, we were expected to, and did, try to see that the positions of the countries with which we were associated were clearly formulated and reflected in the evolving vision of a reformed system. At times the influence went the other way; each of us on occasion tried to influence the deputies of his country or group to alter or adopt positions that were more conducive to a successful reform effort.

The activity of the deputies was characterized by the late Marcus Fleming:

> The method of work adopted by the Deputies and Bureau was one that has seldom been applied in international affairs to such complex and highly technical issues. It was extremely democratic, extremely thorough in its educative effect on the participants, and extremely demanding on the time and energies of all concerned. When the Articles of Agreement of the Fund were hammered out, at and prior to Bretton Woods, it was on the basis of two or three alternative drafts, each elaborated in considerable detail and in self-consistent form by the experts of a major country. On the present occasion, a much more Socratic procedure was adopted. On the basis of general discussion, couched in terms appropriate to the degree of understanding achieved at the time by the senior officials involved, the Bureau sought to elicit points of agreement and clarify points of difference on all the manifold and interrelated issues, and to resubmit the results for further general discussion. Very few of the major countries established coherent national positions over the whole range of these issues, and only one of them, the United States, brought out a fairly comprehensive statement of its position. Even that was not comparable in clarity and precision to the Keynes and White plans of former days. The Europeans handicapped themselves by trying to agree issue by issue on a joint EEC position. The less developed countries made great efforts to agree on a common program of reform through the Group of Twenty-Four, but this agreement was inevitably confined to a few isolated matters of common interest, such as the nature of the link between SDR creation and development finance.[1]

The bureau labored intensively—in spurts—preparing papers for deputies' meetings, which were held on average every other month and lasted anywhere from two to five days. We also prepared papers for the Committee meetings, of which there were six altogether, and assisted Ali Wardhana in planning for them. And we chaired working groups.

When meetings of the deputies or the Committee were held in Paris, Rome, or Washington, we worked in those cities before and after the meetings. But most often we sat together in London around a small table in an office lent to us by the Bank of England.

The three of us who did not reside in London were usually brought in a car each morning to the Bank's "bullion yard," whose sturdy and ancient gate had to be opened by a guard in the pink, swallow-tail coat and black top hat that has been the uniform of his occupation for centuries. Passing through another grilled gate, which was opened only when we were recognized, we climbed two flights of steps and wended our way through the quiet and elegant "parlors" of the Bank to the corridor in which offices had been set aside for us. Here, facing a courtyard with a lawn that remained green even in midwinter, we could neither see nor hear the bustle that characterizes the heart of the city just outside the walls of the Bank of England.

We normally sat all day, interrupted only by lunch and by the delivery of coffee or tea in midmorning and midafternoon. Starting with a first draft prepared by one of us, of whatever it was we were working on at the time, we debated, analyzed, and negotiated until we had produced what we hoped was not only a balanced document but one that would contribute to the creation of a coherent new monetary system. We were conscious then of the fact that a reformed system had to have a coherent design. As George Shultz had said in 1973, "In constructing a world monetary system, we cannot act, as I see it, like merchants in a bazaar bargaining for selfish advantage."[2]

The Issues in Monetary Reform

The issues faced by the Committee of Twenty fell under four major headings: (1) balance-of-payments adjustment, (2) the settlement of payments imbalances, (3) the volume and composition of international reserves, and (4) the special problems of developing countries.

As had been revealed in the IMF report on reform and in the speeches of ministers at the annual meeting, a number of broad propositions relative to the reformed system were already agreed upon when the Committee of Twenty began its deliberations. One was that the international monetary system ought to treat countries with greater uniformity; in particular, the system should be more symmetrical with respect to both balance-of-payments adjustment and the settlement of deficits and surpluses. As an aspect of the greater symmetry, the United States should have both rights and obligations more like those of other countries. It was also broadly agreed that the exchange rate regime should be more flexible than in the past. Finally, the SDR should become the principal reserve asset.

Within the scope of these propositions, there was considerable room for disagreement or, at least, differences in emphasis. Each country or group of similarly situated countries approached reform on the basis of its perception of the deficiencies of the old system. And these perceptions differed.

European officials, supported in a low key by those from Japan, tended to focus on the lack of mandatory convertibility of dollars under the Bretton Woods system. In this view, if the United States were required to use reserve assets (gold, SDRs, and Fund drawings) to finance its balance-of-payments deficits, it would adopt policies to prevent or eliminate such deficits. Said Minister Giscard d'Estaing: "The touchstone of reform is to be found in the area of convertibility. This question outweighs all others, particularly that of adjustment. It raises the fundamental problem of equality in the way rights and obligations are shared within the international community."[3] Those who inclined to this view acknowledged that other changes were also necessary, but to them the establishment of full convertibility, or asset settlement as it was called in the IMF report on reform, was a major objective.

U.S. officials had a different perception of the major defect of the old system. To them the absence of adequate incentives for countries in surplus to reduce or eliminate their surpluses forced the United States into deficit. The United States had been the residual country in the old system, permitting too many other countries to live comfortably with undervalued currencies and therefore balance-of-payments surpluses. It was the U.S. view that a country losing reserves inevitably felt the need to eliminate its deficit, but countries in surplus could go on indefinitely accumulating reserves. What this perception called for was a reformed balance-of-payments adjustment process that would impose more obligations on countries in surplus to correct their positions. This required more than symmetrical asset settlement. On the contrary, as U.S. officials saw it, asset settlement was feasible only if the adjustment process were strengthened.

To turn again to a convenient reference, here is a simplified summary of these differing perceptions:

> some in Europe would say that if convertibility could be restored, balance-of-payments equilibrium would follow; the Americans would say that if a symmetrical balance-of-payments adjustment process could be introduced, convertibility would

be restorable. I do not wish to exaggerate these differences. My main point is that the different viewpoints resulted naturally from the earlier divergent experiences of the parties involved. In fact, however, each recognized the merits of the other's case. And, I happen to believe, the views can be reconciled.[4]

The officials from developing nations, who believed that the breakdown of the Bretton Woods system was no fault of theirs, laid stress on the need to assure a dependable and growing flow of resources to their countries from the more developed countries. There was no disagreement in principle here, but political obstacles to increased development assistance, especially in the United States, were formidable. The representatives of developing countries also took positions on the specific issues concerning adjustment and reserves. In particular they sought to exempt their countries from some of the adjustment and currency arrangements proposed for the new system.[5]

The major issues of adjustment and convertibility gave rise to a number of related questions. For example, the specific means of improving the adjustment process proposed by the United States—a presumptive reserve indicator structure, to be described below—was the subject of protracted debate. There was also disagreement on U.S. proposals that would give countries an option to let their currencies float and to change their par values by small amounts without prior IMF approval. On the European side, the desire for convertibility necessarily led to the controversial question of what to do about existing reserve currency balances, it being obvious, given the relatively small magnitude of U.S. reserves, that these could not be made convertible. Basic differences also existed about capital controls; the Japanese and most Europeans believed that controls on capital flows were necessary and desirable while the Americans were philosophically opposed to them and insisted, at a minimum, that no country should be required to use such controls.

The bargaining power of the United States rested mainly on its willingness to restore convertibility of the dollar—just as its threat to suspend convertibility had been used as a bargaining weapon in the period leading up to August 1971. The desire of American officials to keep their powder dry—that is, not to make their major concession until they had achieved their own objectives in the negotiations—sometimes led others, particularly Europeans, to interpret American coyness as a wish to keep the world on a dollar standard. No doubt some Americans held this position. But I was convinced that the American deputies, Volcker and Daane, were prepared to agree ultimately to an asset settlement system, provided the reform encompassed a satisfactory adjustment mechanism and adequate elasticity in settlement procedures.

Adjustment

In the early meetings of the deputies, discussion of each major topic was guided by an "annotated agenda" prepared by the bureau. Sir Derek Mitchell, the British Treasury deputy, referred to these as "Mr. Morse's examination papers." The papers attempted to identify the salient issues and to put questions designed to stimulate debate—out of which, it was hoped, a consensus could be forged. Individual deputies were free to circulate papers. At the end of the first day of the first substantive meeting, held at the IMF Building in Washington on November 27–29, 1972, the U.S. deputies distributed a paper spelling out both the philosophy and the technical details of the approach outlined by Secretary Shultz in September.[6]

The U.S. Proposal

Taking it as given that in the reformed system most members of the Fund wanted the exchange rate regime to be based on par values or central rates and wanted currencies to be convertible, the U.S. paper proposed an adjustment mechanism that would satisfy these objectives while also safeguarding the United States from the difficulties it had gotten into under the old system.

The essential principle of the proposal was that a system in which currencies were to be convertible into reserves should assure that the "demand" for reserves—reflected in the excess of balance-of-payments surpluses over deficits —did not exceed the supply of reserves available. To implement this principle, a reserve indicator would be utilized to assure consistency between the degree of tolerance for imbalances in the system and the availability of financing for such imbalances. A structure of "reserve indicators" would be established, with a "norm" or base level for each country such that the sum of all "norms" was equal to the total of world reserves (countries' norms would increase over time with the creation of new SDRs). If countries' reserves increased or decreased disproportionately and reached various reserve indicator points, signals of the need for adjustment would be emitted and countries would be expected to adopt policy measures aimed at correcting their surpluses or deficits. Ultimately, if countries failed to take adequate actions to reverse the movement in reserves, "sanctions," or "graduated pressures" as they came to be called, would be applied by the IMF.

The paper stressed that mere consultation was not enough to produce adjustment. This had been demonstrated over the previous decade, when, despite regular consultations in the IMF and the OECD, large payments imbalances had persisted.

The reserve indicators would be "presumptive" rather than automatic signals for adjustment, and provision was made for "overriding" the signals. The concept of presumptiveness gave rise to much confusion, partly because the Americans, anxious that the presumptions be strong, did not initially stress presumptiveness (Shultz had not used the word in September). Perhaps opponents of the U.S. approach found it more vulnerable to attack if they interpreted the reserve indicators as being "automatic" in triggering the need for policy changes and graduated pressures.

Another contentious aspect of the U.S. proposal was that one of the reserve indicator points was a "convertibility point" (later called a "primary asset holding limit"). If a country's reserves passed such a point, it would lose its right to demand conversion of additional accruals of foreign exchange into primary reserve assets. Whether this feature (really a nonconvertibility point) was to be regarded as a sanction or simply an element of elasticity in the settlement system was left in some ambiguity.

While the reserve indicator structure was largely symmetrical (except for the convertibility point on the plus side), the plan explicitly acknowledged that one of its major purposes was to make the adjustment process more even-handed than in the past in the treatment of surpluses and deficits.

In this and other respects, the American proposal (we may call it the Volcker plan) bore a striking resemblance to the Keynes plan of 1943. The Keynes plan was more comprehensive, since it proposed a new institution (a "clearing union") and a new reserve asset ("bancor").[7] In 1972 the institution existed in the form of the IMF, and the SDR served the functions of Keynes' bancor. It was in the rules for adjustment of payments imbalances that the two approaches were so similar. "In recognizing that the creditor as well as the debtor may be responsible for a want of balance, the proposed institution would be breaking new ground" (Keynes in 1943). "Convertibility itself cannot promote adequate or equitable adjustment. Convertibility is in that sense an asymmetrical tool, operating only on deficit countries. In the framework of the U.S. proposal, the inherent link of convertibility to reserve fluctuations would result in broadly symmetrical pressures upon surplus and deficit nations" (Volcker in 1972). Both plans prescribed specific actions that countries in deficit or surplus might take as their creditor or debtor positions cumulated. These actions were quite similar in the two plans.

Paul Volcker did not have the Keynes plan in front of him as he sketched out the U.S. proposal. Although it might seem pertinent, at this point, to cite Santayana's dictum that "those who do not remember the past are condemned to relive it," in this case those who forgot history managed to reconstruct it. The concerns of the United States in the early 1970's were in many ways like those Keynes tried to cope with in the early 1940's. His country and Europe in general feared that the United States, strengthened rather than weakened by World War II, would emerge as a structural creditor in the postwar period and that the full force of balance-of-payments adjustment would fall on the countries of Europe. Keynes' objective was an adjustment mechanism that would work symmetrically while permitting the restoration of currency convertibility and the relatively free, multilateral trade that it was designed to assure.

The Volcker plan of 1972 had the same purposes. Americans put it forward in 1972, after having rejected it in 1943, because the American position had been completely transformed in the interim. Although the parallels are far from perfect—the basic economic strength of the United States in the 1970's was still enormous, in contrast with the position of Europe at the end of World War II—by the 1970's U.S. officials had taken on the mentality that comes from trying to cope with a weak balance-of-payments position. The continental Europeans, in turn, had by then adopted the reverse mentality, similar to the one displayed by Americans in the debates leading up to Bretton Woods.

Apart from the reversal of economic roles, there may have been another explanation for the European resistance to the U.S. proposal of 1972. Some degree of weakness in the U.S. balance of payments was not unwelcome to some Europeans, for such weakness inevitably reflected itself in America's political power. A Europe that was endeavoring to form an economic, and perhaps ultimately a political, union was motivated in part by the desire to place itself on a political plane of greater equality with the United States. An American balance of payments that was strong enough to prevent international monetary turmoil but not so strong as to reestablish American dominance would be consistent with this aim. The same motivation had been present in the negotiations on exchange rate realignment in the autumn of 1971. Then a knowledgable international official had made the point graphically when, putting his finger just beneath his nose, he said to some American officials, "they are trying to keep you in the water up to here."

Reactions to the U.S. Proposal

Having been circulated only after the November 1972 meeting of deputies was under way, the American paper did not receive a full examination until later. *The Economist* was correct in reporting that "the Americans are still out ahead of the field with their adjustment proposals" but "they are still fairly alone in their concentration on reserve movements as the indicator for exchange adjustments"[8] (and, it should have been added, other measures to correct payments imbalances).

Even at the November meeting, several objections were made to reliance on a reserve indicator. It was argued that a country's reserves can change because of short-term capital flows even if its basic balance of payments is in equilibrium. And knowledge by market participants that a reserve indicator was being relied on could provoke speculative capital movements when a country's reserves rose or fell by significant amounts. More broadly, the old issue of "rules versus discretion" was raised. A number of deputies believed that what was required was "assessment" by a deliberative body rather than reliance on simplistic rules. The American deputies responded that they too favored consultation and that the rules could be overridden in the consultation process.

Further discussion at the January 23–25, 1973, meeting of deputies, in Paris, led to a clearer division of views on adjustment. Apart from the American delegation, those who were willing to look with sympathy on "objective indicators" would in most cases have confined their use to triggering consultations in the IMF with countries revealed by the indicator or indicators to be in imbalance. The notion in the U.S. plan that a reserve indicator should also create a presumption of corrective policy actions by countries in imbalance and ultimately of "graduated pressures" applied by the international community received little support. In fact the group was even unwilling at that stage to agree to the establishment of a working party to examine more closely the technical aspects of the use of indicators.

Reserve Assets and Convertibility

In their initial deliberations on settlement and reserve assets, the deputies again agreed on broad principles but disagreed on important aspects of those principles.

Most European deputies favored full convertibility or asset settlement in the reformed system. They differed, however, on how to deal with outstanding balances of reserve currencies, which was a necessary condition for asset settlement. The Italian deputies, Rinaldo Ossola and Silvano Palumbo, presented (and made public) a scheme that would combine asset settlement by reserve centers with voluntary consolidation of existing balances through a substitution account in the Fund.[9] In this scheme, asset settlement would be multilateral, carried out through the IMF, rather than bilateral as in the past. This feature was intended to prevent the sort of political pressure the United States was alleged to have exerted before 1971 on countries that were considering asking for conversion of dollars into gold. Under the Italian proposal, the United States would periodically pay to or receive from the IMF an amount of SDRs equal to its deficit or surplus. Other countries would have the right, but not the obligation, to turn in dollar balances to the Fund in exchange for SDRs. The largely voluntary nature of this provision appealed to representatives of a number of developing countries, who wanted to maintain freedom of choice in the composition of their countries' reserves.

Another approach to convertibility involved a ceiling on countries' holdings of reserve currencies. Amounts above the ceiling would be convertible by reserve centers. Should countries use reserve currencies to finance deficits with reserve centers—thereby reducing the total official liabilities of the latter—the Fund would issue SDRs to the reserve centers in like amount. Adoption of this approach would have led to a gradual reduction in the amount of reserve currencies as an element in total reserves, since the aggregate of ceilings would have moved down as countries used their reserve currencies.

The American deputies showed less than warm enthusiasm for these proposals, though they recognized that even a system of voluntary convertibility would require that something be done to prevent old balances of dollars from being presented for conversion. Part of the hesitance on the U.S. side stemmed from a concern about both the interest rate and the maintenance-of-value obligations that would attach to dollars that were consolidated in a substitution account in the Fund. This concern also led the Americans to favor a low interest rate on SDRs, while many other deputies, wishing to see the SDR as the principal reserve asset, also saw the need for it to bear a more attractive interest rate. These American attitudes no doubt strengthened the suspicion in the minds of others that the United States was anxious to preserve an important reserve currency role for the dollar.

Although there was general agreement that in the reformed system the volume of world reserves should be "controlled" or "managed," this principle seemed to conflict with the desire of a number of countries, especially developing ones, to have freedom of choice in the composition of their reserves. They wished to be able to invest their reserves in ways that would maximize interest earnings and facilitate borrowings from banks. Yet it was difficult to see how the United States could be expected to cease increasing its liabilities if other countries were to be free to increase their claims on the United States.

On the question of interest on SDRs and on consolidating reserve currency balances outstanding, developing country representatives were of two minds. They agreed in principle that the SDR should become the main international reserve asset. But, as net users of SDRs, some were unhappy about the prospect of paying higher interest. And some deputies from developing countries opposed consolidation of dollar balances into SDRs on the ground that creation of additional SDRs by this means, though it would not change the volume of world reserves, might make some developed countries more reluctant to agree to create new SDRs.

With respect to the SDR, there was considerable sympathy for disconnecting its value from that of gold and, in the words of one deputy, making "1 SDR = 1 SDR." Most deputies, including those from the United States, favored removing the existing "encumbrances" on the use of the SDR, such as its ineligibility for payment in connection with increases in IMF quotas and the requirement of reconstitution. These were among the limitations on the SDR agreed to in 1967 and 1968 in the effort to make the new reserve asset palatable to France.

The role of gold in the future system received little attention until the spring of 1973, when the market price rose rapidly and reached $90 per ounce in March. With the market price so far above the official price of $42.22, central banks hesitated to sell gold to each other. This "immobilization" of gold reserves received considerable attention among European central bank governors. A proposal was developed to abolish the official price and permit transactions among monetary authorities at a market-related price. The proposal was opposed by the United States and by most developing countries on the grounds that it would enhance, rather than diminish, the role of gold and would, by effectively increasing the reserves of major gold holding countries, act as a deterrent to the creation of additional SDRs.

Reform Deliberations in a Floating World

Meetings of both the deputies and the ministers of the Committee of Twenty had been scheduled for March 1973 in Washington. The international monetary crisis delayed the deputies' meeting by ten days and led to a change in its agenda. More fundamentally, it altered the existing system profoundly, though no one was sure at the time whether floating exchange rates were to be a temporary aberration or a more long-lasting phenomenon.

At the deputies' meeting on March 22–23, representatives of developing countries expressed resentment over the fact that major decisions affecting the world monetary system had been taken outside the IMF by a limited group of industrialized countries with no opportunity for participation by the rest of the world (though Ali Wardhana and Jeremy Morse had been invited to the Paris meetings of March 9 and 16). The only response that was given, apart from general expressions of sympathetic understanding, was that the pressure of time had dictated the procedures.

The deputies tried to assess the implications of the new developments for the substance of international monetary reform. Among the lessons of the recent experience was the impotence or, at best, limited effectiveness of capital controls in the face of strong speculative incentives to move funds. Another lesson was that markets did not seem to be prepared to wait out the long lags involved in the response of countries' balance-of-payments positions to changes in their exchange rates. Where these lessons pointed, in terms of reforming the system, was not clear.

In a brief second round of discussion of reserve assets and convertibility, the German deputies, Karl-Otto Poehl and Otmar Emminger, pointed out that increases in world reserves in recent times had been the result not only of large U.S. deficits from 1970 through the first quarter of 1973 but also of two other processes: (1) the placement of reserves in the Euro-currency markets (more recently by countries other than those in the Group of Ten, which had ceased making such placements in 1971) and (2) the diversification of reserves out of dollars into other currencies (if, for example, a developing country switched some of its dollar reserves into marks, Germany's reserves increased and no other country's reserves went down).

Given the widespread desire to accelerate the work on reform, the deputies agreed to a five-day meeting in May 1973, at which time the bureau would have prepared a first draft of an outline of a reformed system. Meanwhile two technical groups would meet, one on the use of indicators in the adjustment process, under my chairmanship, and another on disequilibrating capital flows, to be chaired by Jeremy Morse.

Since the Committee itself would be meeting in three days (on Monday, March 26) the bureau would have ready by Saturday morning a report on the work of the deputies to date. Accordingly, the members of the bureau worked all night Friday, March 23, and—thanks to the efficiency of our secretaries and the Fund's technical personnel—the report was available for circulation early on Saturday morning. I managed to get home by about 7:00 A.M. and to snatch a few hours of sleep before a meeting scheduled for noon.

The report summarized the points of agreement and disagreement that had emerged in the deputies' deliberations through January as well as the differing views on the implications of "recent developments" for reform. Under the latter heading, a wider divergence of views on the future exchange rate system had understandably developed.

Before going to Washington for the meeting of the Committee of Twenty, the Finance Ministers of the EEC had caucused in Brussels. As reported in the press (on the basis of a briefing by Belgian Minister de Clercq), they "rejected the American proposal that future revaluations should take place automatically when a country's monetary reserves reach certain limits."[10]

The first substantive meeting of the Committee at ministerial level took place in the Pan American Union building in Washington on March 26–27, 1973. In presenting the "common position" of the EEC countries, Minister de Clercq did not explicitly reject the American approach. Minister Giscard d'Estaing, praising the cooperation that had been exhibited in resolving the crises of February and March, stressed that the move to a floating system did not constitute reform. On the contrary, the recent measures were only transitional. It was necessary to proceed to rebuild the monetary system on a reformed basis, including "fixed but adjustable" exchange rates. The ministers of most developing countries expressed agreement with this proposition.

There was little forward motion on substantive matters; in general the ministers endorsed the work of their deputies. What did emerge was a mandate to the bureau and to the deputies to intensify their work and to "proceed urgently with the preparation of a draft outline of the reform, in which the major issues would be presented to the Committee for decision."

Summarizing the "points" on which discussion had centered, the communiqué mentioned the use of "objective indicators" in the adjustment process. On the exchange rate regime this language was adopted:

> Members of the Committee recognized that exchange rates must be a matter for international concern and consultation and that in the reformed system the exchange rate regime should remain based on stable but adjustable par values. It was also recognized that floating rates could provide a useful technique in particular situations. There was also general agreement on the need for exchange market stability and on the importance of Fund surveillance of exchange rate policies.[11]

An effort to insert the word "temporary" before "floating rates" was resisted by Secretary Shultz, who argued that the matter had not been discussed. But this was as far as he went; he did not object to the proposition that the exchange rate regime in the reformed system "should remain based on stable but adjustable par values" despite the recent turmoil in exchange markets and the inability to maintain a par value system. A lengthy learning process was just getting started in March 1973; the vague semantic compromise on the exchange rate regime that was contained in the communiqué was to be carried over throughout the life of the Committee of Twenty and beyond.

In April and May the two technical groups, on indicators and on capital flows, met in Washington and Paris, respectively. They produced reports in time for the May meeting of deputies.

The report of the technical group on indicators identified various types of objective indicators but focused most of its attention on reserve and basic balance indicators. It explored the technical problems of definition (including whether the appropriate reserve measure was net or gross reserves), data availability, and choices of base levels and other indicator points. It also examined the three possible uses of indicators—to initiate consultations, to induce policy actions, and to induce the application of graduated pressures to countries in persistent imbalance. In this connection attention was also given to criteria for overriding the signals an indicator was giving. The difficulties of applying an indicator to all countries in the Fund were looked at, as were the problems of application in the period of transition to a better balance in world payments.[12]

The report of the group on disequilibrating capital flows analyzed the principal types of flows: leads and lags in commercial payments and receipts and movements of funds through banking systems. It examined the various types of controls that had been utilized in attempts to dampen such capital flows and the possibilities of coordinated action by groups of countries. Movements of official funds were also looked at, notably diversification of reserves out of traditional reserve currencies and placement of dollar reserves in the Eurodollar market. Finally, means of financing and of offsetting flows were examined.[13]

From Exploration to Negotiations

The deputies group met in Washington for a full week, May 21–25, 1973, during which it initiated work on a preliminary outline of reform. The draft of such an outline, together with a detailed commentary on it, had been prepared by the bureau. The deputies changed its procedures by splitting from time to time into smaller groups for less formal deliberation. In general, the deputies moved from the exploratory stage to the stage of negotiation, as Jeremy Morse reported to the press at the end of the week.

The first day was devoted to the special interests of developing countries, a subject that had originally been scheduled for discussion at the March meeting but was postponed because of the February-March crises. The main topics were a possible link between SDRs and development assistance and access of developing countries to capital markets. To no one's surprise, all deputies from developing countries favored the establishment of a link. Those from developed countries were divided both on the basic question and on the form of a possible link—whether the additional financial resources should be in the form of direct allocations of SDRs to developing countries or should be channeled through development finance institutions. It was decided to establish, under the chairmanship of Hideo Suzuki, a technical group on the link and related proposals.

On Tuesday, Wednesday, and Thursday two informal groups of deputies met each morning to consider various sections of the draft outline. Late each afternoon a plenary session received a report on the morning's debate and an opportunity for general discussion was provided. The six subjects covered in the smaller groups were: making the adjustment process more effective, including the use of indicators; intervention and controls; settlement and convertibility; consolidation of outstanding reserve currency balances; the development of the SDR; and the role of gold.

In the group on adjustment, Paul Volcker, arguing that consultation in the Fund was not sufficient to produce effective balance-of-payments adjustment, repeated a story told to him on a recent trip to Southeast Asia: when disagreement arose between the IMF and member countries on the need for policy changes, if the country was small, it fell into line; if it was large, the IMF fell into line; if several large countries were involved, the IMF disappeared. This was, in Volcker's view, a further demonstration of the need for an objective indicator to guide the adjustment process in a way that would be equitable to all countries.

The debate did not succeed in eliminating the objections to the U.S. proposals put forward earlier, but it did bring some convergence of views, including a proposal for "presumptive assessment" in the IMF. Such assessment, it was claimed, would put the burden of proof on the country in imbalance. The notion of applying graduated pressures at some point was also accepted by most, though not all, deputies.

On the question of capital controls, taken up in another group, the basic divergence between the U.S. and most other deputies persisted. The draft outline stated that capital controls would be permitted but not made mandatory. Some deputies would have given the IMF the power to require a country to adopt capital controls. When Jeremy Morse had earlier summarized positions on this question, he characterized controls on capital flows as a necessary evil, with some deputies emphasizing "necessary" and others "evil."

In the consideration of asset settlement, the draft outline presented two forms—a centralized system through the Fund and a bilateral system—and two degrees of stringency—mandatory and voluntary. It turned out that most developing countries tended to favor full asset settlement by reserve centers but freedom of choice for other countries to hold reserve currencies or to present them for conversion.

In general, developing country deputies tended to favor a relatively loose settlement system and a loose adjustment mechanism, at least as applied to them. European and Japanese deputies leaned toward a tight settlement system but rejected U.S. proposals for the adjustment mechanism. American deputies spoke in terms of equal stringency in both the adjustment and settlement systems, but the impression they conveyed was that they preferred a looser settlement system and a stringent adjustment process.

Concerning consolidation of existing reserve currency balances and possible rules limiting the freedom of countries to switch foreign exchange reserves, once again there was a divergence of views. Developing country deputies held out for maximum freedom of reserve management, while some but not all Europeans favored a mandatory consolidation of outstanding dollar reserves, reducing them to working balances. Because of the resistance to mandatory consolidation, consideration was also given to rules on the management of currency reserves. Although it appeared that some rules could probably be agreed upon in this area, the developing country representatives hesitated to make concessions on this, as on other issues, until they had assurance that they would achieve their own objectives in the reform.

The first systematic discussion of gold and the SDR took place in one of the informal sessions. All deputies but those from France and South Africa favored a reduced role for gold, if not demonetization. But they were divided on the desirability of abolishing the official gold price. Abolition would cut the valuation link between gold and SDRs, permitting the latter to take on an independent value. It would also, in some interpretations, serve as a symbol that gold was being dethroned. For others, maintenance of the official gold price combined with the stricture in the IMF Articles on purchases at prices above the official price served the useful purpose of confining central bank gold transactions to *sales* in the market at then prevailing prices; furthermore, it was feared that if the official price were abolished, some central banks might attempt to establish a new higher price for inter-central bank transactions, which would be tantamount to raising the official price.

In a plenary session on the last day of the week, the divisions of opinion on the various issues were clarified further. European deputies continued to reject sole reliance on a reserve indicator, preferring "presumptive assessment," while Paul Volcker stressed the consistency of a reserve indicator approach with the settlement system. He also suggested that it would be a domestic political advantage to policy makers to be able to point to an objective indicator to justify the adoption of policies designed to correct a surplus or deficit. The Europeans in turn noted that decisions to override an indicator would involve a political process similar to assessment. Both the Europeans and the Americans, however, were prepared to put the burden of proof on the country in imbalance, and both agreed to the ultimate use of graduated pressures.

On the question of settlement, Volcker continued to favor voluntary bilateral convertibility, with an opportunity for a one-time initial consolidation of reserve currency balances. Most other deputies supported the Italian proposal for a unified approach to asset settlement and consolidation.

Convergence and Divergence

The deputies met again in July 1973, in Washington, to prepare for a "working session" of ministers scheduled for the end of the month. The deputies did not narrow their divergences on major issues, with one significant exception, but they did clarify the presentation of the issues.

In the course of the debates it became clear that, despite the very large increase in many countries' official dollar reserves after 1970, no deputy regarded the reserves of his country as excessive. This was revealed when the possibility was discussed of consolidating outstanding dollar balances by transforming them into long-term, nonliquid obligations of the United States. There appeared to be no takers. Even the representatives of Germany, whose foreign exchange reserves in mid-1973 were $25 billion (compared with about $4 billion three years earlier) claimed that much of the growth in reserves was matched by increased foreign debts of German citizens, businesses, and financial institutions. If those debts began to be repaid, the Bundesbank would need to use its apparently large reserves. Thus they could not agree to bilateral funding unless there were provision for mobilization of the funded assets.

At the same meeting, the French deputies came forward formally with a proposal that represented an effort to make the adjustment process more symmetrical between countries in deficit and those in surplus. Apparently this resulted from a long chat between Minister Giscard d'Estaing and Secretary Shultz, accompanied by their deputies, during a meeting of their Presidents in Reykjavik, Iceland, in early June 1973.

Shultz and Volcker, aware of the French desire to see a tight form of convertibility in the reformed system, had stressed the asymmetrical effects of convertibility on adjustment. When the French officials returned to Paris, they formulated a new concept of "graduated pressure" which they circulated to the July meeting of deputies. Instead of the U.S. convertibility point, which would have precluded persistent surplus countries from converting foreign exchange earnings beyond that point—thereby requiring them to hold foreign exchange while the country whose currency they held would to that extent be relieved of convertibility obligations—the French officials proposed that beyond a certain point in the accumulation of reserves, surplus countries would deposit additional accruals with the IMF and would be subject to "negative interest" at an increasing rate. In other words, excess accumulations of reserves by countries in surplus would be taxed, but countries in deficit would continue to be subject to full asset settlement. This proposal appeared to add considerable strength to the arsenal of "graduated pressures" already contemplated.

Here again there is a historical parallel with the negotiations that led to Bretton Woods. Keynes' clearing union proposal contained a penalty charge on excess credit or debit balances. (As Harrod put it, "A paradox, to pay interest on your deposit as well as on your overdraft!"[14]) The Americans at that time opposed this as well as the "unlimited liability" of surplus countries to accumulate claims on the rest of the world through the clearing union. This left the adjustment process heavily weighted against countries in deficit, a point that Keynes and his associates pressed on the Americans. In response, the American side came up with a sanction, "the scarce currency clause," designed to introduce greater symmetry. According to Harrod, "This was a very remarkable concession." Reading of it on a crowded night train from London to Oxford, Harrod "felt an exhilaration such as only comes once or twice in a life time." For it was the first time, he said, that the Americans had stated in a document "that they would come in and accept their full share of responsibility when there was a fundamental disequilibrium in trade."[15]

In a similar way, the French in 1973 came forward with a proposal designed to make the system more symmetrical. Whether they were aware that they, like Paul Volcker, were resurrecting a Keynes proposal, I do not know. But, like Harrod, I too felt an exhilaration, and I conveyed my congratulations to my old friend, Claude Pierre-Brossolette, the deputy from the French Ministry of Finance.

The Committee of Twenty met in Washington on July 30–31, 1973, with the understanding that no communiqué would be issued. It had before it a summary of issues and a draft outline of reform, both prepared by the bureau in the light of the deputies' deliberations. Six issues were placed before the ministers:

1. Whether the need for policy action to correct deficits and surpluses should be established by main reliance on a presumptive reserve indicator or by general assessment.

2. Whether graduated pressures on countries in extreme imbalance should include authorization to restrict imports from countries in persistent large surplus that have failed to take adequate corrective measures (a form of the scarce currency clause already contained in the IMF Articles but never used).

3. Whether reserve currency countries should be subject to mandatory convertibility when they are in deficit or to a convertibility requirement depending on whether or not other countries request it (as in the Bretton Woods system).

4. How the value of the SDR should be managed in relation to currencies.

5. Whether transactions in gold between monetary authorities should continue to be ruled out above the official price or whether the official price should be abolished and monetary authorities be free to buy and sell gold at a market-related price.

6. Whether a link should be established between SDRs and development assistance (on which the report of the technical group was available).[16]

The nature of the exchange rate regime was not listed as an issue. The outline continued to carry forward the semantic formula arrived at in March, with no attempt to elaborate it.

The United States was in a minority—in some cases alone—on most of the issues. The reasons for this have already been presented with respect to issues 1, 2, and 3. Concerning the valuation of the SDR, the U.S. preference was for a low interest rate on the ground, as Secretary Shultz explained to his fellow ministers, that American interest rates had historically been lower than those in other countries. A high interest rate on SDRs would give other countries an incentive to borrow dollars in the United States either to acquire SDRs bearing a higher rate of interest or to avoid using high-yielding SDRs to finance a deficit. On gold, the U.S. preference was for measures that would phase out its monetary role. Finally, the United States opposed the SDR link because it would burden the SDR before it had a chance to become the chief reserve asset, a position that Chairman Burns expounded at the meeting.

The minority position of the United States was at least partially explained by its being at the center of the system whose reform was being negotiated. Reform involved change; it was natural that each country wished to minimize the changes in practices and policies that it would have to undertake. "Everybody knows the French talk incessantly about reforms and are said to be clamoring for them, but deep down in their hearts they fear change because it's upsetting. The ideal reforms would be those which put your neighbor's house in order but do not touch you."[17] This observation, if applied to monetary reform, characterized not only the French. As I listened to some of the debates, I couldn't help concluding that "everybody wants reform but nobody wants change."[18]

While the Committee did not fully resolve any of the issues, enough suggestions for bridging the various gaps were offered to create the impression that resolution was possible. Press reports, based on interviews with various ministers, carried an optimistic tone.[19] Thus the deputies were asked to meet again in early September 1973 to try to reach agreement on the questions of adjustment and convertibility. This would be followed by a meeting of the Committee during the IMF annual convocation in Nairobi, Kenya, in late September, when a draft of a first outline of reform might be made public.

After the ministerial meeting, the bureau undertook to revise the draft outline and to present to the deputies, for their September 5–7 meeting in Paris, "models" of adjustment and convertibility systems that might provide the basis for an agreement.

The adjustment model specified that countries would take prompt and adequate action to avoid protracted payments imbalances and would direct policies to keeping their official reserves within limits which would be agreed from time to time in the Fund and which would be consistent with the volume of total liquidity. For this purpose a reserve indicator structure would be established. The model went on to describe the consultation procedures in the IMF and stated that an assessment by the Executive Board would establish whether there is a need for adjustment. The application of graduated pressures was also provided for. Thus the model attempted to blend the approach of the

United States and that of other countries, but it probably leaned toward the U.S. view.

On convertibility, a "mixed system" was spelled out. The idea of such a system, which had come up in the July meetings, was that a group of countries —the industrial ones—would establish a system of multicurrency intervention, similar to what already existed in the EEC "snake." Full convertibility would apply within that group, even if it did not adopt multicurrency intervention, but countries outside the group, which would in any case continue to intervene mainly in dollars, would have the choice of presenting or not presenting dollar accruals for conversion; this choice would, however, be subject to a designation procedure in which the Fund could request countries to convert balances. A substitution facility would be established, and the bureau spelled out the various ways in which "elasticity" could be introduced into the settlement system, including the American proposal for a convertibility point. But, to take account of European objections to this proposal, the convertibility point was put forward on a presumptive rather than an automatic basis; that is, convertibility for a country in large surplus would be suspended at the convertibility point only if the Fund did not decide otherwise.

The presentation of and reactions to these models at the September deputies' meeting in Paris constituted the turning point in the Committee of Twenty negotiations. It was the time of opportunity for convergence. But agreement on the two major issues could not be pulled off.

At the outset of the meeting, the European deputies voiced objection to the models, which appeared to them to accept too much of the American approach to adjustment—particularly a reserve indicator that would presumptively trigger both policy actions and graduated pressures. Although they were not of one mind on the precise form of settlement arrangements, they believed that what the bureau had put forward was not sufficiently stringent. The European deputies were joined by those from Japan and a number of developing countries. Paul Volcker, on the other hand, found the bureau's proposals on adjustment acceptable but was somewhat critical of the convertibility model, though he did not reject it outright. A few deputies found the models acceptable or nearly so.

These different, and apparently irreconcilable, reactions to the effort to bring about a breakthrough on the related issues of adjustment and convertibility were extremely disappointing to the bureau. We had struggled for days in formulating the compromise models. If we had simply tried to encapsulate the majority view, the models would have been much more acceptable to the European deputies. But, all along, the bureau operated on two assumptions that led it to reject this approach. One was that a reformed system had to be designed, not merely negotiated. "After all, there is always a danger in a negotiation that you will put together a compromise rather than a construction."[20] What emerged had to be coherent and workable. A second assumption was that we could not regard the United States as simply one among twenty parties in the negotiations. The central role of the United States and its currency in the system required that the reform proposals be broadly acceptable to the American representatives.

One possible explanation for the nonacceptance of the bureau's models is that by September 1973 it was clear that the U.S. balance of payments had improved greatly. Some European officials may have believed that later on, say in the spring of 1974, the American negotiators would be more relaxed and perhaps ready to give up some of the points that were particularly irksome to others.

Following the disappointing first round of deliberations, various informal discussions were held in small groups. The realization that a complete failure to agree would not only go against the mandate that the Committee had given the deputies but could lead to adverse public reactions resulted in a more conciliatory attitude on all sides. The bureau distributed a somewhat revised set of proposals on adjustment and convertibility, identifying some issues as still unsettled. This provided the basis for accommodation, though it left some major issues open in the hope that they could be resolved at the political level in Nairobi.

As Jeremy Morse told the press, the discussion on the adjustment and convertibility systems had been "quite tough going." The deputies had reached an accord on what should go to the ministers in the sections of the outline dealing with adjustment and convertibility, agreeing on some points and recognizing disagreement on others that required further work.[21]

On this basis the First Outline of Reform was prepared for submission to the IMF annual meeting and for publication. The Committee decided after all that it would not try to resolve the issues of substance during its brief meeting in Nairobi. It did, however, on the suggestion of Minister Giscard d'Estaing, set a deadline of July 31, 1974, for completion of its work. This procedural decision was intended to demonstrate the existence of a "political will" to reconcile differences and agree on a reformed system. The Committee would meet again in January 1974 after the deputies and the IMF Executive Board had worked through the autumn on outstanding issues. Cynics and noncynics alike observed that when politicians cannot agree on substance, they will always come up with an agreement on procedure.

Ali Wardhana's report to the IMF Board of Governors noted that the Outline had "been prepared by the Chairman and Vice-Chairmen of the Deputies" and, "in my view, reflects the stage reached in the Committee's discussions." After recounting what had been agreed, he said that "important issues have not yet been resolved; and further consideration and study must be given to many matters, including the operational provisions of the reformed system. This position reflects the complex and difficult nature of international monetary reform which involves changes in the patterns of countries' behavior that have persisted for many years."[22]

Thus the First Outline of Reform[23] represented not a blueprint but a rough sketch, fuzzy not only around the edges but also in the middle. And the Outline was attributed to the bureau rather than to the deputies or ministers. At a press conference following the Committee's meeting, Morse accepted a reporter's characterization of the Outline as "a tentative unanimous suggestion."

In response to the ministerial decision to finish by July 31, the deputies established four technical groups: (1) on adjustment, with particular reference to a reserve indicator structure and financial pressures; (2) on settlement, with particular reference to a possible multicurrency intervention system; (3) on global liquidity and consolidation; and (4) on the transfer of real resources from developed to developing countries. The bureau was also expected to work on rules for floating while the Executive Board of the IMF would take up the question of the valuation of the SDR.

Reform and the Oil Crisis

Ten days after the Nairobi meeting ended, the Arab-Israeli war broke out. This led in mid-October to the oil embargo and an initial oil price increase of more than 50 percent. The embargo affected economic activity in Europe, Japan, and the United States in a number of ways and led to a sizable strengthening of the foreign exchange value of the dollar. In late December 1973 the Organization of Petroleum Exporting Countries (OPEC) announced a spectacular increase in oil prices, which quadrupled the price of oil from its early October level.

These developments created enormous uncertainty in many areas of life, including the future balance-of-payments positions of oil-importing countries. One consequence of the uncertainty was general agreement—sometimes tacit, sometimes overt—that the regime of floating exchange rates would go on for some time. No country was ready to commit itself to a par value or central rate in the face of the unknowns in its future balance of payments. French officials shared this view, even though they had been among the most orthodox members of the Committee of Twenty in opposing floating exchange rates as anything but a temporary aberration. Now France, and perhaps other countries, could see no alternative to generalized floating but was unwilling to institutionalize or legitimize floating rates. This dilemma was bound to have effects on the course of the reform exercise and on the determination (so widely shared in September) to complete the reform by July 31, 1974.

The deputies and the ministers met in Rome on January 14–15 and 17–18, 1974, respectively. The meetings were overshadowed by current events in the sense that officials were preoccupied with immediate problems and their attitude to long-term reform of the system was necessarily altered. What had been the chief obstacle to early implementation of reforms when the Committee of Twenty was established—namely, the large deficit in the U.S. balance of payments—had by now disappeared. In the second half of 1973, the United States had earned a surplus on goods, services, and private transfers of more than $9 billion at an annual rate. Its overall surplus (on the official settlements basis) came to about the same figure. But now a new factor—the oil crisis—made early action on long-term reform seem unrealistic. It was frequently said that the reform effort had been "overtaken by events."

At their January meetings, the deputies and ministers did not take up directly the perennial issues of adjustment and convertibility in a reformed system, on which the technical groups had been working since the Nairobi meeting but were not yet finished. Rather they concentrated on how to value the SDR, what to do about the structure of the IMF, what guidelines to adopt on floating currencies, how to proceed with the reform exercise and, most important, how to react to the profound changes implied by the large increase in the price of oil. The Committee's communiqué stated:

> Members of the Committee began by reviewing important recent developments including the large rise in oil prices and the implications for the world economy. They expressed serious concern at the abrupt and significant changes in prospect for the world balance of payments structure. They recognized that the current account surpluses of oil-producing countries would be very greatly increased, and that many other countries—both developed and developing—would have to have large current account deficits. In these difficult circumstances the Committee agreed that in managing their international payments countries must not adopt policies which would merely aggravate the problems of other countries. Accordingly, they stressed the importance of avoiding competitive depreciation and the escalation of restrictions on trade and payments. They further resolved to pursue

policies that would sustain appropriate levels of economic activity and employment, while minimizing inflation. They recognized that serious difficulties would be created for many developing countries and that their needs for financial resources will be greatly increased and they urged all countries with available resources to make every effort to supply these needs on appropriate terms. The Committee agreed that there should be the closest international cooperation and consultation in pursuit of these objectives. They noted that the International Monetary Fund, the World Bank and other international organizations are concerned to find orderly means by which the changes in current account positions may be financed, and they urged that these organizations should cooperate in finding an early solution to these questions, particularly in relation to the difficult problems facing non oil-producing developing countries. In particular, while recognizing the uncertainties with regard to future developments in the field of energy, the Committee agreed that the proposal of the Managing Director of the International Monetary Fund for a temporary supplementary facility should be urgently explored. It is recognized that such a facility poses operational problems which must be resolved and would, particularly for non oil-producing developing countries, be only a partial measure, in view of the nature and magnitude of the balance of payments problems created.[24]

In discussing the current situation and formulating the language of the communiqué, the officials of oil-producing countries had defended their actions mainly on the basis that the prices of products they imported had risen. This justification was rejected by others who said that the quadrupling of the price of oil could not be so justified, and, some said, the price of oil would have to come down. But the basic approach to coping with the staggering change in balance-of-payments positions set forth in the communiqué was to be retained and, with a few exceptions, adhered to over the next two years.

On reform, it was decided in effect to shift to a step-by-step or evolutionary procedure. Certain matters requiring early decision would receive priority. These included the valuation of the SDR, on which there was agreement in principle to base it on the average value of a "basket" of currencies; the establishment of a continuing body in the IMF at ministerial level, comparable to the Committee of Twenty; and conditions and rules for floating. "Other aspects of reform could be agreed with the understanding that their operational provisions would be developed and implemented at a later date."[25]

Minister Giscard d'Estaing had relatively little to say at the Rome meeting. The next day, after a cabinet meeting in Paris and a quick visit to Bonn by Giscard, the French announced that the franc would withdraw from the EEC snake and float freely "for six months." France had had to use reserves to the extent of $3 billion in the second half of 1973 to keep its currency in the snake.

In a radio address on the evening of January 19, Giscard cited the fact that there was no chance of reform of the monetary system in 1974 or 1975 as one justification for the decision to float. The other members of the EEC snake decided to continue the arrangement, and German Finance Minister Schmidt disclosed that Germany had offered France a $3 billion credit as an inducement to retain the franc in the snake.[26]

Amidst the turmoil of the early months of 1974 the reform exercise continued. Three of the technical groups completed reports in March, in time for the next meeting of deputies. (Someone compared the continued diligent performance of the technical groups in the face of the crisis precipitated by the oil price increase to the twitching of an animal's lower extremities after its head had been cut off.)

The group on intervention and settlement, chaired by Jeremy Morse, broke new ground in examining the way in which a system of multicurrency intervention among ten or twenty countries might work. It also considered direct market intervention in SDRs by central banks. On settlement, the division persisted between the U.S. proposal for "on demand" convertibility and the European preference for mandatory convertibility at least among the industrial countries. Differences were narrowed slightly, but it was not to be expected that they could be eliminated in a technical group.[27] If the United States was to agree to mandatory asset settlement, that concession would be made at a higher level and only near the end of the entire reform negotiation.

The group on adjustment, under my chairmanship, examined the problems involved in establishing a reserve indicator structure for use in the adjustment process—how it might provide a presumption for consultations, for policy actions, and for the activation of financial pressures against countries in large and persistent imbalance. It tried to clarify the meaning of "presumption" and of "overriding" a presumption. One issue was whether the reserve indicator should be based on net or gross reserves. The American representatives' preference for gross reserves tended to aggravate suspicions that the United States hoped to shield itself from the discipline of the reformed system it was proposing. I tried to resolve this problem by proposing that the indicator structure —norms and various trigger points—would be based on countries' initial gross reserves while *changes* in countries' positions would take account of movements of both reserves and official liabilities. This was not the first or the last time that a member of the bureau acted as an international official rather than as a representative of his country.

The technical group also proposed special treatment for oil-exporting countries; they would inevitably accumulate large reserves and would have to be exempt from the adjustment pressures applicable to other nations.[28]

The group on global liquidity and consolidation, chaired by Alexandre Kafka, examined various criteria for judging the world need for reserves. With respect to consolidation, it was even more evident then that there was little interest in funding reserve currency balances into longer-term nonliquid obligations. Thus various forms, methods, and time patterns of substitution into SDRs were studied.[29]

Final Stages of the Reform Exercise

For the March 1974 meeting of deputies, the bureau produced a revised Outline of Reform with a series of Annexes containing possible operational provisions that were based on the work of the technical groups. When the deputies met in Washington on March 27–29, they debated the usefulness of bringing forth a "vision" of a reformed system, given the uncertainties as to the duration of the interim period characterized by widespread floating and mammoth surpluses of the oil-exporting countries. The majority supported Paul Volcker's position that such a vision—incorporated in an Outline of Reform—should be put before the world as a guide to an evolutionary reform of the system.

At the same time, it was necessary to agree on several more immediate questions requiring "early implementation." These included IMF surveillance of balance-of-payments adjustment during the interim period, guidelines for floating, a declaration against the use of trade restrictions for balance-of-payments purposes, Fund surveillance of global reserves, the valuation and interest yield of the SDR, provisions regarding gold, measures to assist developing countries, an IMF oil facility, and the establishment of an Interim Committee at ministerial level in the Fund.

The deputies from developing countries voiced particular dissatisfaction with the outcome of the reform exercise. This led to a proposal, included in the report of the technical group on the transfer of real resources, chaired by Jonathan Frimpong-Ansah, for the establishment of another ministerial committee, which came to be called the Development Committee.[30]

The debate on guidelines for floating—there were two versions, one put together by the bureau and the other by the IMF—reflected the basic differences of view that had earlier appeared regarding the degree of flexibility in the exchange rate system. In a floating regime, those deputies who leaned toward long-run exchange rate fixity favored a floating guideline that encompassed a zone within which countries would endeavor to keep their exchange rates. Those who leaned more to flexibility had doubts about the feasibility of establishing such zones.

Meeting in Paris on May 7–9, 1974, the deputies polished the Outline of Reform, including a section on "immediate steps" that might be taken. This material was to be submitted to the final meeting of the Committee in Washington on June 10–11. Meanwhile the Executive Board of the Fund had moved toward agreement on the establishment of an Interim Committee at ministerial level, on guidelines for floating, on the valuation and interest rate of SDRs, on an oil facility, on an extended Fund facility for longer-term balance-of-payments assistance to developing countries, and on other matters.

Attendance at the final meeting of the Committee in June revealed a high rate of turnover among finance ministers. Seven of the twenty members who had attended the previous Committee meeting in January were not present in June. Two had moved to higher office: Valéry Giscard d'Estaing was now President of the French Republic and Helmut Schmidt was Chancellor of the Federal Republic of Germany. George Shultz had been succeeded by William Simon as U.S. Secretary of the Treasury, and Anthony Barber by Denis Healey, Labour Chancellor of the Exchequer; Antonio Delfim Netto, for many years Finance Minister of Brazil, had stepped down, to be replaced by Mario Simonsen; and the Finance Minister of Morocco, Bensalem Guessous was succeeded by Abdel-Kader Benslimane.

The meeting began with a statement of behalf of the Group of Twenty-four (the developing countries' counterpart of the Group of Ten) presented by Ismail Mahroug, Minister of Finance of Algeria. The developing countries felt that the Outline of Reform represented an unbalanced approach, since it gave insufficient attention to the interests of developing countries. As for the immediate measures, the ministers of the Group of Twenty-four agreed that any package should include the link of SDRs to development assistance; a solution to the gold problem that did not jeopardize the SDR-aid link or strengthen the role of gold; an extended Fund facility; an increase in the relative share of developing countries in IMF quotas; and establishment of a Development Committee.

As it turned out, the link was not agreed to and nothing was decided on gold. Secretary Simon did agree that the United States would give careful reconsideration to its position on the link. The question of IMF quotas was put off for future consideration. On the other hand, the extended Fund facility was later established and the Development Committee was created.

The final Report of the Committee, together with the Outline of Reform with accompanying Annexes, was made public on June 14. The report repeated the reasons for the switch from what Jeremy Morse called "the grand design" to an evolutionary approach and explained why the "immediate steps" should be taken.

The Outline of Reform itself was characterized, both in the Committee's report and in the preface to the Outline, as recording "the outcome of the Committee's discussion of international monetary reform and indicates the general direction in which the Committee believes that the system could evolve in the future." Thus, in contrast to the Nairobi Outline, the Committee took responsibility for the final Outline of Reform. The Annexes, which were attributed to the Chairman and Vice Chairmen of the Deputies, recorded "the state of discussion" on areas "within which agreement has not yet been reached on some important aspects." The Annexes also provided "illustrative schemes and operational detail." Furthermore, the report envisaged "that arrangements in these areas, as they may be agreed, should be implemented as and when the Fund judges it feasible to do so, and that the Fund might in some cases introduce such arrangements initially on an experimental basis with a view to subsequent agreement on full implementation."[31]

The Outline of Reform set forth the "main features of the international monetary reform":

(a) an effective and symmetrical adjustment process, including better functioning of the exchange rate mechanism, with the exchange rate regime based on stable but adjustable par values and with floating rates recognized as providing a useful technique in particular situations;
(b) cooperation in dealing with disequilibrating capital flows;
(c) the introduction of an appropriate form of convertibility for the settlement of imbalances, with symmetrical obligations on all countries;
(d) better international management of global liquidity, with the SDR becoming the principal reserve asset and the role of gold and of reserve currencies being reduced;
(e) consistency between arrangements for adjustment, convertibility, and global liquidity; and
(f) the promotion of the net flow of real resources to developing countries.[32]

The section on adjustment contained some elements of the Volcker plan, since it provided that countries "will aim to keep their official reserves within limits that will be internationally agreed from time to time in the Fund and which will be consistent with the volume of global liquidity. For this purpose reserve indicators will be established on a basis to be agreed in the Fund." Possible operational provisions and an illustrative scheme were presented in an Annex which drew heavily on the report of the technical group.[33] The section on adjustment also provided for a consultation process in the Fund at the level of both the Executive Board and the ministerial Council of twenty members that was envisaged as a new permanent organ of the Fund. In addition it provided for the application of graduated pressures, and these, as well as modes of activation, were set forth in another Annex.

The objectives of convertibility were stated to be "symmetry of obligations of all countries including those whose currencies were held in official reserves; the better management of global liquidity and the avoidance of uncontrolled growth of reserve currency balances; adequate elasticity; and as much freedom for countries to choose the composition of their reserves as is consistent with the overall objectives of the reform." The specific ways of implementation were spelled out in Annexes. Provision "as necessary" for the consolidation of reserve currency balances was also made.

Regarding primary reserve assets, it was stated that the "SDR will become the principal reserve asset and the role of gold and of reserve currencies will be reduced." The Outline observed that arrangements with respect to gold in the reform system were not settled. Three approaches were identified: monetary authorities, including the IMF, would sell but not buy in the market and would not undertake transactions with each other at a price different from the official price; the official price of gold would be abolished and monetary authorities, including the Fund, would be free to deal in gold with one another on a voluntary basis and at mutually acceptable prices, as well as to sell in the market; and the third approach would also permit purchases in the market. The possibility of a substitution account for gold in the IMF was mentioned.

The alternative forms of an SDR-aid link were identified, though the principle was not agreed. Finally the Outline called for the establishment of a Council with "the necessary decision powers to supervise the management and adaptation of the monetary system."[34]

Part II of the Outline presented the "immediate steps" already discussed.[35]

In broad terms, the final Outline of Reform, apart from the "immediate steps," did not differ greatly from the Nairobi Outline. It was a skeleton and some parts of its structure were not fully articulated, but the Annexes added a considerable amount of flesh to the bones. Although not fully agreed, the material in the Annexes provides the basis, if and when the need is felt, for movement toward a more structured international monetary system.

Postscript on Monetary Reform

An editorial in *The New York Times* on June 15, 1974, quoted the American transcendentalist Margaret Fuller's saying "I accept the universe" and Thomas Carlyle's observation, "By God, she'd better."

This seemed to sum up the general reaction to the conclusion of the work of the Committee of Twenty. The world had changed since the Committee had started on its lofty effort to remake the monetary system. The concerns that had motivated the initiation of the reform effort—the inconvertibility of the dollar, the wish to avoid a repetition of large payments imbalances and frequent crises, and the political desire for a more symmetrical system—had all given way to the more pressing problems generated by the increase in the oil price and by inflation. To many officials a reformed system was conceivable only if it was based on par values, yet the return to par values seemed far away indeed in mid-1974. With a floating dollar, the question of convertibility was virtually irrelevant. For Europeans, the major *raison d'être* of the reform effort had thus evaporated. And the strongest apostle of a par value system—France —was itself floating outside the EEC snake.

Meanwhile the process of learning to live with floating exchange rates went on, though the process was far from smooth. "The evolving monetary system will be the child of the reform discussion and of events: which parent will be dominant, time alone will show."[36]

XV

Learning to Live with Floating Exchange Rates
in a World of Inflation and Recession

The move to generalized floating in March 1973 was widely regarded as a temporary departure from normality. Even George Shultz, a believer in floating rates but sensitive to the viewpoints of other governments—and of some officials in his own government—said in September 1973 that a regime of par values should be the "center of gravity" of a reformed international monetary system.

Regardless of the reasons for, and the expectations as to the duration of, the decision of March 1973, the inflationary infection that overtook the world economy in 1972–1974 made a par value system even more difficult to sustain than before. The higher average rate of inflation created more scope for differences among countries both in the speed of price advances and in interest rates; it therefore brought with it a greater likelihood of movements in exchange rates.

The oil shock at the end of 1973 made an early return to par values seem even less realistic. And the deepest world recession since World War II, caused in part by the increase in oil prices, added to the stresses on countries' external positions. By early 1976, the combination of these shocks and the elapse of time had reconciled even the most ardent exponents of "fixed but adjustable par values" to the acceptance of a system of floating, at least for some time. The questions now concerned the management of floating exchange rates: to what degree and by what methods should they be managed? This chapter examines the developments that brought this shift in attitudes and formed the background for the learning process that occurred in 1973–75.

The Emergence of World Inflation, 1972–1974

With the acceleration of output and income in the U.S. economy in 1972, all the major industrial countries were simultaneously in an expansion phase of the business cycle. In the second half of 1972, real GNP rose at an annual rate of over 7 percent in the seven largest OECD countries (Canada, France, Germany, Italy, Japan, the United Kingdom, and the United States). The growth rate in these countries increased even further—to more than 8 percent —in the first half of 1973. Although the expansion still left capacity utilization in the OECD area lower than at earlier business cycle peaks, the rapid increase in production was accompanied by an unprecedented explosion in world prices of industrial raw materials. In the second half of 1972, *The Economist* index of dollar prices of non-food industrial materials rose at an annual rate of almost 25 percent. Over the next six months, to June 1973, these prices increased more than 50 percent (that is, they more than doubled at an annual rate.)[1]

Coincidentally the Soviet Union's grain crop was poor in 1972; this led to the skillful market operation in which that country managed to purchase an enormous quantity of American grain at remarkably low prices. Crop failures occurred in other countries, and even in the United States food and feed grain output fell in 1972.[2] As a result, the volume of U.S. grain exports increased 70 percent from 1971–72 to 1972–73 and U.S. stocks of grain were drawn down rapidly.[3] From 1972 to 1974, the export price of American wheat more than tripled and the price of corn more than doubled.

The food price problem was further aggravated by the mysterious but well-publicized migration of anchovies, a source of protein feed, from their usual location off the coast of Peru; the sizable reduction in the anchovy catch put additional upward pressure on soybean prices. Sugar and cocoa consumption ran ahead of production and prices for these crops rose too. While growth of demand was a factor, the main explanation for the sharp run-up of prices for grain and other food and feed products in 1972–1974 lay in shortfalls in supply.[4]

The Economist index of world food prices rose about 50 percent in the first half of 1973. Food prices paid by consumers in OECD countries, having risen on average by 5.6 percent from 1971 to 1972, advanced almost 13 percent in 1973 and a further 15.1 percent in 1974. In the first half of 1973, food prices in the United States rose almost 11 percent (an annual rate of nearly 22 percent). In many countries wage increases also accelerated and a vicious circle of price-wage advances began. The response of wages to the inflation was more moderate in the United States than in most other industrial countries.[5]

World food prices, after levelling off in dollar terms in the second half of 1973, skyrocketed again in 1974 as the result of "the worst growing season (particularly for corn) experienced in the United States in a quarter century."[6] Prices reached a peak at the end of 1974 that was three times as high as at the end of 1971.

The advance in prices of non-food industrial materials (excluding fuels), as measured by *The Economist,* slowed in the last six months of 1973—though still rising at an annual rate of almost 50 percent—and reached a peak in April 1974. Prices were then at a level almost 2.5 times that of early 1972. There is reason to believe that the advance in these prices in 1972–1974 was the result not only of the rapid expansion of industrial output but of speculative stockpiling as well.[7]

The quadrupling of oil prices at the end of 1973 had diverse effects, but the impact on inflation rates was clear and immediate. The price of regular gasoline at retail rose between October 1973 and May 1974 by 38 percent in the United States, 41 percent in Italy, 23 percent in Germany, 29 percent in France, 50 percent in Britain, and 54 percent in Japan.[8] Industrial and agricultural costs also rose sharply since petroleum is used not only as a fuel but as a raw material in many industries, including the production of fertilizer. Products that serve as substitutes for petroleum, especially coal, experienced substantial price increases. (In Germany the wholesale price of coal rose 26 percent between October 1973 and May 1974.[9])

The result was that consumer prices in the OECD area as a whole rose by 7.7 percent in 1973 and 13.2 percent in 1974. (See Table 2.) In 1974 the

TABLE 2. **Consumer Prices in Selected Countries**
(Percentage Increases)

	Annual Average 1961–1971	1972	1973	1974	12 Months to December 1975
Canada	2.9	4.8	7.6	10.9	9.5
Japan	5.9	4.5	11.7	24.4	7.6
France	4.3	5.9	7.3	13.7	9.5
Germany	3.0	5.5	6.9	7.0	5.4
Italy	4.2	5.7	10.8	19.1	11.2
United Kingdom	4.6	7.1	9.2	16.0	24.9
United States	3.1	3.3	6.2	11.0	7.0
Total OECD	3.7	4.7	7.7	13.2	9.3

SOURCES: OECD, *Economic Outlook,* various issues; *Main Economic Indicators,* February 1976, pp. 150–153.

increases among the larger countries ranged from 7 percent in Germany to almost 25 percent in Japan. In the circumstances, as Adolfo Diz said, "there is some truth in the nonacademic definition of inflation, which says that you are in an inflationary process when prices that once looked appalling begin to look appealing."[10]

In 1974 Germany was the only large OECD country to avoid "double digit" inflation of consumer prices. Among other OECD countries, Norway had the lowest inflation rate in 1974, a rise of 9.4 percent in consumer prices. Broader measures of prices do not tell a significantly different story from the movement of consumer prices. For the OECD area as a whole, GNP deflators rose on average by 12.4 percent in 1974, compared with the consumer price increase of 13.1 percent.[11]

The surge of inflation had many effects. For our purposes the significant one was the greater variance among countries in price movements (and in expectations about future price movements). Though not the only cause of sharp changes in exchange rates in 1973–1975, the differential rate of inflation was an important one.

The Causes of World Inflation

There is a growing body of professional literature and considerable controversy over the causes of the worldwide inflation that began in 1972. Here it is relevant to examine those alleged causes that stem from the nature and functioning of the international monetary system.[12] One school of thought sees the operation of the monetary system before March 1973 as a major source of world inflation. Another attributes at least the aggravation of inflation to floating exchange rates after March 1973.

In June 1973, Otmar Emminger addressed himself to the subject, "What contribution the international monetary system has made to this process" (of world inflation).[13] He enumerated several ways in which the system contributed to inflation: (1) the resistance or inability of countries in deficit, notably the United States, to adjust their external positions by domestic stabilization measures; (2) the "mechanism of rigid parities," which led to "excessive liquidity creation" as countries in surplus bought dollars to prevent the value of their currencies from rising; (3) the effect of volatile capital movements, in dimensions "never dreamt of," on the monetary policies of recipient countries; and (4) additional sources of reserve creation through Euro-currency markets and diversification of reserves. According to Emminger, these four trends and forces "helped to pervert fixed parities from an instrument disciplining deficit countries to one forcing monetary debauchery on surplus countries."

In elaborating the first cause—the overall U.S. deficit—Emminger repeated the long-standing European argument that Europe and Japan "imported inflation" as a consequence of the excess of American capital outflows over the U.S. surplus on goods and services. Yet in the first half of the 1960's world reserve growth was of moderate proportions.[14] In 1965–1969, the U.S. deficit on official settlements was close to zero on balance. How much, then, did the enormous U.S. deficits of 1970–1972 contribute to world inflation? In these three years, the official settlements deficit of the United States exceeded $50 billion. Of this amount, probably more than half was accounted for by disequilibrating capital flows, which Emminger called "the villain of the piece."

We have already taken note of speculative and other capital inflows to Germany in the early 1970's. To what extent did this phenomenon cause the German inflation and, more important, to what extent does it explain the worldwide inflation?

Robert Triffin, conceding that the "basic roots of the world inflation in which all countries are engulfed today admittedly lie outside the monetary field," argues that "price and wage increases could not have been transmitted to the whole world economy if they had not been underwritten and financed by 'permissive' or 'accommodating' rates of national *and international* monetary and credit expansion far exceeding what could be absorbed by actual increases in production." In support of this thesis, Triffin points out that, measured in dollars, the growth of world reserves in 1970–1972 was greater "than in all previous years and centuries since Adam and Eve."[15]

We need not stop to quarrel with Triffin's methods of estimating world reserves and their creation. More relevant, for our purposes, is the distribution among countries of the increase in world reserves, almost half of which accrued to France, Germany, and Japan. (See Table 3.) The combined reserves of these three countries more than tripled, rising from SDR 14.6 billion at the end of 1969 to SDR 48 billion at the end of 1972. Germany and Japan accounted for the bulk of the increase that the three countries experienced.

To what extent was the acceleration of inflation in Germany a result of the enormous expansion in its foreign exchange receipts? While we cannot answer this question definitively, it is worth recalling that wages of German workers had already increased very sharply in 1969, a year when the United States was reducing, not adding to, world reserves. Wage rates in Germany went up even faster in 1970 and the first half of 1971. Only in late 1971 did the wage advance decelerate; in 1972 it still averaged around 9 percent. In this period when the

TABLE 3. Geographic Distribution of Rest of World's Reserves, 1970–1972
(Billions of SDRs)

	RESERVES END-1969	CHANGES				RESERVES END-1972
		1970	1971	1972	1970–1972	
Total (excluding U.S.)	61.3	16.9 (28)²	32.0 (41)²	23.8 (22)²	72.7	134.0
France	3.8	1.2 (32)	2.6 (52)	1.6 (21)	5.4	9.2
Germany	7.1	6.5 (92)	3.6 (26)	4.7 (28)	14.8	21.9
Japan	3.7	1.1 (30)	9.3 (194)	2.8 (20)	13.2	16.9
Subtotal	14.6	8.8 (60)	15.5 (66)	9.1 (23)	33.4	48.0
Other industrial countries (except U.S.)	23.4	4.5 (19)	9.8 (35)	−0.4 (−1)	13.9	37.3
Other developed countries[1]	7.6	0.9 (12)	3.6 (42)	7.1 (59)	11.6	19.2
Oil exporting countries	4.0	0.9 (23)	2.7 (55)	2.3 (30)	5.9	9.9
Other developing countries	11.7	1.8 (15)	0.4 (3)	5.7 (42)	7.9	19.6

SOURCES: Computed from Table 14, p. 40, IMF *Annual Report*, 1973, and Table 17, p. 38, IMF *Annual Report*, 1974.

[1] Finland, Greece, Ireland, Malta, Portugal, Spain, Turkey, Yugoslavia, Australia, New Zealand, South Africa.

[2] Figures in parentheses show percentage changes. Minus sign denotes reduction in reserves.

wage push moderated somewhat, unemployment was rising in Germany.[16] Wholesale prices rose at an annual rate of only 2.8 percent in the first three quarters of 1972 even though reserves had expanded by $10 billion in 1970–71. Significantly, consumer price advances accelerated during 1972, in large part as the result of what happened to the price of food. With world agricultural prices spurting, food prices paid by German consumers rose at an annual rate of 10 percent in the second half of 1972, compared with 4.1 percent in the first half.[17]

Despite the large increase in reserves in 1970 and 1971, the pressure of *domestic* demand was not strong in Germany. The same was true for *total* demand, until the latter part of 1972, when export orders rose sharply. Over the year from the summer of 1972, domestic orders advanced only about 3 percent while export orders increased 34 percent.[18]

Thus, although the money supply in Germany rose rapidly in 1971–72, domestic demand does not appear to have been buoyant; it was demand from abroad that sparked an upswing in German economic activity in the latter part of 1972.[19]

These observations do not disprove the Emminger thesis, for it may be argued that inflation in other countries, induced by the explosion in reserves, accounted for the increase in demand and prices in Germany in 1972–1973. It is still worth noting, however, that the effect on domestic demand in Germany of the increase in reserves was rather mild. The least one can say is that the facts we have cited do not support Emminger's thesis in a direct way. Gottfried Haberler's observation seems pertinent: "Money managers everywhere have made good use of the international scope of the recent inflation trying to shift the blame for the rise in prices to other countries and to anonymous international markets—as if the inflation bacillus had been flown in from outer space."[20]

In the case of Japan, the evidence against the Emminger view is even stronger. While Japan's reserves increased SDR 13 billion from end-1969 to end-1972, more than quadrupling, wholesale prices over these three years rose about one percent a year.[21] Consumer prices in Japan have always advanced more rapidly than wholesale prices (pp. 111–112), but they too slowed down in the first half of 1972 to show a rise of only 3.2 percent at an annual rate, compared with an average yearly increase of 5.7 percent in the decade of the 1960's.[22] Even more than in Germany, demand and output had been far from buoyant, relative to Japan's normal performance, despite a near-doubling of the money supply from 1969 to 1972. In fact, in 1970–71 Japan experienced its "longest cyclical slump in the postwar period."[23] The acceleration of output in early

1972 was sparked by a 17 percent increase in government spending that was deliberately designed to stimulate the economy. Even though prices began to rise faster in late 1972 and early 1973, the budget remained expansionary.[24]

Wholesale prices in Japan rose significantly in the fourth quarter of 1972, when world commodity prices, other than food, were advancing 12 percent (not an annual rate). And consumer food prices increased at an annual rate of 5.8 percent in the second half of 1972, compared with 1 percent in the first half.[25]

By the second half of 1972—and continuing into the fourth quarter of 1973 —the Japanese economy was booming again. The acceleration of prices can reasonably be attributed to the combination of rising costs of imports (though this was tempered somewhat by the revaluation of the yen) and domestic demand, which had been deliberately stimulated by government policy. Export orders actually fell in 1972, in contrast to Germany's experience. It is thus even more dubious in Japan's case that inflation can be attributed to the functioning of the international monetary system.

No doubt examples of developments in other countries can be found where the Emminger thesis explains the facts; but it is difficult to sustain it in the two countries that accounted for more than one-third of the increase of world reserves in 1970–1972.

The BIS economists, writing on inflation in 1972, said:

> While the acceleration of price increases may be accounted for by developments in commodity markets, there was little visible let-up in the brisk underlying pace of inflation that had already been in evidence during the preceding two years or so. This had broadly been attributed to cost-push pressures, accompanied by the apparent breakdown of earlier relationships between the demand for labor and the rate of wage increase. By the end of 1972 wages in many countries were expanding somewhat faster than twelve months earlier, but this may be ascribed as much to the sensitivity of wage demands to food prices as to a tightening of labor market conditions.[26]

The OECD staff, in an analysis of inflation, stated in 1973:

> Since the years 1971 and 1972 corresponded with the period when, in many countries, price increases remained high or accelerated despite an easing of demand pressures, an *a priori* case could be made for attributing an important causal role to the international monetary transmission process. To make such a case, however, requires the assumption that an abnormally high rate of money creation has a direct impact on price and wage determination, independent of any effect on spending decisions and real demand. While some economists are prepared to make this

assumption, they are generally in a minority. There is, however, one specific causal chain which appears plausible, whereby high rates of monetary expansion have a direct effect on the price of land and other real property, and sharp "speculative" rises in these prices play an important role in pushing up inflationary expectations in the economy as a whole (as well as increasing irritation about the distribution of income).

To summarise, an "international liquidity-monetarist" explanation of the course of inflation in OECD countries other than the U.S. during the period 1965–72 appears rather difficult to reconcile with a year-by-year examination of the facts; even for 1971, when the monetary and price indicators are best in line, the low prevailing level of demand pressures implies the need to resort to a rather extreme (quantity theory) argument.

Whatever may be the difference of views about these questions, it would probably be generally agreed that the large capital inflows into many countries during the last three years have greatly complicated the task of implementing monetary policy, particularly in Germany and Switzerland. Thus, even if it is thought that the amount of inflation imparted directly in this way may be relatively limited, it would remain true that the national authorities' ability to control the course of domestic demand has, to varying degrees, been impaired.[27]

A plausible explanation of the worldwide inflation may be formulated on the basis of the upward pressures from food and industrial commodity prices and their interaction in most countries with wages. The rise in commodity prices, in turn, was a result not only of synchronized expansion in most industrial countries but also of a buildup of inventories in anticipation of higher prices or shortages or both. The accumulation of inventories (including imported products) was equal in 1973 to 14 percent of the increase in real GNP in the six largest OECD countries other than the United States; in the 1960's, inventory accumulation in these countries was equal, on average, to only 1.6 percent of GNP increases.[28] Thus to some extent inflation fed on itself through the expectations it created.

To throw doubt on the monetary explanation offered by Otmar Emminger and others is not to deny that transactions have to be financed and that the increases in various forms of money and credit in some of the countries experiencing inflation was no doubt a necessary condition for the occurrence of the inflation. But that is a rather different matter from identifying the increase in international and domestic liquidity as the main cause of worldwide inflation. Furthermore, given the strong upward push of costs, attempts by central banks to prevent price advances would very likely have plunged the world into an even more severe recession.

Those who find themselves dissatisfied with the foregoing explanations of the great inflation of 1972–1974 may wish to agree with Marina Whitman's observation that, "At present, the international transmission of inflation is a painful phenomenon in search of a theory."[29]

Floating Exchange Rates, 1973–1974

It was when inflation was accelerating in early 1973 that the decision was made to adopt floating exchange rates. In the first two months after foreign exchange markets reopened on March 19, 1973, the EEC snake edged down in relation to the dollar, presumably as earlier speculative positions partly unwound; until mid-May the snake remained within what would have been the established margins around the February central rates. The German mark fell to the lower edge of the snake and tended to carry the other EEC currencies down. The Italian lira and the British pound depreciated against the dollar, and the Japanese yen remained stable only as the result of heavy official sales of dollars by the Bank of Japan. In the second quarter of 1973 as a whole, U.S. liabilities to foreign monetary authorities declined.

Weighted Average Exchange Rates
(Percentage Deviations from Smithsonian Parities)

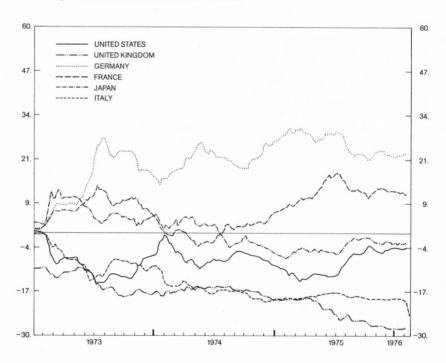

Between May 1973 and the autumn of 1975, the effective exchange rate of the dollar went through three cycles of downswing followed by upswing.[30] (See the chart on page 276.)

Rate Movements in 1973

The exchange rate of the dollar moved down sharply from May to July 1973. Political events in the United States may have played a role, the Watergate affair having reached crisis proportions. On April 30, President Nixon's two chief aides, H.R. Haldeman and John Ehrlichman, resigned following the revelation that some of the Watergate "plumbers," acting on an assignment from Ehrlichman, had earlier broken into the office of Daniel Ellsberg's psychiatrist. On May 17 a committee of the Senate, chaired by Sam Ervin, began its televised and widely publicized hearings. Whether Nixon would be able to hold on to the Presidency was by then a matter of public discussion. This in turn may have created doubts about the ability of the U.S. Government to implement effective economic policies. However, the Watergate episode had no apparent effect either on the working relationship between American and other monetary officials or on the course of the negotiations in the Committee of Twenty.

Meanwhile, short-term interest rates in Germany rose steeply. On May 9 the German Government had announced a stringent program of budgetary restraint designed to combat inflation. It was widely believed that, on top of a tight monetary policy, one result of this program would be to increase Germany's trade surplus and strengthen the mark. Sales of dollars in Europe on May 14 were reported to be of "panic" proportions.[31]

By early June President Pompidou was quoted as saying, "we are witnessing the third devaluation of the dollar."[32]

As the mark pushed against the upper margin of the EEC snake, other snake currencies required support to the extent of more than $1.5 billion. To relieve the pressure and hold the snake together, German authorities revalued the mark by another 5.5 percent on June 29, 1973. (In September, the Dutch guilder was to be revalued by 5 percent.)

In early July the market quotation of the mark, *in terms of dollars,* was almost 25 percent above the level at which the float had started. The dollar value of the Dutch guilder was up about 15 percent and the French franc about 17 percent. But these movements of European currencies in terms of dollars exaggerated the extent of their actual upvaluations, since the currencies of their major trade partners were also rising. The effective exchange rate of the mark, which had revalued twice in addition to floating up, was then 21 percent above its pre-float central rate. The French franc's effective rate was up 11 percent. Over the same period, the effective exchange rate of the dollar fell 10.6 percent.

The effective rate of the dollar fell so much less than its rate against the snake currencies because the dollar exchange rates of Japan and Canada, the two largest trade partners of the United States, had not changed. Japan's huge trade surplus fell from $9 billion in 1972 to less than $4 billion in 1973, and as a result of this and capital outflows, Japan experienced a large overall deficit and the Bank of Japan sold dollars in enormous volume to hold the exchange rate. From February to December 1973, Japan's official reserves fell almost $7 billion.

Nevertheless, President Pompidou's facts were correct; a further 10 percent depreciation of the dollar against the currencies of other industrialized countries had occurred.

In these circumstances, the belief was widespread that the dollar had fallen in value much more than was economically justified.[33] It was understandable that this view was held in Europe, but it was also publicly expressed by U.S. officials. Paul Volcker said on June 26 that the drop of the dollar against the snake "seems overdone and reversible."[34] The next day Arthur Burns told a Congressional committee that the decline in the dollar since May "certainly cannot be justified on any realistic evaluation of international price levels or underlying economic trends."[35]

Yet before the second half of June there had been little pressure from Europeans, and little inclination on the part of Americans, to initiate official operations in foreign exchange markets to counteract the movement in exchange rates. Among the reasons for this may have been a realization that, insofar as Watergate was responsible, there was little chance of bucking the trend. Moreover, European countries would not have welcomed massive official intervention in exchange markets, for this would have undermined their restrictive monetary policies at a time of severe inflation.

In the first week of July, markets for foreign exchange were reported to be chaotic and disorderly. In that week alone the dollar fell in value by 10 percent against the Swiss franc and 9 percent against the German mark and French franc. On Friday, July 6, exchange trading was reported to have ground to a standstill. Over the weekend the central bank governors, meeting in Basle, issued a statement noting that the necessary technical arrangements were now in place to implement the Paris agreement of March 16 regarding official intervention in exchange markets (see page 233). On Monday, July 9, the Federal Open Market Committee held a telephone conference and, with the agreement of the Treasury Department, approved a resumption of exchange operations by the Federal Reserve Bank of New York, to be financed if necessary by drawings on the swap lines with other central banks. The next day an increase in the swap network from $11.7 to $18 billion was announced.[36]

The markets reacted to this announcement and the German mark dropped sharply. But intervention by the central banks was not heavy and European exchange rates advanced again, partly as a result of steeply rising interest rates in Germany; rates on "day to day money" in Frankfurt averaged 15.75 percent in July and on some days exceeded 30 percent. Finally, in late July, as the Bundesbank's financial squeeze relaxed somewhat while U.S. interest rates rose, the dollar started to strengthen.

Following the outbreak of the Middle East War and the imposition of the oil embargo in October 1973, the snake fell steadily against the dollar until mid-January 1974.

It became clear in October that the American balance of payments had experienced a large improvement. The trade surplus for September was almost $800 million, compared with about $50 million in August, and the basic balance (current transactions plus long-term capital) had moved into large surplus in the third quarter. These facts, and the public awareness of them, combined with the belief that the United States was less vulnerable to the oil embargo than Japan and most European countries, led to a strong upward movement in the value of the dollar against all major currencies except the Canadian dollar. From late October 1973 to late January 1974 the effective exchange rate of the dollar rose almost 17 percent.

This upward movement reversed not only the "third devaluation" but most of the February 1973 devaluation. The net result—an effective rate only about 0.5 percent below the Smithsonian rate—reflected diverse movements of other currencies. By late January 1974, the mark, though its effective rate had fallen almost 10 percent from the July peak, was still more than 15 percent above its Smithsonian rate. Other snake currencies were also above their Smithsonian rates. But the pound was down about 17 percent and the lira 15 percent, while the effective rate of the Japanese yen was only about 2.5 percent above its Smithsonian level. France had had to intervene heavily in exchange markets to keep its currency in the snake. In January 1974, just after the Rome meeting of the Committee of Twenty, the French franc dropped out of the snake.

A Second Cycle in Exchange Rates

After the spectacular rise of oil prices at the end of December 1973 and the partial lifting of the embargo, market participants appear to have reassessed the pattern of exchange rates. The view developed that the upward movement of the dollar and the downward float of other currencies had gone too far, just as the opposite movement had seemed excessive in the summer of 1973.

Most European exchange rates began to rise in relation to the dollar in the second half of January 1974. Again there were various influences. U.S. short-term interest rates were declining. On January 29 the U.S. Government announced the dismantling of its restraints on capital outflows. The next day the German authorities announced a relaxation of the restrictions on inflows of capital to Germany. Though the United States was expected to be a large recipient of the surplus funds of OPEC countries, its own growing need for oil imports was beginning to be seen as a heavy burden on its balance of payments. The U.S. trade surplus was diminishing in early 1974 while Germany's trade surplus was increasing. American banks, relieved of the "voluntary" restraint program, stepped up their lending abroad as foreign countries scrambled to borrow in order to finance oil deficits. Meanwhile the advance of consumer prices accelerated in the United States in the first half of 1974 while it decelerated in Germany.

In these circumstances (there was also the approaching climax of the Watergate affair) the effective exchange rate of the dollar fell almost 10 percent from January 28 to May 10, 1974. The German mark returned almost to its July 1973 peak, along with the other currencies in the "mini-snake" (the snake without the French franc). The effective exchange rates of the Japanese yen and the French franc remained unchanged on balance as the upward movement of European currencies was counterbalanced by the downward movement of the dollar; to put it differently, both the franc and the yen rose in relation to the dollar, but by less than the EEC mini-snake.

Industrial production in the United States remained on a plateau until the autumn of 1974. Real GNP crept down in the first nine months of 1974 and then dropped rapidly in the fourth quarter. Unemployment began to rise in May, but inflation accelerated. The Federal Reserve tightened monetary policy beginning in March and the Federal funds rate rose from just below 9 percent in February to 11.25 percent in early May; the rate exceeded 13 percent in early July. In Germany, where final domestic demand—demand for goods and services excluding inventory accumulation and exports—had already decreased at an annual rate of almost 4 percent in the second half of 1973, interest rates in April 1974 fell below those in the United States.[37]

After what appeared once more to be an excessive downswing of the dollar, the markets were ripe for the stories on news tickers on May 14 and in newspapers on May 15 that the American, German, and Swiss central banks were planning to undertake coordinated intervention in the foreign exchange markets. Although the basis for these stories consisted of nothing more than informal discussions, the mark and the Swiss franc fell by more than 4 percent against the dollar on May 14.

From mid-May to early September 1974, the effective rate of the dollar rose fairly steadily for a total increase of about 5.5 percent, again putting it back above the February 1973 level. The mark fell about 6 percent, as did the Japanese yen, whose effective rate by September was below its Smithsonian rate. Japan's huge current account surplus had disappeared even before the rise in oil prices. In the fourth quarter of 1973 the Bank of Japan had let the dollar value of the yen decline while selling dollars to moderate its downward movement.

During 1974, the process of learning to live with floating rates contributed to—but was also affected by—the failure of two large banks and a number of small ones. Sure bets on official exchange rate actions were a thing of the past, but the gambling habit that some foreign exchange traders had acquired was not easy to kick. On June 25, 1974, the Herstatt Bank of Cologne, Germany, was forced to close its doors as a result of heavy losses in foreign exchange trading. This closing left a number of banks around the world with unpaid claims on Herstatt. The result was to introduce extremely cautious behavior on the part of participants in foreign exchange markets, for the Herstatt case showed that "even a spot exchange contract involved a credit risk in which a bank might accept payment on a currency trade but be forced to close its doors before delivering the foreign exchange counterpart. As bank management throughout the world focused on this risk, traders severely limited new transactions to only those names they considered of the highest quality."[38]

During the same period the Franklin National Bank of New York got into serious trouble for similar reasons and was ultimately taken over by another bank. This experience accentuated the caution exhibited by banks and others in undertaking foreign exchange transactions. The result was to make exchange markets "thin" and volatile as participants hesitated to engage in "stabilizing speculation" (buying or selling a currency when its value was judged to have fallen too low or risen too high). It took a while for the markets to recover from these shocks.

The Emergence of World Recession

Until the oil embargo began in October 1973, industrial production had been on an upward trend in most OECD countries. Only in Germany had it levelled off. The large increase in oil prices had a significantly depressive effect on total demand in oil-importing countries. Its impact was similar to that of a huge increase in sales taxes levied on purchasers of petroleum products. For the OECD countries as a group this "oil tax" came to more than $60 billion in 1974, before taking account of the increase in OECD exports to OPEC countries. This was equivalent to a tax roughly equal to 2 percent of the GNP of the OECD countries. A tax increase of this magnitude in the United States would have come to more than $25 billion in 1974 and would have been expected to have a substantial contractionary effect on the economy. In fact, because of the lesser dependence of the United States on imported oil, the "oil tax" in this country amounted to about $17 billion—still a considerable sum.[39]

The oil price rise, plus restrictive fiscal and monetary policies in many countries aimed at containing inflation, plus extended inventory positions, all combined to throw the industrial countries into a recession in 1974—the deepest recession since the 1930's. For the seven largest OECD countries, GNP in real terms fell at an annual rate of 2 percent in the first half of 1974 and 1.7 percent in the second half. It fell further at a rate of 5.8 percent in the first half of 1975, a period in which the trough of the recession was passed in the United States and Japan. In May 1975, 15 million workers were recorded as unemployed in the OECD countries.

Among the several effects of the recession was a reversal in commodity prices. *The Economist* index of industrial materials prices fell by more than one-third in the year from April 1974. Another effect was to reduce sharply the imports of industrial countries, bringing the first yearly reduction in the volume of world trade since World War II. This in turn shifted a good part of the balance-of-payments deficit of OECD countries to the less developed world. The balance-of-payments positions of a number of OECD countries reverted from the oil-induced deficit position of 1974 to a surplus in 1975. Finally, the onset of the recession led to a pronounced alteration in fiscal and monetary policies in the industrial countries, but this change was not synchronized.

Floating Rates in Recession and Recovery

In the autumn of 1974 it became evident that a full-fledged recession was under way in the United States. Manufacturers' new orders had been falling rapidly since midsummer. In November, industrial production dropped 3.5 percent and the unemployment rate jumped from 6.1 to 6.7 percent. After the Federal Reserve began to moderate its restrictive monetary policy in September 1974, short-term interest rates in the United States, already down from peak levels in July, declined sharply over the next few months—more rapidly than in most other countries.

The decline in U.S. interest rates, combined with concern about a movement of funds out of dollars by oil-producing countries in general—and by Arab countries in particular as a precaution against a new outbreak of hostilities in the Middle East—contributed to a reduction in the effective exchange rate of the dollar. The Federal Reserve and other central banks acted to cushion the decline, particularly against the German mark and the Swiss franc, which were subject to corresponding upward pressures. By late January 1975 the effective rate of the dollar had fallen almost 8 percent from its level of early September 1974.

The dollar was again significantly below its February 1973 central rate while the mark, on an effective rate basis, was somewhat above its July 1973 peak and the Swiss franc (reflecting its status as a "haven currency") was almost 17 percent above its July 1973 level and 37 percent above its rate of February 1973. Meanwhile the yen, which had dropped sharply against the dollar in the second half of 1974, was almost 7 percent below its Smithsonian rate on a trade-weighted basis in January 1975. The French franc had been rising in average value from May 1974 as France lagged behind other countries in moving into recession and French interest rates remained relatively high. The strength of the franc was maintained in part by heavy official borrowing abroad by the French government and by nationalized industries.

Once more it was being widely said that the dollar had fallen too far. On February 1, 1975, Federal Reserve Chairman Burns met in London with the heads of the German and Swiss central banks; they agreed on more concerted and more vigorous intervention to maintain "orderly markets." Burns issued a statement saying, "In my judgment, the dollar is basically a very strong currency."[40] In February the Federal Reserve sold more than $600 million of foreign currencies drawn under the swap lines. After a further dip in early March, the dollar remained fairly steady until the end of June. Then, as U.S.

interest rates rose sharply, the effective exchange rate of the dollar increased more than 8 percent by the last week of September 1975. Once again the dollar was above its February 1973 level. From the autumn of 1975 to mid-March 1976 the fluctuations in the effective exchange rates of the dollar were relatively small.

In early 1976, the lira and the pound declined sharply, and the countries in the EEC snake had to undertake heavy intervention to maintain their rate relationships. France dropped out of the snake once again. But the effective exchange rate of the dollar seemed to have stabilized at a level somewhat above where it was after the devaluation of February 1973.

Appraisal of the Floating Experience

If one focuses on the effective exchange rate of the dollar after the advent of generalized floating in March 1973, one sees several large upward and downward swings that appear excessive by most economic standards. The objection to excessive movements in exchange rates, to the extent that they occurred, is that they disturb normal flows of trade and capital—in fact, by this standard one judges whether rate movements were or were not excessive.

Examining the evidence in late 1974, Marina Whitman concluded:

Despite substantial fluctuations, the exchange markets for the dollar and other major currencies do appear to have been dynamically, though cyclically, stable in the period since mid-1971. That is, although fluctuations in rates may well have been larger than would have been required to eliminate underlying disequilibria, the major rate movements appear to have been in the "right" direction, that is, appropriate to actual or anticipated changes in basic economic conditions. . . .

A pattern of speculative behavior which magnifies the amplitude of currency swings, requiring price changes which overshoot equilibrium in order to call forth equilibrating movements of funds, appears to be due to a paucity of continuous stabilizing speculation. . . . there seems to be a widespread feeling that, despite a few widely publicized examples to the contrary, large U.S. banks have become increasingly cautious about assuming net positions in foreign currencies, either spot or forward. Even more marked is an apparent tendency for multinational corporations to overhedge against foreign exchange risk. . . .

Behavior of the sort just described is what one might expect during a learning period, when speculators' views regarding long-run equilibrium values are weakly held and substantial stimulus is therefore required to make them act on them.[41]

A study by two Federal Reserve Board economists of the behavior of exchange rates between March 1973 and September 1975 produced results consistent with these conclusions. Their statistical tests did not rule out the possibility of "bandwagon effects," which would not occur in "efficient markets" where sufficient information is available to market participants to lead to buying or selling that would counteract excessive movements in exchange rates.[42]

Germany and Switzerland

Much of the movement, both up and down, in the effective exchange rate of the U.S. dollar from February 1973 to late 1975 was a reflection of swings in the opposite direction by the EEC snake—dominated by the German mark —and the Swiss franc. On balance, the effective rate of the mark was up about 20 percent and the Swiss franc 40 percent from February 1973 to early March 1976. Germany and Switzerland were among the OECD countries with the lowest rates of inflation in 1973–1975. (The appreciation of their exchange rates undoubtedly contributed to this result.) Insofar as domestic prices affect export performance, there were reasons for the upward movement of their exchange rates.

Germany was the first major country to depress domestic demand in 1973. Thus Germany's surplus on goods, services, and private transfers rose from an average of just under $2 billion per year in 1965–1972 to $6.8 billion in 1973 and, despite higher costs of oil imports, to $11.8 billion in 1974. It is not surprising that there was upward pressure on the mark in this period. Only in 1975 did Germany's current balance decline.

Switzerland's case is a special one because of its traditional role as an international depositary and intermediary for foreign funds. Bank secrecy and all that goes with it has made the Swiss franc a haven currency in times of economic or political uncertainty. The mere expectation that Arab billions might try to move into Swiss francs would be sufficient to drive up the exchange rate.

Commenting in the spring of 1975 on the effects of the upward movement of the EEC snake and the Swiss franc, the BIS pointed out:

Of the four countries whose currencies have appreciated [since May 1971, Switzerland, Germany, the Netherlands, and Japan], only Switzerland is showing signs of having lost ground competitively, though the rapid rise of the [French] franc since mid-1974 is too recent for its full effects to have worked through. The appreciation of the Deutsche Mark has gone hand in hand with an expanding German trade surplus, though export orders have been declining recently.[43]

Floating and World Trade

Those afflicted with "fear of floating," to use Herbert Stein's phrase, have stressed that the uncertainties associated with floating exchange rates would tend to depress both trade and productive capital flows among nations. Robert Roosa gave some specifics in a debate with Milton Friedman in 1967:

> No single trader can know enough about all the developments likely to affect the rate of exchange between his own country and that of his client to make a firm contract without including a substantial allowance for the risk that the rate of exchange between the currencies involved will change while the transaction is underway. Prices in international trade and the costs of doing international business of any kind would thus almost inevitably become higher under a flexible-rate system—higher because the businessman must include a charge for the added element of risk.[44]

Those on the other side of the argument—to be fair to Roosa, we should note that these ideas spread rapidly only after 1967—would stress today that in the period before March 1973 traders and investors could have had no confidence that existing par values would be maintained. The case for and against floating exchange rates must be made in comparison with a realistic alternative. Fixed exchange rates, which businessmen can count on to be maintained for long stretches of time, are not, as our history of the years 1965–1972 has demonstrated, a realistic alternative. The choice lies between floating rates, perhaps managed by monetary authorities, and par values subject to change (perhaps frequently) and sometimes maintained only by heavy use of controls. If these are the alternatives, the debate tends to lose some of its theological and doctrinal flavor.

In any event, world trade does not appear to have been discouraged by the move to floating rates. World trade in real terms (that is, adjusted for price changes) increased 13 percent in 1973, compared with an annual average growth of 8.5 percent in 1960–1970. The growth rate of trade fell to 5 percent in 1974 but world output, which grew at an average annual rate of 5 percent in 1960–1970 and 6.4 percent in 1973, rose only 1 percent in 1974.[45] As Edward Bernstein has pointed out in one of his research papers, the movements in total world trade relative to world output were not very different in 1973–1975 from what they were in 1956–1958, the previous occasion of a near-synchronous cyclical expansion and contraction in the industrial countries.

Available evidence on the increased costs of trade shows that the spread between bid and asked prices in foreign exchange markets has widened. A widening of the spread between the buying and selling prices of foreign exchange is like a tax on international transactions; it could, if it were of significant magnitude, discourage trade and other international dealings. One study shows that in May 1975 the spread for three major currencies, in terms of dollars, was four to eight times what it was in 1970. Even so, the spread did not exceed one-sixth of one percent of the cost of foreign exchange in May 1975.[46] Another study, which goes only through mid-1974, shows similar results for the spread on forward, as well as spot, transactions.[47] Thus the added cost of trade from this source was very small. (The spread between bid and asked quotations has narrowed since these studies were conducted.)

Floating Rates and Inflation

A number of arguments have been put forward over the years to support the proposition that floating exchange rates are likely to create or facilitate more inflation in the world economy than "fixed rates." A traditional argument is that the need to defend a fixed rate or a par value induces monetary and fiscal authorities to take greater care to prevent inflation; if floating rates were adopted, discipline would be weakened and countries would be more likely to pursue inflationary policies.

One answer to this, which seems to have been borne out by recent experience, is that monetary authorities become concerned whenever their country's exchange rate falls in the exchange market, thereby forcing up the domestic prices of imports and import-competing goods, and that this acts as a form of discipline. In any event, it became evident after 1965 that if a par value system was to be workable, countries would have to be prepared to adjust their rates with some frequency. It is doubtful that a workable par value system—if there is one in today's world—imposes more discipline than a floating regime. Otmar Emminger and Gottfried Haberler[48] have recently argued that a fixed rate system is more inflationary than a regime of floating rates.

Another argument is that floating rates produce a type of "ratchet effect" on prices. Countries whose currencies depreciate will experience a rise in prices of imports and tradeable goods and a corresponding acceleration of wages, but when the exchange rate appreciates again these effects will not be reversed, since wages will not fall or slow up as much when prices fall as they rise when prices advance. This argument would apply to a flexible par value system as well, but perhaps not as strongly, since exchange rates might fluctuate less in a flexible par value system than in a managed floating system. The difference appears, at best, to be one of degree. As Walter Salant points out, "If the mechanism invoked by this argument does operate, inflation in the country in question is greater when its currency depreciates than it would be under a fixed exchange rate, but the transmission of inflation to other countries presumably would be less than under fixed rates, so it cannot be concluded that the flexibility of rates would increase inflation in the world as a whole."[49]

Floating Rates and the Autonomy of Monetary Policy

An oft-stated objection to the Bretton Woods system was that central banks' efforts to maintain an exchange rate—to keep it from going above or below the given margins around par values—interfered with or undermined their pursuit of domestic objectives. In his Per Jacobsson lecture cited earlier, Otmar Emminger, looking at the matter from the viewpoint of a country in surplus, gave as the main reason for the "breakdown" of the Bretton Woods system that "the limit of tolerance for the inflationary effect of such currency inflows had been reached."

One of the arguments for wider margins around par values under the old system was that they would provide greater scope for differences in interest rates among countries, since market exchange rates could move up or down within the margins to offset interest rate differentials. As a result, interest-induced flows of funds, and perhaps even speculative flows, would be discouraged because potential movers of funds from one currency to another would face the risk of a larger "recoil" in the market exchange rate, which could turn an expected gain into a loss. This effect would be produced, however, only if there were confidence that the existing par value was going to be maintained. If no such confidence existed—or, more correct, if the probabilities in the minds of market participants that the parity would be held were not reasonably high—the inhibiting effect of wider margins would be weak or nonexistent.[50] Central banks might then have to buy or sell foreign exchange in amounts large enough to interfere with their domestic objectives. This, in fact, is what led to the decision to float in March 1973.

In the period since exchange rates began to float, the wide swings in rates —even in effective rates—have given rise to concerns that have in turn weakened the case for the argument that floating rates permit autonomy for domestic policies. In countries whose exchange rates tended to depreciate, the rising cost of imports aggravated domestic inflation. In countries whose exchange rates were moving up, the actual or potential loss of export markets and the actual or potential increase in imports was seen as undesirable for a variety of reasons.

These effects are more disturbing to countries with more "open" economies—that is, countries more dependent on foreign trade. In a survey of the exchange rate practices of its members in mid-1975, the IMF found, in general, that the larger countries "have mostly inclined to floating" and "smaller countries, with relatively larger foreign trade sectors or with a less diversified production structure, have mostly inclined to a pegging system."[51] By a "pegging system" the IMF meant pegging the exchange rate to another currency, most often the dollar, or to the SDR, or floating jointly as in the EEC snake.

Even for the United States, the least "open" of the industrial countries that are IMF members, it has been estimated that one-fifth of any depreciation in the effective exchange rate of the dollar will show up in the consumer price index; that is, a 10 percent depreciation on a trade-weighted basis will increase the consumer price index by 2 percent.[52]

We can only conclude that while floating rates can remove some of the constraints on monetary policy that were imposed by the par value system, they do not insulate countries from what is happening in the rest of the world nor do they immunize domestic economies from the effects of balance-of-payments adjustment.

XVI

The Impact of OPEC

The quadrupling of oil prices by OPEC at the end of 1973 was probably the most severe shock to the international monetary system—and, more broadly, to the world economy—since World War II. The action had economic, financial, and political effects to which the world will be reacting for some time. Initially the problems were compounded by a widespread lack of comprehension of the true economic effects of the oil price increase. "Never before in the history of economics and finance have so many been thrown into utter confusion by so few."[1] In the first year, 1974, newspapers and airwaves were channels for a variety of apocalyptic predictions. The dire forecasts included the impoverishment of oil-importing countries, a take-over of a good part of the economies of industrialized countries by Arab sheiks now rich beyond their wildest dreams, and an inability of the world's banking system to handle the problem of lending and investing the funds placed with them by OPEC countries.

Those of us who tried to apply rational economic analysis to the problems came to the conclusion that they were manageable.[2] But, trying to reassure those about us who were most concerned, we found ourselves in the uncomfortable position of appearing to defend or to justify the OPEC action. In my view the decision of OPEC to quadruple the oil price (and then to raise it substantially again in 1975) was a monopolistic act by which a small group of countries has been exploiting the rest of the world—developing countries perhaps more, in a relative sense, than developed countries—through their control over the supply of an essential commodity for which substitutes cannot be produced quickly and cheaply. To suggest that the problems thus created can be managed by cooperative international efforts is not in any sense to justify the actions that give rise to them.

Five serious concerns arose for the international economy in general and for oil-importing countries in particular from the OPEC action: What would be the short-term effect on aggregate demand? The long-term effect on real income? The effect on trade balances, in the short and long term? How would oil-importing countries finance their balance-of-payments deficits? And what were the implications of the mushrooming OPEC monetary reserves?

Preconditions for the OPEC Price Increase

World economic conditions were ripe for the action. The worldwide use of liquid fuels as a proportion of total energy use had increased from 34 percent in 1962 to 43 percent in 1971. In Europe the increase was from 36 percent to 57 percent as the production of solid fuels dropped in absolute terms and their share of total energy consumption was cut in half, from 58 to 29 percent. In Japan, use of liquid fuels rose from 43 percent of total energy consumption in 1962 to 71 percent in 1971. Only in the United States did the share of liquid fuels in total energy use not rise in the 1960's.[3] But the big change in the U.S. position was that by the early 1970's the United States had become heavily dependent on imports to meet its petroleum needs. While U.S. output of oil increased nearly 30 percent from 1962 to 1971 (before starting to decline), total petroleum use rose 45 percent. Total imports of oil thus grew from 20 percent of total U.S. use in 1962 to 26 percent in 1971. By 1973 the dependence on imports had increased to 36 percent.

The industrial countries had thus become heavily dependent on oil imported from the thirteen OPEC countries. At the same time, the consumption of oil had widened beyond its use as a fuel. In 1970 non-energy uses of petroleum—including lubricants, petrochemical feedstock, and the base for asphalt—had risen to 10 percent of total petroleum use in North America.[4]

In these circumstances, the demand for oil in industrial countries—the major users—was quite inelastic, at least in the short run. In other words, substitutes for oil were not readily available and a reduction in the supply of oil could have a highly disruptive effect on industrial and social conditions.

These economic circumstances, combined with the political atmosphere engendered by the Arab-Israeli War in October 1973 and the oil embargo, were the background for the two price increases announced by OPEC in the fourth quarter of 1973. Not all oil-producing countries participated in the embargo and not all OPEC members are Arab—facts about which there was much confusion in 1974. Venezuela is usually given credit for having supplied the impetus that forged OPEC into an effective cartel. Growing sophistication in economic analysis in the OPEC countries may also have been a factor. According to Fred Bergsten, "OPEC was reportedly conceived in a bar in Cambridge, Massachusetts, and every country now has its full quota of graduates from prestigious institutions."[5]

One justification that spokesmen for OPEC offered for the price increase was that the costs of products they bought in industrial countries had gone up sharply. A study published by the U.S. Department of Labor throws doubt on this justification. Taking June 1964 as a starting point, one finds that up to June 1970 the prices of U.S. exports to OPEC countries rose almost 10 percent while OPEC oil prices were unchanged. But over the next three years, to mid-1973, oil prices rose 72 percent while U.S. export prices to OPEC countries increased 23 percent. Thus, over the entire period from mid-1964 to mid-1973, oil prices rose 72 percent while U.S. export prices rose 32 percent. In the next year, to June 1974, the price of oil quintupled while the average price of U.S. exports to OPEC increased 21 percent.[6]

It could be argued that the price of oil was too low in 1964 and earlier. In general it is not easy to establish what is an economically justified price for a depletable resource such as oil.[7] Nevertheless, the size of the price hike in late 1973 cannot, by any statistical manipulation, be justified on the basis of what happened to export prices in the United States and other industrial countries.

Effect on Aggregate Demand

In the previous chapter we observed that the internal effects of the oil price increase in an oil-importing country could be regarded as equivalent to a new tax. A paper I had circulated to a number of friends during the Rome meeting of the Committee of Twenty in January drew the attention of *The Economist* for March 23, 1974:

> The problem has been put elegantly by Mr. Robert Solomon, a vice-chairman of the deputies of the Committee of Twenty; he points out that it is useful to visualize the oil price increase as a large sales tax on the use of petroleum products. Internally, that tax has a deflationary effect on demand which is likely to require offsetting action to avoid unemployment.[8]

The magnitude of the "oil tax" in 1974 was about 2 percent of the GNP of the OECD countries as a whole.

When the "oil tax" was imposed, inflation was still raging. In the fourth quarter of 1973, consumer prices in the OECD area were advancing, on average, at 12 percent a year, ranging from a rate of 8.8 percent in the United States to 11.6 percent in Germany, and to almost 20 percent in Japan.

The immediate effect of the oil price action was to give an additional boost to consumer prices. Thus, even though aggregate demand had become less vigorous in the second half of 1973, the officials of most countries were preoccupied with rising prices and overlooked, deliberately or for lack of comprehension, the contractionary effects of the oil price action. One European colleague responded to my analysis of the impact of the oil price increase by saying, "I disagree with your reasoning but if you are right, it is just what the doctor ordered."

It turned out to be more than the doctor ordered. The world experienced in 1974–75 the deepest recession since World War II, and the prospect for a return to reasonably full employment of labor and industrial capacity appears, as of early 1976, to be several years away for most of the larger OECD countries. While it was not the only cause of the recession, the oil price rise was without doubt a major influence. Referring to the United States, George Perry has said, "Higher oil prices, coupled with the failure of fiscal and monetary policies to offset their depressing effect on total demand, have been the primary cause of the present recession."[9]

The impact on aggregate demand was even larger in Western Europe and Japan because of their greater dependence on oil as compared with other energy sources and their almost complete reliance on imports for the oil they use.[10] The direct impact on aggregate demand in developing countries was smaller, since they use relatively less oil. But the effects of recession in the industrial countries on incomes, growth rates, and balance-of-payments positions of developing countries were very large indeed.

One of the ironies in the situation was that the recession in the industrial countries, caused in large part by the price action of OPEC, led to a significant reduction in the demand for oil in 1974–75, well beyond the reduction that would have resulted solely from the higher price. A number of OPEC countries, having stepped up their development programs and consequently their orders for foreign goods (not to mention military equipment), found that their spending abroad was threatening to run ahead of their foreign exchange earnings. Iran, for example, announced in late 1975 that it would be borrowing in foreign markets to cover the gap between its foreign exchange income and outgo.[11]

In OPEC countries the effects of higher oil prices on aggregate demand were the opposite of what they were in oil-importing countries. Most OPEC countries initiated large-scale development plans as their export receipts suddenly jumped in 1974.

> It seems quite likely that these countries will experience rather severe rates of inflation as they attempt to use their new wealth to increase investment in their economies. Even though they will import capital equipment as they increase investment and will import consumer goods as the incomes of their populations rise, some significant part of the increased spending will impinge on the local economy. Both wages and prices will be affected.[12]

It is not too farfetched to compare what is happening in some of the oil countries with what happened in Spain in the sixteenth century when gold and silver poured in from the new world. Consumer prices in oil-exporting countries, as reported by the IMF, rose on average by about 17 percent in both 1974 and 1975—compared with only 4.6 percent in 1972.

Effects on Real Income

The rise in oil prices led to a jump in the oil revenues of OPEC countries of some $75 billion, from about $33 billion in 1973 to about $108 billion in 1974. Saudi Arabia's GNP per capita rose from $540 in 1971 to an estimated $3500 in 1974. For the United Arab Emirates, the rise of per capita income was from $3150 to $19,000.[13]

The effect on real income in oil-importing countries was another phenomenon that was not well understood. The oil-importing countries as a whole were not forced to feel the real costs of higher oil prices—that is, would not be deprived of goods and services that would otherwise be available for domestic use—unless and until OPEC countries came to spend their increased revenues. To the extent that oil-exporting countries simply accumulated financial claims, the rest of the world would not be making transfers of real resources to them.

Thus there was no need for the non-OPEC world to reduce its real income immediately as a result of the oil price increase. The recession did of course lower real income in many countries, but that was not inevitable and it certainly is not permanent. As a matter of fact, if the transfer of real income had occurred immediately—that is, if OPEC countries had been able to increase their imports in 1974 by $75 billion—there would have been no recession in the rest of the world, for the reduction in purchasing power available to residents of non-OPEC countries would have been offset by increased spending in these countries by OPEC residents and governments.

The actual increase in imports by OPEC countries in 1974 came to about

$12.3 billion or roughly one-sixth of the increase in OPEC revenues.[14] Assuming these imports had all come from OECD countries, which is not quite correct, the additional absorption of resources by OPEC countries came to less than one-half of one percent of GNP of OECD countries.

There is considerable uncertainty as to how fast the imports of OPEC countries will expand over future years. This uncertainty explains the widely different guesses as to how long OPEC will continue in surplus and to what figure its unspent income, giving rise to claims on the rest of the world, will grow.

The OPEC countries are far from homogeneous in their economic, political, and social characteristics. One of the differences among them lies in their ability to increase imports. Those with sparse populations and little industry other than the lifting of crude oil from the ground cannot quickly absorb additional imports in large volume. That would require large-scale industrialization programs, which in turn would call for massive immigration. (This might interfere with the social goals of some of these countries.) Other OPEC nations, like Iran and Venezuela, had already made a start on economic development before 1974 and are in a better position to increase their imports rapidly. But even Iran is having trouble absorbing imports; news stories tell of clogged ports and unloaded goods piling up and rusting at dockside.

The largest oil reserves are in the least developed OPEC countries. Saudi Arabia, Kuwait, and Abu Dhabi account for about 45 percent of the world's proven oil reserves. Thus it could be quite a while before imports of OPEC countries as a group begin to catch up with the value of their exports. When they do, the cost in real terms to the industrial countries will be relatively small:

> They imply, not an absolute reduction in living standards [in industrial countries], but a modest reduction for a while in the accustomed rate of growth of per capita consumption. While these losses are sufficiently large to warrant the adoption of policies to reduce them, they should not be viewed as in themselves threatening the prospects for achieving normal rates of growth.[15]

Balance of Payments Effects

The rise in oil prices shifted the current balance of payments of the OPEC countries from an estimated surplus of about $4 billion in 1973 to a surplus of $66 billion in 1974. (See Table 4.) By definition, the current balance of the rest of the world shifted into deficit by about $62 billion. While the distribution of the deficit in 1974 has not been completely accounted for, it appears that

TABLE 4.   Current Balances of Major Group of Countries
            (Billions of Dollars)

	1973	1974	1975
OECD	11	−22	7
OPEC	4	66	42
Non-oil developing countries	−9	−25	−35
Other[1]	−4	−10	−15
Discrepancy	2	9	−1

SOURCE: OECD.
NOTE: Current balances are surpluses or deficits on goods, services and private transfers. Minus sign
        denotes deficit.
[1]Sino-Soviet area, South Africa, Israel, Cyprus, Malta and Yugoslavia.

the OECD countries moved from a surplus of $11 billion in 1973 to a deficit
of about $22 billion in 1974. For the non-oil developing countries the shift was
from a deficit of $9 billion to one of $25 billion. Apparently the Sino-Soviet
area also incurred a large current deficit in 1974.

The industrialized countries of the OECD were accustomed to running
surpluses in their current balances. For the OECD as a whole, the annual
surplus had averaged about $6 billion in 1960–1964 and almost $10 billion
in 1965–1972.[16] It made good economic sense for the world's wealthiest
countries to have surpluses of this sort, for they were thereby enabled to
transfer funds and real resources to developing countries. In 1973 official
development assistance from OECD countries amounted to more than $9
billion; in addition there were flows of private capital from OECD to developing countries.

Once the price of oil was quadrupled, it seemed inevitable that the OECD
countries should be in deficit on current transactions. This required a change
in thinking by residents of the OECD countries. Not only was a surplus no
longer possible, but large current deficits had to be expected and accepted. If
an individual oil-importing country tried to eliminate its deficit by any means
other than the reduction of oil imports, it would simply shift the inevitable
deficit—the counterpart of the OPEC surplus—to another oil-importing country. Such action would be a form of beggar-thy-neighbor, as was recognized
by the ministers of the Committee of Twenty in their Rome communiqué in
January 1974.

It was one thing to recognize this fact of life in principle and another to
accept it in practice. For a while the French Government set itself the goal of
eliminating its trade deficit by the end of 1975. Newspaper stories in the United
States continued to treat trade deficits, when they occurred in 1974, as a

condition to be avoided and trade surpluses, when they reappeared as a result of recession, as a sign of virtue and a healthy economic status.

Because of the effects of the oil price increase on aggregate demand, many of the OECD countries did not have much time to accustom themselves to trade deficits. The recession led to a sharp drop in imports by OECD countries and to a shift back to a current surplus—estimated at $7 billion in 1975, compared with the deficit of $22 billion in 1974. This large shift had its counterpart in a reduction of $24 billion in the surplus of OPEC countries, as the volume of their oil exports fell and their imports grew rapidly. At the same time, the current deficit of non-oil developing countries increased from $25 billion in 1974 to $35 billion in 1975.

The pattern of current balances in 1975 was clearly distorted and unsustainable. It is not feasible for the developing countries to carry over three-fourths of the counterpart of the OPEC surplus. The current deficit of the non-oil developing countries as a group in 1975 had almost quadrupled since 1973. (See Table 4.) About $11 billion of the $26 billion increase in their deficit from 1973 to 1975 can be accounted for by higher costs of oil. An additional burden came in the form of increased interest payments, since the non-oil developing countries had to borrow heavily in 1974 and 1975 to finance their enlarged deficits.

As recovery from recession proceeds in 1976 and beyond, the OPEC surplus is likely to increase again, but not necessarily to its level of 1974. Meanwhile, the current balance of the OECD countries will shift back to deficit, thereby relieving the developing countries somewhat. But even if the OECD countries were to return to high levels of activity quickly, an unlikely prospect as matters look in early 1976, the deficits of non-oil developing countries would remain large.

One expert provided this analysis:

the developing countries are likely to reduce their dependence on imported oil slowly at best, lagging significantly behind the industrial countries in this respect. Of course, some countries that are in a position to develop domestic sources of energy, such as coal, oil and gas, will do so; thus, not all countries will remain as dependent on imports as at present. Therefore, oil imports which in the sixties increased by 9–10 percent a year on an average are expected to grow at a reduced rate in the years to come. Still, with the projected rate of growth of income in the developing countries, it appears unlikely that their oil imports could grow in volume by less than 5–6 percent a year between 1973 and 1985. All this must be taken into account in the assessment of the long-term outlook for the developing countries; reasonable rates of growth in line with actual performance through 1973 can only be achieved with the assistance of large additional foreign exchange resources, both to meet the cost of imported oil and to finance the adjustment investments intended to reduce dependence on imported oil over the long term.[17]

This is why a number of special measures were adopted by the IMF in 1974 and 1975 to ease the financing burden of developing countries.

Financing "Oil Deficits"

The huge balance-of-payments deficits of oil-importing countries had to be financed. And the OPEC countries had to find ways to use the large accumulations of funds that they suddenly came into possession of, as the counterpart of their enormous balance-of-payments surpluses. Thus the OPEC surplus provided the means for its own financing and, accordingly, for financing the deficits of oil-importing countries.

To illustrate this point, as well as other aspects of the relationship between oil-exporting and oil-importing countries, let us suppose that the world is made up of only two countries: PEC, which produces oil and little else and does not have developed financial markets, and PIC, a country self-sufficient in everything but oil while having sophisticated money and capital markets. (This paradigm corresponds roughly to the situation, were the two groups of countries, OPEC and the rest of the world, each united.)

In this two-country world, PEC is selling oil to PIC and buying food and manufactured goods from PIC. When the leaders and wealthier residents of PEC need medical care or recreation they find it convenient to travel to PIC, sometimes renting an entire floor in a luxury hotel. The oil fields in PEC have been developed by giant corporations in PIC, but PEC has begun to buy them out while continuing to depend on their facilities for the distribution of oil in PIC.

Now PEC decides to quadruple the price of oil. PEC has had a surplus of $3 billion with PIC, and it has accumulated each year $3 billion in securities and bank deposits in PIC. PEC's surplus jumps to, say, $60 billion, as does PIC's deficit. Ignoring the internal effects of the higher oil price in PIC, we know that it has to pay almost $60 billion more to PEC than it did earlier. But PEC has almost $60 billion more to invest in securities and bank deposits in PIC. Thus PIC simply borrows the $60 million per year from PEC.

As time goes on, PIC's debt to PEC mounts up. But what can PEC do with its growing financial wealth? It could acquire real estate and even factories in

PIC, but its leaders are cautious in their investment policies. Having national-ized PIC oil company subsidiaries, PEC's leaders are sensitive about acquiring property in PIC. Most of PEC's growing claims on PIC therefore take the form of liquid assets or securities that are not too easily identified as belonging to the government or the wealthy residents of PEC.

Over time, PEC's imports rise. And because of the high cost of oil, PIC gradually develops substitutes for PEC's oil. Such substitutes may take the form of oil supplied from outside PEC as the high price stimulates efforts to find and produce it in PIC, or they may take the form of other types of energy. In time PEC's surplus, which is also PIC's deficit, decreases. But there is considerable disagreement among the experts in PIC as to how rapidly this will happen.

In the meantime, there is no balance-of-payments financing problem as such. PEC has no choice about what to do with the financial proceeds of its surplus. It can only lend or invest in PIC, and this process provides PIC with the means to finance its deficit with PEC. Insofar as PEC places its surplus in banks in PIC, the government or other entities in PIC can borrow from the banks to pay PEC for oil. If PEC prefers to purchase securities in PIC, entities there can issue additional securities and the proceeds can be used to pay PEC for oil.*

Although PIC is going into debt and PEC is accumulating financial claims on PIC, the balance of payments is being financed smoothly. Banks in PIC may become a little nervous; the growing PEC deposits on their books could theoretically be withdrawn at short notice, while the loans they are making to PIC residents have a longer maturity. But it is clear that there is no way for PEC to reduce its total of deposits and other claims except by using them to buy goods from PIC.

Ultimately, when PEC's surplus (and therefore PIC's deficit) has been reversed—as a result of growing PEC imports, reduced PIC purchases of oil from PEC, or a fall in the relative price of oil—PEC will begin to use its accumulated financial assets to finance its deficit with PIC. In this way PIC will begin to repay its debts to PEC. In fact, there is no other way for the debts

*One is reminded of the story of the retired Cape Cod sea captain and his wife. When the wife's sister becomes a widow, the wife suggests to the captain that her sister come to live with them. The captain agrees on the condition that his sister-in-law pay him $10 per week for her room and board. The wife accepts this condition provided the captain will give the $10 to her. Each week, after the widow joins the household, she pays $10 to the captain, who passes it on to his wife. Without telling the captain, the wife returns the $10 to her sister. Thus the process goes on without disrupting the financial arrangements of any of the three parties. (The parallel with the PIC-PEC relationship is not exact, since PIC is incurring a growing debt to PEC.)

to be repaid except as the result of the realization of a deficit in PEC's balance of payments. There can be no question of PIC's creditworthiness; there is no way for it to repay its debts until PEC is in a position to receive repayment. It will be in such a position only when it develops a surplus of imports over exports.

Events in the real world differ from this parable mainly because the actual PIC and PEC each consists of a group of individual countries, and within each group the countries have markedly different characteristics. If each of the oil-importing countries had a deficit and each of the OPEC countries had a surplus (the aggregate deficit being equal to the aggregate surplus), and if the OPEC countries loaned or invested in each of the oil-importing countries an amount exactly equal to the latter's deficit, the balance-of-payments financing process would be as described in our model.

Problems arise because some of the oil-importing countries are more attractive creditors than others. Thus some of them receive a share of the OPEC financial surplus greater than their deficit with OPEC and, as a result, others receive or are able to borrow an amount of OPEC funds less than adequate to finance their deficits. This requires a reshuffling of funds among oil-importing countries, and a considerable amount of such reshuffling has occurred. In 1974 OPEC countries are estimated to have invested about $11 billion in the United States, when it had not a deficit but a small surplus ($2 billion) on current transactions. At the same time, however, American banks loaned more than $13 billion to foreign countries, of which more than $3.5 billion went to Latin America, $5.5 billion to Japan, and more than $2 billion to countries elsewhere in Asia and Africa.

Also in 1974, OPEC countries are estimated to have placed a net amount of $23 billion in the Euro-currency markets. The Euro-currency banks loaned $7 billion to Japan, more than $5 billion to Latin American countries, and about $1.5 billion to Australia, New Zealand, and South Africa. Loans to European borrowers were also of some magnitude.[18]

While a substantial amount of such reshuffling continued in 1975, questions of apparent creditworthiness began to arise, which could bring on some future problems. The developing countries incurred very large deficits as a result of the recession, and their financing needs exceeded by far what would have been required to meet the higher costs of oil imports. This is a major problem for 1976 and beyond.

The point has been made. The balance-of-payments deficits created by the increase in oil prices are financeable if sufficient imagination, innovation, generosity, and international cooperation are employed. The OPEC countries are in a position to provide, directly or indirectly, the funds to finance these deficits. They cannot avoid it.

Up to now, direct financing of developing countries by OPEC appears to have been less than ample. In 1974, when the oil bill of developing countries increased by $11 billion, OPEC countries provided them with $4.6 billion in various forms: direct assistance to military allies ($1.2 billion), concessional loans to other countries, directly or through multilateral agencies ($1 billion), purchases of World Bank bonds ($2 billion), and loans or subscriptions to other multilateral financing institutions ($0.4 billion).[19] This meager flow raises questions as to the continued solidarity, evident in various international organizations since early 1974, between non-oil developing countries and the members of OPEC. (As officials of non-oil developing countries appeared to rejoice at the consequences of the OPEC action, I pictured a person up to his neck in quicksand cheering as he sees someone else fall in up to his ankles.)

The Nature of OPEC "Reserves"

From the beginning of 1974 through December 1975, the reserves of major oil-exporting countries, as measured by the IMF, increased by more than SDR 37 billion, from SDR 12.0 billion to SDR 48.3 billion. (In terms of dollars, the increase came to about $42 billion.) Over the same period, world reserves rose by just over SDR 42 billion. Thus virtually all of the growth of world reserves accrued to OPEC countries in this period. The SDR 6 billion increase in the reserves of other countries represented a rise of about 4 percent over two years.

We have seen that the reserves of OPEC countries are usable only when and if those countries develop a deficit in their trade (and other transactions) with the rest of the world. That day is some distance off. It is reasonable, in fact essential, to treat OPEC reserves as a special case when judging either the adequacy of world reserves or their effect on world inflation. Rather than "reserves" in the usual sense, OPEC claims on the rest of the world should be treated as long-term investments.

XVII

Further Evolution of the International Monetary System

In June 1974 the Committee of Twenty completed its work and published an Outline of Reform which included a series of "immediate steps" that would be taken "to begin an evolutionary process of reform, and to help meet the current problems facing both developed and developing countries."

By the time of the annual meeting of the IMF—September 30 to October 4, 1974—the various industrial countries were either on the brink of or in serious recession, yet rates of inflation were still very high. The financing of large payments imbalances brought about by the oil price increase continued to be a matter of grave concern. In the circumstances, the mood of the annual meeting was generally characterized as "somber." Jean-Pierre Fourcade, the new French Minister of Finance, told the IMF Governors assembled in Washington that their annual meeting was marked by anxiety, "an anxiety that centers on four major themes: payments imbalances caused by the rising cost of essential raw materials; inflation; international capital movements; and development financing."[1]

The International Monetary Issues, 1974–1975

As provided for in the Outline of Reform, the Board of Governors of the IMF passed a resolution establishing an Interim Committee of the Board of Governors on the International Monetary System, similar in form to the Committee of Twenty. John Turner, Canada's Finance Minister, was chosen chairman. The Interim Committee, as its name implies, would function in an advisory capacity until the Fund's Articles of Agreement were amended to authorize formally a permanent Council in the Fund at ministerial level. The Interim Committee's assigned task was to "advise and report" to the Board of Governors with respect to the functions of the Board of Governors in: (1) supervising the management and adaptation of the international monetary system, including the continuing operation of the adjustment process, and in this connection reviewing developments in global liquidity and the transfer of real resources to developing countries; (2) considering proposals by the Executive Directors to amend the Articles of Agreement; and (3) dealing with sudden disturbances that might threaten the system.

The resolution establishing the Interim Committee did not mention "deputies." In fact there were to be no formal meetings of deputies to the "members," who were of ministerial rank. The IMF Executive Board was expected to do the preparatory work and to receive the views—in practice, the decisions—of the Interim Committee.

At its initial meeting, on October 3, 1974, the Interim Committee addressed itself to the problem of "recycling" surpluses of oil-exporting countries and asked the Fund's Executive Directors, "as a matter or urgency," to consider "the adequacy of existing private and official financing arrangements, and to report on the possible need for additional arrangements, including enlarged financing arrangements through the Fund, and to make proposals for dealing with the problem." Britain's Chancellor of the Exchequer Denis Healey had suggested a sizable enlargement of the Fund's Oil Facility, which had been established earlier in the year, but the American and German Ministers were less than enthusiastic about this proposal.

Among other issues, the Committee identified "the adjustment process, quotas in the Fund, and amendments of its Articles, including amendments on gold and the link," as subjects to which it would give priority.[2]

Over the period from October 1974 to January 1976, the Interim Committee and the Executive Board of the Fund were to concern themselves mainly with (1) the financing of massive payments imbalances, (2) an increase in IMF quotas, (3) the exchange rate regime, and (4) the treatment of gold. Over the same period, the Executive Board would complete a revision of the IMF Articles of Agreement—the first major overhaul of the Articles since Bretton Woods, apart from the additions to the Articles at the time the SDR facility was established.

On the exchange rate regime, a change in attitudes was becoming evident. In their addresses to the 1974 annual meeting neither Japanese Finance Minister Masayoshi Ohira, nor Indian Minister Y.B. Chavan, nor Nicaraguan Governor Roberto Incer (who spoke for twenty Latin American countries), expressed a wish to move from floating rates back to a par value system.

French Minister Fourcade and Belgian Minister Willy de Clercq were among the very few who mentioned a return to a "stable exchange rate regime" and "stable but adjustable parities." Fourcade said that floating rates, though "an inevitable evil for the time being, will never constitute an acceptable response to the profound exigencies of a sound international payments system." French views on this matter were to shift over the next year, but before they did, a European official quipped at an EEC meeting, where the French representative was insisting on a program for a return to fixed exchange rates, that eight of the nine EEC members were isolated on this issue.

On gold, U.S. Treasury Secretary Simon, in his speech to the 1974 annual meeting, referred briefly only to the objective of removing it from a central role in the system "and of assuring that the SDR becomes the basis of valuation for all obligations to and from the Fund."[3] He referred to the SDR not as a reserve asset but as a unit of account. In a press conference, however, Simon did say that "we wish to see gold removed from the center of the monetary system; and replaced by the SDR." The apparent U.S. coolness to the SDR —a mystery I am unable to explain—plus the stated objective of diminishing the role of gold, led some Europeans to believe that the Americans were trying to establish the dollar as the dominant reserve asset.

Minister Fourcade, saying that the question of gold should be approached "in a more pragmatic than doctrinaire manner," called for elimination of the "special status of gold" so that it would be treated "like any other monetary asset." In the French text of his address, Fourcade used the word *banalization* to characterize the process he had in mind for the treatment of gold. This would require abolition of the official price and freedom of central banks to buy and sell gold "at a price derived from the market." Further, "our wish is for the special drawing right to constitute the center of the new system."[4]

In a series of meetings over the next fifteen months—January 15–16, 1975, in Washington; June 10–11 in Paris; August 31 in Washington; and January 7–8, 1976, in Kingston, Jamaica—the Interim Committee resolved the major issues identified above. Those issues involved both the current financing of payments imbalances and the longer term reform of the system.

Financing Facilities

An issue that had been carried over from the Committee of Twenty was the link of SDRs to development assistance. Secretary Simon informed the other members of the Interim Committee in January 1975 that, after careful reevaluation, the United States still could not agree to the SDR-aid link. He was supported by the German Finance Minister. This ended serious consideration of the link during the period under review.

At the same meeting, the Interim Committee agreed to an extention of the IMF Oil Facility for another year on a somewhat enlarged basis. In withdrawing its initial opposition, the United States won approval for a review of IMF policies that would make it possible for the Fund to use, in its lending operations, the currencies of a greater number of its members. This would effectively increase the lending capacity of the IMF without requiring it, as in the case of the Oil Facility, to seek loans from countries in surplus (particularly OPEC countries). Agreement on the broader use of currencies of IMF members was not reached until January 1976.

The Interim Committee also agreed to the establishment of a special account in the Fund—to be financed by contributions from oil-exporting and developed countries—for the purpose of subsidizing the interest rate paid by the "most seriously affected" Fund members when they borrowed from the Oil Facility. Most seriously affected (MSA) countries were those with very low incomes and large balance-of-payments deficits owing to the higher price of oil.

Under the 1974 Oil Facility, 40 countries borrowed a total of SDR 2.6 billion, of which Italy took 26 percent and Spain about 12 percent. The lenders were several OPEC countries—Iran, Kuwait, Nigeria, Oman, Saudi Arabia, Abu Dhabi, and Venezuela—plus Canada and the Netherlands.[5]

For 1975, SDR 4.3 billion was available, including SDR 464 million left over from the 1974 facility. The United Kingdom and Italy together borrowed SDR 1.8 billion and other developed countries took SDR 1.1 billion. A total of 45 developing countries borrowed the remaining SDR 1.4 billion. The lenders included those that contributed in 1974 (except Abu Dhabi and Canada) plus Austria, Belgium, Germany, Norway, Sweden, Switzerland, and Trinidad and Tobago.[6]

To provide assistance on concessionary terms (that is, with interest rates and repayment schedules more favorable than would be available on loans from other sources) to the most seriously affected developing countries, Secretary Kissinger and Secretary Simon proposed in November 1974 the establishment in the IMF of a Trust Fund, to be financed in two ways: from contributions by OPEC states "and other sources" and from the profits on sales of some of the Fund's gold in the private market. At that time the market price of gold was close to $190 per ounce, while gold was carried on the books of the Fund at $42.22 per ounce.

Kissinger and Simon also proposed a $25 billion "financial solidarity fund" among OECD countries to perform the functions of a "safety net"—that is, to give assurance to lenders that OECD borrowing countries had an official financing facility to fall back on. The negotiation of this fund, which came to be called the Financial Support Fund, was completed in April 1975. Its ratification by the U.S. Congress is in some doubt at this writing.

The IMF Trust Fund was discussed by the Interim Committee in June 1975, when it was looked at as part of a package of proposals concerning the future role of gold and the treatment of the Fund's own gold holdings.

IMF Quota Increase

The Articles of Agreement of the Fund call for a review of quotas at intervals of not more than five years. Quotas had been raised across-the-board in 1959, 1966, and 1970. As new members joined the Fund, the total of quotas had crept up. Total quotas increased from SDR 8 billion in 1948 to SDR 29 billion in early 1976 (equal to about $34 billion at the dollar value of the SDR at the end of 1975).

The Executive Board of the Fund began its required review of quotas in 1974, and the matter was considered by the Interim Committee during 1975. Before the Interim Committee met in January 1975, the EEC Finance Ministers announced that they favored a doubling of the combined share of OPEC countries in Fund quotas, from 5 to 10 percent. While indicating also that the share of developing countries should not be reduced, the EEC Ministers did not indicate how the reduction in the share of developed countries should be distributed.

The proposal to double the share of OPEC was intended to reflect the enhanced political and economic importance of these countries and, in the process, to increase their capacity to make financial resources available to other countries through the IMF. (Another instance of the recognition of the increased political influence of the OPEC countries was the decision to begin the Fund's 1975 annual meeting on September 1 in order to avoid an overlap with Ramadan, the month-long Moslem holy period. September 1 was Labor Day in the United States in 1975, and many of us had to disrupt our normal August vacations in order to prepare for and be present at the annual meeting.)

The United States did not oppose the EEC proposals. But the necessary decrease in the share of developed countries in IMF quotas created problems. The United States was reluctant to see its own share of quotas (and its percentage of votes in the Fund, which differs slightly from its share of quotas) decline very much. Decisions in the Fund on major questions required a weighted majority vote of 80 percent or more; the U.S. share of total votes was 20.8 percent in 1975, which gave the United States a veto it was reluctant to lose. It was evident, however, that even if the United States managed to retain more than 20 percent of IMF votes in this round of quota increases, its share would probably fall below that figure in the future as Fund membership increased (if Switzerland, China, Russia, or, following Rumania's example, some of the Eastern European countries decided to join the Fund). The U.S. concern over its voting share was eased by a decision to change the required percentage of weighted votes on major questions to 85 percent.[7] This decision also gave the EEC a veto. The remaining problems relating to the distribution of quotas were ironed out in the autumn of 1975.

The quota increase will become effective only when it and the amended Articles of Agreement (which, among other things, eliminate the requirement to pay gold to the Fund in partial subscription of increased quotas) are ratified by the IMF membership. (In the United States, and many other countries, such ratification involves legislative action.) The result will increase total quotas to slightly over SDR 39 billion (about $45 billion). The U.S. voting share will drop to 19.96 percent, on the basis of present IMF membership.

The Exchange Rate Regime

The doctrinal dispute over the nature of the future exchange rate regime continued throughout the year following the 1974 annual meeting. The communiqués of the Interim Committee in January and June 1975 once again stated that provision should be made for "stable but adjustable par values and the floating of currencies in particular situations." This semantic compromise, which had its origin at the March 1973 meeting of the Committee of Twenty, showed remarkable survival power; in practice, positions on the exchange rate regime became unfrozen in the course of 1975.

The American stance, under William Simon and Jack Bennett at the Treasury (Bennett was succeeded as Under Secretary for Monetary Affairs by Edwin H. Yeo III in the summer of 1975) shifted, in emphasis if not in substance, to a more explicit advocacy of floating as an available long-run option for countries that wished to avail themselves of it. This shift was a result both of conviction and of pressure from the Congress, notably Henry Reuss. He wrote to Secretary Simon in August 1974, objecting strongly to the provisions on exchange rates contained in the Outline of Reform of the Committee of Twenty and arguing that countries should be permitted "to choose floating exchange rates as their normal regime." Reuss went on to state, in an underlined sentence: "A new plan of reform should be drafted that would permit IMF members to opt for either fixed parities under one set of rules or floating rates under another set of guidelines."[8] Congressman Reuss had reacted in a similar manner to the Nairobi Outline.[9]

In his reply to Reuss, Secretary Simon, while defending the position adopted by the U.S. representatives in the Committee of Twenty, expressed agreement on the "basic elements" of the U.S. position on floating. He went on to say:

> My own observations do not reveal, however, a drift in thinking among international financial officials toward a return to fixed exchange rate parities. A large number of officials continue to look forward in the hope that some day—which all recognize could not be soon—par values will represent the center of gravity of the exchange rate system, but the experience over the past year and a half with generally floating rates has in fact probably led to a much wider recognition of the contributions which floating rates can make.[10]

While Secretary Simon was being pushed toward floating exchange rates by Henry Reuss, Valéry Giscard d'Estaing, as French Finance Minister and then as President of the Republic, had Michel Debré pulling him in the other direction from the French National Assembly. Debré, an important figure in the Gaullist party, the support of which was necessary for Giscard's parliamentary majority, took an orthodox line on exchange rates, stressing the "disorder" in the international monetary system brought about by floating rates.

Nevertheless, France's position became more supple, though the timing of its concessions on exchange rates was no doubt governed by the evolution of the agreement on gold. President Giscard d'Estaing proposed that the heads of government of the major industrial countries should meet to take up monetary questions. Finance Minister Fourcade said in August 1975 that France was making "a better system of floating" its first priority, conceding that it might be two to four years before the world would be ready for "fixed but adjustable" exchange rates. What France now envisaged was a transition by degrees to a par value system.[11]

Meanwhile, the IMF Executive Directors had before them what appeared to be irreconcilable proposals from the French and U.S. Directors for a revised Article on exchange rates. This led the Fund staff to produce a compromise version which was available for both the June and August 1975 meetings of the Interim Committee. At the August 31 meeting there seemed to be a consensus that if the Americans and French could agree on language for the

Fund Articles regarding the exchange rate system, the result would be acceptable to others.

In his address to the 1975 annual meeting, Minister Fourcade stressed that although the final objective must be defined "without ambiguity or mental reservation," France would take "a pragmatic approach to the modalities" of a return to exchange rate "stability" in stages.[12]

Secretary Simon expressed the U.S. position:

> We believe strongly that countries must be free to choose their own exchange rate system and that all countries, whatever choice they make, must be subject to the same agreed-upon principles of international behavior. The right to float must be clear and unencumbered. In view of the great diversity in political systems, institutional arrangements, size of national economies, and degree of dependence on foreign trade and investment, our world requires an open mind about the future.[13]

In the next three months, intensive negotiations were conducted by Jacques de Larosière and Edwin Yeo, the deputies to the French and American Finance Ministers. The American position was no doubt strengthened by the fact that in their addresses at the 1975 annual meeting of the Fund neither the German nor the Japanese Finance Minister had mentioned a Fund-wide system of "fixed but adjustable" par values. On October 15, 1975, according to a Reuters dispatch, German Minister Hans Apel told a press conference that he saw no real alternative to floating exchange rates at the time. A similar dispatch, on November 11, said Japan's central bank Governor Teiichiro Morinaga was advising the Prime Minister to be cautious about proposals for changing the present floating exchange rate system. Japan had learned to live with floating.

While the secret Franco-American negotiations continued—Ed Yeo was crossing the Atlantic with dizzying frequency—further signs appeared of a shift in the French position. President Giscard d'Estaing, in a lecture at the Ecole Polytechnique on October 28, 1975, called for a return to a system of "stabilized parities, to a system that has a degree of viscosity instead of fluidity when it comes to changing parities." In the context it seems clear that he was using the word parities *(parités)* to mean exchange rates, not necessarily declared par values, for he went on to say, "Right now, the parities among currencies, at least for certain exchange rates, fluctuate as if in a vacuum— every movement is of an exaggerated magnitude."[14]

By November 12, Giscard was saying (in a press interview) that at the upcoming Presidential summit meeting France would avoid a theoretical debate: "compared with our traditional position we have come to envisage a limited flexibility of the system."[15]

During November 15–17, the heads of government of France, Germany, Italy, Japan, the United Kingdom, and the United States met at the Château de Rambouillet, 30 miles southwest of Paris. Built in the fourteenth century, this château was where François I died in 1547 and where Napoleon spent the last night before his exile to St. Helena in 1815. In the present century it has been a summer residence of Presidents of the Republic and a place to entertain foreign heads of government. In the splendor of this château in November 1975, the six Presidents and Prime Ministers devoted themselves to economic problems. The agenda, quietly negotiated by a group of special representatives (including George Shultz) of the governmental leaders, was broader than had been proposed initially by Giscard; it covered not only monetary matters but economic questions in general.

The "Declaration of Rambouillet" of November 17 was characterized by Leonard Silk of *The New York Times* as "written in resonant and cadenced prose/poetry."[16] The declaration stressed the importance of assuring recovery from the recession without "another outburst of inflation," of encouraging world trade and avoiding trade restrictions, of accelerating trade negotiations, of increasing economic relations with socialist countries in a number of ways, and of reducing dependence on imported energy while cooperating with producer countries.

In the monetary area, the heads of government welcomed the "rapprochement, reached at the request of many other countries, between the views of the U.S. and France on the need for stability that the reform of the international monetary system must promote." And, "our monetary authorities will act to counter disorderly market conditions, or erratic fluctuations, in exchange rates."[17]

It was emphasized at various press conferences that the French-American agreement had two elements: a new Article IV on exchange rate arrangements under the IMF Articles of Agreement and new procedures for frequent consultation among central banks and finance ministries of the larger countries on intervention in exchange markets to prevent "erratic fluctuations" unrelated to underlying economic factors.[18]

The new Article IV, polished and refined with the help of the Fund's estimable General Counsel, Joseph Gold, was made public in January 1976. It begins with a carefully balanced statement of the general "obligations of members," stressing both the "orderly underlying conditions that are necessary for financial and economic stability" and the obligation of IMF members "to collaborate with the Fund and other members to assure orderly exchange arrangements and to promote a stable system of exchange rates." In particular, each member shall (1) endeavor to direct its policies "toward orderly economic growth with reasonable price stability," (2) "seek to promote stability by fostering orderly underlying economic and financial conditions and a monetary system that does not tend to produce erratic disruptions," (3) "avoid manipulating exchange rates or the international monetary system in order to prevent effective balance-of-payments adjustment or to gain an unfair competitive advantage over other members," and (4) "follow exchange policies compatible with" these undertakings.

The Article goes on to provide that "Under an international monetary system of the kind prevailing on January 1, 1976," countries may adopt exchange rate arrangements that include (1) the maintenance of a value for currencies in terms of the SDR "or another denominator, other than gold," (2) cooperative arrangements by which they maintain the value of their currencies in relation to the value of the currency or currencies of other members, or (3) other exchange arrangements of a member's choice (this option implicitly sanctions floating). Further, "To accord with the development of the international monetary system," the Fund, by an 85 percent majority, "may make provision for general exchange arrangements without limiting the right of members to have exchange arrangements of their choice consistent with the purposes of the Fund and the obligations" under the first section of Article IV, summarized above.

The new Article also provides that the IMF shall exercise "firm surveillance over the exchange rate policies of members, and shall adopt specific principles for the guidance of all members with respect to those policies." To these ends, the Fund would be supplied with appropriate information by member countries, and members would be obliged to consult with the Fund on their exchange rate policies when so requested by the Fund.

The Fund, by an 85 percent majority, may determine that "international economic conditions permit the introduction of a widespread system of exchange arrangements based on stable but adjustable par values." This determination would be made "in light of the evolution of the international monetary system, with particular reference to sources of liquidity, and, in order to ensure the effective operation of a system of par values, to arrangements under which both members in surplus and members in deficit in their balances of payments take prompt, effective, and symmetrical action to achieve adjustment, as well as to arrangements for intervention and the treatment of imbalances." (This language was a reflection of the work of the Committee of Twenty on adjustment.)

Although the possibility of a widespread return to par values is envisaged, there is provision, in a separate schedule, that any "member that does not intend to establish a par value for its currency" shall "consult with the Fund and ensure that its exchange arrangements are consistent with the purposes of the Fund" and with Article IV.

Thus stands the compromise on the constitutional aspects of the exchange rate regime. It is delicately balanced in a number of ways: It gives the United States a veto on determination by the Fund that par values should be adopted on a widespread basis and, if such a determination is made, it permits countries, including the United States, to continue to float. The French can interpret the agreement as being consistent with their objective of a staged return to par values. And the second part of the French-American agreement—not yet made public—provides for close consultation among countries with floating rates and appears to envisage more active intervention in exchange markets to preserve stability of exchange rates.[19]

In trying to assess the significance of the exchange rate agreement, one is torn between calling it a major accomplishment and simply regarding it as an acceptance of the inevitable. On the one hand, France abandoned a long-held doctrine by agreeing to include in the IMF Articles a provision that sanctions floating without limit of time. On the other hand, France had neither the support of its EEC partners to press for more stringent conditions nor the means to force the United States to abandon floating. When France moved once again from an extreme position to the consensus view, its action appeared as a mighty concession. What the French gained was apparent agreement by the United States to accept greater responsibility for the movement of its exchange rate in the market and U.S. acceptance of language that envisages the possibility of an eventual return to stable but adjustable par values.

The outcome on exchange rates was closely related to the agreement on gold.

The Treatment of Gold

In 1964 the report of the Group of Ten had stated that "gold will continue to be the ultimate international reserve asset" (see page 67). In the course of the two-year reform exercise of the Committee of Twenty, the French position on gold came around to join that of the majority—who believed that the role of both gold and reserve currencies should diminish while the SDR became the principal reserve asset. By 1975 the word "demonetization" was being used frequently by finance ministers and other officials during the debates in the Interim Committee. (In 1968 I had shocked some people by characterizing the results of the Washington and Stockholm meetings of March as demonetizing gold at the margin.)

For a while French officials used the term *banalization* to describe the process of dethroning gold. The use of this word gave rise to confusion. Some, including Under Secretary Bennett, thought it was consistent with treating gold like any other commodity, though this interpretation hardly jibed with the fact that central banks do not buy, sell, or hold commodities. It turned out that what the French had in mind was that, instead of being the main reserve asset—as it had been characterized by President de Gaulle in 1965—gold would become another reserve asset to be held and used in the same manner as currency reserves. They and some other Europeans wanted to be in a position to use gold in transactions among monetary authorities instead of having it remain "immobilized" as a result of the large discrepancy between the official and market prices. They wanted to restore gold to some role in the system. The French in particular were unwilling to accept the possibility of using gold only for sales in the market, given the strong interest of French citizens in the market price of their hoarded gold.[20]

In line with the shift in their position on the appropriate role of gold, French officials came up with the idea that gold held by the Fund might be returned to member countries at the price at which they had paid it over to the Fund in partial subscription of quotas and quota increases. The logic by which this conclusion seemed to be reached was rather puzzling: if gold were no longer to be at the center of the international monetary system, the IMF, the central institution of the system, should not continue to hold gold, since this would somehow conflict with the aim of reducing gold's importance; the Fund should accordingly return its gold to member countries ("restitute" was the word that came to be used, implying, incorrectly, that the gold did not fully belong to the Fund). How this proposal could be consistent with the proposition that, in French eyes, gold would still be a reserve asset, if not the chief one, was unclear. To call the proposal crass would be rude, but it is difficult to interpret it in any other way than as a grab for the capital gain represented by the increased market value of the Fund's gold. The crassness, if such it was, was tempered somewhat by a proposal by French officials that part of the capital gain be passed on indirectly to developing countries, possibly via the proposed Trust Fund.

An alternative or perhaps supplementary explanation for the position on restitution adopted by French officials was that they feared that the United States and developing countries would push for more and more sales of IMF gold on the market as a means of raising funds to assist developing countries.

The Trust Fund, proposed by the United States, was the first step in this direction. Given their traditional concern about the market price of gold, the French may have regarded restitution to member countries as a way of forestalling massive sales of the Fund's gold on the market.

A number of ministers, including some from the EEC, initially opposed the restitution proposal, but sometime in the spring of 1975 Secretary Simon seems to have agreed with his French counterpart on partial restitution of IMF gold, perhaps as a way of getting French approval of the Trust Fund.

The American attitude toward gold also changed. In the Committee of Twenty's Outline of Reform, three alternatives had been presented, and the United States had opposed the options that would have permitted freedom of transactions among monetary authorities at market-related prices.

At the January 1975 Interim Committee meeting, Secretary Simon moved toward the less than clear-cut, less than unanimous EEC position—which had emerged from a meeting at Zeist in the Netherlands on April 22–23, 1974—that the official price be abolished and that monetary authorities be permitted to engage in transactions with each other and possibly with the market.[21]

Everyone at the January 1975 Interim Committee meeting agreed that the obligation to pay gold to the Fund for quota subscriptions or other purposes should be ended. The communiqué stated:

> Much progress was made in moving toward a complete set of agreed amendments on gold, including the abolition of the official price and freedom for national monetary authorities to enter into gold transactions under certain specific arrangements, outside the Articles of the Fund, entered into between national monetary authorities in order to ensure that the role of gold in the international monetary system would be gradually reduced.[22]

The lack of elegance in the language was the result, it can be imagined, of hasty negotiations at the end of a long meeting.

Informal discussions proceeded during the spring of 1975, with the French pushing for maximum freedom for monetary authorities to deal in gold while U.S. officials wanted sufficient limitations on such transactions to assure that a new official price would not be established and that gold would gradually move out of official hands.

Shortly before the June Interim Committee meeting, Treasury Under Secretary Bennett was quoted in the press as saying that the chances of any agreement were less than fifty-fifty because of an "extreme" attitude on the part of France on gold. A French official is said to have commented that no agreement could be reached while the United States was represented by Bennett.[23]

For better or worse, the broad outline of an agreement was reached in June. By then the French had apparently accepted the position of "certain delegations" at Zeist that "gold transactions with the free market should not, over a certain period of time, lead to a net increase of the combined official stocks." The main disagreement centered on an American proposal that transactions between monetary authorities should be confined to circumstances in which the selling government was faced with an extreme financial need.

The outcome was reported in the communiqué:

> The Committee held a detailed discussion of the role of gold and there was widespread agreement that a solution would have to be based on the following broad principles:
> (i) The objective should be an enhancement in the role of the SDR as the central asset in the international monetary system and, consequently, a reduction of the role of gold.
> (ii) The official price of gold should be abolished.
> (iii) Obligations to use gold in payments between the Fund and members should be abrogated.
> (iv) There should be the sale of a portion of the Fund's gold at the approximate market price for the benefit of developing members in general, and particularly those with low income, and the sale of another portion to members at the present official price.
> (v) With respect to the rest of the Fund's gold, there should be a range of broad enabling powers, exercisable with a high majority.
> (vi) A reasonable formula should be found for understandings on transactions by monetary authorities with each other and in the market, which would include understandings that would be designed to avoid the re-establishment of an official price and would deal with the volume of gold held by monetary authorities.
> (vii) An appropriate formula should be found for collaboration with the Fund in connection with the understandings among monetary authorities. Some countries felt that this collaboration should relate also to the reduction of the role of reserve currencies in the international monetary system.
>
> The Committee was of the view that the Executive Directors should be asked to study the question of gold further in order that a final agreement can be reached on the basis of these principles.
>
> The Executive Directors should study the establishment of a gold substitution account through which members would be able to exchange a part or all of their gold holdings for SDRs issued by the Fund for this purpose.[24]

On the afternoon before the August 31, 1975, meeting of the Interim Committee, the finance ministers and central bank governors of the five largest IMF countries were invited by Secretary Simon for a cruise on the Potomac River aboard the Presidential yacht Sequoia. Despite a reported high noise level from the engines, a deal was worked out on gold that seemed to give something to everybody present. This agreement was accepted the next day by the Interim Committee. As reported in the communiqué, it was agreed that one-sixth of the Fund's gold (25 million ounces) would be sold for the benefit of developing countries and another one-sixth would be restituted to member countries. The countries of the Group of Ten, plus others wishing to agree, would observe, during a two-year period, these arrangements:

1. That there be no action to peg the price of gold.
2. That the total stock of gold now in the hands of the Fund and the monetary authorities of the Group of Ten will not be increased.
3. That the parties to these arrangements agree that they will respect any further conditions governing gold trading that may be agreed to by their central bank representatives at regular meetings.
4. That each party to these arrangements will report semi-annually to the Fund and to the BIS the total amount of gold that has been bought and sold.
5. That each party agree that these arrangements will be reviewed by the participants at the end of two years and then continued, modified, or terminated. Any party to these arrangements may terminate adherence to them after the initial two-year period.

The communiqué continued:

Many members from developing countries expressed concern that the proposed arrangements for gold would give rise to a highly arbitrary distribution of new liquidity, with the bulk of gains accruing to developed countries. This would greatly reduce the chances of further allocations of SDRs, thereby detracting from the agreed objective of making the SDR the principal reserve asset and phasing out the monetary role of gold. This aspect should be studied, and measures explored to avoid these distortions.[25]

The market price of gold, which had been above $160 per ounce in mid-August, fell about $30 in September, presumably in anticipation of sales in the market by the Fund.

Secretary Simon hailed the gold agreement and revealed that the United States had made "substantial concessions" by dropping a demand for individual country limits on acquisitions of gold.[26] He also made it known that the administration would not submit the new agreements—on gold and IMF

quotas—for Congressional ratification until the third element in the package
—the exchange rate question—had been settled satisfactorily. This was part
of the leverage that led to the November 1975 agreement at Rambouillet.

Other reactions to the gold agreement were diverse. An article in *Le Monde*
on September 9 bore the headline, *"Démonétisons l'or, vive l'or!"* (Let us
demonetize gold, long live gold!). *The Economist* observed: "The Americans
believe gold is being phased out of the monetary system by the steps proposed
at the IMF. But they just might have been taken for a ride."[27]

Congressman Henry Reuss attacked that part of the agreement providing
for restitution of IMF gold "at a cut rate of $42 an ounce to an 'insiders list'
of distributors [sic] which almost exactly corresponds to the world's wealthiest
countries, with the poor countries getting a few crumbs."[28]

Meanwhile in Paris Michel Debré accused Minister Fourcade of signing
an agreement forbidding central banks to buy or sell gold for two years.
Fourcade replied that he had faced the danger of IMF sales in the market
without central banks being able to buy; his effort was to assure that freedom
for central bank purchases and IMF sales would begin at exactly the same
time.[29] This question of "simultaneity" would become increasingly important
to French officials, especially as the market price of gold fell.[30] But there was
the obstacle that the IMF Articles, before amendment, ruled out official purchases of gold at a price above the official price.

At hearings before Representative Reuss' subcommittee, former Treasury
Secretary Henry Fowler expressed opposition to the gold agreement: "The
fatal flaw in the tentative agreement is the combination of an abolition of the
official price for gold for official monetary transactions with the implicit freedom in the complementary understanding among the Group of Ten that, *after
two years,* any national central bank may buy gold from another central bank
at *any price* or from the private market *at any price* and in any amount." This
could result, Fowler claimed, in making "gold again the principal component
of monetary reserves" and at a higher value. It would also involve an inequita-
ble distribution of the increase in international liquidity and jeopardize the
future of the SDR. Fowler advocated, as an alternative to the August 31
agreement, exploration of a gold substitution account in the IMF.[31] At the
same hearing, Professor Fritz Machlup denounced the agreement as a betrayal
of "the principles of the reform of the international monetary system that had
been hammered out in arduous discussions over a period of twelve years."

In a letter to Representative Reuss, dated November 1, 1975, Secretary
Simon commented on Reuss' September 17 speech and, implicitly, on
Fowler's concerns. He argued that a new pegged price for official transac-

tions was unlikely, given the large element of risk in purchases of gold. "The myth of a high and rising gold price has been broken" and "elimination of the official price of gold is essential to its demonetization." He rejected the charge that developing countries were being treated inequitably. As to a substitution account, he expressed an open mind but noted that some proposals for such an account would have the effect of putting a floor under the price of gold.[32]

Jamaica Agreement

The series of negotiations was wound up at the Interim Committee meeting in Kingston, Jamaica, on January 7–8, 1976. The issues regarding exchange rates had already been settled in substance and no new decisions were needed. The agreement on IMF quotas arrived at by the Executive Board was endorsed.

On gold, it was agreed that sales of gold on behalf of the Trust Fund should take place in public auctions over a four-year period and the proceeds used to provide balance-of-payments assistance, on concessionary terms, to IMF members with low per capita incomes—initially those with annual incomes not above SDR 300 per person. The communiqué noted that the BIS, not a Fund member, would be able to bid in these auctions.*

The most contentious issue at Jamaica concerned the question of additional credit facilities for developing countries with large balance-of-payments deficits resulting from the combination of the high oil price and the recession in industrial countries. After considerable wrangling both in the meeting room and elsewhere, it was agreed that, in the period until the quota increase became effective, countries' potential borrowing rights at the IMF would be increased by 45 percent. In addition, the Executive Board had already agreed to a liberalization of the Compensatory Financing Facility, under which countries could borrow when they experience a shortfall in export income.

The communiqué stated that the amended Articles of Agreement should include a provision by which Fund members would "undertake to collaborate with the Fund and with other members in order to ensure that their policies with respect to reserve assets would be consistent with the objectives of promoting better surveillance of international liquidity and making the special

---

*This seemed unnecessary and irrelevant; if the BIS were planning to buy gold for its own account, it would be acting like any other investor and there would be no reason to single it out; if it were going to buy as agent for central banks (thereby technically violating the IMF Articles), that too did not justify singling out the BIS, since central banks could use other agents.

drawing right the principal reserve asset in the international monetary system."[33]

Subject to ratification by 60 percent of IMF members (77 countries) having in the aggregate 80 percent of the total voting power in the Fund, the Amendments to the Fund's Articles of Agreement will become effective. Precedent suggests that the necessary formalities may not be completed before late 1976 or some time in 1977, but unless some unexpected change in the international situation occurs, ratification in due course can be expected.

A headline in *The New York Times* of January 10 read: "Currency Reform Is Seen Achieved." Secretary Simon was reported as saying he did not foresee any further "major initiatives" in world monetary reform for the indefinite future." Otmar Emminger observed, "lo and behold, we suddenly have an *international monetary system* again."[34]

Question marks still hang over each of the two main issues, whose resolution was no doubt interlinked and whose principal disputants were the United States and France. The precise implementation of the exchange rate agreement is uncertain and, as Secretary Simon has frankly admitted, there are likely to be differences in interpretation between the United States and other countries. So it is with the gold question. During the two-year period, the ability of central banks to support the price, if they should wish to do so, is limited by the ceiling on gold holdings. What will happen when the two-year period ends? Will France and other countries agree to an extention of the agreement? If they do not, will central banks undertake to follow the recommendation of a few European officials and establish a range for the market price of gold—a floor and a ceiling within which they would hold the market price by buying and selling?

Given these questions concerning the two key areas in which France and the United States forged agreement, thereby beginning a new era of Franco-American amity in the monetary field, it is no wonder that a number of observers expressed surprise over the French concessions on the exchange rate issue and the U.S. concessions on the gold issue. These uncertainties may explain Representative Reuss' reaction to the Jamaica agreement. After several exchanges of letters with the Secretary of the Treasury, he announced on January 26 that he would not raise any serious objection to the Jamaica agreement but would "hold my nose and ratify it with a few exceptions."

XVIII

The Present and Future of the System

As these words are written (March 1976) the ink is hardly dry on the Jamaica agreement. A number of questions remain regarding the implementation of that agreement. The resolution of these questions will be the product of evolving experience rather than of once-and-for-all decisions across a negotiating table in the IMF, the Group of Ten, the Group of Five, or even what has been called the Group of Two—France and the United States.

Some may fear that the decisions will be made by the Group of One—the United States.* But there seems to be sufficient evidence that the United States, though it wishes to avoid the straitjacket in which it found itself in the 1960's and early 1970's, is committed to international cooperation and multilateral decision-making in the IMF. The Jamaica agreement, and the consultations that led to it, demonstrate an American willingness to adapt to the perceived desires of other countries in an effort to preserve international monetary and political harmony.

Where We Stand in 1976

As a prelude to thinking about the future, let us compare the nature of the economic and monetary problems that preoccupied officials (including heads of government) in early 1976 with their concerns at the beginning of the 1960's.

---

*The tendency of Americans at times to universalize their interests or concerns was pointed out in a friendly way when Finance Minister W. F. Duisenberg of the Netherlands, at a Committee of Twenty meeting, observed that the purely American sports event in which one of two baseball teams becomes the champion is called the "World Series."

In the United States the two periods were similar in that recovery from recession was a major goal of policy. But the rate of inflation was higher and the fear of a revival of inflation greater in early 1976 than they had been fifteen years earlier.

A striking difference was apparent on the international side. Constant concern over the U.S. balance of payments had become a thing of the past, for two reasons: the two devaluations of the dollar had strengthened the underlying U.S. balance-of-payments position, and the structure of the international monetary system had been fundamentally altered. The move to floating exchange rates and the cessation of convertibility of the dollar into gold permitted American officials to abandon the nervous and defensive stance they were compelled to adopt in the early 1960's when President Kennedy coupled his fear of nuclear war with his worry over the U.S. balance of payments.

In Europe, changes in attitudes and concerns were also evident. Much of the bickering over monetary matters between European and American officials in the early 1960's had been based on misconceptions and on the "growing pains" of the EEC as it felt its way toward confidence in the durability of its economic strength. Europe was no longer saddled with President de Gaulle's efforts to utilize international monetary weapons and to shape the international monetary system in order to further his political objectives. The issue of the role of the dollar in the world had shed much of its emotional, doctrinal, and even political connotations on both sides of the Atlantic.

Japan had come of age as a world power, and its spectacular rise to that status was no longer creating problems in its relationships with the United States and other countries. Japan had begun to turn its attention to the domestic problems it had neglected during the period when its industrial production and its foreign trade expanded so rapidly.

In general, the leaders of the major countries in 1976 were concerned with real—not imagined or obsolete—economic problems in their relationships with each other and in the developing world.

Among developing countries, the evolution from the early 1960's was anything but uniform. The oil-producing countries had, of course, transformed their position markedly. Other developing countries as a group had managed to accelerate their rates of growth and a number of them had increased the degree of industrialization of their economies. But some of them continued to be plagued by excessive birth rates and abject poverty.

The Problems

Chapter I stressed the relevance of economic interdependence. In the short time since that chapter was first drafted, the term "interdependence" has become a cliché. But that makes it no less real; on the contrary, the fact of world economic interdependence has come to be more widely and more deeply perceived. Like so much else in life, economic interdependence is not an all-or-nothing concept. One has to go back centuries to find a period when economic interdependence among countries did not exist. However, the degree of interdependence and, equally important, the appreciation of its existence have never been greater than today.

Again and again, in the history we have traced, the monetary officials of nations have sat down together in the face of crisis and have worked out cooperative solutions to common problems that were threatening the shared well-being of their countries. What held them together and motivated the successful resolution of crisis was the knowledge that all were in the same boat, that "going it alone" could only make everyone worse off.

Recognizing interdependence is one thing; working out its implications is another. As Joseph Nye has stated:

> to declare on the two-hundredth anniversary of our independence that the third century will be an era of interdependence is true but trivial. Interdependence does not provide clear guidelines for a new foreign policy. There is still a "necessity for choice." Interdependence just makes the choices harder. The choices will be about how to organize ourselves so that both the "domestic and foreign" aspects of interdependence receive their share of attention.[1]

The central questions for the future of the international monetary system have to do with reconciling the fact that economic policy is made by politically independent governments with the fact that the economic welfare of the people over which these governments preside has become increasingly dependent on events and policies in other countries. These central questions have both substantive and organizational aspects, and we shall be concerned mainly with the substantive. But how these questions are dealt with inevitably involves the organization of international decision-making. It is impossible for the 128 members of the IMF to act in the manner of a New England town meeting. Consequently, the Fund now has the equivalent of an executive committee of its 128-member board of directors. This new organ of the Fund—the Interim Committee, which may be succeeded by a permanent Council—has been and will presumably continue to be the forum for major decisions concerning the structure and management of the system.

With this introduction, let us consider the future of the international monetary system.[2]

The Exchange Rate System

The monetary system envisioned in the Outline produced by the Committee of Twenty was more managed than the one that preceded it. The balance-of-payments adjustment process, the settlement of imbalances, and the volume of international reserves (and to some extent its composition) would have been subject to rules and centralized decision-making in the Fund.[3] The fatal flaw in the Committee's endeavors was the unwillingness of its members to focus on the exchange rate regime (as we saw in Chapter XIV). Now we have an exchange rate regime that seems better adapted to the realities of the times. Equally important, policy makers and the public have now come to accept the exchange rate system they were unwilling to face up to in 1973–74. But the international monetary system as a whole appears to be considerably less managed than either its predecessor or the system contemplated in the Outline of Reform produced by the Committee of Twenty. Is a greater degree of management desirable? Is it possible?

The present hybrid system of individual and bloc floating is likely to persist as far into the future as it is reasonable to try to see.* In my view, the existing exchange rate regime should not be regarded as completely different in kind from a workable—that is, flexible—par value system. The difference between a flexible par value system and a regime of managed floating is one of degree. On the spectrum of different exchange rate systems, completely fixed rates are an impossibility in a world of politically independent nations—an impossibility even in the EEC snake, where occasional changes in established exchange rates have been and will again be necessary because the price levels, interest rates, and other variables in the member countries will often diverge.† At the other end of the spectrum, freely floating rates have been ruled out by international

---

*In late 1975 most developing countries were pegging their exchange rates either to another currency (52 of 97 developing countries were floating with the dollar, 6 with sterling, and 13 with the French franc) or to a group of currencies (either the SDR or a basket of currencies of their own invention). All such rates can be adjusted from time to time in relation to the peg.[4]

†This was illustrated again, as this chapter was being completed, when the French franc dropped out of the snake and the Benelux "worm" was abandoned on March 15, 1976.

agreement. Somewhere in between, a flexible par value system and managed floating are neighbors.

As we observed in concluding Chapter XV, the system of floating exchange rates—while a significant improvement on the overly rigid par value regime that preceded it—does not "insulate countries from what is happening in the rest of the world." Interdependence continues to exist.

In these circumstances, to what degree and by what means should floating exchange rates be managed? That they should be managed has been agreed (as we saw in the previous chapter). But much remains to be done in implementation of this agreed principle. Criteria must be developed that will permit identification of "erratic" movements in rates and distinguish them from movements based on underlying economic factors. The latter, presumably, are rate movements that facilitate economically justified balance-of-payments adjustment.

Some aspects of this distinction are clear. If a country has an inflation rate significantly higher or lower than that of its trade partners, its effective exchange rate will be expected to decline or rise. (If it is a member of the EEC snake, it will have to devalue or revalue from time to time.) Should a country's competitive position change for other reasons—if "Urbania" suddenly finds that it is the possessor of a large reserve of petroleum—it may be desirable for its exchange rate to move up. Another basic economic change justifying an upward or downward movement of a floating exchange rate might be an alteration in a country's capacity to export or import capital. A country that became more attractive to long-term foreign capital on a net basis would appropriately let its exchange rate rise so that it could absorb real resources corresponding to the new inflow of funds.

Cyclical Movements

More controversial questions arise concerning the movements of exchange rates in response to differences among countries in their business cycle positions. A country that goes into recession while its trade partners do not will experience an increase in its current surplus (or a decrease in its current deficit), but in today's world of mobile capital this is likely to be swamped by outflows of funds if its interest rates fall relative to those in other countries.[5] Thus its exchange rate will tend to decline. The extent to which exchange rates will move in such circumstances will depend in part on the degree to which market participants look "over the valley" of the recession to the next upswing and take positions in the currency that is temporarily depressed in a recession.

Such stabilizing speculation could well occur and could moderate cyclical movements in exchange rates.

If such stabilizing speculation does not occur in significant volume, the monetary authorities of the countries concerned have three choices: (1) to let exchange rates move to reflect differential cyclical developments among them, (2) to try to limit exchange rate movements by gearing monetary policies— notably interest rate policies—to maintaining more stable exchange rates, and (3) to moderate exchange rate changes by intervening in exchange markets, buying or selling foreign exchange.

There are arguments both for and against letting exchange rates respond to differential cyclical movements among countries. If a country goes into recession, the reduction in its exchange rate will, with a time lag, tend to offset some of the fall-off in domestic demand by stimulating exports and discouraging imports. In this way, the recessionary tendencies will be transmitted to other countries. Because the country in recession will have "exported" some of its problem—more of it than under a stable exchange rate—it may be less active than it should be in adopting the needed domestic counter-recessionary measures. Similar considerations apply to a country that moves into a phase of excess demand relative to its trade partners.

A further problem is that movements in exchange rates in response to cyclical fluctuations may lead to shifts in the use of domestic resources that will appear unjustified when the recession ends and the exchange rate goes back up. Again, the question is whether and to what extent economic entities will look over the valley of the recession and anticipate the recovery of the country's economy and its exchange rate. Assuming that stabilizing speculation will not be complete, the disadvantages of cyclical movements in rates could be reduced by official actions (1) to affect interest rates, (2) to affect the exchange rate directly by market intervention, or both.

Each of these approaches has disadvantages. In the first case, either the country in recession or its trade partners will be giving up, or at least limiting, the use of one tool of domestic demand management—monetary policy—to the extent that they try to keep interest rates close enough together to prevent a significant international flow of capital. One solution to this dilemma would be for countries to use fiscal policy more actively to regulate domestic demand while they aimed monetary policy at external stabilization. This in turn would require more flexible procedures for altering fiscal policy than have been possible in most countries in the past. Such a change would be desirable even apart from international considerations; but it seems far off.

An alternative to coordination of monetary policies would be a form of regulation over capital flows along the lines of the interest-equalization tax used in the United States from 1963 to 1974. The purpose would be to offset the incentive to move funds in or out of a country when its interest rates exceed or fall short of rates abroad. This approach would not find favor with the business community, either in the United States or elsewhere. To be effective such a tax or similar incentive might well require a panoply of controls, particularly on corporate financing across national boundaries.

Intervention in the exchange markets to prevent cyclical movements in exchange rates would affect domestic monetary conditions in most countries. Heavy intervention could throw us back to the difficulties that beset Germany and other countries in the late 1960's and early 1970's. A major reason for the move to floating in March 1973 was to put an end to the undermining of monetary policy in Europe that accompanied heavy central bank purchases of foreign exchange designed to prevent change in exchange rates.

There are no simple solutions to these problems. And they are not confined to a system of floating exchange rates; a workable system of par values would have to involve frequent changes in the par values. Similar difficulties would arise if (as is possible under the Fund's new Article IV on exchange rates) many countries return to par values at some future time.

Other Exchange Rate Movements

Apart from clearly observable business cycle swings, we know from experience that there will be shorter-term movements in exchange rates. These will raise questions about the operational definition of "erratic." Some part—but not all—of the large swings in the effective exchange rate of the dollar from March 1973 to the autumn of 1975 was no doubt erratic.

Various proposals have been made and will no doubt continue to be made governing central bank behavior in the management of floating rates.[6] The problems to be addressed involve not only the degree of management but the specific techniques of management. The countries of the EEC snake, for example, in acting to keep their currencies within the agreed 2.25 percent band, often intervene by buying or selling dollars rather than one another's currencies. The result is to shift the entire snake up or down in relation to the dollar, whether this effect is desirable or not—and perceptions may well differ on the desirability of such movements.

Similarly, if central banks whose currencies are under downward pressure in exchange markets sell dollars to prevent or cushion the downward movement while countries in the opposite position do not buy dollars, the effective exchange rate of the dollar will tend to fall. Or the reverse could happen, and the dollar would strengthen. These examples, all drawn from actual experience, illustrate the types of questions that need to be addressed as the Fund exercises "firm surveillance over the exchange rate policies of members" and adopts "specific principles for the guidance of all members with respect to those policies," as called for in the new Article IV.

By now it should be clear that floating exchange rates have not eliminated the need for international cooperation and management.

The Role of Reserves

Is any sort of settlement or convertibility mechanism necessary or desirable among countries with floating currencies? Is deliberate creation of reserves necessary? To what extent and in what form? Conversely, is there a need to control the nondeliberate creation of reserves? Does the composition of world reserves raise problems for the future functioning of the system?

Convertibility

The term convertibility has more than one meaning. Applied to the dollar in the period up to August 15, 1971, it meant the conversion of dollar balances held by foreign monetary authorities into another form of reserve: gold, SDRs, or IMF positions. This form of convertibility, provided for in the Bretton Woods agreement, reflected the asymmetrical nature of the system: in general the monetary authorities of other countries bought or sold dollars against their own currencies in the foreign exchange market in order to maintain their exchange rates within the established margins around their declared par values; the United States stood ready to supply or absorb dollars in exchange for other reserve assets in transactions with foreign monetary authorities. Both the United States and other countries—except those pegging their exchange rates to a single currency or a group of currencies—have now abandoned the old ways of making their currencies convertible.

But some degree of convertibility still exists. Whenever a central bank with a floating currency intervenes in the exchange market to buy its own currency (by selling a foreign currency) it is facilitating the conversion of its currency into another. The alternative to official intervention—hence conversion—would have been for the exchange rate to fall until some private party found it attractive to buy the country's currency in exchange for another currency or until the transaction was no longer profitable or attractive to the potential seller.

In general, the sort of convertibility that characterized currencies other than the dollar before floating now takes place only to the extent that monetary authorities decide to intervene in exchange markets. And it remains to be seen to what extent countries will find it desirable, or will be obligated by international agreement, to intervene. In any event, private participants can always convert one currency into another in a floating system (in the absence of capital controls imposed by some countries); the question is, at what price?

The convertibility that applied to the dollar before August 1971 has less of a role in the present system. The Committee of Twenty's Outline of Reform provided that "All countries *maintaining par values* will settle in reserve assets those official balances of their currencies which are presented to them for conversion." (Emphasis added.) It was accepted, without much controversy, that countries with floating currencies would be free of the obligation to convert. What may not have been envisaged when this language was agreed to was a system of widespread floating, though that was the reality in September 1973 when the deputies of the Committee of Twenty put this provision into the draft Outline of Reform.

What function would be served by a resumption of convertibility of the dollar into other reserve assets under floating rates? One function of such convertibility under the par value system was seen in the Outline of Reform as "the better management of global liquidity and the avoidance of uncontrolled growth of reserve currency balances. . . ."

Apart from the special case of OPEC reserves, uncontrolled growth of reserve currency balances would occur only in the event of persistent intervention by monetary authorities to prevent the exchange rate of the reserve currency (for all practical purposes, the dollar) from depreciating or to prevent their own currencies from appreciating. To the extent that countries are able to transform such acquisitions of dollars into other reserve assets, they might be tempted to engage in excessive intervention and, in consequence, to restore an excessively rigid exchange rate regime. Thus, under a floating rate system as under the sort of par value system envisaged in the Committee of Twenty Outline, convertibility and the adjustment process are intertwined. It seems reasonable to conclude that a restoration of convertibility by the United States should be predicated on the adoption of adjustment principles of the type put forward in the Volcker plan (see Chapter XIV).

Aside from new acquisitions of dollars, some individual countries might want to convert some of their existing dollar reserves into other reserve assets, particularly at a time when the dollar is, or is expected to be, weakening in exchange markets. This function, however, could not be performed on a very large scale without exhausting the reserves of the United States. A substitution account in the IMF would be needed for this purpose.

There is a broader case for a substitution account under a floating exchange rate regime. At present, dollars make up a large fraction of countries' foreign exchange reserves. At the end of 1974, official holdings of dollars in the United States and in Eurodollar markets were about SDR 95 billion out of a total of SDR 125 billion of foreign exchange reserves.[7] In these circumstances, countries intervening in foreign exchange markets to prevent their own currencies from depreciating are likely to sell dollars. Countries intervening to buy foreign currencies in order to prevent their own exchange rates from appreciating may buy currencies other than dollars. The consequence of all this could be downward pressure on the exchange rate of the dollar at times when this is not in the interest of either the United States or the world at large.

One way to give countries a wider choice of intervention currencies is to provide a mechanism for converting existing dollar reserves into SDRs through a substitution account in the Fund. Then, when a country needs to sell foreign exchange to keep its own currency from depreciating, it can exchange its SDRs for any other currency and will not be confined to selling dollars. The same result is achieved if countries lend to each other to finance intervention. In both cases, the monetary effects of intervention will arise.

The Supply of Reserves

In the three years from the advent of generalized floating to March 1976, world reserves, as measured by the IMF, increased by SDR 54.1 billion or about 36 percent. But almost three-fourths of the increase accrued to OPEC countries.

> The reserves being accumulated by OPEC countries are, in my view, qualitatively different from reserves accumulated by other countries. OPEC reserves are more in the nature of long-term foreign investments, being held against the day when the oil wells run dry. It is not in the power of most OPEC countries to spend their reserves, for there is a limit to their capacity to expand their imports, given the nature of their economies. Furthermore, when OPEC countries finally do achieve a level of imports that exceeds their exports and use their reserves to finance the resulting deficits, the reserves they have accumulated will, to a large degree, be extinguished, since the counterpart of much of their reserve buildup is debt incurred by oil-importing countries.[8]

The point to be stressed is that the reserves available to non-OPEC countries increased only 10 percent in three years. (A significant portion of that growth occurred in the first quarter of 1976, when Germany made large loans to other EEC countries in an effort to preserve the snake.) To argue that international liquidity has been out of control in this period makes little sense.

Few oil-importing countries have been willing to use reserves to finance their deficits since the quadrupling of oil prices in late 1973. This is understandable; reserves are normally used to finance temporary imbalances, and it was expected that the oil-induced deficits would go on for a number of years. Most countries would deplete their reserves if they tried to use them to finance their deficits. Therefore oil-importing countries decided to borrow and to use the proceeds to finance their deficits. This process then led to the recorded increase in world reserves, concentrated in OPEC hands.

Given the slow growth of reserves of non-OPEC countries, it may well be that a case can now be made for deliberate creation of reserves. Italian Minister Emilio Columbo suggested at the 1975 annual meeting of the IMF that "we should give consideration to resuming SDR allocations, with a more favorable distribution for developing countries."[9]

The Composition of Reserves

Much of the increase in world reserves in recent years has been in the form of dollars, held either in the United States or in the Eurodollar market. In the years 1970–1972, the U.S. balance-of-payments deficit led to a sharp expansion of world dollar holdings. Since early 1974, the rapid increase in the reserves of OPEC countries has to a large degree taken the form of dollar claims. In 1974 alone, when OPEC reserves increased by about $33 billion, deposits of these countries in the Eurodollar market increased about $19 billion.[10] Another $10 billion is estimated to have been invested in the United States.

Just as OPEC reserves should be viewed in a different way from the reserves of other countries, their investments abroad have a special quality. Although acquisition of financial assets in the United States by OPEC countries shows up as a deficit in the U.S. balance of payments, this statistical result is quite misleading. These investments are much more in the nature of long-term capital flows than of reserves. If they were treated in this way, the U.S. balance of payments would show a smaller deficit or a larger surplus. And, as noted, world reserve totals would be smaller. Thus the treatment of OPEC financial claims on other countries causes statistical as well as analytical confusion.

The Role of the Dollar

A goal of President de Gaulle was to reduce the "exorbitant privilege" of the United States that resulted from the special status of its currency. Since the mid-1960's, when de Gaulle's views were most strongly expressed, foreign official holdings of U.S. dollars have increased enormously. Foreign dollar reserves held in the United States have risen from about $16 billion in 1965 to almost $80 billion at the end of 1975. Of this increase of about $64 billion, $55 billion occurred in the 39 months from the end of 1969 to March 1973. Since then, most of the remaining growth has been accounted for by OPEC countries.

Despite this startling increase in world dollar holdings, the attitudes of other countries toward the dollar seem to have changed. There was some enthusiasm, during the Committee of Twenty deliberations, for consolidating dollar balances in an IMF substitution account. (To some degree this enthusiasm, where it existed, was motivated by the knowledge that convertibility could not be restored unless something were done to protect U.S. reserves against the conversion of existing dollar balances.)

The oil crisis and the emergence of the large OPEC surplus, together with the corresponding deficits elsewhere, have made countries more comfortable about their dollar holdings. This sense of comfort with official dollar holdings strengthened after the effective exchange rate for the dollar stabilized in the autumn of 1975.

Today the role of the dollar in the international monetary system is a matter that calls neither for national pride on the part of Americans nor for political distaste on the part of non-Americans. For many years, going back to Bretton Woods, the American attitude toward the world's use of its currency has been schizophrenic. The New York banking community and even the Federal Reserve Bank of New York were originally opposed to establishing the IMF, preferring the "key-currency" approach advocated by Professor John H. Williams of Harvard, who was also a vice president of the Federal Reserve Bank of New York. The economists at the Federal Reserve Board, however, favored a more universalist approach, through the IMF.[11]

Some residue of this difference in approach within the Federal Reserve System survived through the years. Although the New York Federal Reserve Bank came to accept the IMF, it has always shown great concern over the role of the dollar as a world currency. Its senior officers had little enthusiasm for the SDR during the period of its negotiation, though, again, they came to accept—grudgingly—the new reserve asset once it was in existence. Alfred Hayes, former president of the New York Reserve Bank, said in 1975:

> I wonder how much scope there is for an internationally issued paper asset in today's world. The use of SDRs as the world's main reserve asset is, of course, intellectually attractive. Translating this into practice, however, involves enormous pitfalls. The political aspects seem particularly difficult, involving as they do the role of reserve currencies as well as the question of national sovereignty in general.[12]

Schizophrenia about the role of the dollar has not been entirely absent from Washington, as was revealed in the U.S. Treasury's attitude during the early 1960's and the later negotiations in the Committee of Twenty (see Chapters III and XIV). It is worth noting the historical parallel with British attitudes when the Bretton Woods agreements were being negotiated: apparently a majority of the directors of the Bank of England were opposed, partly because "sterling exchange will be replaced by dollar exchange."[13]

Whether the reserve currency role of the dollar is of significant material benefit to the United States is doubtful. The notion that the United States needs the ability to create "international money" to finance American political or military activities abroad is easily exaggerated. When the United States was unable to change its exchange rate, this money-creating ability may have been an advantage (though many may have wished that it had not been so easy to finance our Vietnam venture). But under floating exchange rates, or even under a flexible par value system, it is difficult to think of a political or—one is reluctant to say—military activity abroad that could not be financed by a moderate increase in the U.S. export surplus brought about by a correspondingly moderate depreciation of the dollar. The United States need not be dependent on foreign borrowing, in the form of increased dollar reserves held by foreign monetary authorities, to carry out its international responsibilities.

Much of the emotion has gone out of the question of the special role of the dollar as a currency reserve. It is not a great advantage or a great disadvantage to the United States—or to other countries. If there is a wish to convert outstanding dollar reserves into SDRs through a substitution account in the IMF, there seems little reason for the United States to object, assuming the terms applicable to the dollars that would move into the Fund would be no more onerous to the United States than they are when the dollars are in the hands of foreign monetary authorities. There may even be sound technical reasons, related to intervention in exchange markets, for establishing a substitution account.

The Role of Gold

Much has been written about gold and the attitudes and emotions that surround it. Shakespeare, in whose works one finds a rich variety of characterizations of gold, called it the "common whore of mankind."[14] Keynes in the 1920's referred to the gold standard as a "barbarous relic."[15]

With equal if not greater fervor, others have either praised or been awed by gold's monetary role. When in April 1933 President Roosevelt agreed to a Congressional measure (the Thomas amendment) that, among other things, permitted him to raise the dollar price of gold—a move interpreted at the time as "going off the gold standard"—Lewis Douglas, FDR's Budget Director, is reported to have said: "Well, this is the end of Western civilization."[16] On March 30, 1943, *The New York Times,* in an editorial opposing Keynes' proposed Clearing Union, said: "The gold standard was, without any international agreements, the most satisfactory international standard that has ever been devised." President de Gaulle paid his respects to gold's role in 1965, though his motives may have been largely political. And *Pravda,* the daily newspaper of the Communist Party in the USSR, has advised Western nations to return to the gold standard.[17]

Those who are worshipful of gold (gold bugs or, more politely, chrysophilites) are usually motivated by one or more of these concerns: particular economic theories now held by a small minority of economists, distrust of government, international political objectives (there is discernible among non-Americans a correlation, far from complete though it is, between attachment to gold and anti-Americanism), and, last but not least, hope of personal or national pecuniary gain.

We are concerned here, of course, with gold's role as an official reserve asset. In its private role, it will undoubtedly continue to be widely used, given its remarkable properties of indestructibility, ductility (an ounce of it can be drawn into a fine wire fifty miles long), beauty, resistance to corrosion, and high conductance of electricity.[18]

We noted in the previous chapter that the Jamaica agreement left a question mark hanging over the future role of gold, one that relates mainly to what will happen after two years, when the Group of Ten gold agreement comes up for review.

Attitudes toward the role of gold as a monetary asset have altered markedly over the decade from the mid-1960's to the mid-1970's. Yet, despite the lip service paid to the SDR as the principal reserve asset of the future, there persists in some circles in Europe a desire to preserve a significant role for gold. The basis for this view is difficult to pin down, for it is never articulated publicly. It seems to involve, in the last analysis, a fear that international cooperation may some day founder and the IMF become unworkable or, at least, that it might function in a manner inimical to the interests of Europe. Those who hold this view would therefore not want a large fraction of Europe's reserves held in the form of SDRs, a liability of the Fund, since they see a remote danger that reserves in that form might become unusable. For similar reasons, they are unhappy to see so much of Europe's reserves held in dollars. In a period of monetary hostility, if worse came to worst, the use of both SDRs and dollars could be blocked. This leads them to see the preservation of a significant role for gold as a fall-back or fail-safe mechanism in the event that international cooperation should give way to international monetary enmity.

Those who hold this view are able to point to the fact that a large proportion of the reserves of the United States is already in the form of gold. Thus the United States is not taking many risks as to the future usability of its reserves. If American officials wish to combat the position just described, one way to do so would be to exhibit a greater enthusiasm for SDRs, including the exchange of gold reserves for SDRs in a substitution account in the IMF.

The fears described above are held by a small minority; the probability of their realization is not high. But it is understandable that some Europeans, having lived through much more political and social turmoil than most Americans, are somewhat more skeptical, even cynical, about the durability of international cooperation.

Although a few European officials would like to see established what would effectively be a new official price for gold, it seems unlikely that this will come about. As long as the United States does not change its basic approach to gold as an international reserve asset, a European attempt to peg a new price in the market would have to contend not only with the vagaries of private demand and supply of gold but also with the possibility of gold sales in the market by the U.S. Government. The sharp fall-off in industrial uses of gold at the high market prices of 1974–75 is an indication of the risks involved in an official attempt to place a floor under the price.[19] Even the market price of March 1976 (about $130 per ounce) may be like the Cheshire cat, fading away and leaving only a grin behind.

What seems likely is that gold will continue to remain "at the bottom of the pile" of countries' reserves. On occasions when their reserves in other forms become depleted, countries will either sell gold in the market if the price is attractive, or borrow using gold as collateral (as Italy did from Germany in 1974). Gradually gold is likely to seep out of official reserves and into the market, where it will become available to jewelers, dentists, artists, and industrial users for whom substitutes for gold are less readily at hand than for monetary authorities.

The Role of SDRs

The SDR is in a way a symbol of the move toward international monetary integration, toward a more symmetrical international monetary system, and toward the eventual conversion of the IMF into a world central bank.

Although only about SDR 9 billion is outstanding in SDRs in early 1976, the time may be near when it will be appropriate to create additional SDRs. In a system of managed floating, countries will continue to feel a need for reserves and, as income and trade increase, this need will grow. In addition, a case can be made for establishing a substitution account in the IMF for reserve currencies and for gold. Such actions would substitute SDRs for other forms of reserves. With dollars unlikely to be added to countries' reserves in large amounts over time (apart from the special case of OPEC) and with gold, too, unlikely to provide significant additions to reserves, the SDR has a future.

The Future System in Broader Perspective

An interpretation of the lessons to be drawn from our review of exchange rate developments since Bretton Woods is that interdependence has become so great that some insulation is needed in the interaction of national economies. Controls were tried in the late 1960's and early 1970's, and that form of insulation did not work. Now floating exchange rates are being used as a means of partially shielding countries from excessive influences from abroad. Given the political independence of countries and the consequent divergencies in policies and economic developments, "something" has to be able to give in their economic interrelationships. For the present and foreseeable future, that "something" is likely to be the exchange rate.

Flexibility in exchange rates does not, however, provide complete insulation. Cooperation and joint management—what the French call *concertation* —are still necessary. One of the immediate tasks is to work out a set of guidelines and criteria for such joint management.

What have we learned that can help those who will be formulating "specific principles for the guidance" of IMF members with respect to exchange rate policies and other aspects of the future system?

The international system has tended to follow the evolution that has occurred within individual countries' monetary systems. One of the major lessons
learned in the thirties—some would identify it as the essence of the "Keynesian
Revolution"—is that the pursuit of self-interest by individual entities in an
economy does not necessarily bring about optimal results for the economy as
a whole. A number of homely examples illustrate this principle: If a fire breaks
out in a theatre, the individual may be motivated to dash for the nearest exit;
if everyone dashes, disaster can result. Similarly, the individual sitting along
a parade route may improve his view if he stands up; if everyone stands up,
no one is better off. A common example from the economics textbooks is that
the individual may feel he is bettering himself if he spends less and saves more;
if everyone follows his example in an economy that is not experiencing excess
demand, total real income will fall and all will be worse off.

One of the consequences of this lesson for individual economies was the
assumption of responsibility for the maintenance of "full employment" and
price stability by fiscal and monetary authorities. Governments took on the
task of "demand management," sometimes supplemented by other policies,
particularly incomes policies to influence prices and wages directly.

To some extent, a similar lesson was learned about international economic
relations. In the 1930's, the efforts of countries to deal with their domestic
unemployment problems by increasing trade surpluses turned out not to be in
the general interest. An important purpose of those who designed the IMF was
to prevent the use of such beggar-thy-neighbor policies.

This lesson can be generalized. The pursuit by the policy makers of individual countries of what they perceive to be the self-interest of their economies
may turn out to be self-defeating. This was recognized by the Committee of
Twenty in the immediate reaction to the oil price increase.

Just as there is a need in each country for economic policies aimed at high
employment and price stability, there is a need, at the international level, for
a similar effort to make the policies of individual countries compatible with the
well-being of the world economy. Since there exists no international authority
that can directly perform this function, it can be done only by means of
consultation and cooperation among representatives of independent nations
meeting together in established international fora. Such consultation, aimed at
reconciling the policies of nations in order to make them consistent with the
general well-being, can be assisted by agreed objective criteria, such as those
put forward in the American plan submitted to the Committee of Twenty in
November 1972.

Walter Bagehot, the essayist and editor of *The Economist,* said in 1873 that "money does not manage itself." He was concerned with money in an individual economy; it is clear today that the same dictum holds true in the international sphere.

A corollary of this general proposition is that small countries, too, need to pursue policies that are compatible with the general welfare. There is a tendency for officials of small countries to believe, or at least to say, that what they do has little effect on the world economy but their economy is acutely sensitive to the impact of developments in the larger countries. Yet the actions of smaller countries do cumulate and can have a major impact on the world economy.

An incidental lesson of the history we have reviewed is that international monetary arrangements ought to be fashioned in such a way as to be relatively immune to the public statements of officials. We saw again and again in the late 1960's and early 1970's that large speculative flows and even crises were set off by public pronouncements of finance ministers, legislators, and others. Since no conceivable reform will prevent politicians and other officials—or influential private individuals—from making public statements, the only solution to this problem is to make the international monetary system less vulnerable to shocks of this kind.

Finally, though we have focused very little on the problems of developing countries in this book, we may properly conclude it by reminding ourselves that the world's most serious economic problem is to be found in the misery in which too large a fraction of the population of the so-called third world lives. The international monetary system can make, at best, a marginal contribution to the alleviation of this misery. Let us remember that it exists and endeavor to see that a well-functioning international monetary system will provide a framework in which the urgent problem of poverty can be attacked.

International Monetary Chronology

1944

July 1–22   International Monetary and Financial Conference of the United and Associated Nations at Bretton Woods, New Hampshire, agrees to establish International Monetary Fund (IMF) and World Bank (IBRD).

1945

July 31   Bretton Woods Agreements Act signed by President Truman.

September 1   Lend-lease aid terminated by U.S.

September 11   Export-Import Bank authorizes loan of $550 million to France.

1946

March 8–18   Inaugural Meeting of Boards of Governors of IMF and IBRD, Savannah, Georgia.

May 6   Executive Directors of IMF take up their functions.

June 19   Export-Import Bank authorizes an additional loan of $650 million to France.

July 15   President Truman signs bill approving Anglo-American Loan Agreement, providing loan of $3.75 billion to U.K.

1947

March 12   President Truman asks Congress for $400 million special assistance to Greece and Turkey in addition to $350 million requested earlier for other countries.

May 8	IMF extends its first loan: $25 million to France.
June 5	Secretary of State Marshall, in speech at Harvard, proposes European Recovery Program (ERP).
July 15	U.K. restores convertibility of pound.
August 20	U.K. suspends convertibility of pound.
November 17	President Truman asks a special session of Congress to provide $597 million "interim aid" for Austria, China, France, and Italy until the European Recovery Program can get under way.

1948

January 25	France abandons its par value and adopts a multiple exchange rate.
April 5	IMF decides that countries receiving U.S. assistance under ERP should not normally borrow dollars from Fund.
June 28	President signs bill appropriating initial $4 billion for European Recovery Program and $2 billion for other foreign assistance.

1949

| September 18–29 | Exchange rates of European countries devalued in amounts ranging from 30.5 percent for pound sterling to 12.3 percent for Belgian franc. Many non-European countries also devalue. |

1950

| July 1 | European Payments Union (EPU) established by recipients of ERP assistance. |
| September 30 | Canada adopts floating exchange rate. |

1952

| August 13 | Japan joins IMF. |

1956

| October 17 | France is extended IMF standby credit of $263 million. |
| December 22 | U.K. borrows $561 million from IMF and is extended a standby credit of $739 million. |

1957

| February–June | France draws $263 million from Fund. |
| August 12 | France devalues the franc by 16.7 percent. |

1958

January 1	European Economic Community (EEC) comes into existence.
January	France is extended IMF standby credit of $131 million.
March–June	France draws $131 million from Fund.
December 27	Ten European countries restore the convertibility of their currencies for nonresidents. Five other European countries soon follow. EPU eliminated.
December 29	France devalues the franc by 14.8 percent.

1959

September 9	IMF quota increase agreed.

1960

October	Price in London gold market rises, touching $40 per ounce.
October 31	Presidential candidate Kennedy denies that he would devalue the dollar.
November	U.S. and seven other countries begin to sell gold in London market.
November 16	President Eisenhower issues directive instituting measures to reduce U.S. balance-of-payments deficit.

1961

March 6–7	Germany and the Netherlands revalue their currencies upward by 5 percent.
March	U.S. Treasury initiates operations in foreign exchange markets.
September 30	Organization for Economic Cooperation and Development (OECD) formally comes into existence.

1962

January 5	Proposal for IMF to borrow from ten industrial countries—General Arrangements to Borrow (GAB)—approved.
February 13	Federal Reserve adopts procedures for foreign currency operations.
May 1	Canada reestablishes a par value for its currency.

1963

July 18	President Kennedy proposes interest equalization tax on American purchases of foreign securities.
October	Deputies of Group of Ten begin a nine-month study of "functioning of the international monetary system and of its probable future needs for liquidity."

1964

June 30	International study group of 32 economists completes report, *International Monetary Arrangements: The Problem of Choice.*
July	Group of Ten Study Group on Creation of Reserve Assets organized.
August 10	Group of Ten issues report on functioning of international monetary system.
October 17	Newly elected Labour Government decides against devaluation of sterling.
October 26	U.K. imposes 15 percent surcharge on imports of manufactures.
November 20	First use of GAB as U.K. borrowing of $1 billion from IMF is announced.
November 23	Bank of England raises Bank rate from 5 to 7 percent.
November 25	Credits of $3 billion extended to U.K. by U.S. and ten other countries, plus BIS.

1965

February 5	President de Gaulle calls for return to gold standard.
February 10	President Johnson announces extension of restraints on U.S. capital outflows to bank loans and corporate investment overseas.
April 1	IMF quota increase agreed.
May 12	U.K. draws additional $1.4 billion from IMF.
June	Report of Study Group on Reserve Assets circulated to governments.
June 15	French Finance Minister Giscard d'Estaing rejects a return to gold standard.
July 10	Secretary of the Treasury Fowler proposes an international monetary conference to consider "improvements in international monetary arrangements."
August 10	Report of Study Group on Reserve Assets published.
September 2	U.K. Government announces new wage-price policy.
September 10	Federal Reserve and other central banks enter exchange markets to support sterling.
September 28	Group of Ten instructs deputies to undertake "contingency planning" to meet future reserve needs.
December 6	Federal Reserve raises discount rate from 4 to 4.5 percent.

1966

January	Valéry Giscard d'Estaing replaced by Michel Debré as French Minister of Economy and Finance.
February 25	President de Gaulle meets with his senior officials and adopts stand against "contingency planning" for a new reserve asset.

July 20	British Government announces drastic stabilization program.
September 13	Increase in credit lines to Bank of England from Federal Reserve and other central banks.

1967

January 8–9	French Finance Minister Debré in an interview in *Le Monde* raises possibility of a future increase in official price of gold.
January 10	President Johnson calls for 6 percent temporary income tax surcharge.
January	Bundesbank begins to ease restrictive monetary policy.
March	U.K. completes repayment of debts to Federal Reserve and other central banks.
April 17–18	Finance Ministers of EEC, meeting in Munich, agree on joint position on SDR.
May 2	Germany's agreement not to buy gold from the U.S. announced.
May 17	President de Gaulle rejects proposal that U.K. join EEC.
June 5	Six day Arab-Israeli war begins.
July	U.K. draws on central bank swap lines again.
July 17–18, August 26	Ministers and Governors of Group of Ten meet in London to iron out differences on SDR.
August	President Johnson asks for 10 percent income tax surcharge.
September	Outline of SDR Facility approved at IMF annual meeting in Rio de Janiero.
November 11–12	Magnitude of a possible British devaluation discussed at Basle meeting of central bank governors.
November 14	British government announces October trade deficit, the largest on record.
November 16	British Cabinet formally decides on devaluation.
November 17	Bank of England sells more than $1 billion in foreign exchange market to support sterling exchange rate.
November 18	Britain announces 14.3 percent devaluation of pound, from $2.80 to $2.40. President Johnson issues statement reaffirming intention of U.S. to maintain official price of gold at $35 per ounce.
November 26	Governors of central banks of active members of gold pool meet in Frankfurt and agree both to continue pool sales and to support existing pattern of exchange rates.
November 30	IMF provides standby credit of $1.4 billion to U.K.

1968

January 1	President Johnson announces stringent balance-of-payments program involving mandatory capital controls.
February 28	Senator Javits issues statement calling for suspension of convertibility of dollar and abandonment of gold pool.
March 7	Canada exempted from U.S. capital controls.
March 9–10	Central bankers meet in Basle and are persuaded by Chairman Martin to continue gold pool.
March 14	FOMC agrees to increase Federal Reserve swap network by $2.8 billion.
March 15	London gold market closed.
March 16–17	Meeting of active gold pool members in Washington establishes two-tier gold arrangement and abandons gold pool.
March 19	U.K. introduces stringent budget.
March 29–30	At Stockholm, Group of Ten, with France reserving its position, resolves final issues on establishment of SDR.
April 1	London gold market reopened.
May	Student and worker uprisings in France.
June 5	France draws $100 million on Federal Reserve swap.
June 18	France sells $400 million of gold to U.S. and three European countries.
June 28	Income tax surcharge and expenditure ceiling is signed into law by President Johnson.
August	Speculation in exchange markets on a revaluation of German mark.
September 9	Basle arrangements to guarantee sterling balances announced.
November 1–19	Speculation on exchange rate changes in Europe; Bundesbank takes in $2.8 billion.
November 13	President de Gaulle says devaluation of franc would be "worst form of absurdity."
November 19	France announces cut in budget; Germany announces increased taxes on exports and reduced taxes on imports.
November 20–22	Ministers and Governors of Group of Ten meet in Bonn to deal with foreign exchange crisis.
November 24	In nationwide address, President de Gaulle announces refusal to devalue franc. President Johnson supports him.

1969

April 4	U.S. eases controls on capital outflows.
April 28–June	After losing referendum, President de Gaulle resigns and is succeeded in June by Georges Pompidou. Giscard d'Estaing reenters cabinet as Finance Minister.

April 29	German Finance Minister Strauss suggests publicly that Germany might revalue mark as part of a multilateral realignment.
April 30–May 9	Bundesbank takes in $4 billion in order to hold exchange rate.
May 9	German cabinet rejects revaluation "for eternity."
May 12	Germany introduces new controls on inflows of funds.
July 28	SDR amendment enters into force.
August 8	France devalues the franc by 11.1 percent.
September 29	Germany lets the mark float.
October 24	Germany establishes new par value, up 9.3 percent.
October–December	Germany's reserves fall by more than $5 billion, including sale of $500 million of gold to U.S.

1970

January 1	First allocation of SDRs, in the amount of $3.4 billion.
February 9	IMF quota increase agreed.
June 1	Canadian dollar floats.
June 9	EEC sets 1980 as target date for monetary and economic union.
September 13	IMF publishes report on *The Role of Exchange Rates in the Adjustment of International Payments.*
January–December	U.S. has balance-of-payments deficit of $9.8 billion.

1971

January 1	Second allocation of SDRs—$3 billion.
April 4	U.S. Treasury official tells press that the U.S. expects no change in exchange rates.
April	Germany acquires $3 billion of foreign exchange, in holding exchange rate.
April 26	German Economics Minister Schiller proposes joint float of European currencies to Hamburg meeting of EEC Finance Ministers. French Minister Giscard d'Estaing proposes devaluation of dollar.
April 28	Bundesbank suspends purchases of dollars in forward market.
May 3	German economic research institutes recommend that the mark float.
May 4	Bundesbank takes in $1 billion. Secretary Connally issues statement saying "no change in the structure of exchange parities is necessary or anticipated."
May 5	Bundesbank takes in $1 billion in first hour and then suspends official operations in foreign exchange market.
May 8–9	EEC Finance Ministers meet in Brussels and again reject Schiller's proposal for joint float.

May 9	Austria revalues by 5 percent and Switzerland by 7.1 percent.
May 10	Germany and the Netherlands let their currencies float.
May 28	Secretary Connally declares, in a speech at Munich: "We are not going to devalue. We are not going to change the price of gold."
June 4	Japan announces "eight point program" to reduce its balance-of-payments surplus.
August 2	President Nixon meets with Connally and Shultz and quietly decides that a drastic change in U.S. policies, domestic and international, is needed.
August 7	Subcommittee of Joint Economic Committee recommends revaluation of foreign currencies or float of dollar.
August 13	President Nixon and top economic officials go to Camp David.
August 15	President Nixon announces price-wage freeze, 10 percent import surcharge, and suspension of convertibility of dollar into gold and other reserve assets.
August 16–20	Bank of Japan takes in $2 billion in attempt to hold exchange rate.
August 19	France rejects German proposal for joint float of European currencies and establishes two-tier foreign exchange market.
August 23–27	Bank of Japan takes in another $2 billion and then decides to let yen float.
August 23	Schweitzer, on "Today" television program, suggests devaluation of dollar in terms of gold as a U.S. "contribution" to restoration of monetary stability.
September 3–4	Deputies of Group of Ten meet in Paris and U.S. unveils its objective to achieve a swing of $13 billion in its balance of payments.
November 30–December 1	Group of Ten meets in Rome and discusses "hypothetical" devaluation of dollar but fails to agree on a realignment of exchange rates.
December 6	Canadian Prime Minister Trudeau announces that Canada's dollar would float even after a realignment of other currencies.
December 13–14	Presidents Pompidou and Nixon meet in the Azores and announce agreement on a devaluation of the dollar and a revaluation "of some other currencies."
December 17–18	Group of Ten meets at Smithsonian Institution in Washington and agrees on a realignment of currencies, including devaluation of dollar.

1972

January 1	Third allocation of SDRs—$3 billion.
March 1	Germany imposes "Bardepot"—a disincentive on borrowing abroad by German businesses.
March 7	EEC decides to narrow margins for their currencies to 2.25 percent to form EEC "snake" in the Smithsonian "tunnel."
May 1	U.K. decides to join EEC snake.
May 12	In speech at Montreal, Chairman Burns sets out ten elements of a reformed monetary system and calls for prompt "rebuilding process."
May 16	John Connally succeeded by George Shultz as Secretary of the Treasury.
June 23	U.K. leaves EEC snake and floats, after losing $2.5 billion of reserves in 6 days.
June 26	After "closing" exchange markets, EEC Finance Ministers meet and decide to maintain snake, apart from Denmark's withdrawal, but to permit Italy to intervene and settle in dollars.
June 28–July 14	European central banks and Bank of Japan purchase $6 billion to hold exchange rates.
June 29	German Government, over objection of Economics Minister Schiller, adopts an exchange control measure—prohibition of sale of German bonds to foreigners.
July 2	Schiller submits resignation and is later succeeded by Helmut Schmidt.
July 19	Federal Reserve undertakes operations in foreign exchange markets for first time since August 15, 1971.
July 26	Formation of IMF Committee on Reform of the International System (Committee of Twenty) approved.
September 6	IMF publishes report on *Reform of the International Monetary System.*
September 26	Secretary Shultz presents to IMF annual meeting the broad outlines of a U.S. proposal for international monetary reform.
November 27–29	Deputies of Committee of Twenty, meeting in Washington, begin substantive work on reform.

1973

January 1	U.K., Ireland, and Denmark become EEC members.
January 11	U.S. announces end of Phase 2 of price-wage controls.
January 20	Italy establishes two-tier foreign exchange market.
January 23	Swiss franc permitted to float.
February 4	Germany announces additional exchange controls.
February 5–9	Bundesbank purchases $5 billion in effort to hold exchange rate.

February 7–12	Under Secretary Volcker visits major capitals on 31,000-mile trip.
February 12	Foreign exchange markets "closed" in Europe and Japan. U.S. announces 10 percent devaluation of dollar.
February 12	Japan adopts floating exchange rate, followed by Italy and Switzerland.
February 14	Exchange markets reopen.
March 1	European central banks purchase $3.6 billion and "close" foreign exchange markets.
March 4, 8	EEC Finance Ministers meet in Brussels to consider joint float and requests for U.S. actions.
March 9	Finance Ministers of 14 countries meet in Paris.
March 11	EEC Ministers announce joint float of "six" currencies (while Britain, Italy, and Ireland float independently). Germany revalues mark by 3 percent.
March 13	Austria revalues its currency by 2.25 percent.
March 16	Finance Ministers of 14 countries meet again. Sweden and Norway associate their currencies with EEC snake.
July 10	Federal Reserve resumes intervention in foreign exchange markets and expands swap network.
September 24	Committee of Twenty releases First Outline of Reform and agrees to July 31, 1974, deadline for completion of its work.
October	Oil embargo imposed and oil price raised during Arab-Israeli War.
November 12	Central bank governors, meeting in Basle, terminate two-tier gold agreement.
December 23	Oil price raised again, quadrupling it from level of early October.

1974

January 17–18	Committee of Twenty, meeting in Rome, decides to adopt evolutionary approach to reform.
January 19	French franc drops out of EEC snake.
January 29	U.S. terminates controls on outflows of capital.
January 30	Germany relaxes restrictions on inflows of capital.
April 22–23	EEC Finance Ministers, meeting at Zeist in the Netherlands, adopt a position on the future role of gold.
June 14	Committee of Twenty issues Outline of Reform, including "immediate steps," and concludes its work.
June 25	Herstatt Bank of Cologne (Germany) fails.
October 3	New Interim Committee of IMF holds its first meeting.

1975

February 1	Central bank governors of Germany, Switzerland, and U.S. meet in London and agree on more concerted intervention to maintain orderly markets.
February	Federal Reserve sells $600 million of foreign currencies, drawn under swap network.
July 10	French franc rejoins EEC snake.
August 31	Interim Committee and Group of Ten, meeting in Washington, agree on treatment of gold.
November 15–17	Six heads of government, meeting at Rambouillet, acknowledge "rapprochement" between France and U.S. on exchange rate system.

1976

January 7–8	Interim Committee, meeting in Kingston, Jamaica, completes interim reform, with agreement on IMF quota increases, exchange rate system, treatment of gold, Trust Fund.
March 15	France drops out of EEC snake.

Source Notes

I. The International Monetary System: What It Is and Why It Matters

1. *The New York Times,* July 2, 1975, p. 14.
2. International Monetary Fund, *Summary Proceedings,* Annual Meeting, 1973, p. 71.
3. Miriam S. Camps, *The Management of Interdependence: A Preliminary View,* Council on Foreign Relations (1974).

II. Recovery and Renewal: The System from Bretton Woods to the End of the 1950's

1. The authoritative biography is R. F. Harrod, *The Life of John Maynard Keynes* (New York: Harcourt Brace Jovanovich, 1951). See also *Essays on John Maynard Keynes,* ed. Milo Keynes (New York: Cambridge University Press, 1975).
2. David Rees, *Harry Dexter White: A Study in Paradox* (New York: Coward-McCann, 1973).
3. On the necessity of distinguishing clearly between postwar relief and reconstruction on the one hand and "long run currency stabilization" on the other, see the various articles written in 1943 and 1944 by Professor John H. Williams and reprinted in his *Postwar Monetary Plans and Other Essays* (New York: Knopf, 1945).
4. "European Initiative Essential to Economic Recovery," Remarks by the Secretary of State on the occasion of commencement exercises at Harvard University, June 5, 1947, reprinted in *The Department of State Bulletin,* 16: 415 (June 15, 1947), pp. 1159ff.
5. For a full description and analysis, see Richard N. Gardner, *Sterling-Dollar Diplomacy* (New York: McGraw-Hill, 1969), pp. 188–254.
6. "Proposals for an International Clearing Union," reprinted in *The International Monetary Fund, 1945–1965,* Vol. III: Documents (Washington: International Monetary Fund, 1969), pp. 19–36.
7. Lord Keynes, "The International Clearing Union," speech delivered before the House of Lords, May 18, 1943, reprinted in *The New Economics,* ed. S.E. Harris (New York: Knopf, 1947), p. 365.
8. Harrod, *The Life of John Maynard Keynes,* pp. 543ff.
9. In "The International Monetary Fund," speech before the House of Lords, May 23, 1944, reprinted in *The New Economics,* p. 373.

10. Quoted by Joseph Gold in "The Institution," *The International Monetary Fund, 1945–1965,* Vol. II: Analysis (Washington, International Monetary Fund, 1969), p. 513.

11. Austin Robinson, "A Personal View," in *Essays on John Maynard Keynes,* p. 19.

12. See W. McC. Martin, "Toward a World Central Bank?" 14 September 1970, *The Per Jacobsson Foundation.*

13. Henry Fairlie, *The Kennedy Promise* (Garden City, N. Y.: Doubleday, 1973), pp. 122–123.

14. Raymond Aron, *The Imperial Republic* (Englewood Cliffs, N.J.: Prentice-Hall, 1974), p. 178.

15. *Foreign Relations of the United States, 1947,* Vol. III (Washington: Department of State, 1972), p. 255.

16. Agency for International Development, *U.S. Overseas Loans and Grants* (Washington, May 1974).

17. Aron, *The Imperial Republic,* p. 191.

18. Charles P. Kindleberger, *The Dollar Shortage,* (Cambridge, Mass.: M.I.T., Technology Press, and New York: Wiley, 1950), p. 24.

19. Ibid., pp. 166–167.

20. Alfred E. Kahn, *Great Britain in the World Economy* (New York: Columbia University Press, 1946).

21. Organization for European Economic Cooperation (OEEC), *Problems and Progress of the European Economy,* Fifth Annual Report, January 1954, p. 291.

22. IMF, *Annual Report, 1953,* Washington, pp. 20–21.

23. OEEC, *Twelfth Annual Economic Review,* September 1961, pp. 185–186.

24. Commission on Foreign Economic Policy, *Report to the President and the Congress,* January 1954, pp. 3–5 and passim.

25. Ibid.

26. U.S. Department of Commerce, *Survey of Current Business,* various issues.

27. Angus Maddison, *Economic Growth in the West* (New York: Twentieth Century Fund, 1964), p. 25.

28. Ibid., p. 37.

29. Ibid., p. 62.

30. OEEC, *Twelfth Annual Economic Review,* p. 150.

31. Maddison, *Economic Growth,* p. 161.

32. IMF, *Annual Report, 1959,* p. 47.

33. W. Fellner, M. Gilbert, B. Hansen, R. Kahn, F. Lutz, and P. de Wolff, *The Problem of Rising Prices,* OEEC, May 1961, p. 22.

34. Ibid.

35. The change of attitudes and practices in the French business community is well described by John Ardagh, *The New France,* 2nd ed. (Baltimore: Penguin, 1973).

36. A. Lamfalussy, *The United Kingdom and the Six* (Homewood, Ill.: Irwin, 1963), pp. 116–117 and passim. France joined the virtuous circle only in 1958.

37. IMF, *Balance of Payments Yearbooks.*

38. IMF, *Annual Report on Exchange Restrictions, 1958,* pp. 9, 145–149.

39. IMF, *Annual Report on Exchange Restrictions, 1959,* pp. 4–5.

40. U.S. Department of Commerce, *Survey of Current Business,* various issues.

41. OEEC, *Statistics of National Accounts, 1950–1961,* Paris, 1964.

42. *Report to the President on Foreign Economic Policies* (Gray Report), Washington, 1950, pp. 45, 47.

43. United Nations, *Monthly Bulletin of Statistics,* various issues.

44. *Facts and Figures on the Japanese Economy* (Tokyo: Japan Development Bank, 1966), p. 19.

45. Ibid., pp. 10, 11.

46. Computed from United Nations, *Monthly Bulletin of Statistics,* December 1959, p. 7.

47. As measured at the time; see IMF, *International Financial Statistics,* June 1960.
48. IMF, *Annual Report on Exchange Restrictions, 1959.*
49. IMF, *Annual Report, 1960,* p. 62.
50. *Economic Report of the President,* January 1960, p. 51 and passim.
51. *Federal Reserve Bulletin,* 46: 10 (October 1960), pp. 1095–1096.
52. OEEC, *Europe and the World Economy,* Eleventh Annual Economic Review, April 1960, p. 9.
53. Albert O. Hirschman, "Invitation to Theorizing About the Dollar Glut," *Review of Economics and Statistics,* 42:1 (February 1960).
54. IMF, *Annual Report, 1960,* p. 38.
55. Ibid., pp. 4, 5.
56. For a survey of the literature, see J. Williamson, "International Liquidity: A Survey," *The Economic Journal,* 83: 331 (September 1973).
57. R. Triffin, *Gold and the Dollar Crisis* (New Haven: Yale University Press, 1960). Triffin had made his point earlier in a governmental report and in Congressional testimony.
58. See, for example, Samuel I. Katz, "Leads and Lags in Sterling Payments," *The Review of Economics and Statistics,* 35:1 (February 1953).
59. *Public Papers of the Presidents of the United States,* Dwight D. Eisenhower, 1960–61, pp. 868–869.

III. The First Half of the 1960's: The United States on the Defensive

1. Board of Governors of the Federal Reserve System, *Supplement to Banking and Monetary Statistics,* Section 15, International Finance, Washington, 1962, pp. 6–8.
2. *The Economist,* London, 197: 6110 (October 1, 1960), pp. 60–61.
3. Ibid. 197:6114 (October 29, 1960), pp. 475–477.
4. "A Statement by Senator John F. Kennedy on the Balance of Payments," Philadelphia, Pennsylvania, October 31, 1960, reprinted in Robert V. Roosa, *The Dollar and World Liquidity* (New York: Random House, 1967), pp. 265–270.
5. Roosa, *The Dollar,* p. 23.
6. Board of Governors of the Federal Reserve System, *Annual Report* covering operations for the year 1960, pp. 5, 67, 69.
7. *Economic Report of the President,* January 1961, pp. 39–40. In early 1961, the prohibition on the holdings of gold by U.S. citizens was extended to their holdings abroad.
8. Arthur M. Schlesinger, Jr., *A Thousand Days* (Boston: Houghton Mifflin, 1965), p. 126.
9. Gilbert Burck, "A Dillon, A Dollar," *Fortune,* February 1961, p. 221.
10. Theodore C. Sorensen, *Kennedy* (New York: Harper & Row, 1965), p. 406; Schlesinger, *A Thousand Days,* p. 130.
11. Bank for International Settlements (BIS), *Annual Report, 1968,* p. 31.
12. Based on a conversation and correspondence with Professor James Tobin, then a member of President Kennedy's Council of Economic Advisers.
13. Roosa, *The Dollar,* p. 13.
14. *Report to the Honorable John F. Kennedy by the Task Force on the Balance of Payments,* December 27, 1960, the John F. Kennedy Library, Waltham, Massachusetts.
15. Gilbert Burck, "A Dillon, A Dollar," p. 222.
16. Roosa, *The Dollar,* pp. 14–15.
17. Sorensen, *Kennedy,* pp. 280, 409.
18. "The United States Balance of Payments and the Gold Outflow from the United States," A message from President Kennedy to the Congress, February 6, 1961, reprinted in Roosa, *The Dollar.*

19. *The Economist,* 198:6129 (February 11, 1961), pp. 533–535, 553.
20. Arthur M. Okun, "Monetary Policy, Debt Management and Interest Rates: A Quantitative Appraisal," *Stabilization Policies,* Commission on Money and Credit, (Englewood Cliffs, N. J.: Prentice-Hall, 1963), pp. 331–380.
21. See *The Gold Pool,* IMF, *Annual Report, 1964,* pp. 31–32.
22. *The International Monetary Fund, 1945–1965,* Vol. I: Chronicle, pp. 507ff.
23. National Advisory Council on International Monetary and Financial Problems, *Special Report to the President and to the Congress on Special Borrowing Arrangements of the International Monetary Fund,* U.S. Government Printing Office, January 1962, p. 9.
24. Ibid., Annex B, Exchange of Correspondence between M. Wilfrid Baumgartner, Minister of Finance and Economic Affairs of France, and Douglas Dillon, Secretary of the Treasury, Paris, France, December 15, 1961.
25. *The International Monetary Fund 1945–1965,* Vol. I: Chronicle, p. 514.
26. Ibid.
27. Schlesinger, *A Thousand Days,* pp. 652–654.
28. See, for example, *Economic Report of the President,* January 1964, p. 38.
29. *The Washington Post,* January 23, 1962, p. A17.
30. *Federal Reserve Bulletin,* 49: 7 (July 1963), p. 946.
31. U.S. Department of Commerce, *Defense Indicators,* various issues.
32. "Bank Credits to Foreigners" *Federal Reserve Bulletin,* 51: 3 (March 1965), pp. 361–370.
33. BIS, *Annual Report, 1962,* pp. 8–9.
34. IMF, *Annual Report, 1964,* pp. 50–52.
35. BIS, *Annual Report, 1961,* pp. 16, 146.
36. Ibid., p. 147.
37. See Gisele Podbielski, *Italy: Development and Crisis in the Postwar Economy* (Oxford: Clarendon Press, 1974), pp. 24–37.
38. BIS, *Annual Report, 1964,* p. 10.
39. See Robert W. Gillespie, "The Policies of England, France, and Germany as Recipients of Foreign Direct Investment" in *International Mobility and Movement of Capital* (Fritz Machlup, Walter S. Salant, Lorie Tarshis, eds.) (New York: National Bureau of Economic Research, 1972), pp. 397–431.
40. *The New York Times,* August 27, 1970, p. 17.
41. Sorensen, *Kennedy,* p. 409.
42. *The Economist,* 214:6337 (February 6, 1965), pp. 567–569.
43. Stephen D. Cohen, *International Monetary Reform, 1964–69, The Political Dimension* (New York: Praeger, 1970), p. 50.
44. *The United States Balance of Payments in 1968* (Washington: Brookings, 1963).
45. Ibid., p. 259.
46. IMF, *Annual Report, 1964,* pp. 26–28.
47. IMF, *Annual Report, 1965,* pp. 9–12.
48. *Economic Report of the President,* January 1964, p. 139. The passage quoted was probably written by me, though the entire section of the report was a matter of considerable negotiation with the Treasury Department.
49. Robert V. Roosa, *Monetary Reform for the World Economy* (New York: Harper & Row, 1965), pp. 26–32.
50. OECD, *The Balance of Payments Adjustment Process,* A report by Working Party 3 of the Economic Policy Committee, August 1966.
51. *The United States Balance of Payments,* Statements by Economists, Bankers and Others on the Brookings Study, "The United States Balance of Payments in 1968," materials submitted to the Joint Economic Committee, Congress of the United States, U.S. Government Printing Office, Washington, 1963, pp. 210–214.

52. Sorensen, *Kennedy,* p. 408. Paul Samuelson is on record as having advocated devaluation of the dollar as far back as 1959.

53. *The United States Balance of Payments,* p. 111.

54. See H.S. Houthakker, "Exchange Rate Adjustment," in *Factors Affecting the United States Balance of Payments,* Compilation of Studies prepared for the Subcommittee on International Exchange and Payments of the Joint Economic Committee, Congress of the United States, U.S. Government Printing Office, Washington, 1962, pp. 287-304.

IV. Stirrings of International Monetary Reform

1. IMF, *Summary Proceedings,* Annual Meeting, 1962, pp. 61-68.

2. Roosa, *The Dollar,* pp. 33-34.

3. This article is reprinted in Roosa, *The Dollar,* pp. 93-108.

4. Ibid., p. 34.

5. "The Balance of Payments," A Special Message From President Kennedy to the Congress, July 18, 1963 (reprinted in Roosa, *The Dollar,* pp. 317-334).

6. Group of Ten Communiqué, October 2, 1963, reprinted in *Federal Reserve Bulletin,* 49: 10 (October 1963), pp. 1357-1358.

7. IMF, *Summary Proceedings,* Annual Meeting, 1963, pp. 55-63.

8. This French proposal was apparently an adaptation of an earlier proposal of E. M. Bernstein. (See Model, Roland & Co., *Quarterly Review and Investment Survey,* 4th Quarter 1963.)

9. *Ministerial Statement of the Group of Ten and Annex Prepared by Deputies,* August 1964, reprinted in *Federal Reserve Bulletin,* 50: 8 (August 1964), pp. 975-999.

10. Ibid.

11. *Minutes of the Federal Open Market Committee (FOMC), 1964,* p. 577.

12. *International Monetary Arrangements: The Problem of Choice,* Report on the Deliberations of an International Study Group of 32 Economists (Princeton, N. J.: Princeton University Press, 1964).

13. IMF, *Summary Proceedings,* Annual Meeting, 1964, pp. 38-46.

14. Ibid., pp. 203-209.

15. Ibid., pp. 198-202.

16. Statement of Arturo Perez Galliaro of Guatemala, speaking for 19 Latin American countries and the Philippines, ibid., pp. 49-52.

17. Some of these are summarized in the *Economic Report of the President,* 1964, pp. 144-148.

18. *Report of the Study Group on the Creation of Reserve Assets* (Rome: Bank of Italy Press, 1965), pp. 26-29, reprinted in *Balance of Payments—1965,* Hearings before a Subcommittee of the Committee on Banking and Currency, United States Senate, 89th Congress, First Session, Part 2, U.S. Government Printing Office, Washington, 1965, pp. 1103-1204.

19. Ibid., pp. 54-57.

20. Ibid., pp. 29-32.

21. Ibid., pp. 33-39.

22. Ibid., p. 71.

23. Ibid., pp. 86-87.

24. Ibid., pp. 38-43.

25. Ibid., pp. 43-46.

26. Roosa, *Monetary Reform for the World Economy.*

27. Ibid., p. 67.

28. *1965 Joint Economic Report,* Report of the Joint Economic Committee, Congress of the United States on the January 1965 Economic Report of the President, March 17, 1965, U.S. Government Printing Office, Washington, pp. 10-15.

29. Remarks by Honorable Henry H. Fowler, Secretary of the Treasury, before the Virginia State

Bar Association, Hot Springs, Virginia, July 10, 1965, reprinted in *Balance of Payments— 1965,* pp. 1020–1075.

30. Memorandum from the President to the Secretary of the Treasury, June 16, 1965, reprinted in Lyndon Baines Johnson, *The Vantage Point: Perspectives of the Presidency* (New York: Holt, Rinehart & Winston, 1971), pp. 597–598.

31. *Minutes of the FOMC, 1965,* p. 780.

32. IMF, *Summary Proceedings,* Annual Meeting, 1965, pp. 41–42.

33. "Liquidity: No Stop, No Go," *The Economist,* 217: 6371 (October 2, 1965), pp. 67–68.

34. IMF, *Summary Proceedings,* Annual Meeting, 1965, pp. 121–129.

35. Ibid., pp. 100–109.

36. Ibid., pp. 75–82.

37. "Communiqué of the Ministers and Governors of the Group of Ten issued on September 28, 1965," reprinted in *Federal Reserve Bulletin,* 51: 10 (October 1965), pp. 1407–1408.

38. "Liquidity: No Stop, No Go," pp. 67–68.

V. The Travail of Sterling, 1964–1968

1. OECD, *Main Economic Indicators,* Historical Statistics 1955–1971, March 1973.

2. IMF, *Balance of Payments Yearbooks.*

3. IMF, *Annual Report, 1965,* pp. 83–84; BIS, *Annual Report, 1965,* p. 121.

4. Henry Brandon, *In the Red: The Struggle for Sterling 1964–66* (London: Andre Deutsch, 1966), p. 28.

5. According to Richard Crossman, these included Thomas Balogh, Nicholas Kaldor, and Robert Nield. "The Crossman Diaries," *The Sunday Times,* February 2, 1975, p. 15.

6. Brandon, *In the Red,* pp. 39–40.

7. Ibid., pp. 40–44.

8. Ibid., p. 64.

9. Ibid., p. 70.

10. *Minutes of the FOMC, 1965,* pp. 602–611.

11. Ibid., p. 783.

12. OECD, *Main Economic Indicators,* Historical Statistics 1955–1971, p. 470.

13. Brandon, *In the Red,* pp. 85–98.

14. Ibid., pp. 100ff.

15. *Minutes of the FOMC, 1965,* pp. 937–938.

16. Ibid.

17. Brandon, *In the Red,* p. 114.

18. "Treasury and Federal Reserve Foreign Exchange Operations," *Federal Reserve Bulletin,* 52:3 (March 1966), pp. 318–322.

19. Fred Hirsch, *The Pound Sterling: A Polemic* (London: Gollancz, 1965), p. 134, footnote.

20. "The Crossman Diaries," *The Sunday Times,* March 16, 1975, p. 33; Harold Wilson, *A Personal Record: The Labour Government 1964–70* (Boston: Little, Brown, 1971), pp. 255–257.

21. "Treasury and Federal Reserve Foreign Exchange Operations," *Federal Reserve Bulletin,* 53: 3 (March 1967), p. 357.

22. *Minutes of the FOMC, 1967,* p. 1025.

23. Ibid., p. 757.

24. Ibid., p. 854.

25. Ibid., p. 1038.

26. Ibid., p. 1039.

27. Ibid., p. 1026.

28. See Harold Wilson, *A Personal Record,* p. 454; "Devaluation: Chronology of a Crisis," *The New York Times,* December 17, 1967, p. 14F; *Minutes of the FOMC, 1967,* p. 1304.
29. *Minutes of the FOMC, 1967,* pp. 1221–1222.
30. Ibid., p. 1216.
31. Ibid.
32. Ibid., p. 1304.
33. Ibid., pp. 1332–1333.
34. Ibid., pp. 1300–1301.
35. Ibid., p. 1335.
36. Ibid., p. 1342.
37. Harold Wilson, *A Personal Record,* p. 513.
38. BIS, *Annual Report, 1969,* p. 117.
39. For an account of this struggle reflecting the viewpoint of Alfred Hayes and Charles Coombs of the Federal Reserve Bank of New York, see John Brooks, "In Defense of Sterling," *The New Yorker,* March 23 and 30, 1968.
40. *Minutes of the FOMC, 1968,* pp. 610–633, 711–718.
41. BIS, *Annual Report, 1971,* p. 130.
42. This conclusion is supported by the analysis of Jacques R. Artus, "The 1967 Devaluation of the Pound Sterling," IMF, *Staff Papers,* 22: 3 (November 1975), pp. 595–640.

VI. The Build-up of Monetary Crisis: The United States, Germany, and Japan

1. *Minutes of the FOMC, 1965,* p. 861.
2. Ibid., pp. 1113–1117.
3. Ibid., p. 1118.
4. Ibid., pp. 1272–1276.
5. Arthur M. Okun, *The Political Economy of Prosperity* (Washington: Brookings, 1969), pp. 66–69.
6. Ibid., p. 70.
7. Ibid., pp. 71–72.
8. Kermit Gordon, "Inflation: A Non-Apocalyptic View," for delivery at a Williams College Convocation, September 14, 1974, p. 8 (mimeo.).
9. *Federal Reserve Bulletin,* various issues.
10. "Treasury and Federal Reserve Foreign Exchange Operations," *Federal Reserve Bulletin,* 52: 9, 53:3 (September 1966, March 1967).
11. All data from Annual Reports of Council of Economic Advisers, *Economic Report of the President,* various issues.
12. Okun, *The Political Economy of Prosperity,* p. 85.
13. Ibid., pp. 88–89.
14. A summary of these measures and the official rationale for the balance-of-payments program are set forth in U.S. Treasury Department, *Maintaining the Strength of the United States Dollar in a Strong Free World Economy,* U.S. Government Printing Office, Washington, January 1968.
15. *Minutes of the FOMC, 1968,* pp. 108–110.
16. *Federal Reserve Bulletin,* 55:4 (April 1969), p. 197.
17. *Annual Report of the Board of Governors of the Federal Reserve System,* 1969, p. 260.
18. Okun, *The Political Economy of Prosperity,* p. 92.
19. *Economic Report of the President,* February 1971, p. 73.
21. The dangers were not veiled from the eyes of Federal Reserve officials, nor others in Washing-

ton. In briefing the Federal Open Market Committee on April 2, 1968—just after a Group of Ten meeting at which agreement was reached on establishing the SDR—I sketched two "scenarios" of future developments. The second one, which assumed continuation of inflation in the United States, could involve growing doubts about the dollar, heavy conversions of dollars into gold and "a suspension of gold payments by the United States" (*Minutes of the FOMC, 1968,* pp. 404–405). See also presentation on October 8, 1968, by Arthur Hersey (Ibid., pp. 1159–1163).

22. All data from OECD, *Main Economic Indicators,* Historical Statistics, 1955–1971.
23. See Walter Heller et al., *Fiscal Policy for a Balanced Economy,* OECD, December 1968, pp. 42–49.
24. OECD, *Main Economic Indicators,* Historical Statistics 1955–1971, pp. 90–123.
25. Ibid.
26. IMF, *Annual Report, 1969,* p. 47.
27. Leon Hollerman, "Foreign Trade in Japan's Economic Transition," in *The Japanese Economy in International Perspective,* ed. Isaiah Frank (Baltimore: Johns Hopkins Press, 1975), p. 171.

VII. The Great Gold Rush of 1967–1968

1. *Minutes of the FOMC, 1967,* p. 1213. Of this amount the U.S. share was 50 percent until France stopped contributing in June; then the U.S. share went to 59 percent.
2. *Minutes of the FOMC, 1967,* pp. 1389–1390.
3. Ibid., pp. 1302, 1379.
4. "The Price of Gold is not the Problem," reprinted in *Federal Reserve Bulletin,* 54: 2 (February 1968), pp. 115–121.
5. *Minutes of the FOMC, 1968,* pp. 253, 394.
6. Ibid., p. 405.
7. Ibid., pp. 357–380.
8. Ibid., pp. 393–394.
9. *Minutes of the FOMC, 1967,* p. 1379.
10. Johnson, *The Vantage Point,* pp. 318–319.
11. Reprinted in *Federal Reserve Bulletin,* 54:3 (March 1968), p. 254.
12. *Minutes of the FOMC, 1968,* pp. 607–608.
13. Ibid., p. 403.
14. See my article, "A Two-Tier System: Permanent or Temporary?" in *The Gold Dilemma,* Banking and Finance Seminar, November 17–18, 1968, Oklahoma State University.
15. IMF, *Annual Report, 1970,* pp. 127–128.
16. *Minutes of the FOMC, 1968,* pp. 819–821.
17. See, for example, *The New York Times,* July 9, 1968, p. 49.
18. *Minutes of the FOMC, 1968,* p. 1358.
19. Ibid., p. 1144.
20. *The Washington Post,* October 5, 1968, p. C7.
21. IMF, *Annual Report, 1970,* pp. 184–189.

VIII. Gestation and Birth of the SDR, 1965–1969

1. *Minutes of the FOMC, 1966,* pp. 97–98.
2. Ibid., pp. 282–283.
3. See, for example, Otmar Emminger, "The Gold-Exchange Standard and the Price of Gold"

in *Monetary Reform and the Price of Gold,* ed. Randall Hinshaw (Baltimore: Johns Hopkins Press, 1967), p. 98.

4. IMF, *Annual Report, 1966,* pp. 18–20.
5. *Minutes of the FOMC, 1966,* pp. 480–481.
6. *The Washington Post,* May 10, 1966, p. D6.
7. Statement to the Press by Mr. Otmar Emminger, Chairman of the Deputies of the "Group of Ten," Frankfurt am Main, May 12, 1966.
8. Group of Ten, *Communiqué of Ministers and Governors and Report of Deputies,* July 1966.
9. Ibid. The communiqué is reprinted in *Federal Reserve Bulletin,* 52: 8 (August 1966), pp. 1149–1150.
10. *Minutes of the FOMC, 1966,* p. 1363.
11. Ibid., pp. 1365–1366.
12. *Minutes of the FOMC, 1967,* p. 4.
13. Ibid., pp. 166–167.
14. Based on Communiqué issued by Finance Ministers of six members of European Economic Community, Munich, April 18, 1967.
15. *Minutes of the FOMC, 1967,* pp. 422–423.
16. Transcript of Press Conference conducted by Otmar Emminger, Chairman of the Deputies of the Group of Ten, and Pierre-Paul Schweitzer, Managing Director of the Fund, Paris, June 21, 1967.
17. Cohen, *International Monetary Reform, 1964–69,* p. 134.
18. *The Washington Post,* August 28, 1967, p. A-13.
19. "International Monetary Reform," address by Otmar Emminger, September 11, 1967, Montreal, Canada.
20. *Minutes of the FOMC, 1967,* pp. 949–950. Professor Fritz Machlup later made the same point in *Remaking the International Monetary System: The Rio Agreement and Beyond* (Baltimore: Johns Hopkins Press, 1968), pp. 8–12.
21. *Le Monde,* August 29, 1967.
22. *The Washington Post,* August 29, 1967, p. C6.
23. Reprinted in IMF, *Annual Report, 1968,* pp. 171–174, and *Federal Reserve Bulletin,* 53: 11 (November 1967), pp. 1877–1882.
24. *The New York Times,* March 23, 1968, p. 41.
25. *The Economist,* 227: 6502 (April 6, 1968), p. 62.
26. Lyndon B. Johnson, *Public Papers of the Presidents of the United States,* 1968–69, Book I, p. 472.
27. *Minutes of the FOMC, 1968,* pp. 407–408.
28. IMF, *Summary Proceedings,* Annual Meeting, 1969, p. 58.
29. IMF, *Annual Report, 1969,* pp. 14–30.
30. A summary of the Working Party 3 discussion of this matter may be found in *Minutes of the FOMC, 1969,* pp. 475–478.
31. See, for example, my article, "The International Monetary System in the 1970's," *Business Economics,* 5:1 (January 1970).
32. See Milton Gilbert, *The Gold–Dollar System: Conditions of Equilibrium and the Price of Gold,* Essays in International Finance, No. 70, November 1968, International Finance Section, Princeton University, Princeton, New Jersey.
33. *Minutes of the FOMC, 1969,* p. 649.
34. Ibid., pp. 746–747.
35. Ibid., pp. 837–838.
36. IMF, *Summary Proceedings,* Annual Meeting, 1969, pp. 275–298.

IX. The "Events of May" 1968 in France and the French-German
Currency Crises

1. For one attempt, see Stanley Hoffmann, *Decline or Renewal? France Since the 1930's* (New York: Viking, 1974), pp. 145–184.
2. Edward L. Morse, *Foreign Policy and Interdependence in Gaullist France* (Princeton, N.J.: Princeton University Press, 1973), p. 133.
3. For a view of these events by one of the more revolutionary of the student leaders, see Daniel Cohn-Bendit, *Le Grand Bazar* (Paris: Pierre Belfond, 1975), pp. 33–50.
4. *The Wall Street Journal,* May 31, 1968, p. 3.
5. *Minutes of the FOMC, 1968,* p. 809.
6. IMF, *Annual Report, 1969,* pp. 34–35.
7. *Minutes of the FOMC, 1968,* p. 704.
8. BIS, *Annual Report, 1969,* p. 15.
9. OECD, *Main Economic Indicators,* Historical Statistics 1955–1971, pp. 225–227.
10. Ibid., pp. 224–235.
11. Johnson, *The Vantage Point,* pp. 23–24.
12. "Treasury and Federal Reserve Foreign Exchange Operations," *Federal Reserve Bulletin,* 55: 3 (March 1969), pp. 214–216.
13. *Minutes of the FOMC, 1968,* pp. 1372–1373.
14. *The New York Times,* November 19, 1968, p. 1.
15. See my article, "Reflections on the International Monetary Crisis," *Review,* Federal Reserve Bank of St. Louis, 50: 12 (December 1968), pp. 20–21.
16. Wilson, *A Personal Record,* p. 582.
17. *Minutes of the FOMC, 1968,* pp. 1367–1373.
18. *The New York Times,* November 26, 1968, p. 68.
19. *Minutes of the FOMC, 1968,* p. 1369.
20. *The New York Times,* November 24, 1968, p. 70.
21. Johnson, *The Vantage Point,* p. 321.
22. *The New York Times,* May 10, 1969, p. 1. A friend who saw this announcement on television said there was a touch of irony in its presentation. In cold print in the next day's newspapers, the statement looked both earnest and ridiculous.
23. IMF, *Annual Report, 1970,* pp. 56–57, 83–84.
24. *The Economist,* 245: 6745 (December 2, 1972), Survey, p. 14.
25. "Treasury and Federal Reserve Foreign Exchange Operations," *Federal Reserve Bulletin,* 56: 3 (March 1970), pp. 230–231.
26. Ibid., pp. 232–233.
27. OECD, *Main Economic Indicators,* Historical Statistics 1955–1971, p. 268.

X. The Exchange Rate System: A Reform That Failed

1. "The Value of Money and the International Monetary System," speech delivered by M. W. Holtrop, President of the Netherlands Bank and President and Chairman of the Board of the Bank for International Settlements, before the "Wirtschaftsforum Hessen" in Frankfurt am Main on November 29, 1965, reprinted in M. W. Holtrop, *Money in an Open Economy* (Leiden: H.E. Stenfert Kroese N.V., 1972), pp. 322–336, and summarized in BIS, *A Collection of Central Bankers' Speeches (1964–65),* Basle, March 1966.
2. *Guidelines for Improving the International Monetary System,* Report of the Subcommittee on International Exchange and Payments of the Joint Economic Committee, Con-

gress of the United States, U.S. Government Printing Office, Washington, 1965, pp. 19–21.

3. *The New York Times,* November 26, 1968, p. 1.

4. "Reflections on the International Monetary Crisis," pp. 20–21.

5. For example, George N. Halm, *The "Band" Proposal: The Limits of Permissible Exchange Rate Variations,* Special Papers in International Finance, No. 6, International Finance Section, Princeton (1965); Fellner, Triffin, Machlup et al., *Maintaining and Restoring Balance in International Payments* (Princeton, N.J.: Princeton University Press, 1966); John Williamson, *The Crawling Peg,* Princeton Essays in International Finance, No. 50 (December 1965) and "Exchange Rate Policy and the Future," *Moorgate and Wall Street,* Spring 1967; J. Carter Murphy, "Moderated Exchange Rate Variability," *National Banking Review,* 3: 2 (December 1965); Fred Hirsch, *Money International* (London, 1967); J. E. Meade, "Exchange Rate Flexibility," *Three Banks Review,* June 1966; and J. Black, "A Proposal for the Reform of Exchange Rates," *The Economic Journal,* 76:302 (June 1966).

6. See, for example, Roy Blough, "The Adjustment Process and the International Role of the Dollar," *Journal of Finance,* 24: 2 (May 1969), and my discussion of this article in the same issue.

7. Committee on Finance and Industry (Macmillan *Report*), H.M. Stationery Office, June 1931.

8. *Approaches to Greater Flexibility of Exchange Rates,* ed. George N. Halm (Princeton, N. J.: Princeton University Press, 1970).

9. IMF, *Annual Report, 1969,* pp. 30–32.

10. Francis M. Bator, "The Political Economics of International Money," *Foreign Affairs,* 47:1 (October 1968), p. 62.

11. Gottfried Haberler and Thomas D. Willett, *A Strategy for U.S. Balance of Payments Policy,* American Enterprise Institute, February 1971, p. 15.

12. IMF, *Summary Proceedings,* Annual Meeting, 1969, pp. 54–55.

13. Ibid., pp. 59–60.

14. Ibid., pp. 154–155.

15. *Minutes of the FOMC, 1969,* pp. 1359–1362.

16. IMF, *The Role of Exchange Rates in the Adjustment of International Payments,* Washington, 1970.

XI. The Road to Camp David

1. IMF, *Summary Proceedings,* Annual Meeting, 1970, p. 18.

2. "Treasury and Federal Reserve Foreign Exchange Operations," *Federal Reserve Bulletin,* 57:3 (March 1971), pp. 190–192.

3. IMF, *Annual Report, 1971,* pp. 23–24.

4. *The New York Times,* April 5, 1971, p. 49.

5. IMF, *Annual Report, 1971,* p. 98.

6. *The Washington Post,* April 28, 1971, p. A19.

7. *The New York Times,* May 4, 1971, p. 65.

8. Resolution adopted by EEC Council of Ministers, May 9, 1971.

9. Paul Volcker later countered this simile by noting that an elephant is "the beast of burden who goes around doing a lot of work for people, who is able to serve because he has a steadiness of purpose" (*The New York Times,* May 26, 1971, p. 55).

10. Remarks of the Honorable John B. Connally, Secretary of the Treasury, at the International Banking Conference of the American Bankers Association, Munich, Germany, May 28, 1971.

11. *The Balance of Payments Mess,* Hearings before the Subcommittee on International Exchange and Payments of the Joint Economic Committee, Congress of the United States, 92nd

Congress, First Session, June 16, 17, 21 and 23, 1971, U.S. Government Printing Office, 1971, p. 2.

12. Ibid., pp. 82, 84.
13. *The New York Times,* July 12, 1971, p. 39.
14. *The Journal of Commerce,* July 14, 1971, p. 1.
15. *The Baltimore Sun,* July 15, 1971, p. A7.
16. *The Christian Science Monitor,* July 16, 1971, p. 1.
17. *The New York Times,* July 24, 1971, p. 1.
18. "Excerpts from Deposition Taken From Nixon by Lawyers," *The New York Times,* August 21, 1975, p. 26.
19. Henry Brandon, *The Retreat of American Power* (Garden City, N. Y.: Doubleday, 1973), pp. 221–222; Juan Cameron, "How the U.S. Got on the Road to a Controlled Economy," *Fortune,* January 1972, p. 77.
20. Peter Kenen, "Convertibility and Consolidation: A Survey of Options for Reform," *The American Economic Review,* 63:2 (May 1973), p. 193.
21. *The New York Times,* August 8, 1971, p. 1.
22. The Department of the Treasury, "Memo to the Press," August 6, 1971.
23. Hendrick S. Houthakker, Speech at DePaul University, November 22, 1971; Cameron, "How the U.S. Got on the Road," p. 76.
24. Brandon, *The Retreat of American Power,* p. 225.
25. This paragraph and what follows are based on conversations with Arthur Burns, Paul Volcker, and Dewey Daane, and on William Safire, *Before the Fall* (Garden City, N.Y.: Doubleday, 1975), pp. 509–528; see also Brandon, *The Retreat of American Power,* pp. 218–246.
26. Richard Nixon, Address to the Nation Outlining a New Economic Policy: "The Challenge of Peace," August 15, 1971, *Public Papers of the Presidents of the United States,* Richard Nixon, 1971, pp. 886–891.
27. Press Conference by Georges Pompidou, President of the French Republic, at the Elysée Palace, September 23, 1971, Ambassade de France, Service de Presse et d'Information.

XII. From Camp David to the Smithsonian, August-December 1971

1. *The Washington Post,* September 6, 1971, p. A4.
2. *The Wall Street Journal,* August 27, 1971, p. 4.
3. IMF press release, August 20, 1971.
4. *The Washington Post,* August 25, 1971, p. A5.
5. Charles Ashman, *Connally* (New York: Morrow, 1974), p. 69.
6. *The New York Times,* April 11, 1975, p. 35.
7. Arthur Schlesinger, *A Thousand Days,* p. 1020.
8. Brandon, *The Retreat of American Power,* p. 350.
9. Press Conference by Georges Pompidou, President of the French Republic, at the Elysée Palace on September 23, 1971, Ambassade de France, Service de Presse et d'Information.
10. IMF, *Summary Proceedings,* Annual Meeting, 1971, p. 3.
11. Ibid., pp. 194–197.
12. Ibid., p. 219.
13. *The New York Times,* October 7, 1971, p. 69.
14. "Treasury and Federal Reserve Foreign Exchange Operations," *Federal Reserve Bulletin,* 57: 10 (October 1971), p. 786.
15. *Congressional Record,* October 1, 1971, pp. S15619–15621.
16. *Congressional Record,* September 21, 1971, pp. H8611–8615.

17. *The New York Times,* October 19, 1971, p. 61.
18. *The Journal of Commerce,* October 19, 1971, p. 1.
19. Ibid., October 18, 1971, p. 11.
20. *The Washington Post,* October 22, 1971, p. A20.
21. Ibid., October 24, 1971, p. L1.
22. *The Journal of Commerce,* October 28, 1971, p. 3.
23. *The Wall Street Journal,* November 2, 1971, p. 3.
24. *The New York Times,* November 5, 1971, p. 59.
25. *The Journal of Commerce,* November 10, 1971, p. 1.
26. *The New York Times,* November 11, 1971, p. 91.
27. Remarks by the Honorable John B. Connally, Secretary of the Treasury, before the Economic Club of New York, at the Waldorf-Astoria Hotel, New York, November 16, 1971.
28. Brandon, *The Retreat of American Power,* pp. 235–236.
29. *The New York Times,* November 25, 1971, p. 41; *The Wall Street Journal,* November 26, 1971, p. 3.
30. *The Journal of Commerce,* November 26, 1971, p. 9.
31. Brandon, *The Retreat of American Power,* p. 232.
32. *The Wall Street Journal,* November 30, 1971, p. 3; *The Washington Post,* December 1, 1971, p. A1.
33. *The Journal of Commerce,* December 8, 1971, p. 1.
34. *The Wall Street Journal,* December 10, 1971, p. 4.
35. *The New York Times,* December 10, 1971, p. 65.
36. *The Baltimore Sun,* December 14, 1971, p. A1.
37. Henry Brandon's report that all this was decided at a dinner on December 13 is subject to doubt; on the morning of the 14th, neither Giscard nor Connally knew what the precise figure was; Brandon, *The Retreat of American Power,* p. 241.
38. *The Journal of Commerce,* December 15, 1971, p. 1.
39. *The New York Times,* December 19, 1971, p. 1.
40. Press Communiqué of the Ministerial Meeting of the Group of Ten on December 17–18, 1971, in Washington, reprinted in IMF, *International Financial News Survey,* 23:50 (December 22–30, 1971).
41. These results are very close to those derived by William H. Branson, "The Trade Effects of the 1971 Currency Realignments," *Brookings Papers on Economic Activity,* 1:1972.
42. See "U.S. Balance of Payments and Investment Position," *Federal Reserve Bulletin,* 58: 4 (April 1972), pp. 333–336.
43. "The New World Economic Order," Address by Valéry Giscard d'Estaing, President of the French Republic, at the Ecole Polytechnique, Paris, October 28, 1975, Ambassade de France, Service de Presse et d'Information.
44. *Federal Reserve Bulletin,* 58: 3 (March 1972), p. A-86.
45. BIS, *Annual Report, 1972,* pp. 162–163.

XIII. The Crumbling of the Smithsonian Agreement, 1972–1973

1. Statement by Arthur F. Burns, Chairman, Board of Governors of the Federal Reserve System, before the Joint Economic Committee, February 9, 1972, reprinted in *Federal Reserve Bulletin,* 58: 2 (February 1972), p. 123.
2. *Economic Report of the President,* January 1973, p. 19.
3. Ibid., p. 4.
4. Ibid., p. 82.
5. *The New York Times,* March 4, 1972, p. 33.

6. *The Washington Post,* March 13, 1972, p. D10.
7. Some Europeans saw in the arrangement the beginning of a lessened dependence on the dollar as both a reserve and a vehicle currency. See A. de Lattre, "Problems Faced By a Bank of Issue in the Creation of a Common Currency," Faculty of Law and Economic Sciences, Nice, May 29–30, 1970 (mimeo.).
8. A Committee of Governors had been proposed by Richard Gardner in *Sterling-Dollar Diplomacy,* Introduction to 2nd edition (New York: McGraw-Hill 1969), p. xxxvi, and had certainly been considered by the IMF staff.
9. *The New York Times,* March 15, 1972, p. 69.
10. "Some Essentials of International Monetary Reform," Remarks of Arthur F. Burns, Chairman, Board of Governors of the Federal Reserve System, before the 1972 International Banking Conference, Montreal, May 12, 1972, reprinted in *Federal Reserve Bulletin,* 58: 6 (June 1972), pp. 545–549.
11. *The New York Times,* May 13, 1972, p. 1; *The Wall Street Journal,* May 15, 1972, p. 4.
12. Budget Statement of the Chancellor of the Exchequer (Mr. Anthony Barber), March 21, 1972.
13. *The New York Times,* June 21, 1972, p. 59.
14. *The New York Times,* July 19, 1972, p. 47.
15. *The Economist,* 244: 6726 (July 22, 1972), p. 32.
16. Translation from *Die Zeit,* August 4, 1972.
17. "Treasury and Federal Reserve Foreign Exchange Operations," *Federal Reserve Bulletin,* 58: 9 (September 1972), p. 758.
18. Ibid., pp. 758–759.
19. *The Wall Street Journal,* July 21, 1972, p. 4.
20. *The New York Times,* July 20, 1972, p. 1.
21. IMF, *Summary Proceedings,* Annual Meeting, 1972, pp. 353–356.
22. *The New York Times,* September 19, 1972, p. 89.
23. IMF, *Summary Proceedings,* Annual Meeting, 1972, p. 167.
24. Indeed, heavy selling of dollars in Tokyo followed revelation of the plan; see *The New York Times,* September 28, 1972, p. 77.
25. IMF, *Summary Proceedings,* Annual Meeting, 1972, pp. 34–44.
26. Ibid., p. 72.
27. Ibid., pp. 163–171.
28. IMF, *Annual Report, 1972,* p. 31.
29. IMF, *Summary Proceedings,* Annual Meeting, 1972, pp. 153–161.
30. *The New York Times,* September 28, 1972, p. 69.
31. *The New York Times,* September 30, 1972, p. 39.
32. See comments of Frank Southard, Deputy Managing Director of the IMF, in *Key Issues in International Monetary Reform,* ed. Randall Hinshaw (New York: Marcel Dekker, 1975), p. 32.
33. *The Washington Post,* January 30, 1973, p. D11.
34. *The Journal of Commerce,* February 5, 1973, p. 1.
35. Ibid., February 6, 1973, p. 1. *The New York Times,* February 6, 1973, p. 59.
36. "Treasury and Federal Reserve Foreign Exchange Operations," *Federal Reserve Bulletin,* 59: 3 (March 1973), pp. 146–163.
37. "Statement on Foreign Economic Policy" by Secretary of the Treasury George P. Shultz, February 12, 1973.
38. IMF, *Annual Report, 1973,* pp. 28–29.
39. *The New York Times,* February 16, 1973, p. 53.
40. BIS, *Annual Report, 1973,* p. 119.

41. *The Economist,* 246: 6759 (March 10, 1973), p. 15.

42. Ibid., p. 99; *The New York Times,* March 9, 1973, p. 49.

43. *The Wall Street Journal,* March 12, 1973, p. 3.

44. *The New York Times,* March 10, 1973, p. 46.

45. *The New York Times,* March 13, 1973, p. 59.

46. OECD, *Main Economic Indicators.*

47. *The New York Times,* March 17, 1973, p. 41.

XIV. International Monetary Reform: The Committee of Twenty, 1972–1974

1. J. Marcus Fleming, *Reflections on the International Monetary Reform,* Essays in International Finance, Number 107, December 1974 International Finance Section, Princeton University, pp. 9–10.

2. IMF, *Summary Proceedings,* Annual Meeting, 1973, p. 55.

3. Ibid., p. 74.

4. "International Monetary Reform," by Robert Solomon, a talk before the Canadian Institute of International Affairs, Toronto, Canada, March 13, 1974, partially reproduced in IMF *Survey,* March 18, 1974, pp. 81–82.

5. A collection of papers on the viewpoint of developing countries on reform may be found in UNCTAD, *Money, finance and development: papers on international monetary reform,* United Nations, New York, 1974. For an analysis of reform issues as they affect developing countries, see William R. Cline, *International Monetary Reform and the Developing Countries* (Washington: Brookings, 1976).

6. This paper was published in an appendix to the Annual Report of the Council of Economic Advisers, *Economic Report of the President,* January 1973, pp. 160–174.

7. "Proposals for an International Clearing Union" (April 1943), reprinted in *The International Monetary Fund, 1945–1965,* Vol. III: Documents, pp. 19–36.

8. *The Economist,* 245: 6745 (December 2, 1972), p. 83.

9. See *The Economist,* 246: 6753 (January 27, 1973), p. 72. An earlier version of this proposal was included in IMF, *Reform of the International Monetary System,* p. 28.

10. *The American Banker,* March 26, 1973, p. 3.

11. Communiqué of the Committee of the Board of Governors on International Monetary Reform and Related Issues, March 27, 1973, reprinted in *IMF Survey,* April 9, 1973, p. 100, and in IMF, *International Monetary Reform: Documents of the Committee of Twenty,* p. 214.

12. IMF, *International Monetary Reform: Documents of the Committee of Twenty,* pp. 51–77.

13. Ibid., pp. 78–94.

14. R.F. Harrod, *The Life of John Maynard Keynes* (New York: Harcourt Brace Jovanovich, 1952), p. 542.

15. Ibid., pp. 544–545.

16. IMF, *International Monetary Reform: Documents of the Committee of Twenty,* pp. 95–111.

17. "Dialectic instead of decision" by Pierre Viansson-Ponte, *Le Monde,* December 5, 1975, reprinted in English in *Manchester Guardian Weekly,* 113: 24 (December 14, 1975), p. 13.

18. *Key Issues in International Monetary Reform,* ed. Randall Hinshaw (New York: Marcel Dekker, 1975), p. 39.

19. See, for example, *The Wall Street Journal,* August 1, 1973, p. 3.

20. "International Monetary Reform—The Shape of Things to Come," by C.J. Morse, Chairman of the Deputies of the Committee of Twenty, International Monetary Fund, speech to National Foreign Trade Council, New York, November 12, 1973, partially reproduced in IMF *Survey,* November 23, 1973.

21. IMF *Survey,* September 21, 1973, pp. 273–274.

22. IMF *Survey,* October 8, 1973, p. 305.
23. Ibid., pp. 305–308, and IMF, *Summary Proceedings,* Annual Meeting, 1973, pp. 353–367.
24. Communiqué of Committee of Twenty, January 18, 1974, reprinted in IMF *Survey,* January 21, 1974, p. 17, and in IMF, *International Monetary Reform, Documents of the Committee of Twenty,* pp. 216–219.
25. Ibid.
26. IMF, *Survey,* February 4, 1974, p. 40.
27. The report of the group is published in IMF, *International Monetary Reform, Documents of the Committee of Twenty,* pp. 112–140.
28. Ibid., pp. 141–161.
29. Ibid., pp. 162–182.
30. Ibid., pp. 183–210.
31. Ibid., pp. 3–6.
32. Ibid., p. 8.
33. Ibid., pp. 9, 24–28.
34. Ibid., pp. 7–18.
35. Ibid., pp. 18–22.
36. C.J. Morse, "The Evolving Monetary System," speech to International Monetary Conference, Williamsburg, June 7, 1974, partially reproduced in IMF *Survey,* June 17, 1974, pp. 186–189.

XV. Learning to Live with Floating Exchange Rates in a World of Inflation and Recession

1. *The Economist,* 250: 6810 (March 2, 1974), pp. 86–87, and 256: 6889 (September 6, 1975), pp. 80–81.
2. John A. Schnittker, "The 1972–73 Food Price Spiral," *Brookings Papers on Economic Activity,* 2:1973, pp. 498–506.
3. Fred H. Sanderson, "The Great Food Fumble," *Science,* May 9, 1975 (General Series Reprint 303, Washington: Brookings, 1975).
4. Edward R. Fried, "International Trade in Raw Materials: Myths and Realities," *Science,* 191: 4228 (February 20, 1976), pp. 641–646.
5. The contrast in the behavior of wages in the United States and other countries in 1973–74 is discussed in George L. Perry, "Understanding World Inflation," *American Economic Review,* 65: 2 (May 1975), pp. 121–122.
6. Sanderson, "The Great Food Fumble."
7. Richard N. Cooper and Robert Z. Lawrence, "The 1972–75 Commodity Boom," *Brookings Papers on Economic Activity,* 3:1975, pp. 671–723.
8. CIA, "International Oil Developments," *Statistical Survey,* 15 January 1976.
9. United Nations, *Monthly Bulletin of Statistics,* 28:9 (September 1974), p. 172.
10. "Inflation and the International Monetary System," 16 June 1973, *The Per Jacobsson Foundation,* p. 50.
11. OECD, *Economic Outlook,* December 1975, p. 113.
12. Various channels by which inflation may spread internationally are identified and examined in Walter S. Salant, "The International Transmission of World Inflation," Paper prepared for the Conference on World Inflation, at the Brookings Institution, November 21–23, 1974, Washington.
13. Otmar Emminger, "Inflation and the International Monetary System," 16 June 1973, *The Per Jacobsson Foundation.*
14. The Managing Director of the IMF has characterized the growth of world reserves in the

fifties and sixties as "rather modest." See Johannes Witteveen, "The Control of International Liquidity," address to The Conference Board, Frankfurt, Germany, October 28, 1975, reprinted in IMF, *Survey,* October 28, 1975, pp. 313–316.

15. Robert Triffin, "Size, Sources and Beneficiaries of International Reserve Creation: 1970–1974," May 27, 1975 (mimeo.).

16. OECD, *Economic Outlook,* various issues.

17. Ibid., July 1973, p. 97.

18. OECD, *Main Economic Indicators.*

19. BIS, *Annual Report, 1973,* pp. 53–56.

20. G. Haberler, "Inflation as a Worldwide Phenomenon—An Overview," *Weltwirtschaftliches Archiv,* 10: 2 (1974), p. 181.

21. OECD, *Economic Outlook,* July 1973, p. 99.

22. Ibid., p. 23.

23. BIS, *Annual Report, 1973,* p. 46.

24. Ibid., p. 48.

25. OECD, *Economic Outlook,* July 1973, p. 97.

26. BIS, *Annual Report, 1973,* p. 10.

27. "The International Transmission of Inflation," OECD, *Economic Outlook,* July 1973, p. 90.

28. OECD, *Economic Outlook,* July 1974, p. 11.

29. Marina v.N. Whitman, "The Payments Adjustment Process and the Exchange Rate Regime: What Have We Learned?" *American Economic Review,* 65: 2 (May 1975), pp. 133–146.

30. The effective exchange rate of a country is the weighted average rate against the currencies of its major trade partners. For a discussion of this concept and of various approaches to its measurement, see Annual Report of the Council of Economic Advisers, *Economic Report of the President,* February 1974, pp. 220–226, and Rudolf R. Rhomberg, "Indices of Effective Exchange Rates," IMF, *Staff Papers,* 23:1 (March 1976), pp. 88–112.

31. *The Journal of Commerce,* May 15, 1973, p. 1.

32. *The Washington Post,* June 6, 1973, p. A1.

33. For explanations, see Walter S. Salant, "The Post-Devaluation Weakness of the Dollar," *Brookings Papers on Economic Activity,* 2:1973, pp. 481–496.

34. *The Wall Street Journal,* June 27, 1973, p. 3.

35. *The New York Times,* June 28, 1973, p. 67.

36. "Treasury and Federal Reserve Foreign Exchange Operations," *Federal Reserve Bulletin,* 59: 9 (September 1973), p. 623.

37. OECD, *Economic Outlook,* December 1974, p. 83.

38. "Treasury and Federal Reserve Foreign Exchange Operations," *Federal Reserve Bulletin,* 60: 9 (September 1974), pp. 637–638.

39. Robert Solomon, "The Allocation of 'Oil Deficits,' " *Brookings Papers on Economic Activity,* 1:1975, p. 64.

40. *The Washington Post,* February 4, 1975, p. D6.

41. Marina v.N. Whitman, "The Payments Adjustment Process and the Exchange Rate Regime: What Have We Learned?" pp. 137–138.

42. Michael P. Dooley and Jeffrey R. Shafer, "Analysis of Short-Run Exchange Rate Behavior, March 1973 to September 1975," *International Finance Discussion Papers,* 76, February 1976, Board of Governors of the Federal Reserve System.

43. BIS, *Annual Report, 1975,* p. 29.

44. Milton Friedman and Robert V. Roosa, *The Balance of Payments: Free Versus Fixed Exchange Rates,* American Enterprise Institute for Public Policy Research, Washington, 1967, pp. 38–39.

45. IMF, *Annual Report, 1975,* pp. 3, 11.

46. Charles Piggott, Richard James Sweeney, and Thomas D. Willett, "Some Aspects of the Behavior and Effects of Flexible Exchange Rates," paper presented at the Conference on Monetary Theory and Policy, Konstanz, Germany, June 1975 (processed).

47. Frank McCormick, "Transactions Costs in the Foreign Exchange Market under Fixed and Floating Exchange Rates," paper presented to the Western Economic Association Annual Conference, San Diego, California, June 26, 1975 (mimeo.).

48. G. Haberler, "Inflation as a Worldwide Phenomenon—An Overview."

49. Salant, "The International Transmission of World Inflation."

50. See, for example, IMF, *The Role of Exchange Rates in the Adjustment of International Payments,* A Report by the Executive Directors, 1970, pp. 56–58.

51. IMF, *Annual Report, 1975,* pp. 23–24.

52. S. Y. Kwack "The Effects of Foreign Inflation on Domestic Prices and the Relative Price Advantage of Exchange Rate Changes," *International Finance Discussion Papers,* 35, November 21, 1973, Board of Governors of the Federal Reserve System.

XVI. The Impact of OPEC

1. "Impacts of Higher Oil Prices," Address by Robert Solomon before The Fourth European Institutional Investor Conference, London, December 3, 1974.

2. I made four speeches on the subject in 1974. See, for example, *The New York Times,* May 14, 1974, p. 47, and June 22, 1974, p. 35; *The American Banker,* November 8, 1974, p. 2. The fourth speech, given in London on December 3, succeeded in escaping notice by the press. An appraisal along similar lines may be found in Hollis Chenery, "Restructuring the World Economy," *Foreign Affairs,* 53: 2 (January 1975), pp. 242–263.

3. Joseph A. Yager and Eleanor B. Steinberg, *Energy and U.S. Foreign Policy* (Cambridge, Mass.: Ballinger, 1974), pp. 443–446.

4. OECD, *Oil: The Present Situation and Future Prospects,* 1973, p. 45.

5. C. Fred Bergsten, "The New Era in World Commodity Markets," *Challenge,* September-October 1974, p. 42.

6. Edward E. Murphy and Jorge F. Perez-Lopez, "Trends in U.S. Export Prices and OPEC Oil Prices," *Monthly Labor Review,* November 1975, p. 40.

7. See William D. Nordhaus, "The Allocation of Energy Resources," *Brookings Papers on Economic Activity,* 3:1973, pp. 529–574.

8. *The Economist,* 250:6813 (March 23, 1974), p. 7 of Survey.

9. "The United States," in *Higher Oil Prices and the World Economy,* ed. Edward R. Fried and Charles L. Schultze (Washington: Brookings, 1975), p. 103.

10. George Basevi, "Western Europe," ibid., p. 107.

11. *The New York Times,* December 9, 1975, p. 59.

12. "The International Monetary Situation," Address by Robert Solomon before the Atlanta Society of Financial Analysts, Atlanta, Georgia, November 6, 1974.

13. John Williamson, "The International Financial System," in *Higher Oil Prices and the World Economy,* p. 217.

14. Edward R. Fried and Charles L. Schultze, "Overview," ibid., p. 13.

15. Ibid., p. 66.

16. Solomon, "The Allocation of 'Oil Deficits.' "

17. Wouter Tims, "The Developing Countries," in *Higher Oil Prices and the World Economy,* p. 185.

18. BIS, *Annual Report, 1975,* pp. 139–142.

19. OECD, *Development Cooperation, 1975 Review,* Report by Maurice J. Williams, Chairman of Development Assistance Committee, November 1975. For a discussion of OPEC aid

programs, see Maurice J. Williams, "The Aid Programs of the OPEC Countries," *Foreign Affairs,* 54: 2 (January 1976), pp. 308–324.

XVII. Further Evolution of the International Monetary System

1. IMF, *Summary Proceedings,* Annual Meeting, 1974, pp. 92–93.
2. Press Communiqué, Interim Committee of the Board of Governors on the International Monetary System, October 3, 1974, reprinted in ibid., pp. 383–384.
3. Ibid., p. 89.
4. Ibid., pp. 96–99.
5. IMF, *Annual Report, 1975,* pp. 53–55.
6. IMF, *Survey,* April 5, 1976, pp. 97, 102.
7. Press Communiqué, Interim Committee of the Board of Governors on the International Monetary System, August 31, 1975, reprinted in IMF, *Summary Proceedings,* Annual Meeting, 1975, pp. 299–304.
8. Letter of August 16, 1974, to The Honorable William E. Simon from Representative Henry S. Reuss, Chairman of the Subcommittee on International Economics of the Joint Economic Committee, reprinted in *Hearings* before the Joint Economic Committee, 93rd Congress, Second Session, October 11, 16 and 18, 1974, U.S. Government Printing Office, Washington, 1974, pp. 31–38.
9. *Congressional Record,* November 5, 1973, pp. H9582–9584.
10. See note 8.
11. *The Wall Street Journal,* August 22, 1975, p. 6.
12. IMF, *Summary Proceedings,* Annual Meeting, 1975, p. 101.
13. Ibid., p. 117.
14. "The New World Economic Order," Address by Valéry Giscard d'Estaing, President of the French Republic, at the Ecole Polytechnique, Paris, October 28, 1975, Ambassade de France, Service de Presse et d'Information, p. 14.
15. *Le Figaro,* November 12, 1975, p. 2.
16. *The New York Times,* November 19, 1975, p. 51.
17. Declaration of Rambouillet, November 17, 1975.
18. See, for example, *The New York Times,* November 19, 1975, p. 51.
19. The headline on the front page of *Le Monde* for November 19, 1975, referred to a more stable dollar.
20. France is said to have more gold in private hands than any other country; the amount was estimated at $5 billion (at $35 per ounce) in 1972; *The Economist,* 245: 6745 (December 2, 1972), Survey, p. 27; see also Ray Vicker, *The Realms of Gold* (New York: Scribner, 1975), p. 173.
21. *Official Journal of the European Communities,* 18: C174 (July 31, 1975), pp. 19–20.
22. Press Communiqué, Interim Committee, January 16, 1975, reprinted in IMF, *Annual Report, 1975,* pp. 97–99.
23. *The Journal of Commerce,* May 29, 1975, p. 4.
24. Press Communiqué, Interim Committee, June 12, 1975, reprinted in IMF, *Annual Report, 1975,* pp. 99–101.
25. Press Communiqué, Interim Committee, August 31, 1975, reprinted in IMF, *Summary Proceedings,* Annual Meeting, 1975, pp. 299–304.
26. Reuters dispatch, September 1, 1975.
27. *The Economist,* 256: 6889 (September 6, 1975), p. 99.
28. *Congressional Record,* September 17, 1975, pp. H8776–8778.
29. Unclassified report from U.S. Embassy, Paris, September 19, 1975.

30. *The New York Times,* November 8, 1975, p. 35.
31. Statement of Henry H. Fowler, before the International Economics Subcommittee of the Joint Economic Committee, U.S. Congress, October 10, 1975 (processed).
32. *Department of the Treasury News,* Letter from Treasury Secretary William E. Simon to Representative Henry S. Reuss, Chairman, Subcommittee on International Economics of the Joint Economic Committee, November 7, 1975.
33. Press Communiqué of the Interim Committee, January 8, 1976, reprinted in IMF, *Survey,* January 19, 1976, pp. 18–19.
34. "The Quest for Stability—National and International Monetary Problems," Remarks by Otmar Emminger, Deputy Governor of the Deutsche Bundesbank, before the European-Atlantic Group, London, February 19, 1976.

XVIII. The Present and Future of the System

1. Joseph S. Nye, Jr., "Independence and Interdependence," *Foreign Policy,* 22 (Spring 1976), p. 160.
2. Several of the issues considered in this chapter are discussed by Edwin M. Truman, "The United States and the International Monetary System: Some Issues and Alternatives," in *Trade, Inflation and Ethics* (Lexington, Mass.: D.C. Heath, forthcoming).
3. See "Outline of Reform," June 14, 1974, IMF, *International Monetary Reform, Documents of the Committee of Twenty,* Washington, 1974, pp. 7–48.
4. IMF *Survey,* February 2, 1976, pp. 35–39.
5. In the early postwar period, it was commonly believed that when a country went into a recession its balance of payments would strengthen because its imports would fall relative to its exports. Later, as capital flows assumed growing importance, it became evident that they usually overwhelmed the trade balance effect, as we have seen. This phenomenon is not new. John H. Williams observed in 1932: "Recent investigation of the prewar movements of gold show, in the case of both England and the United States, a clearly defined tendency for gold to flow inward during prosperity and outward during depression." John H. Williams, "The Crisis of the Gold Standard," *Foreign Affairs,* January 1932, reprinted in his *Postwar Monetary Plans and Other Essays* (New York: Knopf, 1945), p. 156.
6. See, for example, Wilfred Ethier and Arthur I. Bloomfield, *Managing the Managed Float,* Essays in International Finance 112, October 1975, International Finance Section, Princeton University; and Michael P. Dooley and Jeffrey R. Shafer, "Rules for Intervention Without Fixed Parities," International Finance Discussion Papers, February 1976, Board of Governors of the Federal Reserve System.
7. IMF, *Annual Report, 1975,* p. 39.
8. "On the Past and Future of the International Monetary System," Address by Robert Solomon before the Seminar on Financial Problems of International Firms, Graduate School of Business, University of Chicago, October 2, 1975 (processed).
9. IMF, *Summary Proceedings,* Annual Meeting, 1975, p. 41.
10. IMF, *Annual Report, 1975,* p. 39.
11. For an account of these divergent attitudes toward the Bretton Woods proposals, see Alfred E. Eckes, Jr., *A Search for Solvency* (Austin: University of Texas Press, 1975).
12. Alfred Hayes, "Emerging Arrangements in International Payments, Public and Private," August 31, 1975, *The Per Jacobsson Foundation.*
13. Richard N. Gardner, *Sterling–Dollar Diplomacy,* p. 123.
14. *The Life of Timon of Athens,* Act IV, Scene 3.
15. John Maynard Keynes, *Monetary Reform* (New York: Harcourt Brace Jovanovich, 1924), p. 187. In *Paradise Lost,* Milton speaks of *"Barbaric* Pearl and Gold."

16. Frank Freidel, *Franklin D. Roosevelt, Launching the New Deal* (Boston: Little, Brown, 1973), p. 334.
17. *The New York Times,* November 6, 1974, p. 67.
18. See Vicker, *The Realms of Gold.*
19. See Edward M. Bernstein, "The Monetary Stock of Gold and the Free Market," *Economic Review,* Shields Model Roland, April 1, 1976.

Index